Madame De Staël

MADAME DE STAËL

*HER FRIENDS, AND HER INFLUENCE
IN POLITICS AND LITERATURE.*

BY

LADY BLENNERHASSETT.

WITH A PORTRAIT OF MADAME DE STAËL.

In Three Volumes.

VOL. I.

LONDON: CHAPMAN AND HALL
LIMITED.

1889.

WESTMINSTER:

PRINTED BY NICHOLS AND SONS,

25, PARLIAMENT STREET.

TRANSLATOR'S NOTE.

The following pages are a slightly-abridged translation of LADY BLENNERHASSET'S work " FRAU VON STAËL IHRE FREUNDE UND EHRE BEDEUTUNG IN POLITIK UND LITTERATUR".

J. E. GORDON CUMMING.

February 12, 1889.

PREFACE.

" La première loi d'une portrait est de ne pas le faire dans un ton
opposé à celui du modèle "—SAINTE-BEUVE.

HARDLY any important book of an historical tendency
has been written concerning the period between 1789
and 1815 without bringing in the name of Anne
Germaine Necker, Baronne de Staël-Holstein.

Born on the 22nd April, 1766, in the midst of the
culture of the eighteenth century; brought up under
the direct influence of Jean Jacques Rousseau's ideas,
and in active intercourse with all the celebrated
people of her day, from Voltaire to Mirabeau, from
Turgot to Bonaparte, she never concealed her predi-
lection for them; and in a manner took part in the
whole Revolution. Her share in politics chiefly
occurred in the ten years between 1789 and 1799.
When this period came to an end, her actual literary
career began with her book, *On Literature*, and only
ceased at her death, which took place on the 14th
July, 1817.

This career is marked by the immense success of
Corinne, by the publication of her book *On Germany*,
an intellectual feat of importance that can scarcely
be over-estimated; and lastly by the political legacy

she bequeathed, in the *Reflections on the French Revolution*, which inspired the flower of the sons of France with a desire to secure the blessings of liberty for their country, in attempting which their predecessors went to their death in 1789—conquered, but unconvinced.

The life of one whose existence combined all the vicissitudes of a woman's lot, and whose nature was endowed with a special capacity for suffering, was sure to arouse an equal degree of sympathy and interest.

Thus an essay on Madame de Staël has ever been a favourite theme with French authors. Men no less distinguished than M. J. Chénier, Barante, J. de Maistre, Thiers, Villemain, Châteaubriand, Lamartine, Nettement, Nisard, Ch. de Rémusat, Gustave Planche, Gérusez, Ch. de Mazade, Amiel, Brunetière, Caro, O. Feuillet, Guizot, Taine, failed not, were it but incidentally, to lower their flag before her.

More detailed studies, taking her for their subject, have been written by Madame Necker de Saussure, Benjamin Constant, Alexander Vinet, and above all by Sainte-Beuve, the master of modern criticism; and they belong to the most skilled portraiture in French prose. All these studies are chiefly, however, of a literary character. The numerous accounts of the political position and importance of Madame de Staël, spreading over the literature of the French Revolution, generally lack authenticity, or they are imperfectly verified.

This literature is so voluminous that it is almost impossible to look through all the memoirs, biographies, letters, and histories it includes..

And yet the portrait of this wonderful woman could only be examined in connection with the framework of the current thoughts and events surrounding her. In the words of one of our greatest historians, we should rather prefer the repetition of what is already known to the risk of inaccuracy induced by an incessant effort to be original.

Owing to the difficulty of separating Madame de Staël's personal history from that of her surroundings, the various attempts, especially the English attempts, to produce an exhaustive and life-like portrait of her, have utterly failed.

Seventy years have elapsed since her death, and one of the most important figures in modern times has hitherto found no adequate biographer.

Whilst in pursuit of entirely different studies, the authoress of the following work became sensible of this void in the history of the nineteenth century. That she should have felt herself constrained to set these studies aside, in the endeavour to fill up the deficiency, is amply explained by the wealth of material, and its connection with so many of the episodes and leading figures of the Revolution, of the Empire, the German classical era, the Restoration; and finally it is explained by the central figure itself, which owed its powers of attraction more to its irresistible worth than even to its genius.

And there was an additional motive.

Madame de Staël saw Germany in the hour of its deepest political debasement. Undeterred by passing events, she chose that hour to acquaint the world with its intellectual worth and renown.

Schiller, and Goethe, Charles Augustus, and the Duchess Louise, William and Alexander Humboldt, were her friends, and she was the patroness of A. W. Schlegel. Grillparzer's *Sappho* was inspired by *Corinne*. Her picture hung above Baron de Stein's library table, as that of an ally in the struggle against the oppressor.

Such memories have their responsibilities. Taking this into consideration, we trust that the story of Madame de Staël, traced by a German hand, may be accepted with indulgence as a contribution to the German literature of the centenary of 1789. No one more deeply valued all that was good and enduring in the weighty experiment of that date than she, to whom liberty was more precious than all other gifts in life.

Munich.

CONTENTS OF VOL. I.

CHAPTER III.

CHAPTER IV.

CHAPTER V.

MADAME DE STAËL.

French crown during the next reign, although retaining all the typical attributes of his own nationality.

Berwick, an Englishman, fought the battles of Louis

MADAME DE STAËL.

CHAPTER I.

The Necker family—James Necker goes to Paris—The Economists—
Necker's attention directed to Public Affairs—His marriage—
Mademoiselle Curchod under the parental roof—Her visit to
Lausanne—Gibbon, Moulton, and J. J. Rousseau—Mademoiselle
Curchod at Ferney—Goes to Paris—The Neckers first friends—
Madame Necker's friendship for Buffon—Gibbon in Paris—Birth
of Anne Germaine Necker, April 22, 1766—Influence of the social
atmosphere in Paris upon Madame Necker—Literary import-
ance of the Necker *salon*—Madame Necker a mother to the poor.

THE excitable and jealous patriotism of the French,
so often serving as an example to other nations, and
not unfrequently as a useful incentive to the extension of their own strength, has nevertheless been
powerless to prevent the direction of the State from
falling into the hands of foreigners.

In this, the principal share fell to the Italians; to
Concini, under Louis XIII.; and to Cardinal Mazarin,
who added so much to the brilliancy and glory of the
French crown during the next reign, although retaining all the typical attributes of his own nationality.

Berwick, an Englishman, fought the battles of Louis

XIV. The Scotchman, Law, managed the finances of the Regent. The Revolution accepted help from Thomas Payne, an Englishman ; from Marat, a native of Neuenburg ; from the Prussian Anacharsis Clootz ; from the German Prince of Hessen Rheinfels; from Buonaparte, the Corsican. Stofflet, a Suabian, fought in the cause of the Vendée; and Lückner, a native of the Upper Palatinate, in that of Louis XIV. The German element preserved its own individuality less than any other, on foreign soil, from the field-marshal Maurice de Saxe down to the author Grimm, in whose praise it is cited that he had become quite French. The same cannot be said of his friend and contemporary, James Necker, the Genevan, who at a moment of direst need undertook the financial direction of the affairs of the French government, and who, ten years later, further undertook to save it from utter destruction, on the eve of the most dreadful storm that hitherto had burst upon a European nation.

Necker never entirely lost the traces of his German origin, dating only a generation back, and it is recognizable in the merits and good qualities as well as in the failures and mistakes to which the miscarriage in 1789 of this enormous double task must be ascribed.

The Necker family was of Irish descent, and this is equivalent to saying that they claimed noble blood, although drawing a line at those royal honours which float in the fanciful brain of every true Irish Celt, as a fragment of his stolen birthright.

All traces of the family disappeared from Ireland

in the time of Queen Mary, to appear again in Pomerania, where members of it filled offices in the Church.

The son of Martin Necker, a preacher in the parish of Wartenburg, not far from Pyritz, became an advocate at Küstrin. His son, named Charles Frederic, born in 1685, soon relinquished a similar narrow line of existence, although it had originally been his own choice, and first accompanied a young Count Bernstorff, a godchild of George I., to the Geneva university, subsequently visiting the various capitals of Europe with him. About the year 1724 he arrived in London with his pupil, and there the King rewarded his exertions with a yearly salary of 100*l*., on condition that he should organize a school at Geneva for young Englishmen. To this Necker consented, and shortly afterwards the Grand Council of the university conferred the honorary title of Professor of Law upon him. In 1726 he married a sister of Gautier, the Chief Secretary and a Member of Council, who belonged to a refugee Huguenot family, tracing its origin through the Gallatins and Tuderts to Jacques Cœur, the great financier of the fifteenth century. In the same year he obtained the privileges of a citizen, and being, as the decree expressed it, "priceless by reason of his services," was elected shortly afterwards to the High Council, became a member of the reformed Consistory in 1742, and at the same date published a treatise on the "Constitutional Law of the High Council of the German Nation," a translation of which appeared simultaneously in Frankfort and Leipzig in 1764.

Although Necker had specially notified that the pamphlet contained " nothing that could be displeasing to princes," the High Council of the Republic thought it wiser to decline the dedication, in consideration of its monarchical surroundings. It nevertheless assured the author of its special goodwill.

The proceeds of his school enabled him to become possessed of a country-place, to which he gave the name of " Germanie " in memory of his native land.

He appears to have taken no small interest in the welfare of his adopted country, and it was whilst endeavouring to calm the excitement arising out of an election in the church of St. Peter's, then disturbed by violent disputes, that in 1762 he suddenly fell lifeless to the ground.* He had reached the age of seventy-seven years, and left two sons behind him, Louis and James.

Louis Necker, the elder of the two, born in 1730, and doctor of law, originally followed the same path as his father had done. He first accompanied one of the counts of Lippe Detmold to the university of Turin, was afterwards tutor to the Baron von Wassenaër, of an old Netherland family, and went with him in that capacity to the Utrecht university. Being appointed professor of natural history in the university of his native town, he busied himself with

* Senebier, *Histoire Littéraire de Genève*, 1786, iii. 90. Galiffe, *Notice Généalogiques sur les Familles Genevoises*, ii. and iv. Dr. J. Hermann, Oberlehrer, *Zur Geschichte der Familie Necker*, Berlin, 1886.

—

several works for the Encyclopædia, and carried on his father's school, but after his first wife's death found himself obliged to leave Geneva, in consequence of some legal disputes. He gave up his professorship, and went to Marseilles, where he assumed the surname of de Germanie, and with the help of his brother, James Necker, started a banking business, which in a few years enabled him to retire into private life, and go back to Paris with two million livres. There, through their common love of physical science, he became the friend of Benjamin Franklin, and there also he married a Mademoiselle de Hauteville.

This second marriage proved childless, but a son of the first marriage entered the French army, and a daughter married and settled in Geneva, where in 1804, and in the same year as his brother, Louis Necker died.[*]

A very different career, comprising all the changes and chances of human greatness, and their inevitable disappointments, was allotted to James Necker, born September 30th, 1732, the younger son of Frederic Charles.

Victor de Bonstetten, his friend in later years, speaks of a characteristic trait in his early youth in Geneva, which was otherwise undistinguished by any special event. It had been related to him, that when young Necker played with his companions he always

[*] *The Necker Family*, by C——r, and *Jacob* Necker, by A. W. Schlegel. Both notices printed in the newspaper *The Contemporaries*. 1816-1817 and 1818-1819.

managed that the forms of government of which he had read should be represented in miniature, and thus he obtained an opportunity of framing laws for them.*

In the Switzerland of that date young and old busied themselves with politics ; and the various cantons each represented various forms of government, and of political theories in miniature. This appears all the more surprising when we remember the apathy prevalent throughout the length and breadth of Germany, their next-door neighbour. This was so complete, that in 4700 letters—interchanged from 1722-1756 between the Gottscheds and half the rest of the world—politics with the exception of one or two casual allusions are barely mentioned.† Notwithstanding the almost universal interest taken by the Swiss in public affairs, the second half of the eighteenth century was a period of decadence in the history of Switzerland. A number of small states divided the land, from the monarchy of the Prince Bishops down to the absolute democracy of the small cantons in the mountains; but the aristocracy, nevertheless, prevailed in public life; whilst even the democracy in the small cantons did not hesitate to have their dependants.

Besides the thirteen cantons, there were three smaller communities, represented in the Diet by the name of the united towns. Amongst these, the

---

* Bonstetten, *Letters to Frederike Brun*, published by Matthison, i. 205.   † Danzel, *Gottsched and his Times*, p. 279.

republic of Geneva enjoyed the most flourishing industrial development ; whilst the aristocratic families in Berne, Lucerne, Freiburg, Solothurn, were already in a state of decline.

In 1760 the Swiss secured themselves an intellectual centre by the formation of the Helvetic society on the occasion of the Jubilee of the Basle university. At its head came Iselin, with Geszner, Hirzel, and Schinz, from Zurich ; later on they were joined by Bodmer, Lavater, Pestalozzi, and Bonstetten.

Encouragement of patriotism and civil virtue, as well as the furtherance of the public welfare, was their ostensible aim ; politics were insensibly added as the times grew stormier. In like manner Geneva took up a special position from an intellectual stand-point. The historian J. von Müller calls it "comparatively the most enlightened town to be met with far and wide."

"After a long servitude," he says, "Calvin introduced the shadow of political freedom by the powerful rule of the Protestant clergy, and succeeding generations brought it still further to perfection. Envied by more than one neighbour, this town was an immense industrial centre, and that of a comparatively immense concourse of intellectual people; but when the joys of liberty are the most talked about they are the nearer being lost." "Never is a native of Geneva put to confusion," he adds, "by giving his opinion."[*]

In his *Reminiscences* Bonstetten confirms this state-

* J. von Müller, *Letters. Complete Works*, xvi. 42, 55.

ment. He tells us that so much was never written for
and against aristocracy and democracy in any place
as in Geneva. He says, "Aristocracy was in the
constitution and in the position of the town, democracy
in some of its customs. The whole power of the aristocracy was united in the 'Little Council,' and all
the patrician families lived on the hilly portion of the
town, whilst the plebeians lived at their feet in the
lower town. And yet there was no recognised difference
of classes; no real boundaries divided the reigning
families from their subordinates. A purely ideal conception of power existed; it therefore came to pass that
in no country were the smallest rights more tenaciously
adhered to than in this republic. One of these imaginary rights was that of living on the hill. How often
I was annoyed by the slighting remarks applied by
the inhabitants of the upper town to the residents in
the lower town, in whose houses I had occasionally
danced.

"This universal jealousy produced universal culture
in every class. The women were amiable, the men
well-educated, even learned, and education was altogether more advanced than in any of the greater
nations.

"As the unusual intellectual cultivation in Geneva
sprang from ancient civil and religious controversy,
and from a commercial spirit, the character of the
Genevese was altogether serious, and more disposed
for calculations and accounts than for enjoyment and
merriment.

"Voltaire says of Geneva, ' *Cité sournoise, où jamais l'on ne rit.*' The puritanical spirit of the clergy had banished all amusement, especially public plays, from their midst, as doubtful abominations. The serious nature of the Genevese made them all the more vigorous in a dispute, so that even the most insignificant political question produced a storm of words and pamphlets.

" I remember that the greatest praise that could be bestowed in the days of my childhood was commendation for good behaviour. To be well-behaved, meant keeping as quiet as an old grandfather or as stiff as a councillor. My father had recommended me to the notice of Cramer, an excellent man, and then Syndic of the Republic. I saw him first in his kitchen, dining with his wife and servant-girl. The venerable old man wore a wig, too, which reached his stomach like a splendid mane. These good manners thawed by degrees, like ancient glaciers, at the time of Voltaire's appearance, and he was not entirely innocent of bringing about this result."* The owner of Ferney subsequently boasted that he had corrupted Geneva; † but in the days of Necker's youth Bonnet, the great and modest natural philosopher and *savant*, who tried to find a middle path between the philosophical problems of the day and the Christian faith, in the same way as Necker afterwards endeavoured to do, was the most influential man in his native town. Whilst suc-

* Bonstetten, *Reminiscences of Youth.*
† *Voltaire to d'Alembert,* i. 184.

cessfully pursuing his studies in the atmosphere of patriarchal simplicity and austerity peculiar to Geneva, James Necker, in compliance with his father's wish, was obliged, at the age of sixteen, to give up the university, and went to Paris, there to make his livelihood in mercantile pursuits.

It has been rightly observed that this interruption left a permanent gap in his education.* At first he seemed unlikely to succeed. Far other matters than those connected with money claimed young Necker's interest; he loved his books, eagerly read all the leading literature of the day, and in his leisure moments wrote short pieces for the theatre, more especially comedies in verse, which later on he congratulated himself he had never published.

A mere chance led to the discovery that this merry young fellow, full of jokes and play, was nevertheless possessed of very special talent for the calling he so unwillingly pursued.

His father had placed him with Vernet, the Genevese banker, with whom he stood in friendly relations. The head of the bank lived in the neighbourhood of Paris, and only attended on certain days. During his absence an important business offer came from Holland. Decision was urgent; Necker, who was now eighteen years old, undertook the transaction, and on Vernet's return unfolded not only a carefully-prepared, but a suitable, scheme, to which he gave his entire approval.

* Madame de Charrière, *Lettres, Mémoires. Revue Suisse*, p. 777.

In the following three months his clerk had learnt Dutch, and thus all the management of important business with the great Dutch commercial houses passed into his hands.

His fortune was made, and when Vernet retired from business in 1762 he entrusted a sum of money to James Necker, which enabled him, in partnership with the Genevan Thélusson, to found a bank, which very soon became the most important in France, and made a new departure in banking. This firm did not adhere to mere mercantile transactions or to the management of the State revenues, as hitherto had been customary, but struck out an independent line of its own and undertook important monetary operations. Speculation in corn was its first opportunity. The corn trade had been freed in 1764 by Choiseul, and this economic revolution was the result of the interest awakened, towards the middle of the century, in everything connected with domestic economy. It found expression in the economic literature started between 1750 and 1760, and aroused the same passionate discussions as a short time previously could only have been effected by religious discussions."

" The nation," wrote Voltaire, " wearied of verses, tragedies, comedies, operas, romances, novels, moral reflections still more romantic than the above, and theological disputes upon Grace and the *Convulsion-naires*, began to turn its attention to grain, and even to neglect renown in order to talk of nothing but corn and wheat."

If we compare these remarks with the testimony of the current literature, and the course of events in the capital, they can scarcely be considered exaggerated. For even at Versailles, in the heart of the monarchy, under the king's roof, the Marquise de Pompadour busied herself in advancing the theories of her old doctor Quesnay, the founder of the physiocratic system. Latour had already painted her with a volume of *L'Esprit des Lois* in her hand.

In the epigraph that he places at the beginning of his famous book,* *Pauvres paysans, pauvre royaume ; pauvre royaume, pauvre roi*, he pleads for his favourite idea—the alliance of an absolute monarchy with the peasant classes, which, if rightly understood, might have given another turn to the history of the century, and, notwithstanding Quesnay's apparent defence of despotism, might have extended to personal liberty, by means of the security of property.†

Whilst the elder Mirabeau, recognizing his own future ideal in this union between the sceptre and the plough, sought to adapt Quesnay's theories to his own class, and aspired to a nobility that should live on its own property, renounce all luxury, give itself up to the landed interest, prove itself determined to uphold religion, and its duty to its home and country, Gournay accomplished for commerce and trade what Quesnay and his friends had undertaken for agri-

---

* *Maximes genérales du Gouvernement économique d'un royaume agricole*, 1760.

† Lavergne, *Les Économistes Français au xviii siècle.*

culture. He introduced the celebrated axioms "*Laissez faire*," "*Laissez passer*," into the administrative methods of his day, and the term "*Bureaucratie*" was also coined by Gournay.* His influence and Quesnay's extended far beyond the borders of France, whilst the physiocratic theories and system of governing by the laws of nature were adopted by the most enlightened men of the day and of the most varied nationalities, amongst whom were numbered the Grand Duke Leopold of Tuscany, afterwards Emperor, the Margrave Charles Frederick of Baden, the Chancellor Chreptowicz, and, in some degree, Joseph II. himself.

In Paris, which set the fashion, the economists owed their success in a great measure to the protection and influence of women. Although the authors who expounded the theories of the " Sect," as it was called, were dull and almost unintelligible, their ponderous writings nevertheless described the direction of the current opinion, and won the active support of the educated world. The heaviest farming questions were discussed in elegant boudoirs; the Duchess d'Enville, mother of the distinguished Duc de la Rochefoucauld, a victim of the Revolution, was reputed one of the best authorities on these subjects; in their favour Madame d'Epinay forgot her love affairs; irreconcilable quarrels were put aside for discussions on the elder Mirabeau's *L'ami des hommes*, or Quesnay's *Maximes*.   The

* Grimm et Diderot, *Correspondance Littéraire, Philosophique, et Critique, adressée à un Souverain d'Allemagne*. Paris, 1830. Première partie, iv. 146. New edition by M. Tourneux. Paris, 1885.

Dauphin, father to Louis XVI., called the first-named
work "The breviary of honest people," and, in the
firm theories of the old nobleman, found something of
the exalted spirit of reformation which had pervaded
Fénélon's attitude to his grandfather, the Marcellus
of his dynasty.

On the other hand, Melchior Grimm, who belonged
to the philosophical party, jokingly called the *Philosophie Rurale* (Mirabeau's last work, which had
appeared in 1763) the "Pentateuch of the Economists,"
and, with consummate ability, the Abbé Galliani, who,
after Voltaire, was the cleverest and wittiest man of
the day, undertook to discuss the exaggerations and
extreme views of the physiocrats, with their boundless
theories as to free trade in corn, and made China the
scene of action in an imaginary sketch of their ideal
of an agricultural state in his *Dialogues sur les blés*,
which were esteemed equal to the *Lettres des Provinces* by the enthusiasts of the time.

Galliani's book embraces the whole of the period
we are now considering, and is, therefore, more than
any other, worthy of notice as encouraging the discussions and free criticism of many subjects beyond
the purely economic question.

Even in 1729 " Freedom and inviolability of property," wrote Voltaire, who had returned from England, " this is the device of the English, and it is just
as good as ' Mont-joye ' and 'Saint Denis.' "

Other glances than his had since been directed across
the channel, and one work succeeded another during

the following twenty years, shattering the decaying foundations of the old kingdom. In 1748 Montesquieu led the way with *L'Esprit des Lois*. The essay *Sur les mœurs* followed in 1756. The year 1762 brought the double gift of the *Contrat Social* and of *Emile*.

Meanwhile the Encyclopædists arrayed their powerful artillery against the existing state of things. Diderot, the very genius of revolution, promulgated all its doctrines. Wherever a spark of it was to be found those ideas were bound to be set alight, and, attracting or repelling, to set the whole spiritual atmosphere in commotion, whilst the outward calm did but increase the inward ferment.

It has been remarked, that, although Necker had shown no inclination for his calling, circumstances subsequently counteracted this, and fortune so favoured him that when barely thirty-three years of age he had secured what in those days was a very considerable fortune, amounting to several millions.

His outward circumstances being thus free from anxiety, his thoughts again turned to the plans and aspirations of his youth. On reaching manhood he aspired to exchange the counting-house for the outer world, and possess things more precious to him than riches and material comfort.

Fortune had still further favoured him in the fact that the experience gained in his commercial life proved the best preparation for the sphere of his subsequent labours.

At the age of thirty-two Necker met and married Mademoiselle Susanne Curchod, and to this he not only owed the happiness but the dignity of his life. This lady made herself an independent name in the society of the eighteenth century, but her best claim to be remembered by posterity is that she was the loving, yielding, unselfish wife of a distinguished man.*

Stirred perhaps by the memory of his own experiences, Goethe asserts in his *Dichtung u. Wahrheit*, that no more beautiful theme for a modern idyll can be found than in the home of a country clergyman.

The home in which Pastor Curchod's daughter began her existence on the 2nd of June, 1737, answered to this description, not so much from its poetical surroundings as from its high moral standard.

Her modest whitewashed home, with its green shutters, stood in the Pays de Vaud, close to the borders of France, in the small parish of Crassy, where her father was minister. Her mother traced her decent to a banished Huguenot family, the d'Alberts of Montélimart. She had been very beautiful in her youth, and these traditions of noble descent seem later on to have induced her daughter when in Paris to take her mother's name for a short time instead of her own.† Susanne had no brothers or sisters, and the Pasteur Curchod could therefore

* *The Necker Family*, by C——r. *Jacob Necker*, by A. W. Schlegel, vol. i. and iv. or the *Contemporaries*. *Notice sur M. Necker*, par le Baron de Staël, son petit-fils. Madame de Staël, *Vie privée de M. Necker*. *Œuvres Complètes*, xvii. ·1.

† D'Haussonville, *Le Salon de Madame Necker*, i. 11.

devote his whole fatherly care to his one daughter. When barely sixteen she wrote a Latin letter to one of his friends, who praises her style as Ciceronian; she studied physics and geometry, cultivated music, and described herself as a slight blonde girl, with merry blue eyes, refined features, and a winning smile, but as betraying her modest village origin in her appearance.

This attractive personality failed not to find admirers. The pulpit in the small church at Crassy soon attained a popularity amongst the young theologians not altogether due to their anxiety for the spiritual welfare of the community in that village. Letters from friends are extant reproaching her for having encouraged the young men by her coquetry; she herself confessed afterwards that she had been too inexperienced to display the necessary worldly wisdom, and further that the commendation lavished upon her had turned her head.

The feelings she inspired found expression in verse; one lover makes moan over

" Votre eternelle morale
Qui me fut toujours si fatale ; "

to another she appears in a dream ;

" Ne vous alarmez pas, Suzette,
Vous grondâtes, l'amour se tut,
Mon sommeil aima sa conquête,
Et mon reveil votre vertu "

is the concluding stanza of one of the best specimens perpetrated by her poetical adorers.

The memorable episodes in the youth of Susanno Curchod did not however take place in her early years at Crassy, but in Lausanne, where her parents used to take her as often as circumstances allowed.

D'Haussonville has given us an ample account of the style of social amusement prevalent in the old imperial town known to us chiefly as the resort of tourists in the present day. Although reduced to 9,000 inhabitants, the society of Lausanne had nevertheless separated itself into two groups, which only met from time to time. One was represented by the old aristocratic families, whose interests gravitated to the seat of government at Berne, and who led a patriarchal existence of quiet hospitality on the shores of their beautiful lake, but at times condescended to mix with the people, and to take its share in their pleasures. The other set was made up by the professors and students of the university, and was joined by a number of young girls calling themselves *La Société du Printemps*, and these amused themselves in winter with dancing and parties, and in summer with excursions and games.

The advent of Mademoiselle Curchod, and the reputation of her great talent, gave rise to the institution of an Academy which took its name from the wells of La Poudrière near the town, and imposed literary essays with the tenderest problems of the heart for their subject.

At one time the members of the Academy would busy themselves in asserting woman's right of possession "over the hearts of men—which might be compared like the New World to fallow, uncultivated land." On another occasion, to the question " What gives greater pleasure than anything else?" they unanimously answered " Making an unhappy person entirely happy, without being forced in any way to do so by outward circumstances."

In all these subtilties in the taste, or rather in the absence of taste, belonging to that time, Susanne Curchod took the liveliest share; and here again she was lauded, worshipped, adored, either as Sappho or Suzette, and reproached with the fact that she liked it all. In any case her nature gave no sign of the strong pedantry of her later years. About this time a young foreigner made his appearance in Lausanne, and joined in all this amusement and philandering with love. He appeared much struck by the young girl, and succeeded in exciting a reciprocal interest in her heart, an interest that entwines itself around the memory of the historian of the *Decline and Fall*, like the ivy on a time-honoured edifice.

Gibbon was sent by his father to the pastor Pavillard, in Lausanne, at the age of sixteen, in hopes that he might be induced to recant from the Catholic faith, which, guided "by a noble hand," he had embraced at Oxford a short time previously.[*]

The cure proved only too successful; with his ecclesiastical creed Gibbon lost all Christian belief,

[*] A passage from the writings of Bossuet had persuaded him to take this step. *Memoirs of my Life and Writings*, chap. iii.

and thus metamorphosed, at the age of eighteen, he first met Mademoiselle Curchod.

Later on, his external appearance gave rise to many good stories—for Gibbon became a shapeless, fat, little man, with short legs, and an utter absence of profile.* A certain M. de Bièvre used to say that when he required exercise he walked three times round Gibbon.† Further it is known, that, when again in Lausanne, he sank on his knees to make a declaration to the authoress Crousaz (afterwards Baroness Montolieu), and was quite unable to comply with her request that he would get up and say no more on the subject. " Ah ! if I only could," groaned the unfortunate Gibbon, and a servant had to be called in to assist him to his legs again. This was more than a quarter of a century later ; Mademoiselle Curchod knew a different Gibbon, before he had attained his renown, but possessed of all the attraction of youth. She speaks of his beautiful hair, his distinction and charming manners, and lays stress upon the clever and ever-varying expression of his countenance.

In his own incisive style Gibbon has immortalized the portrait of the young girl. He thus writes, " The personal attractions of Mademoiselle Curchod were embellished by the virtues and talents of her mind, and in her short visits to some relations in Lausanne her wit, beauty, and erudition commanded the universal

---

* Marquise du Deffand, *Letters to Horace Walpole.*
† Duchess d'Abrantes, *Histoire des Salons de Paris*, ii. 365.

appreciation of those around her. The report of such a prodigy awakened my curiosity. I saw and loved. I found her learned without pedantry, lively in conversation, pure in sentiment and elegant in manners, and the first sudden emotion was fortified by the habits and knowledge of a more familiar acquaintance.

"She permitted me to make her two or three visits at her father's house. I spent a few happy days in the mountains of Burgundy,* and her parents honourably encouraged the connection.

"In a calm retirement the gay vanity of youth no longer fluttered in her bosom; she listened to the voice of truth and passion, and I might presume to hope that I had made some impression on a virtuous heart.

"At Crassy and at Lausanne I indulged my dreams of felicity, but on my return to England I soon discovered that my father would not hear of this strange alliance, and that without his consent I was myself destitute and helpless. After a painful struggle I yielded to my fate."

Then follows the classical sentence, "I sighed as a lover, I obeyed as a son. My wound was insensibly healed by time, absence, and the habits of a new life. My cure was accelerated by a faithful report of the tranquillity and cheerfulness of the lady herself, and my love subsided into friendship and esteem." †

* As d'Haussonville remarks, he is mistaken. Crassy was on Swiss territory.

† Gibbon, *Memoirs of my Life and Writings*, chap. iv.

Chance so ordained that when Mademoiselle Curchod's great-grandchild examined the archives at
Coppet he came upon fresh proof of the small love-
affair, described in these measured terms, and naturally
drew a rather different conclusion from the discoloured
letters of young Gibbon ; for Susanne Curchod's love
was the deeper of the two, and endured long after his
had grown cold.

D'Haussonville published several letters written by
Gibbon to the young girl in the first flush of awakened
interest.

In them he compares himself, because separated
from her, to an oriental prince suddenly imprisoned
in the darkness of a dungeon—to Adam driven out of
Paradise. After spending a few weeks in pastor
Curchod's home, he speaks of the treasures of the
beautiful mind he found there, to which the possession
of a kingdom or even philosophy was not to be compared.

Just as Socrates thanked the gods that he had been
born a Greek, so in the same way Gibbon gave thanks
that he had become acquainted with this best and most
enchanting of beings.

He was so much in love that Julia de Bondeli,
Rousseau's and Wieland's friend, tells us that Gibbon
was met near Lausanne with a naked dagger in his
hand, stopping the country people, and demanding of
them at the point of the dagger whether a more beautiful or loveable creature existed than Mademoiselle
Curchod of Crassy.*

* Bodemann, *Julie von Bondeli*, pp. 217-218.

The young girl was at that time actually engaged to him, but not without many doubts and fears, which he tried vainly to calm, as to the durability of his faith.

When she learnt that his father was opposed to their union, Gibbon never again entirely succeeded in quieting the heart he had conquered. But Susanne Curchod was far from thinking that their engagement would be broken off, when in the spring of 1758 the young man's father summoned him back to England.*

In the course of the next four years almost the only sign Gibbon made to the neglected girl, to whom he was engaged, and whom he had left behind in the Swiss mountains, was the despatch to her of an essay on the study of literature with a formal dedication to herself.

Her father had meanwhile breathed his last, and she had gone to Geneva, where she supported herself and her mother by giving lessons. According to local tradition, she used to ride about the neighbourhood to her pupils, and sometimes lecture or distribute prizes to them from a small pulpit of twigs and moss.†
She was universally respected, was considered un-usually cultivated, and carried on a correspondence upon the literary topics of the day; amongst other subjects she and Julie Bondeli discussed the *Nou-*

---

* D'Haussonville, *Le Salon de Madame Necker*, i. 39-55.
† Sainte-Beuve, *Madame Necker, Causeries de Lundi*, iv. 240.

velle Héloïse.[*] She frequently looked back with pleasure to this period, for although her means were limited, and her future undecided, she still had many happy hours, which, in the days of her prosperity, she sought in vain to recall.[†]

But this chapter of her life was destined to be brief. Three years after the death of her father she lost her mother, and in her deep distress she reproached herself for impatience and indifference to her during the last days of her life. This exaggerated self-reproach was due to the burden of trouble and the trials which had so sorely taxed her strength, for in the meanwhile the engagement to Gibbon, which she still considered binding, had come to an end.

The pen, at that time so famous, found no better phrase whereby to break this to her than the well-known formula of our school-days.

"Mademoiselle, I hardly know how to begin; and yet it must be," he continued. "You will already guess what I have to say to you. Spare me from further detail; yes, I must give you up for ever! The fiat has gone forth; my heart grieves over it, but everything must give way to duty. When I reached England inclination and interest alike advised me to win back my father's affection and to disperse the clouds which had estranged it from me for a time. I flatter myself that I have succeeded in this. His whole

[*] Bodemann, *Julie von Bondeli.* Two letters to Susanne Curchod in Geneva, 1761.

[†] Golowkin, *Lettres recueillies en Suisse.*

attitude, the tenderest attention, the most especial
kindness, convince me of it. At one moment, when
he assured me that my happiness occupied his every
thought, I took advantage of the opportunity and
begged that he would permit me to marry the girl by
whose side, under any sky or in any land, my life
would be equally happy, and without whom they would
all alike be distasteful to me.

"This was his answer: 'Marry your foreign girl;
you are independent; but remember, before you do
it, that you are the son of an Englishman.' He enlarged upon the subject of deserting him and bringing
his grey hairs prematurely to the grave; upon the
cowardice of trampling down all the duties I owed to
my country. I withdrew to my chamber and remained
there two hours; I will not attempt to describe my
position to you; I left it to tell my father that I would
sacrifice the happiness of my life to him. May you,
mademoiselle, be happier than I can ever hope to be.
I shall always pray for this, and find consolation in
it. Would that my wishes might accomplish it! I
tremble to hear of your fate, and yet do not leave me
in ignorance of it. Pray assure M. and Madame
Curchod of my respect and my grief. I shall always
remember Mdle. Curchod as the best and most delightful of women; may she not utterly forget the man
who did not deserve the despair which has come upon
him. Farewell!—This letter must appear strange to
you in every sense. It is the true representation of
my mind. Twice I wrote to you, on the way to

England from a village in Lorraine, from Maestricht, and finally from London. You never received my letters. I do not know whether I should hope that this letter will reach your hands. And this, Mademoiselle, is why I have the honour to remain, with remembrances which are the torment of my life, and with respect which nothing can alter,

"Your sincere and obedient servant,

"GIBBON.

"Beriton, Aug. 24, 1762."

Gibbon's descriptions of his life in England during the year after his return from Switzerland do not in the least correspond with the passion contained in this letter, affected though it may be. They depict a life spent amidst cheerful and pleasant occupations, giving itself up more and more to serious study and wide literary designs, in which love and sad recollections certainly played a very subordinate part, if, indeed, any part at all.

In like manner Susanne Curchod had apparently schooled herself to accept a fate to which she had become accustomed, with resignation, and without ill-will towards the man who had brought it upon her, when suddenly, in the following May, 1763, the news reached her that Gibbon had returned to Lausanne.

It seems never to have entered into his head that this unexpected return might deeply move the poor girl. Then he received the following letter, dated from Geneva, in which her long pent-up feelings at length break forth.

"Sir.—I, myself, blush at the step I am now venturing to take; I would fain hide it even from myself and from you. Great Heaven! is it possible that an innocent heart can thus abase itself? What humiliation! I have had sharper suffering, but have never felt it so deeply as now. I owe it to my peace of mind to take this step. If I lose this chance, peace can never again be possible for me. Can I enjoy any such, whilst my self-tormenting heart mistakes the indications of your increasing indifference towards me for the signs of affection? During five long years I have sacrificed myself to this chimera with singular and incomprehensible constancy; but at last my too romantic nature has awakened from its self-deception, and I beg you on my knees to enlighten this foolish heart. Confirm your entire indifference, and my spirit will know how to submit. Certainty will restore that peace for which I sigh. You would be the most despicable of men did you refuse to answer me frankly, and God, who knows my heart, this God, who without doubt loves me although He has tried me so terribly, will punish you if, heedless of my prayer, there should be the least dissimulation in your answer, or should your silence make sport of my peace. If ever you should make this undignified step of mine known to a single creature, were it even to your best friend, the bitterness of my punishment would be in proportion to my error. I should then regard it as a crime the extent of which I had not taken into consideration in all its horror.

"I already feel how greatly my former reserve and my present sentiments are violated by this abasement of my maidenly pride."

The fact that this letter, addressed to "Mr. Gibbon, English nobleman at M. de Mezeray's in Lausanne," was found with its black seal broken, in the house at Coppet, leads to the conclusion that it is the original which he had returned to her. The sender of it afterwards added at the end of it, "A thinking soul is punishment enough, and every thought draws blood."

Although Gibbon's feelings were not influenced by this outbreak of her burdened heart, the verdict of posterity certainly was. Madame Necker's portrait gained not a little, in womanly grace and human sympathy, by assimilation with that of Susanne Curchod.

A second letter he received from Geneva, written in a very different tone, in acknowledgment of his answer, leaves very little doubt as to its contents, although they are unknown to us.

The young girl had by this time mastered her feelings, and writes:—

"Five years of separation could not work the change which now has suddenly taken place within me. It might have been well that you had spoken earlier, or in a different strain to me. Do not, however, grieve over my fate. My parents are dead, and what do I care for outward prosperity? Not to you did I sacrifice my existence, but to an ideal being, who could only exist in such a romantic head as mine was ever wont to be ; from the position of the only man I ever could have loved, you at once fell back, on receipt of the letter that opened my eyes, to the rank of an ordinary mortal, and I now have become more indifferent to you than to any other, as you cease to resemble the sentimental swain of my dreams.

"It now lies with you to offer compensation.

"Follow the plan you propose to me, add your regard to that of the rest of my friends, and you will receive an equal share of my friendship and confidence. Believe that these words do not proceed from any bitterness, but from a wish to help you; my conduct and feelings have deserved your respect, and your friendship ; I count on both. In the future there must be no further allusion to our past relations, and I will close them with a few necessary remarks.

" Since the losses I have had, this neighbourhood has become unbearable to me, and friends who are ready to help me recommend me to leave it. I cannot accept their offers without humiliation, and I cannot refuse them without hurting their feelings.

" I had thought of going to England, whence I had had a situation offered me, but the information I gathered as to the position of a lady companion, and the customs of the country, is so conflicting, that I still hesitate between going there and accepting a place at one of the German courts. You could help me to a decision. I depend as much upon your judgment as upon your taste.

" At the time your book appeared I put one or two

ideas on paper which had been suggested by it. I venture to send you these as the first proofs of my friendship; it will not be my fault if I do not give you others; I desire to assure you of this verbally when you come to Geneva, and justify the praises I have there lavished upon you.

"I hear that various English people are betaking themselves to Motiers from Paris. If this is your reason for coming to my country, and you should wish for a letter to Rousseau, I must beg you to let me know, as my best friends are most intimate with him. I should be really indebted to you if you would put my admiration of your talents to the test."

Amongst the friends she mentions in this letter was one whose feelings for Mademoiselle Curchod had gone through another stage, but without meeting any encouragement. Later on, whilst still mindful of her, he asserts that he had always loved, and always should love her, even were he never permitted to add to her happiness. This was the Pastor Moultou,[*] so well known to all readers of J. J. Rousseau's *Confessions*. He had been married, a short time before, to a friend of Susanne Curchod's youth, and thus was in a position to offer her the hospitality of his roof, under pretext of requiring her assistance in organising his new household.

He did not allow her outwardly calm appearance to deceive him, but, on the contrary, made a last effort in favour of the unhappy attachment, which he knew she had not relinquished.

---

[*] Aimé Steinlen, *Charles Victor de Bonstetten*, p. 36.

Jean Jacques Rousseau had lived for some time at Motiers Travers, not far from Neuenberg, under the protection of King Frederick of Prussia. Now that it was given back to him, the home he had longed for when in a distant land no longer ministered to his happiness. He wrote to the Marshal of Luxembourg that he had expected to come back to what had charmed him in youth, but the landscape, the sky, the men, all were changed. Even the hills that had enchanted his eyes at the age of twenty were now unrecognisable.*

Here, as in a fever—at variance with himself and the whole world—lived the man who inspired such confidence in his contemporaries that some came to him as a law-giver, who could re-establish tottering institutions; others as to a physician of souls, who could heal wounded spirits.

Among the latter was Moultou, who related the story of his young friend's misplaced love to the hermit of Val-de-Travers, and how she had sacrificed all her prospects by reason of her troubles, only to find the originator of them cold and unfeeling, as utterly cured of his passion as she was not. "She has written a letter that wrings my heart," added Moultou. "You, who so well know the torments of the mind, would certainly pity the poor girl. But you can do more, and help her. Speak to Gibbon when he comes to you of the reputation she enjoys in Geneva, not only on account of her knowledge and

* *Jean Jacques et le Pays Romand*, p. 68. Geneva, 1878.

intelligence but also on account of her spotless reputation and blameless life. I assure you, my honoured friend, that I know of nothing purer or more heavenly than this womanly soul; and I am entirely impartial, as I am the very one who would fain help her to leave us for ever and go to England."*

Meanwhile, after three weeks' reflection, Gibbon had answered Mademoiselle Curchod's last letter, with all reserve, declining regular correspondence as "too dangerous for his peace of mind," and above all, although with every profession of friendship, offering no opposition to the intentions of the girl he was once engaged to on the subject of going abroad.

He never went to J. J. Rousseau, who differed from Moultou in the following words: "You have given me a commission for Mademoiselle Curchod, of which I shall acquit myself ill, precisely on account of my esteem for her. The coldness of Mr. Gibbon makes me think ill of him. I have read his book.† It is deformed by the perpetual affectation and pursuit of brilliancy. Mr. Gibbon is no man for me. I cannot think him well adapted to Mademoiselle Curchod. He that does not know her value is unworthy of her; he that knows it, and can desert her, is a man to be despised."

Gibbon could afford quietly to ignore the literary censure, as it was unjust; with respect to the judgment on his personal behaviour, he had good grounds

* J. Levallois, *J. J. Rousseau, ses Amis et ses Ennemis*, p. 1.
† *Essai sur l'Étude de Littérature.*

for being sensitive.   Years afterwards he tried to defend himself.* The breach was however widened still further between him and Mademoiselle Curchod, and this time under Voltaire's roof.

The latter had betaken himself to Switzerland in 1756, after the well-known passages between him and his friend and patron, Frederick.

He spent the first two years of this exile of his own choosing in Lausanne, where he led the brilliant life of supremacy and hospitality, in allusion to which he used to say that he had been the hotel-keeper for all Europe, and had received between three and four hundred Englishmen at his house, who were so devoted to their own country that hardly any of them ever remembered him after their departure.†

Amongst these Englishmen was Gibbon, who saw Voltaire act his tragedies, supported by a troupe of ladies and gentlemen from Lausanne, trained by himself, in the theatre at his villa of "Mon Repos."

Whilst Rousseau addressed his letters to d'Alembert "on the dangers of the theatre for a small town, where the customs are still pure," Voltaire, in the first flush of success, was also sending him news that "Zaire" was better played on the shores of the Lake of Geneva than in Paris: he had an audience of two hundred people, who were just as well able to give an opinion as any other public in Europe, and he had drawn tears from all these Swiss eyes.

* Gibbon, *My Life and Writings*, chap. iv.
† *Voltaire to Madame du Deffand*, i. 219.

From Lausanne Voltaire went to Geneva, which place ventured to show more opposition to his influence, and in consequence was set down by him as inhabited by 24,000 argumentative beings, a ridiculously anti-quated town.

This "*petitissime, parvulissime, et pedantissime re-publique*" he soon exchanged for Ferney, and thence summoned his friends in Geneva, and any strangers who might be there, to share in its pleasures.*

These included the Duchess of La Rochefoucauld d'Enville, and through her and Moultou (who had accomplished the apparently impossible feat of living in friendly relations both with the Patriarch of Ferney and with the Hermit of Motiers) Mademoiselle Curchod was introduced to Voltaire. She made such a good impression on him that he received her into the envied band of his correspondents, and many of the graceful fanciful letters which, even in his ad-vanced years, he found time and inclination to write to women, bore her address, and appeared later on in Grimm's literary correspondence.

At one of the Ferney theatrical representations, Mademoiselle Curchod once again met Gibbon.

This unexpected encounter revived the scarcely allayed storm in her breast, and his behaviour con-firmed the old saying, that those who have inflicted an injury seldom, if ever, can forgive.

He was so neglectful, she says herself "so cruel,"

* Lucien Perey et Gaston Maugras, *La Vie intime de Voltaire aux Delices et á Ferney.* Paris, Calman Levey, 1885.

that she once more thought it necessary to write to him and allude to the past.[*]

But of what avail are reproaches and complaints in such a case? As no further understanding could be possible between this cold-blooded young man and the still romantic girl of six-and-twenty, it naturally followed that a further residence in her own country under these circumstances became unbearable to her.

Just about that time a young widow, Madame de Vermenoux, arrived from Paris to consult Tronchin. She spent a very sociable winter at Geneva, and, amongst others, she saw a good deal of young Bonstetten, and Moultou, who lived in the same house as she did. In this way she further made the acquaintance of Mademoiselle Curchod, who, on first acquaintance, was set down by Bonstetten as "tall, handsome, but a little affected."[†]

As the time drew near for her return to Paris Madame de Vermenoux proposed that she should accompany her as lady-companion. To this she unhesitatingly consented, and went with her to Paris in the spring of 1764.

The ladies got on very well together, and Mademoiselle Curchod had only to be careful that the requirements of her position in the house of the rich young woman should not exceed the possibilities of her own modest income. In the month of July she first mentions the name of Necker in a letter to Moultou,

[*] For these and all earlier letters, d'Haussonville, *Le Salon de Madame Necker*, i. 39-55, 70-76, 86.

[†] V. Bonstetten, p. 8.   Golowkin, *Lettres recueillies en Suisse.*

as that of a visitor who might be of interest to her correspondent as a native of Geneva.

In Paris people knew a great deal more of the reasons that took the rich financier to the house of Madame de Vermenoux, and it was said that before she started for Switzerland he had proposed marriage to her.

Her first marriage had been by no means happy; she had besides contracted other ties, and therefore, whilst retaining his friendship, she refused Necker's offer.

After her death he spoke of the extraordinary fascination of his adored friend,* but, according to the letter Mademoiselle Curchod addressed to Moultou at Geneva, he did not long grieve as her rejected suitor. Necker had gone to Geneva during the summer, and there the chances of his engagement to Mademoiselle Curchod were already discussed.

"My dear friend," she wrote, confessing the interest that Necker had aroused in her, " he is too much in public life to be led by one voice; he must be governed only democratically, by the greatest number, and thus during his whole life he will never find happiness." This was the first and last time she spoke in this objective way of the future minister. In her next letter her heart was implicated, and she was obliged to recant, for on his return from Geneva Necker sought and obtained her hand in marriage.

Soon afterwards, when she had learnt to know him

---

* Grimm et Diderot, *Correspondance Littéraire*, xiv. 19-20, 1788, Necker to Meister.

better, she thus wrote, "Never ask, my dear James, for the expression of my feelings. Let me enjoy my happiness without thinking about it. In admitting it I shall fear to lose it, and I cannot reflect upon the blessings of my life without dreading that they should come to an end. Think at least of the responsibility you are taking upon yourself. I fear I shall turn you into the most unthankful of men. If you are not one of the best, read no further. Turn away your eyes and tear up this letter; it is going to be an indictment against you. Yes, my friend, you are the chain that binds me to this earth. The moment you leave off loving me I shall be estranged from the whole creation. Ponder deeply as to what my happiness consists in. Is it not the magic of your love, which makes everything attractive in my eyes? I can only see a faint reproduction of our bond in the consolations of friendship; the splendour of your fortune only reminds me of the trouble it has cost you to earn it. Vanity tempts me to hope that I shall please you, and that by my intellectual pursuits I may be able to retain your affection and withstand the ravages of time. When I lie down to rest I say to myself, 'He loves me.' When I awake my first impulse is to thank Heaven for such love. But my soul can never again be divided from yours, and a greater faith in God is added to it by this union. My friend, never let your feelings towards me grow cold, as mine will never alter towards you. I should regard the day of my death as the most beautiful of my life if I knew it to be the day on which your love for me had reached its highest limit." *

In one word, Mademoiselle Curchod was in love, and, what was still rarer, she was, and remained, a happy wife, giving happiness in return.

Chance so seldom separated the husband and wife, and then only for so short a time, that, with a few unimportant exceptions, no further correspondence took place between them. But from daily experience Necker could prove how entirely her love for him filled every moment of her existence.

They were married quite quietly, without even letting Madame de Vermenoux know the day and the hour. Whilst it was said in Paris that this lady had brought about the marriage to free herself from an inconvenient adorer, who could now bore himself with his wife,† Madame Necker no longer showed any reserve as to her affection. "I am the wife of a man whom I should take to be an angel if his liking for me did not betray his weakness."‡

Six months later she writes :—" I should be the most ungrateful of human beings if I did not offer up prayers of thankfulness every moment of my life."

Under Necker's own eyes she sketched the following portrait of him for her correspondent. " Imagine

---

* D'Haussonville, *Le Salon de Madame Necker*, ii. 7.

† Baronne d'Oberkirch, *Mémoires*, i. xiii.

‡ Golowkin, *Lettres recueillies en Suisse*, 244, 283. *Madame Necker to Madame de Brenlès.*

the most literal creature in the world, so happily convinced of his own superiority that he never notices
mine, so certain of his perspicacity that he is constantly taken in, so positive that he in himself combines every talent in all its perfection that it never
occurs to him to seek a pattern in others.   The insig-
nificance of others surprises him, because his own
greatness suffices him, and he constantly compares
himself with others that he may satisfy himself that
he is incomparable.

"He mistakes stupid for clever people because he
considers himself to be on a summit whence all those
at his feet appear equally lowly; he nevertheless
gives preference to the stupid people, because he holds
that they are an excellent foil to his genius.

"Furthermore he is as capricious as a beautiful
woman, and just as inquisitive. I flatter myself,
however, that the harmless medicine which I proffer
to him by means of this letter (he is reading it over
my shoulder) may cure him for a time of this insuffer-
able malady."*

This sketch of character is only meant for a joke.
But even at that date Madame Necker had so little
idea of joking that a good many of the traits she
touches upon are accepted as authentic in his biographies, especially in one of the most life-like and
faithful—that written by his friend H. Meister, only
published long afterwards, although, even then, he
knew him intimately.

* D'Haussonville, *Le Salon de Madame Necker*, i. 115.

Necker's undeniable self-appreciation was best held in check by Madame Necker's opinion of her husband; after the sad experience of her early days she could not but draw comparisons between him and others, and the result was that the grateful affection Necker had inspired in her rose to passionate adoration.

She did things for his sake that she would not have considered desirable for her own; she sacrificed her personal inclinations, time, strength, repose, and health, to turn the eyes of the world upon him, and to gather an influential and distinguished social circle around him.

Herself unknown, and without connection or high rank to aid her in her task, this was no easy matter for a young foreigner to undertake. It must have been all the more difficult for Madame Necker, as it was only by degrees, and not without an effort, that she gave herself up to the fascinations of a Parisian life. As early as 1765 she thus writes to her friend, Madame de Brenlès, in Switzerland: "The only aim of existence in Paris is to cultivate the taste, but this is done at the expense of genius." The men she considered superficial, the women vain; their corrupt morals went against her better feelings. "It is easy to resist temptation of a base description," she wrote, "but it is much more difficult to keep the temptation to ambition at a distance, because this passion is so intermingled with the best qualities and the firmest convictions that it is almost impossible not to be possessed by it in Paris." *

Ambitious she had long been, if not for herself for another. For his sake she undertook to form a *salon* which was to be above all things literary. When the result of Madame Necker's social endeavours and efforts, after scarcely two years of Parisian life, came to the ears of her friends in Switzerland, these concealed neither their astonishment nor their anxiety; and Moultou, as her most intimate friend, inquired what was to become of her Christian convictions in such surroundings. " My dear friend," she replied, "how can you mistrust me for a single moment ? The reasons of my faith came to me at my birth, and, although they are the foundations of my happiness, you can think me capable of giving them up. You may accuse me of exaggerated enthusiasm, but ought you to be the one to complain that I honour everything that is right and good ? I receive a few authors, but I lost no time in acquainting them with my views, neither are theirs disturbed in my presence. At my age nothing is easier than to regulate the tone of a pleasant domestic circle. I certainly come in contact with a great many atheists, but their arguments have never made the smallest impression upon me, and, if ever they penetrated to my heart, they could only cause a shudder."†

* Golowkin, *Lettres diverses recueillies en Suisse*, 264. Genève, 1827.

† D'Haussonville, *Le Salon de Madame Necker*, i. 164.

Looking back upon this period she wrote later on to the author Thomas: "Do you remember how I found myself twenty years ago in the midst of all those distinguished people of European reputation, when I used to hear all the ideas upon which my happiness rested treated as chimeras? It cost me a severe struggle to retain my convictions against this stream of unbelief."*

Under certain circumstances she did not hesitate to stand up for what was sacred to her with a courage that even her opponents, such as Grimm, fully appreciated. During one of her Friday dinners, being led into a discussion that could no longer be kept within bounds, with Grimm himself, and having argued a long time without being able to convince him, she at length burst into tears, but felt herself obliged to write before the end of the evening, to beg him to forgive her for what had occurred.† However, it was not with men who pursued that particular line of thought that she formed the ideal friendships so necessary to her mental tendency and warmth of feeling. The names which must always be linked with hers besides that of Moultou are those of Thomas and Buffon. In the eighteenth century, Buffon was considered equal in fame to Voltaire, and with Rousseau and Montesquieu he takes the first rank among his contemporaries.

"The form of an athlete and the mind of a

* Madame Necker, *Mélanges*, iii. 213.
† D'Haussonville, *Le Salon de Madame Necker*, i. 150.

philosopher," as Voltaire describes him.   Mallet du
Pan sets him down as the type of a philosopher; just,
rather than generous, reasonable in all things, loving
order, and promoting it around him.   From the age
of thirty-two, when he was appointed director of the
Royal Gardens, he dedicated his whole life to natural
history, and not quite fifty years later he finished a
work of thirty-six volumes, which opened new paths
to the learning of that time, and was like a poem
written in prose.   The Château de Montbard in
Burgundy is inseparably connected with the name of
Buffon, as Ferney is with the memory of Voltaire;
Les Charmettes, or the Hermitage at Montmorency,
with that of Jean Jacques Rousseau; the Château de
la Brède and its English park, with the original plan
of *L'Esprit des Lois.*   There he usually led a retired
existence, divided between his work-room, in a
secluded tower on the property, and looking after his
garden.   This was now and then interrupted by visits
to the capital.   On one of these latter occasions, at
the age of sixty-seven, having just lost a much-loved
wife, he made acquaintance with Madame Necker.   This
first meeting, arranged by a mutual friend, led to an
intimacy which lasted till Buffon's death.   " I adore
you so sincerely," he once wrote to her, "that you
cannot fail to be thankful for it.   I love you for this
life and the next, and even for Eternity, if your views
concerning it are more settled than mine, which it is
to be hoped they are."   As far as it lay in mortal
hands, Buffon proved his words.   As his end drew

nigh, Madame Necker left her own house to be near
him in his last moments. He had her picture beside
him, painted on a snuff-box, which she had given him.
Necker's book, *On the Importance of Religious Conviction*, had appeared shortly before, and Buffon listened
with great pleasure whilst his son read it aloud to
him.* When Madame Necker entered, he deplored
the tragedy he had to offer her. In the brief moments
of repose granted to him during his terrible sufferings,
he found comfort in clasping her hand, and in telling
her how happy he was made by the sight of her, at a
moment when nothing else could any longer give him
either pleasure or joy.† In the sketch she left behind
her of the last moments of her great friend she carefully asserts that he departed openly acknowledging
his acceptance of the Christian faith.‡ But when she
looked back upon his scientific knowledge she arrived
at a very different conclusion, by no means so consoling
to her. It has been remarked of a greater man than
Buffon that he resembled one who had wandered
through and admired all the interior of a splendid
palace, and then had forgotten to leave his card on
the master of it.§ Buffon did not quite do this,
inasmuch as the name of the Creator is frequently
mentioned in his works. But it is well known that
in his remarks against Hérault de Seychelles he said

* Madame Necker, *Mélanges*, iii. 253, 318, 376.
† Buffon to Madame Necker two days before his death.
‡ Nadault de Buffon, *Correspondence Inedité de Buffon. Madame
Necker on Buffon's death.*
§ *Flier Letters*, 47.

that it was only necessary to insert the term "Creative Power of Nature" where he had used the word "Creator."

In the spring of 1765 Gibbon again returned to Paris, and was hospitably received by the Neckers. He speaks of this renewal of acquaintance in the terms he generally selected when alluding to Madame Necker, terms which were not exactly well chosen.

"The Curchod," he writes, "I saw at Paris. She was very fond of me, and the husband particularly civil. Could they insult me more cruelly? Ask me every evening to supper, go to bed, and leave me alone with his wife. What an impertinent security! it is making an old lover of mighty little consequence. She is as handsome as ever, and much genteeler, seems pleased with her fortune rather than proud of it. I was (perhaps indiscreetly enough) exalting Nanette d'Illen's good luck, and her fortune. 'What fortune?' (said she with an air of contempt) 'not above 20,000 livres a year.' I smiled, and she caught herself up immediately. 'What airs I give myself in despising 20,000 livres a year; why, a year ago I looked on 800 livres as the summit of my wishes.'" *
The pendant to this letter is another from Madame Necker to her friend Madame de Brenlès in Switzerland, written November the 7th, 1765: "Have I told you yet that we have seen Gibbon here? His arrival gave me special pleasure, not that I had the least

* Gibbon, *Memoirs of my Life and Writings*, 68, 79, note 10.

affection left for a man who deserved it so little, but
because it was such a complete and well-deserved
satisfaction to my womanly pride.   I saw him almost
daily; he was gentle, agreeable, and reserved almost to
shyness, a daily witness of my husband's affection for
me, his mental superiority, his amiable disposition. The
warmth of his admiration for the outward splendour
surrounding me for the first time made me value that
to which I had hitherto been indifferent, and which I
had even found disagreeable."*

Years passed on, the youth and maiden who once
had met on the shores of the Lake of Geneva, and
who with their different dispositions had loved and
misunderstood each other, were now grown old.   In
the summer-house on his terrace at Lausanne, Gibbon
put the finishing strokes to a work the like of which
but few achieve. · Even in that hour, in sharp contrast
to the joy of success, came the sensation of mutability
in all things earthly, and the comparison between the
undying reputation of the work and the short period
of life's enjoyment still left to its author.† Gibbon
was then fifty years old, and stood solitary in his
fame.   He found it so irksome that five years afterwards he thought of a tardy marriage.   The last
letter he received from Madame Necker was on this
subject.   She had gone back to Switzerland with her
husband during the Revolution, and spent the winter

---

* Golowkin, *Lettres diverses recueillies en Suisse*, 265.
† Gibbon, *Memoirs of my Life and Writings*, 190.

at Geneva, as did also Gibbon.   On the 15th of
June in that year she wrote from Coppet: "We often
think of the enjoyable hours we spent with you when
by the favour of Providence the object of the pure
and precious affection of my youth was brought into
contact with that other which secured such an envi-
able lot to me in this world.   This unusual combination
and your unequalled powers in conversation led me
into enchanted realms; the link between the past
and the present caused truth to take the form of a
dream.   Could you not decide on prolonging it?
Coppet is at its best; I will not add anything more,
for we live quite in retirement; the Genevese remain
in the town, and owing to bad times they leave their
country-houses empty.   Even M—— has felt constrained
to marry again and we hardly ever see him . . . .
I therefore pray you to avoid any such tardy union;
the marriage that brings happiness to our riper years
must be contracted in early youth; then only is the
union complete.   Inclinations blend with each other,
sentiments assimilate, ideas are shared, the intellectual
qualities are modelled on each other, the pleasure of
life is doubled, and youth is prolonged; for the impressions of the mind govern the eye, and even vanished
beauty does not lose its power.   Who would venture
to find a worthy companion for you, who have reached
the highest mental development, whose whole life is
spent in a fixed pursuit?   An unsatisfactory union
always reminds me of the statue of Horace: you are
wedded to fame, and your friends who love you look

on the bond without envy as it is reflected on themselves." *   And thus the intercourse between Gibbon
and Madame Necker drew to a harmonious conclusion.
Born in the same year he was destined to end his
days but a few months before she did; he died un-
married on the 17th February, 1794, not quite 'fifty-
seven years old.   Fate had not been unjust; according to Goethe's favourite saying, "To each in old
age was apportioned in full measure what they had
wished for in youth; solitary greatness to the man,
to the woman the happiness of a deep and reciprocated
affection."

In the second year of her marriage Madame Necker's
daughter and only child was born on the 22nd of
April, 1766, and named Anne Louise Germaine. After
a few years the Neckers were obliged to exchange their
house in the Rue Michel le Comte for the Hôtel le
Blanc in the Rue Cléry, considered one of the finest
in Paris, but pulled down in the year 1842 when the
Rue Mulhouse was built.   The Necker family continued to live there until they exchanged it for their
residence in the Contrôle-générale.†   The choice of
a summer resort soon followed. At first Necker used to
hire the small Château of Madrid built by Francis I.
in the Bois de Boulogne after his release: then he
bought the beautiful Château de Saint Ouen on the
banks of the Seine, with its terraces and park, and
which was near enough to Paris to allow his guests

* Madame Necker, *Mélanges*, i. 360.
† Sainte-Beuve, *Causeries de Lundi*, xii. 210, note.

to return there late at night.   All their pleasantest memories were associated with this place.   Madame Necker herself could not withstand the seductions of this new existence.   "One could and might be happier elsewhere" (she wrote to her friend in Switzerland), "but in order to be so one must never have known the fascination, which, although it does not actually constitute happiness itself, still poisons any other form of existence.   We are like the gourmands, whose pampered palates weary of every delicacy and yet can never go back to a good simple diet.   Both bodily and mental taste is marvellously indulged in this place, and we, physically and morally, work out the story of that young sybarite who was prevented from sleeping by a crumpled rose-leaf."*

She does not conceal the difficulty she had in adapting herself to this new world.   "It is quite true that I do not hold to the same ideas as when I first came to this country.   I held that literature was the key to everything: that a man only made mental progress by means of books, or became great and remarkable by the extent of his learning: but I now recognise that an author only knows certain subjects, which are of no use to him under any other circumstances, and this has been my own invariable experience where those I chance to meet did not possess general ability. In society I had nothing to say; the speech in use was ever unknown to me: although forced, woman-

* Golowkin, *Lettres*, &c., 413.   *Madame Necker to Madame de Brenlès*, Paris, April 6, 1773.

like, to win men's approval, I was unable to understand
all the gradations of self-love, and gave offence where
I sought to flatter. What would be called sincerity
in Switzerland in Paris goes by the name of selfishness.
Here carelessness in small matters is called ignorance
of good manners ; in one word, as I never found the
right tone, and, above all, was not quick at repartee,
as my own constant blunders only made me shyer,
and I saw that my own ideas would never amalgamate
with those around me, I resolved to bury my small
capital and never to resuscitate it, and thus, if possible,
to live more in harmony with my surroundings." *
The Neckers' circle had nevertheless the greatest influence even in relation to literature; it is very closely
connected with the intellectual movement of the second
half of the eighteenth century in France,† and some
of the best-known episodes in the history of the times
are intertwined with its memories. It was Madame
Necker who invited a select audience to listen to the
first reading of Paul and Virginia by Bernardin de
Saint Pierre in her *salon*, but this gem in French prose
was not appreciated on its first appearance, and the
author, who enjoyed the special friendship of Necker
and his wife, had to go through this experience. When
Buffon was seen to be asleep and another to be laughing a few of the ladies in the company hastened to

---

* Golowkin, *Lettres*, &c., 400. *Madame Necker to Madame de
Brenlès*, Paris, 31 August, 1771.

† *Le Salon de Madame Necker. Revue de Deux Mondes*, 1833,
ii. 691.

conceal their tears, and the romance fell flat. Only
in the last few years of their existence in 1787 did
discriminating society make good its mistake, but the
book now belonged to another period and helped to
usher in a new epoch in literature. No less famous
is the dinner of April 17th, 1770, to which Madame
Necker invited Diderot, Suard, the Marquis de Chastellux, Grimm, de Schomberg, Marmontel, d'Alembert,
Thomas, Saint Lambert, Saurin, Helvetius, Raynal,
and the Abbés Arnauld and Morellet, and on which
occasion, at the instigation of their hostess, the idea
was started of erecting a statue of the Patriarch of
Ferney, to be executed by Pigalle. Concerning the
design, to be supplied by the sculptor, a long dispute
took place, in which verses to Madame Necker from
Voltaire find a place. They are reproduced in a
milder form in Beuchot's edition of his letters, but
the original lines found afterwards amongst Suard's
papers read differently.* Notwithstanding strenuous

---

* Vous craignez, beauté délicate
  Que ce Pigalle trop ingénu
  Ne me présente à vous tout nu,
  Mais pardonnez-lui, s'il me flatte.

  Quand son ciseau vous sculptera
  Ne soyez pas si renchérie;
  Ou tout le monde lui criera
  Otez moi cette draperie.

  Les grâces n'en eurent jamais;
  L'habillement les défigure,
  Et vouloir cacher leurs attraits,
  C'est un péché contre nature.

E 2

opposition the undertaking succeeded, owing to the support of the King of Denmark, with that of the Empress Catherine and Frederick the Great. By the advice of Diderot, who at that time upheld the antique, Pigalle produced an undraped Voltaire, with marvellously life-like features and startlingly faithful.* This statue, treated in the manner of an anatomical study, was certainly never exhibited; later on it came into the possession of a nephew of Voltaire's, who in 1816 presented it to the library of the Institute, where it still is to be found, in company with the heart of the philosopher.† It is more to Madame Necker's credit that she supported every work of mercy and charity than that she corresponded with Voltaire, inspired the muse of Thomas, and was the friend of Buffon. After her death Necker had the consolation of referring to many such undertakings, some of which had been successfully called to life and others personally carried out by her unselfish efforts.‡ It is worthy of remark that Madame Necker was the first to enlist the assistance of sisterhoods in this work, which she carried on simultaneously with her efforts to ameliorate the conditions of prison-life. She spent much energy upon the reception and bringing-up of foundlings, but, above

> Je consens qu'un lourd vêtement
> Couvre ma chétive machine,
> Mais quant a vous, objet charmant,
> Prenez la gaze la plus fine.

* Grimm et Diderot, *Correspondance Littéraire*, i. 118, 164, 465; iii. 249.　　　　　　　† Morellet, *Mémoires*, i. 195.

‡ Madame Necker, *Mélanges*, i. *Notice sur Madame Necker*, xxxv.

all, her name is inseparably connected with sweeping
reforms with regard to the better nursing and treat-
ment of the patients in hospitals. At the period when
she first came to the capital, priding itself on every
refinement of luxury, sufferers in hospital were not
even given separate beds, but as they arrived were
added to the ranks, and indifferently shared a bed
with those on the road to recovery and those who
were dangerously ill, the poorly or the dying, a patient
with an infectious disease or another merely temporarily indisposed.   The most frightful scenes and
fatal results were the daily consequence of this state
of things in the dreaded refuges provided for earthly
suffering. The unfortunate human race was sacrificed
under the very eyes of the nurses and doctors in a
way that happily is now unknown.   For many years
Madame Necker's interest in this matter had been
aroused, and when Necker was first appointed Minister
to Louis XIV. she succeeded in obtaining a monetary
grant for the establishment of the small hospital which
still bears her name ; and further secured the help of
twelve sisters of mercy, who undertook the care of
the patients under the direction of the vicar of Saint
Sulpice.   Although the Archbishop of Paris was the
sworn enemy both of the Jansenists and the Philosophers, he was so entirely of the same mind as Madame
Necker, on the mutual ground of love to our neighbours, that when he won a considerable sum in a law-
suit against the city of Paris he gave it over to Necker,
begging him, with remarkable tolerance, to devote it

to charitable purposes, and merely to account for it
to the king.*   It was principally through the instru-
mentality of his wife that Necker, after a very few
years of married life, came into pleasant and satisfactory relations both with the great world and the no
less influential literary world, and obtained sufficient
insight into his surroundings to enable him to take
his place on the perilous stage of Parisian life and
his share in the ever-increasing excitement of the day.

---

* Necker, *Œuvres complètes*, iii. 497, &c.   Auguste de Staël,
i. clix. *Œuvres complètes*.   Henri Martin, *Histoire de France*.

CHAPTER II.

In 1768 the position Necker had made for himself as
a man of business induced his native town of Geneva
to confide the management of its affairs into his
hands. As set forth in the business-like style of his
official answer to the " Magnificent little Council,"
Necker undertook this with a request that " regard
might be had to his talents," and he declined to
accept any remuneration. The post in itself was not
very important, but it procured him access to Court
and frequent intercourse with the Prime Minister
Choiseul, who personally esteemed him and became
much attached to him. The only diplomatic difficulty
Necker experienced in the outset of his labours consisted in moderating the zeal of his government for
the good of the little Republic, and in making it

understand that the affairs of Geneva could have only a comparatively small claim on the attention of the French Minister.* He had, however, plenty of opportunities of serving his native town, and afterwards he looked back on this first post as that whence he had derived the most unalloyed satisfaction.† Shortly after this nomination Necker joined the administration of the East India Company.

Just at the time when the Government threatened its existence, and in the name of Free Trade attacked its privileges through the Abbé Morellet, Necker published a special statement in defence of the shareholders. He did not, however, succeed in saving the Company, which was dissolved by royal decree in 1770. Shortly after its dissolution he carried out his plan of quitting the bank, and retired in the year 1772 with a fortune of seven and a half million francs, surrendering all share in the business. De Germany, his brother, and Girardot, undertook to carry it on, and eventually the son of the great physiologist and poet, Albert von Haller, joined Girardot in a partnership, which under the Convention and the Directory embarked in various bold ventures, and obtained the contract for the Italian army from Bonaparte.‡ Necker used often to say how easy it would have been for him, with his intimate knowledge of the European

* D'Haussonville, *Le Salon de Madame Necker*, ii. 84.

† Baron Auguste de Staël, *Notice sur Necker*, i. xii. *Œuvres complètes*.

‡ *Revue Suisse*, 1856, 658, &c. *Die Zeitgenossen*, 1816-1817 and 1818-1819, vols. i and iv.

markets, still further to increase his fortune, but having reached the age of forty he decided on following the mode of life he most inclined to. His unselfishness and indifference in money matters were so sincere that, his wife asserts, from that moment the whole management of his immense fortune fell into her hands, and she had to buy and sell, farm, build, and manage everything, without being able to induce him to talk over these matters with her. " The comic result is," she continues, " that at last the dependants have become so accustomed to taking all their orders from the mistress of the house, that they imagine Necker to have no knowledge of money matters, seeing that he keeps so entirely aloof from them."* This indifference to money is a fine trait in Necker's character, and outweighs many weaknesses.

On the 10th of May, 1774, the corpse of the old king was carried, without any kind of state, to the vault at St. Denis, amidst the insults of the people, and Louis XVI. began to reign, not having reached the age of twenty. The young monarch was met by the question—no longer to be evaded—as to whether he alone would obstruct the impulse now actuating France; a question partly influencing the best traditions of the monarchy. The greatest and most successful of the sovereigns of that dynasty had had Sully by his side; under his grandson Fénélon, Vauban, and Bois Guilbert had in vain planned the outlines of a policy which would have saved him

* Madame Necker, *Mélanges*, ii. 372.

from shipwreck; even under Louis XV. the reforming element had not disappeared which d'Argenson
and more especially Machault represented in the
king's council. The serious youth of Louis XVI.,
and his well-known conscientiousness and kindness of heart, gave rise to the hope that his reign
would be a contrast to that of his grandfather. His
first selection did not justify this expectation. He
passed over the enlightened and experienced Machault,
and chose Maurepas, who was alike frivolous and old.
Maurepas entrusted the Foreign Affairs to the Count
de Vergennes, and next sought for some one to fill the
post of the outgoing Minister of Marine. Chance,
the powerful ally of the *ancient régime*, directed his
choice towards Turgot, the last of the great statesmen
of the monarchy.

Turgot was forty-seven years old, and so handsome
that his features recalled the noblest creations of the
antique; once seen he could not easily be forgotten.
He was first appointed Minister of Marine, and in
August 1774 became Controller-General, which meant
Finance Minister, and Secretary of State for most of
the Home Affairs.

" If good does not come of this," writes d'Alembert
to Frederick, "it shows that good does not exist."
One of his biographers writes, " This man raises
ambition into a virtue." His appointment was considered as a concession to the philosophers, as he
agreed with some of their ideas, and laboured for
toleration in religious matters, for the triumph of

humane principles in administrative and economical questions, and for the universal spread of education. His political doctrine offered a most emphatic contrast to the revolutionary doctrine, as he exacted nothing beyond a reformation of the existing state of things, and instead of losing himself in a perilous Utopia he was content to deal with the present situation, declining to abolish even the worst abuses without offering compensation to those who might be injured by their abolition.* When an attempt was made to prejudice Louis XVI. against him, by pointing him out as an encyclopædist, the king, to the joy of Voltaire, replied, " He is an honest man and that is enough for me." Unfortunately, the distinguishing feature in the life of Turgot was his persistent ill-luck. The fruits of his exertions as Intendant of Limoges were entirely destroyed by the famine of 1770-1771, which sent up the public debt to a million, and this after he had done his very utmost to diminish it. In the beginning of 1775, when still in office, he was seized with illness, at a moment when every interest threatened to combine against him at Court. Next a rise in prices was artificially brought about by the operations of financiers, and, in consequence, the so-called "guerre des farines" broke out in various parts of the kingdom, being purposely originated in Paris by those who had obtained a monopoly of the corn-trade through Turgot's legislation, which had taken off all

* Foncin, *Ministère de Turgot*, 548-549.

restrictions in that direction.* Prosecution of the
culprits was suppressed by the king's command, as it
would have entailed far-reaching and painful disclo-
sures. Turgot himself believed in the complicity of
the Prince of Conti. By an unintentional but most
unfortunate coincidence, Necker's book on the "Corn
Laws and Trade" came out just at this time. It rejected
unconditional free trade in corn, not only in foreign
countries but also in the interior, and therefore added
to the ferment by making Turgot's administration
answerable for the momentary increase of distress.
Necker's sentence directed against the Economists—
" anatomical experiments should not be attempted on
living bodies"—took unto itself wings. Unfortunately
he further excited public attention by attacking
property, in favour of cheap bread for the poor. He
described the rich as " devouring the substance of the
poor," and put sentences, such as these, into the
mouth of the people—" What care we for your laws
concerning property? we possess none. Your laws
of equity? We have nothing to defend. Of freedom?
If we do not work to-morrow we must die."†

The coronation of the young king took place at
Rheims in the June of the year thus unhappily
begun. Turgot had proposed that the sentence in the
oath should be omitted wherein the king solemnly

* *Idem*, 214. Droz, *Histoire de Louis XVI.* i. 166.

† *De l'Administration de Monsieur Necker par lui-même, Œuvres
complètes*, vi. 8. De Lavergne, *Les Economistes Français au 18ième
siècle*, 147. Necker, *Du Commerce et de la Législation des Grains.*

promises a thorough extirpation of heresy. Louis XVI. endeavoured to meet the difficulty by murmuring a few unintelligible words at that particular moment. On their return from Rheims, Turgot submitted the memorandum on toleration to him, that his conscience might be quieted and his position freed from any misapprehension.   Owing to circumstances and to the existing scarcity, Turgot had to put off his intended reforms until better times: they were to include the entire remission, by means of momentary compensation, of all feudal rights upon property belonging to the nobility and clergy, as well as their total abolition on the Crown domains.   These better times came no more as far as he was concerned.   The queen could not forgive the retrenchment of her establishment, and became the centre of all the Versailles cabals. Count Creutz, the Swedish ambassador, wrote in April 1776 to his royal master, Gustavus III. that "all the great people, all the Parlements. the entire financial clique, and the ladies of the Court, had leagued them-selves together in a powerful combination against Turgot."*   Mercy-Argenteau, Maria Theresa's ambas-sador, tried in vain to restrain her royal daughter.† There remained the king.   In February 1776, when the waves of opposition ran high, he spoke the his-torical words, " *Il n'y a que M. Turgot et moi qui aimons le peuple.*"‡   Two months later his power of

* Foncin 513.   Geffroy, *Gustav III. et la Cour de France.*

˙ † Geffroy et Arneth, *Marie Antoinette, &c. Correspondance,* ii. 439, April 13, 1776.

‡ Foncin, *Ministère de Turgot,* 422.

resistance was exhausted. Turgot handed him a
fresh memorial in the beginning of May, and after he
had spoken the king asked coldly if that were all.
On receiving an affirmative answer he replied, "Well,
so much the better," and thereupon turned his back
on his minister. The Count of Provence described
the king's disposition as consisting of smooth billiard-
balls, and these had now fallen asunder. The king
did not again receive Turgot, who was dismissed on
the 12th of May. The queen could scarcely be dis-
suaded from sending him to the Bastille. Mercy
asserts that she it was who decided Turgot's fall.*
The letter which the Emperor Joseph addressed to
her in July referring to these matters is well known
— "You interfere, dear sister, to depose ministers;
have you thoroughly considered your right to interfere with the government of France? Have you had
sufficient experience?" † Nevertheless it was unjust
to lay the whole blame on her and on the privileged
classes: the people rejoiced in like manner when it
heard of the fall of its best friend, and thanked the
king with effusion for it. Turgot's inexcusable error
lay in his idea that he only needed to be in the right
and to have the wish to benefit others. Frederick the
Great and Maria Theresa agreed with Voltaire about
Turgot. Voltaire was in Paris in 1778, and on meet-

* Mastier, *Vie de Turgot*, 593, &c. Geffroy et Arneth, *Marie
Antoinette*, &c. ii. 442.

† Arneth, *Marie Antoinette, Joseph II., et Leopold II. Letters*,
1-3.

ing Turgot seized his hand, crying: "Let me kiss the hand which has worked the salvation of the people."

At the age of fifty-four he died a victim to gout, and still more to the results of mental over-work. At the time of Turgot's fall Necker had gone with his wife and friend Suard to make a short stay in England. "How Necker will rejoice to hear this," wrote Madame du Deffand to the Duchess of Choiseul at Chanteloup.[*] Meanwhile Gibbon was doing the honours of London to the French guests, and Walpole those of his delightful property Strawberry Hill.

Necker's writings contain nothing about this visit, but Madame Necker eagerly read Milton and Pope, Bolingbroke and Chesterfield, translated Gray's *Elegy* for a literary collection of Suard's, and wished herself back in Westminster Abbey, to enjoy everything over again with her friend the author Thomas.[†] The Neckers had been back in Paris several months when Clugny (Turgot's successor) died.

No one knew the state of the public finances better than Necker did. All means had failed since Turgot's retirement. The Dutch would lend no more money. Necker himself had already come to the rescue of the king's financial necessities during the administration of the Abbé Terray in 1770, and without receiving interest he had advanced money, and thereby ren-

---

[*] Garat, *Mémoires sur Suard*, ii. 318. Madame du Deffand, *Correspondance*, iii, 217.

[†] Madame Necker, *Mélanges*, iii. 172. Querard, *La France Littéraire*, ix. 280.

dered the purchase of corn possible for the provinces where the distress was greatest. In 1772 he had once more lent several millions.

"We implore you to come to our assistance in the course of the day. Time presses, you are our last resource; we reckon on your support to save the royal credit." The French financial Secretary of State found it necessary to apply to Necker in this tone.* And now in the spring of 1776 the great question of a rupture with England and the intervention of France in favour of the American colonies pressed for an answer, for the second time in the same year, and the "first gunshot was synonymous with the bankruptcy of the State."* When Necker undertook to restore confidence, and even in the event of war to meet the requirements of royalty, the treasury was exhausted, but it did not appear practicable that he could be appointed *Contrôleur-Général*, that is, Finance-Minister. A compromise was therefore found, and Taboureau des Réaux retained the title, whilst Necker administered the finances as Director of the Royal Treasury. Hitherto the post had always been filled by *Parlementeers*; and, moreover, until 1776 Protestants were merely tolerated in France; they had no rights of citizenship, and their children were not considered legitimate. Nevertheless the king gave his consent, and signed the appointment on the 22nd of October, 1776. The money-market greeted

* A. de Staël, *Notice*, i. xi. xxi.-xxiii.
† Quoted from d'Ivau, Terray's predecessor.

this as it had done that of Turgot with a considerable rise. The Genevese rejoiced over the success of their fellow-citizen. In his honour the "magnificent little council" struck the first of the eighty-two medals which he was to receive in the course of his public career,[*] and the literary history of Geneva says of Necker's works that they should be the hand-book of all princes who desire the good of their people.[†] The Court only saw in Necker the opponent of his hated predecessor, and flattered itself with the hope that such financial talent would carry out its aim without cutting down expenses. The bishops made objections to the choice of a Protestant. "I will sacrifice him," replied Maurepas, "if the clergy will undertake to pay off the French national debt." But among the members of the French episcopate Necker was to find true friends and upholders of his work. Finally, the people rejoiced that Necker had undertaken the conduct of affairs.

Thus began Necker's first ministry. He took up a different position to that of Turgot. What the latter had not succeeded in it was impossible for Necker to attempt. As a Protestant he had beyond all things to consider the clergy; as a foreigner he had to use the utmost discretion in his courtly relations; belonging to the middle class he had to protect the privileged classes—those of parliamentary as well as hereditary nobility—if he were not to fall a

[*] D'Haussonville, *Le Salon de Madame Necker*, ii. 109.
[†] Senebier, *Histoire Littéraire de Genève*, iii. 164.

victim to the opposition which was certain at once to
arise against his first efforts in any new direction.
The natural result of finding himself in such an exposed position was, that as far as possible Necker
restricted himself in the first years of his ministry to
financial affairs, and renounced any projects for far-
reaching reform; * and here we must recall the fact
that, under the *ancien régime*, home-affairs in France
were almost entirely under the control of the Finance
Minister, † but even this limited sphere was not easy
to manage. Hardly a year had elapsed after his
appointment when a difference of opinion between
him and Taboureau resulted in the retirement of the
latter; and on the 22nd of June, 1777, Necker was
named Director-General of Finance. He stipulated
that he should receive no salary, and to this Louis
XVI. reluctantly gave his consent. Even with this
new qualification he remained subordinate to Maurepas, and, what was still more remarkable, he continued
to be debarred from attending the Councils held in the
king's presence, or from himself laying his plans
before the king, a frightful disadvantage in those days
when the personal decision of the king was the only
guarantee of continuance in office.

In the eighteenth century republicanism was not
thought much of in Europe, whereas absolute monarchy
had many supporters in the days of Frederick and

---

* A. de Staël, *Notice*, i. 46. Necker, *Œuvres complètes*, iii.
Premier Ministère.

† Leser, *Necker's Second Administration*, 12.

Catherine, of Maria Theresa, Charles III., and Leopold of Tuscany.

Side by side with the theory of princely supremacy and omnipotence of the state, almost exclusively held in Germany during the second half of the eighteenth century, there arose a new doctrine, the progress and development of which were in close connection with the spread of ideas and theories which, in 1688, had extended their sway in England, and had now been attentively received by the French. Across the sea it had needed all the inconceivable blindness, and consequent misconception, of the last crowned representative of the old dynasty to shake the conservative adherence of the English people to the House of Stuart. The excellently-written history of English party-spirit in the eighteenth century sets forth nothing with greater distinctness than the fact that the hardest triumph of Liberty was not over external foes but over prevailing popular opinion.* Long after the struggle between unconditional obedience and liberty for the people was decided in favour of the latter, the permanency of the change worked by William of Orange hung upon mere chance, whereas, once the English theories on political freedom were spread over France, they received unconditional support. The period at which English influence in literature began to prevail over that of Italy and Spain we may gather from a novel of Prévost's, *Mémoires d'un Homme de Qualité*, as well as from other works of that

---

* Lecky, *History of England in the Eighteenth Century*, i.

time. The scene in the first part of the book is laid in
Spain in 1731, and in its course the hero praises the
English constitution, and gives an excellent opinion
upon Shakespeare. French translations followed of
Daniel de Foe, Steele, Swift, and Addison. Prévost
himself undertook to render Richardson's *Pamela,
Clarissa*, and *Grandison* into French, and prepared
the way for the *Nouvelle Héloïse.** The pioneers
of the intellectual movement in the eighteenth century — Voltaire, Buffon, Montesquieu, Rousseau,
and with them a considerable number of other authors
and learned men — found a hospitable reception in
England, at times spent years in that country, and
on their return retailed the English ideas as their
own.† Montesquieu, who principally contributed to
this movement, says that the ministry of his day knew
no more of England than children of six years old.
This was not the case at the time of his death. In
1748 the book on *L'Esprit des Lois* had been
printed abroad without the author's permission, and
had to be brought surreptitiously into France; in
1755, when Montesquieu died, Louis XV. asserted
that such a man could not be replaced.‡ It is rela-
tively unimportant to Montesquieu's reputation and
influence upon his times that his greatest work is more
an interpretation of the various laws—the obsolete as

---

* Brunetière, *Etudes sur le* 18*ième siècle. Revue des Deux Mondes,*
15th Feb. 1885, p. 829.

† Buckle, *History of Civilisation.* John Morley, *Voltaire,* iii.

‡ Louis Vian, *Montesquieu, sa Vie, ses Ouvrages.* Droz, *Histoire de
Louis XVI.* i. 82.

well as those still in existence—more a physiology of
the state than an actual foundation of constitutional
law or a complete system of government. Neither
need we consider whether his conception of the state
is a false one when he takes it to be the creation of
personal despotism, or whether his leading thoughts
on the division of power refer more to the politics of
former days than to the philosophers and statesmen
of England. Montesquieu's special claim to distinction
lies much more in the fact that he brought his contemporaries to a knowledge of the necessity of fixed
laws and a steady government, and that in the celebrated sixth chapter of the eleventh book on the
English constitution he describes it as, in his opinion,
the happiest of all existing solutions of the problem
of political freedom. Montesquieu's views concerning
history, and the idea represented by him that the
quality of the physical nature of a country has dis-
tinct influence upon the character of its inhabitants,
and acts upon its habits, laws, and constitution; his
repeatedly-expressed conviction that a nation owes
something to its antecedents, that its past requires a
certain duty from it, and therefore that its future cannot
be shaped without taking this into consideration,—all
these doctrines, brought into notice by this clear and
superior mind, the immediate precursor and founder of
the new historical teaching of the eighteenth century,
at once exclude the thought that he aimed at a servile
imitation of foreign institutions. The practical aim
of his political teaching lay in the adaptation of

representative forms of government to the now historically-established circumstances of his own country. Nurtured in the highest circles of society and in the Paris *salons*, it soon directed fashion, taste, and literature. One of the cleverest women of the day, Mademoiselle de l'Espinasse,* Turgot's friend, only expressed the universal opinion when she wrote, " How can we sufficiently deplore the fact of living under a government like ours ? As far as concerns a weak, unhappy creature such as I am, I would rather be the most insignificant member of the English community than the King of Prussia." The question arose as to what practical realisation this teaching could find in the French monarchy, and the answer was sought in the history of its ancient institutions.

Until the days of Richelieu the greater number of the provinces forming the French nation had had their own representative assemblies, for the imposition of taxation and its distribution. Most of these assemblies were dissolved by that powerful minister, and set aside in favour of what were called Intendants, who governed, or rather misgoverned, the thirty-two generalities into which the kingdom was divided. Only a few provinces—Brittany, Burgundy, Languedoc, part of Provence, Flanders, Artois, and a few of the smaller Pyrenean districts — retained their old mode of representation, and were called

* Mademoiselle l'Espinasse to Guilbert. Foncin, *Ministère de Turgot*, p. 127.

pays d'état, whilst the rest, deprived of all representative form of government, were most inappropriately termed *pays d'election.** Louis XIV. ratified the absolute nature of Richelieu's work, and extended the power of the intendants over life and death. Noble and enlightened men directed all their efforts in favour of the reform of this example of crowning absolutism. Bois Guilbert and Vauban, Boulainvilliers and Saint Simon, and finally Fénélon, branded the rule of these privileged tyrants, who had become the scourge of the population, and who, at the price of draining the money and blood of their dependants in the provinces to minister to the ends of the king's treasury, had obtained exemption from punishment for their own extortions and those of their satellites.

Boulainvilliers, Saint Simon, and Fénélon had already sought the redress of such miserable abuses by calling together the States-General, which were to be fed by the provincial assemblies. D'Argenson and the Marquis Mirabeau required that Louis XV. should reinstate the latter, and Mirabeau ventured to remind the king that his father had already decided on this.† Still more important than the movement in favour of the re-establishment of the provincial assemblies was that for the revival of the representation of the states by the separate orders. The French *états-généraux* had not met since 1614.

---

* Lavergne, *Les Assemblées Provinciales*, 2.

† Mirabeau, *L'Ami des Hommes.* D'Argenson, *Considérations sur le Gouvernement de France.*

Necker's first attempt gradually and individually to call together the provincial assemblies dates from May, 1778. They were to decide on the imposition or abolition of taxes, the making or repairing of roads, the maintenance and improvement of farming and industry. The intendants of the several provinces were to be permanent; Necker even added to their powers, but in future they were not to resign their post without the king's permission, and the new provincial assemblies were to watch over their efficiency. They were not to re-establish any former conditions of government, but in most directions they were to regulate matters in a way that suited the surrounding necessities better than the antiquated institutions of the Middle Ages. These, however, did not exist in more than the few provinces we have already named.

In place of election on the basis of a given income, and without regard to rank, Necker went back to the principle of representation of the three orders.

In the States-General, as well as in the representative provincial assemblies, each class worked separately; and when the highest in rank—the nobility and clergy --- banded together they were always in the majority against the *Tiers-État*. One province only formed an exception to the rule. In Languedoc, where all the members met in one hall and voted by persons, the *Tiers* was composed of as many members as the two other classes together. Fénélon had already proposed the mode of election now chosen by Necker.

Not without due reflection did the king give his consent to it.* The first attempt to introduce the new
institution was made in Berry, one of the smallest
and poorest provinces of the monarchy. The Assembly
consisted of forty-eight members—twelve of the nobility, twelve of the clergy, twelve representatives of
the towns-people, and twelve of the country proprietors. The king chose sixteen deputies, who in
their turn elected the remaining thirty-two, and the
whole was presided over by the Archbishop of Bourges.
It was to meet together every second year for the
space of a month, and in the intermediate space of
time its decrees were to be carried out by a bureau
formed of seven members under a president. This
attempt, in the event of its success, was to serve as a
pattern for other similar institutions throughout the
land, and was to endure as long as "it so pleased the
king."

Its principal utility consisted in relieving the
taxation and in its just distribution, and in superin-
tending the road-making, carried out hitherto by the
hated bondage of the *Corvée*. It further assisted
charitable institutions, and encouraged trade and
industry. Necker's special innovation lay in the
appointment of a fourth party, by adding twelve
landed proprietors, that is, twelve peasants, to the
Tiers-État. The next provincial assembly was to be
introduced in Dauphiné in 1779. This province had
formerly had a representative assembly and lost it

* Lavergne, *Les Assemblées Provinciales*, 18.

under Richelieu; it therefore raised difficulties, and demanded that its ancient rights should be restored instead of the new regulations offered to it.

Necker left the Government before the quarrel was smoothed over : only in 1789 did it come to an end, allowing the representatives of Dauphiné to fill an important part in the events of the period.

The introduction of a provincial assembly in the *généralité* of Montauban (now called Haute-Guienne, after the old style) proved a success, although it was a failure in 1780 at Moulins, for Bourbonnais, Nivernais, and La Marche.

The two provincial assemblies in Berry and in Montauban lasted until 1786, and fully justified Necker's expectation, "that an interest in the general prosperity would thereby be aroused, and the people secured by the newly awakened sense of prosperity and confidence in the Government." * These useful results are the brightest spots in the history of Louis XVI.

As far as mortals may foresee, the development of affairs in France would have been very different had Necker been allowed time to widen and strengthen the institution of provincial assemblies, but this was not to be.

The American War annually cost the Treasury about four hundred millions. These unheard-of sums could not be raised without help from fresh sources.

* Necker, *De l'Administration de Finances. Œuvres complètes*, iv. 21, 86.

In the year 1780 there existed very nearly four thousand posts, the purchase of which conferred nobility. Most of these were small appointments at Court, sold by those who held the highest positions about the throne, and who unlawfully dealt in them to their own profit and advantage. Necker proposed that the king should abolish some and cut down others, and this was carried out. The share of the *fermier général* in indirect taxation was at the same time lessened, and the number of financial appointments reduced. The further sum of fourteen millions, which the altered and increased revenue of the *ferme générale* brought in in 1780,* was only a drop in the ocean compared to the requirements of the State, and new means had to be found for obtaining credit. Necker came back upon his favourite idea of winning public opinion through a clear explanation of the affairs of the State, and raised the hitherto impenetrable veil which had covered the finances of the French monarchy since the days of Richelieu. His *Compte-rendu*, dedicated to the king, appeared in January 1781, and was the greatest novelty in the government of the ancient monarchy. In this financial report he indicated a surplus of ten millions in the State revenue in excess of its expenditure, a disappearance of deficit, and increased prosperity in the land. The next result of this statement of accounts was Necker's new loan, which brought more than two

* Auguste de Staël, *Notice sur M. Necker. Œuvres complètes*, i. cxxi.

hundred and sixty-three millions in a few months. His influence from a moral standpoint was no less remarkable. The detailed statement of existing abuses pledged the Government to remove them, and demanded the support of public opinion to help the king to carry out the work of reformation required by justice. This support alone could lend him the necessary strength to carry it through, but at the same time it forced him to adhere to it. The *Compte-rendu* has long been proved erroneous from a financial point of view. The statement Necker produced had reference merely to the ordinary revenue and expenditure, and excluded the extraordinary burdens imposed by the war.* Neither was Necker's budget that of any particular year, but a sort of fiction, an average budget, giving the regular state of the income and expenditure during the course of a year, but ignoring the possible deficiencies, extraordinary expenditure, or the current deficit. Moreover, neither the necessary administrative information, nor any system resembling the modern system of accounts, existed at that time to facilitate an exact statement of the income and expenditure. Thus the State revenue in 1781 amounted to four hundred and thirty millions, whereas Necker's return reckoned them only as two hundred and sixty millions, because no reliable account of the other sources of income had been given. It was simply taken for granted that they had attained the maximum

* Necker, *De la Révolution Française. Œuvres complètes*, x. 229.

average returns.* Necker's appreciation of the power
of public opinion was visible in everything he wrote,
and in all his dealings. His friends' enthusiasm might
deceive him as to the extent of the opposition which
had arisen against him, but he was perfectly aware
of its existence. In the Provinces † the highest aristocracy willingly helped on his reforms, but the nobility
at Court forgave Necker as little as it had tolerated
Turgot, and continued in the practice of the most
pernicious abuses as if they were inherited rights.
At such a time the queen's influence was not to be
undervalued; she remained constant to Necker under
every circumstance. The fact that it was to her influence that the two ministers, De Castries and Ségur,
owed their portfolios in the War and Marine departments, made it all the more difficult for Maurepas to
forgive her. Vergennes, who equally opposed all
innovations, shared his antipathy; the old minister
required and obtained a secret memorial from the
latter addressed to the king, wherein it was set forth
as highly dangerous " to leave the most complicated
adminstration of the kingdom in the hands of a republican and a Protestant." The peace maintained
entirely by the exertions of a so much wiser minister
was thereby threatened. Meanwhile there appeared
a newly-written pamphlet against the *Compte-rendu*.
The author of it filled the post of treasurer to the
Comte d'Artois. In those days the attacks of the

* Droz, *Histoire de Louis XVI.* i. 294, &c.
† Lavergne, *Les Assemblées Provinciales.*

press were more felt than they now are, and moreover Necker's whole strength lay in the respect and confidence of the public. He therefore demanded proof of the slander, and, as the inquiry before three of his colleagues resulted in his complete exoneration, he then demanded the right of attending the ministerial deliberations. In his own account of his first ministry he does not attempt to conceal how bitterly he was mortified by the attacks of his enemies, and by the doubts cast on the purity of his intentions, nor did he attempt to conceal it from his wife. To her it seemed unbearable that in place of the universal recognition he so well deserved he should allow the most unjust and unworthy accusations to go forth against him, and she was led in consequence to commit the greatest possible tactical mistake. Without acquainting Necker with her intention, she went to Maurepas, who, as Madame de Staël writes, "In any exhibition of real feeling only saw an opportunity for exposing the weak point," * and she demanded that the pamphlets attacking her husband should be suppressed. This enabled the minister thoroughly to gauge how surely those arrows, mostly directed by himself, had gone home. He now went a step further, and not only refused the entry to the ministerial council demanded by Necker, but added the insulting suggestion that Necker could overcome the objection by changing his religion, and lastly he begged his colleague to withdraw his resignation. Filled with

* Madame de Staël, *Notice sur la Vie privée de Monsieur Necker.*

the desire to continue in his course of usefulness,
Necker did not hold the new proposals as final. He
requested an examination into the army and navy
expenditure, the dismissal of the refractory Intendant
of Moulins, and the forcible introduction of the edict
calling together a Provincial Assembly for the Bourbonnais, which the Parlement in Paris had rejected.
Maurepas refused this also, and Necker now wrote
to the king that with heartfelt regret he must part
from him.* His resignation dates from May 19, 1781.
Turgot had died two months earlier, and only in the
following November, Maurepas, who had been an
invalid for years, died also. There would not have
been long to wait for his death. Necker's plan of
government never replaced Turgot's carefully thought
out and compact system, resting as it did on the
firmest principles. He chiefly gained his political
experience at the expense of the State. But he was
an administrator, the like of whom was not to be
found in France at that time.

A united ministry headed by Necker would have
been the best choice for the monarchy in 1781.
Curiously enough the queen had a suspicion of this
at the time. Her correspondence with Maria Theresa
does not, it is true, definitely mention him, but she
repeatedly expresses her displeasure with reference to
Maurepas and Vergennes, whose attitude during the
Bavarian war of succession showed but little defer-

* Auguste de Staël, *Notice sur M. Necker. Œuvres complètes*, i.
clxxvi. Droz, *Histoire de Louis XVI*. i. 302.

ence to her sympathies for her country and family,
and against whom, moreover, her mother and Joseph
II. continuously endeavoured to arouse the influence
of the young queen.* But her partizanship for
Necker, to whom she herself conceded the diminution
of her courtly state,† contributed none the less to
hasten his fall, just as a year before her dislike had
contributed to that of Turgot. At Versailles, during
the space of an hour, she endeavoured to persuade
Necker to withdraw his resignation. It was getting
dark towards the end of their interview, and he did
not notice the tears in the queen's eyes; later on he
declared that had he done so he would not have had
the courage to withstand her. His withdrawal from
public life brought about a reaction in his favour, in
the face of which the abuse of his opponents was
silenced; men forgot to criticise in remembering the
good he had worked or desired. Catherine II. (who
alluded to the finances of the most Christian king as
"*une matière tout-à-fait dégoutante*"), the Queens
of Naples and of Poland, begged him to assume the
management of their affairs.

The King of Sardinia wrote, "I wish my people
deserved to be governed by him."‡ Joseph II. did
not remain behind the rest; he wrote to Mercy that

---

* Arneth, *Maria Theresa and Marie Antoinette. Lettres,* 1778.
Correspondance Secrète entre Marie Thérèse et Mercy, 1778.

† *Idem.*

‡ Madame de Staël, *Sur le Caractère de M. Necker et sur sa Vie
privée.*

he had retained the friendliest recollection of Necker ever since he had met him in Paris in 1778, and at the same time he commanded his ambassador to remind Necker of this interview, and to assure him of the esteem his character and capabilities had inspired in him.* In the latter days of his official position Maria Theresa gave the Neckers a very flattering token of her regard, "As you often meet Necker," wrote the empress to Mercy, "I wish you to convey to him the favourable impression I have of his capacity, and to add that I always read the accounts of his financial operations with much interest, and that I am convinced that we might adapt them with profit to our own, although they are not in such a critical condition as those of France. You might at the same time inform Madame Necker that some years ago the Genevese painter Liotard was in Vienna, and that I expressed a wish to see his pictures; one that especially pleased me was the portrait of a very good-looking young person in a pretty attitude, holding a book in her hand. I took such a fancy to the picture that I bought it. It is Madame Necker's portrait, and I often look at it with pleasure: when Liotard was last here he regretted that he had let the picture go, and begged me to allow him to copy it, to which I consented, but I retained the original, which is now in my study."† "The Neckers," replied the ambas-

* Geffroy et Arneth, *Marie Antoinette, Correspondance secrète de Marie Thérèse et du Comte de Mercy-Argenteau*, iii. 405, note. Letter of March 4, 1780.

† Geffroy et Arneth, *Marie Antoinette, Correspondance secrète de*

sador, " deserve this distinguished mark of favour: the
husband for his unimpeachable honesty and talents,
the wife for the impersonification of every virtue."*

When, however, Madame Necker expressed a natural wish to possess a copy of the letter from the
empress, Mercy refused it to her, and the empress
approved his refusal, "that," as she expressed it,
" too great ostentation might not be engendered." †
Necker himself made no secret of the grief it was to
him to be interrupted in his course of usefulness ; he
writes that he had not sufficient vanity to simulate
indifference, and, when looking through his papers,
the sheet upon which he had drawn up his plans for
the future caused him a flood of tears.‡ Very few
occupations had any charm for one who had given his
mind to public life, and who had become so much
attached to it. Country life and its solitude could
alone console him. Assurances of general esteem and
sympathy followed him, not only from the capital
but from the whole of France. People flocked to
St. Ouen to honour the fallen minister in his retirement. Public opinion, which he so frequently recognised and referred to, had on this occasion justified
his confidence ; whilst it approved of his transactions
and his views and vindicated the past, it seemed, in
like manner, to guarantee the future : only he over-

Marie Thérèse et du Comte de Mercy-Argenteau, iii. 405. Maria
Theresa to Mercy, 3 March, 1780.

   * *Idem.*   † *Idem.*

   ‡ *De l'Administration des Finances. Œuvres complètes*, iv. 98.

looked the fact that even whilst turning its approving gaze towards him this public opinion had itself moved on.

We have already alluded to the part Montesquieu played in the history of the eighteenth century, and to the political development upon which his theory rested, pointing convincingly to the example of England as the land in which it was more fully carried out than in any other. There alone had Montesquieu's axioms been corroborated, "that the laws must be determined by custom," and "what this can determine should never require to be enforced by the law." His definition of freedom, as consisting "of the right to do everything allowed by the law," precluded any dangerous experiments by its cool firmness. It well represented the mind of the man who declared that he desired nothing except "that the earth should continue to revolve on her axis," and who found compensation for all the chances of fate in the consciousness of true merit.

The treaty between Louis XVI. and the United States, now at war with England, was signed on the 6th February. It was a reluctant tribute to public opinion on the part of Maurepas. For years public opinion had sided with the American colonies in their struggle with the mother-country.

Admiration for the English Government had not modified the natural prejudice against the English themselves, and it only required encouragement from outside to fan the dormant hatred so long subsisting

between the two nations into a vivid flame. In this
respect there was little difference between the disposition of the educated upper classes and that of the
people, and it was by no means confined to France.
Marie Antoinette gave expression to the popular
opinion when she wrote to her mother, "Just as
Frederick the Great is a bad neighbour to Austria,
so are the English to the French; the sea has never
hindered them from injuring us in every way." *
The sentiments of the empress did not lessen this
apprehension. When the Emperor Joseph's journey
to London was frustrated in June 1780 by a rising of
the population of London directed against the Catholics,
and known as "the Gordon Riots," she wrote to her
daughter, "This then is the much-vaunted freedom—
the pattern constitution ; without morals or religion
nothing avails." In Germany curses were invoked
upon the subsidiary treaty with England, and the
news that German troops had been taken prisoners
by Washington in 1776 was received with exultation.†
Diderot found ways and means, in a treatise concerning Seneca, to forsake the position he had taken up
with regard to the American colonies that he might
advocate a war with England. The sympathies of
his countrymen were easily enough won now that
the cry for liberty no longer had any connection with
England, but, on the contrary, was raised in opposition to her, and now that the American colonies

---

* *Maria Theresa and Marie Antoinette*, May 17, 1773.

† Niebuhr, *Geschichte des Zeitalters der Revolution*, i. 75.

replied to the demands they had found unbearable
by their Declaration of Independence. At this juncture French enthusiasm was aroused; ovations were
prepared for Franklin. The young La Fayette was
followed across the sea, and the king and his ministers
were forced to go to war. It now seemed as if liberty
was only obtainable by means of uproar and by opposition to monarchical rule.

Both Turgot and Necker deprecated war with
England, seeing that any participation therein would
certainly lead to utter confusion in the finances.
Their opinion was however unheeded, the national
feeling was in favour of revenging the wrongs of 1763,
and above all the loss of Canada. The result of this
alliance between the oldest monarchy and the youngest
republic was gradually to make itself felt upon home
politics. The military and diplomatic results were
by no means so important a sequence of the French
intervention as the impression brought home by the
returning warriors.

It is now proved beyond contention that at the
bottom of these impressions lay one of the most
destructive and fatal misunderstandings ever chronicled, contributing more than any other to unavoidable revolution.

When the youth of France went forth to this
struggle as to a feast it imagined that in the rising
of the colonies it recognised revolt against the existing
state of things, reaction against monarchy, enthusiasm

for republican conditions; in one word, an awakening
of democracy.

In reality very little if any of this was to be found.
The fundamental principle that no one should be
taxed without having a voice in the matter, which
was the starting-point for the conception of political
liberty, was entertained by the subjects of the British
Crown, across the seas and at home, in an equal
degree. The conduct of the English Government had
impugned this theory, and therefore challenged opposition. Not until long after the outbreak of hos-
tilities was the thought of an entire separation from
the mother country entertained by American statesmen. As late as in the year 1774, Franklin,
Washington, and even Jefferson, who was of a much
more revolutionary tone of mind, could truthfully
assert that it was not the wish of the colonies to
separate from England. Chastellux emphatically
remarks, that the first difficulty encountered by the
American statesmen was that of inducing the people
to give up a monarchical government, and he adds,
that although the new constitution was democratic it
could do nothing to change the aristocratic tone of
the government of the nation.* The delegates of
the foremost states of the union in 1775 spoke to the
same effect. Their original aim was to redress past
wrongs, not to establish their independence; they

---

* Chastellux, *Voyages dans l'Amérique du Nord* (English translation), i. 331, and ii. 177. Lecky, *History of England in the Eighteenth
Century*, iii. 412, 414.

were still the descendants of the Puritans of old, who had sorrowfully torn themselves from their homes for conscience' sake. Political freedom was as holy and solemn a matter to the descendants of the Pilgrim Fathers as religious freedom had been to them in 1629. Without it there was no security of property, life was valueless, and conscience lost its hold. Their resistance had the same origin in manly and Christian conviction, they held firmly to laws, customs, and descent, and they only decided to separate from the mother country when forced to do so. Only when blood was once spilt, and the die cast, did the unavoidable stream of revolution, mingle in their resistance; and, according to one of the best judges, the American revolution, like most others, was the work of an energetic minority forcing the majority step by step into a position whence no escape and no return was possible.*

Once separation was decided upon, to which the unity of the English people eventually fell a sacrifice, it again became evident how little of the spirit of revolution characterised the statesmen of the new nation. Unlike the French, who in 1789, when the Government was overthrown, seemed possessed by the desire to begin everything at the beginning, and to show no deference to any of the institutions sanctioned by time and experience, the fathers of the American Union unhesitatingly referred to the national constitution, against which they had only lately

* Lecky, *England in the Eighteenth Century*, iii. 443.

risen. Beyond the English constitution the only authority carrying any weight in America was that of Montesquieu, and to his influence may be attributed the most original and one of the most influential institutions of the United States government, that of their highest court of law, in which his doctrine concerning the distribution of power is carried out and perfected. In all its former and substantial attributes the American government is an off-shoot of the British government as it was in operation in the space of time between 1760 and 1787, and it certainly interpreted it in a conservative and not in a radical sense.* The former subjects of George III. had no king to set at their head, neither did they desire one. No dynasty sprang from the Union, but, as far as concerned the overwhelming majority, the struggle it undertook against King George III. and his Parliament certainly arose from no antagonism to monarchy any more than it arose from opposition to constitutional system or to parliamentary government. Their president is the copy of an English monarch, with all the attributes of power enjoyed by such until the year 1789, and which, by a curious coincidence, began to be restricted in England at the very time when the American executive came into operation, March 4th, 1789. The temporarily-chosen president at the White House, although only there for a definite and limited space of time, exercises far

---

* Sir Henry Maine, *The Constitution of the United States. Quarterly Review*, January, 1884.

greater authority than any of the constitutional princes in Europe. In the organisation of their representation the conservative sense of the American statesmen is clearly observable, and it always favours liberty rather than equality. Not only do they adopt the system of the Two Chambers, but their Senate is one of the most powerful political corporations, and above all it is permanent. It repudiates equality by the mode of its composition, although, on the other hand, it guarantees equal rights for every State in the Union, including the rights of the lesser States. The smaller and more insignificant are represented by the same number of deputies in the Senate as the greater and more populous; and in the same way as the president is a representation of the English king, the Chamber of Deputies represents the Lower House as it existed in England in the eighteenth century. Its privileges are much less extensive than those adopted by its English prototype in the last hundred years; it has remained a merely legislative assembly, whereas England is, in point of fact, ruled by the Lower House. The much-prized and envied equality of the citizen and the politician promised by the United States constitution was the equality of a dominant race, which, with the hierarchical Anglo-Saxon feeling, knew even now how to defend and hold fast the social position which adds weight in public life. This equality was compatible, in the wide sphere of the Union, with the extirpation of the outlawed Indian and with the slavery of the imported negro.

As the United States constitution even now appears
to be the ideal of democratic government to superficial observers, we can scarcely wonder if Washington's French friends, with their newly-acquired political opinions, formed an erroneous idea of the real
nature of it in their blind republican partizanship;
they mistook the wings for the stage—the prologue
for the play—the proclamation of the rights of the
people for the kernel and substance of the constitution.

In their thoughtless enthusiasm they imagined that
these ordinary propositions meant the glorification of
natural laws after the doctrines of Rousseau, instead
of a departure from the absolute Anglo-Saxon rights
of the people, which was the actual state of the case.
They cared not for establishing the rights of American
citizens, but only those of the human race : the
rhetorical embellishments of the lawgivers, whose
principles accommodated themselves to the maintenance of slavery, were set aside in favour of absolute
doctrines, in which no mercy for the existing state of
things was to be found.   Those amongst American
statesmen who were of a republican turn of mind
strengthened this error; Franklin made use of it in
Paris, with crafty calculation, in favour of his political aims, which were in truth of a very practical
nature ; and Jefferson, who drew up the " Declaration
of Independence," wrote with a satisfaction easily
understood, " The American revolution appears to
have awakened the thoughtful section of the French

people out of the sleep of despotism. Authors, rich middle-class people, the young generation amongst the nobility, were now found ready to follow the teaching of sound reason and justice for all." * Lessing, the great pioneer of freedom, warned the Germans in the midst of the tumult against those "who wanted to put out the lights before daylight." †

When Gustavus III. of Sweden received news of the French alliance with America he wrote to the Count Creutz in Paris that the behaviour of the French ministry appeared alike to forsake the principles of justice, the interests of the nation, and the maxims upheld by the Government during so many centuries.

" I cannot admit," he continued, in the fulness of his kingly dignity "that it can be right to support rebels against their king; the example which endeavours to upset all the restrictions of power will only be too readily followed."‡

"My business is to be royalist," said Joseph II. during his stay in the French capital, and when pressed to express an opinion on the subject by the American insurgents. But even his warnings were useless. On the second triumphal return of La Fayette, Marie Antoinette conveyed his wife in her own carriage to meet him, and the Parisian Parlement

* Jefferson, *Complete Works, Correspondence,* ii. 67, 535. 1786 and 1787.

† Lessing, *Dialog Ernst and Falk,* v. quoted by Niebuhr, 16.

‡ Geizer, *Gustave III. Nachgelassene Papiere,* ii. 111.

imagined it could prepare no more gratifying spectacle for the Czarewitch Paul than the sitting in which it offered honorary places in their midst to the heroic companions-in-arms of George Washington. In more than one instance these distinctions were well earned. If La Fayette had misunderstood the spirit in America, he understood that of the new France all the better; it was he who gave expression to its inmost thoughts when he later on declared that, saturated with the American tone of thought, he had always been, and would always continue to be, an advocate of equality.

Necker was again Minister when this revolution was completed.

Whilst the young republic over the seas took the English constitution as its pattern, and chose Montesquieu's political doctrine as its rule, monarchical France took the social contract in hand, and familiarized itself with Rousseau's teaching concerning the sovereignty of the people.

Nothing indicates that Necker would have been quicker than those around him to realize that the struggle for liberty tended towards equality, and that the conception of reform tended towards revolution. He found however that public opinion, to which he attached so much importance, had reached this point of view when it once more placed him at the head of affairs after his seven years' retirement.

CHAPTER III.

DURING this transition from riches and consideration to influence and power, and back again to the comparative quiet of a simple private life, the Neckers' only child grew up; and it seemed as if no mere ordinary career could be in store for one so gifted and possessing such extraordinary talents.

Anne Louise Germaine, whose third name recalls the old German home, and in a manner foretells her future destiny, spent a very happy childhood. The first person of any note who mentions her is her godmother Madame de Verménoux, who, when Necker and his wife betook themselves in 1770 to Spa, the fashionable resort of all real and fancied invalids in the eighteenth century, used to go and see the little girl, aged four, at the Château de Madrid, which the

Neckers at that time were in the habit of hiring for the summer; and wrote to the mother that Germaine had won not only her own admiration but that of all who saw her, amongst others that of various old gentlemen, including an abbé.

At the same period Madame Geoffrin begged the Neckers' acceptance of a specially comfortable arm-chair, and another of equal size followed very shortly for the daughter of the house, "that she might not have recourse to blows to obtain possession of their chair. Both the chairs, I may add," she writes, "come from the sale of Philemon and Baucis." *

The next celebrity who especially took an interest in the child was Madame d'Houdetot, a neighbour at St. Ouen, who used to make it her regular resort when Necker and his wife were not there. In her letters to the child's mother she speaks of her as if she were her own, praises her merry ways and her wonderful eyes, and reassures her parents as to a trifling irregularity in her growth, as she says that a slight rise in the right shoulder is only due to the constant use of the right arm; and she had therefore charged her attendants to be careful in making her use her left hand.

To this circumstance is attached an anecdote in which Victor de Bonstetten was the victim.

After a long residence in Holland at the Leyden university and then in England, where he had com-

---

* D'Haussonville, *Le Salon de Madame Necker*, i. 121, 122, and ii. 26.

pleted his studies, the studious young man, now five-
and-twenty years old, came to Paris, where he spent
the greater part of the year 1770, and amongst other
friends found Madame Necker, late Mademoiselle
Curchod, and her husband, who received him with the
utmost hospitality.   On one occasion whilst visiting
them at St. Ouen he went for a stroll in the park.   A
sharp blow was suddenly dealt him with a stick, as
sudden as it was unexpected.   Turning towards his
assailant he discovered the little four-year-old Anne
Germaine, who satisfactorily explained to him that
she was recommended to use her left hand as much
as possible.

This commenced a friendship between the two,
only terminated by death.*   Bonstetten has left us
details which are of interest on other subjects ; amongst
other things they comfort succeeding generations
with the fact that the *salons* in the eighteenth century were not always entertaining.

"On the appearance of a new piece Madame
Geoffrin, Madame Necker, or Mademoiselle de l'Espinasse, are visited, and whatever is pronounced upon
it by Diderot, d'Alembert, Marmontel, or Thomas, is
treasured up.   Visits are paid the same evening; at
least sixty people are encountered to whom the same
thing is repeated.   These sixty people do the same
thing in their turn, the result being that the following day judgment is given and promulgated throughout Paris.   The decision of men of taste is in reality

* Simond, *Voyage en Suisse,* i. 269.

public opinion, divined by instinct by those of
superior discernment. It becomes modified and perfected in passing from lip to lip. The necessity of
daily pronouncing an opinion on the last new thing in
art and literature obliges each family circle to include
a *bel-esprit*, or some one who will furnish it with an
opinion or judgment on every subject that may arise.
These *bels-esprits* form among themselves an invisible
aristocracy which goes on descending in scale by im-
perceptible gradations. The heads have their tribunals,
the subalterns their departments.

" If any one ventured to speak of himself amidst
these surroundings he would be thought unbearable
by the rest, for no one in Paris takes the slightest
interest in the affairs of his fellow-creatures; the first
care must always be to increase the self-approbation
of others, and never to forget that if they appear to
interest themselves in you it is only out of politeness,
and on condition that you should also understand it
in this light and not take advantage of it. To these
causes may be attributed the pleasant style of intercourse and the interchange of trifles and commonplaces
which produce the unusually agreeable women, and the
really few good mothers and wives."

Comparing the state of things in France and England, Bonstetten decided unhesitatingly in favour of
the latter. He considered that in France the author's
intelligence and general knowledge developed new
and striking ideas, but possessed very little method.

In England it was just the reverse; nothing could

be better than to clothe the ideas there originated or brought over from Geneva in French forms; for the Englishman begins by laying in a store of sound reason, whereas the Frenchman reserves this to the very last, and often dies without having attained it at all. In France all depends on interest; in England merit decides everything. The English strive to serve their country; the French to secure a few influential persons; in England abuses are the exception, in France they are the rule.* In letters to his friends Bonstetten gives pleasant descriptions of the country-life in France; as for instance, in the Château de Rocheguyon belonging to the Duchesse d'Enville, where every kind of amusement and distraction was provided—"carriages, hacks, hunters, hounds, tennis, billiards, theatre, concert-room; the hostess and her daughter-in-law only desiring that their guests should be thoroughly amused." A library of fifteen thousand volumes helped towards this, and the young Swiss gives the palm to the inhabitants of this château for personal simplicity, purity of morals, nobility of thought, and intellectual taste.†

Unenlivened by the love of hunting and shooting peculiar to the old French nobility, the life at St. Ouen was much quieter, the tone was always more serious and studied, and the presence of the little girl was in truth the only diversion. Her picture, the work of some unknown hand, represents her as rather dark

* A. Steinlen, *Charles Victor de Bonstetten*, pp. 75, 78.

† *Idem*, pp. 80, 81.

in complexion, with lively irregular features and the
promise of mind and virtue shining even then out of
her large dark eyes.

Although at a subsequent period Madame Necker
tried in vain to keep her daughter from the influences
of J. J. Rousseau, she began like the rest of the women
of her day. "I bring up my daughter to be like
Emile and not like Sophie," she wrote in 1768, "and
hitherto Nature seems more attractive in the child
than any art could be."*   She wished as much as
possible herself to direct the child's education, especially as Necker's duties obliged him to follow the
court to its various places of residence and left more
time at her disposal.   "During thirteen of the best
years of my life," she wrote on this subject to her
husband, "you know that I have never let my daughter
be out of my sight; I have taught her several languages, especially her own, and endeavoured to cultivate her memory and understanding by means of
the best books.   During your stay at Versailles or at
Fontainebleau I went alone to the country with her ;
there I used to walk with her, read with her, and
pray with her.   When she was unwell I encouraged
the efforts of her doctor by my care and nursing ;
and I have since been told that she used often to ex-
aggerate her cough in case she should be ·deprived of
my loving care.   In one word, I sought to nurture
and encourage every gift of nature, as I hoped to im-

* Golowkin, *Lettres recueillies en Suisse*, p. 359.

prove her disposition and as I had thrown my whole pride into it."*

She strove in her educational method to lead her daughter's habits and disposition in the straight path of duty and industry. Highly educated, for a woman of her time and station, she might even be considered learned. Therefore she did not hesitate to lay a severe burden of work upon the gifted girl, and to awaken her interest in every possible branch of learning, which in those days was far in advance of the plan of education then in vogue for young ladies.

She hoped by this means that she should best be able to combat the influence of certain materialistic ideas, and by a severely methodical education to prepare the way for the decided supremacy of religious views; but she went to work like many others who are in the habit of living by strict rule themselves, and who forget to reckon with individual requirements and youth.

This restraint was specially likely to be almost unbearable in the case of Mademoiselle Necker. She was more than ordinarily lively, straightforward, and sensitive, craving for love as well as praise and encouragement. Even as a child her love for her father was a curious mixture of merriment and irritability, easily turned to tears, out of all proportion to her years.

She was hardly eleven years old when her mother

* D'Haussonville, *Le Salon de Madame Necker*, ii. 85.

selected Mademoiselle Huber, a young relation from Geneva, as her governess. Mademoiselle Huber, who was subsequently known as the beautiful and accomplished Madame Rilliet-Huber, remained the young girl's intimate friend. Mademoiselle Huber describes their first meeting, giving prominence to the impression made upon her by her pupil's grace and versatility of expression, which almost approached eloquence.

" We never used to play like children," she continues; " she at once inquired about my hours of instruction and the various languages I was fluent in, and whether I often went to the theatre. When I replied that I had only been two or three times at the latter she expressed her astonishment, and, promising that we should very shortly go and see a comedy, she added that after each play we must write down our recollections of it and what we thought of it, as this was her habit. We also promised to write to each other every morning. We then went into the drawing-room. Beside Madame Necker's arm-chair there was a small wooden chair, upon which her daughter had to sit quite still and upright. Then a few old gentlemen came in who seemed to take the utmost pleasure in amusing her."

Whilst still a child Mademoiselle Necker wrote sketches and studies of character, according to the prevailing fashion, and there soon followed verses, essays, and plays. Before she was fifteen years old she looked over a copy of *L'Esprit des Lois*, and made marginal notes. A short treatise by her on the

Edict of Nantes caused the Abbé Raynal to express
a wish to incorporate it in the next edition of his
History of the Indies. After the *Compte-rendu* was
published she handed an anonymous composition on
the subject to Necker, who, however, recognised his
daughter's style of writing.

Her own originality enabled her to withstand the
severe educational system to which she was sub-
jected.

On the occasion of one of Gibbon's visits to Paris
in 1776 Necker and his wife expressed a wish that
this clever and distinguished individual might remain
among them. Thereupon the little maid of ten years
old proposed to her mother, in all good faith, that
she should marry the shapeless celebrity, and by this
desperate step secure him to the family for ever, for
in her restless, active nature the development of the
heart kept pace with that of the mind.

Thus she passionately loved Mademoiselle Huber;
the excitement of meeting distinguished men would
bring tears to her eyes and make her heart beat; the
books she read transported her into another world.
Her description is well known of the impression made
on her by Richardson, the greatest novelist of the
day. "The elopement of Clarissa," she says, "was
the principal event of my youth." Her first and best
biographer, Madame Necker de Saussure, says she was
always young but never a child.

" Here blossom the joys of your life," wrote Madame
d'Houdetot to Madame Necker; "strive to enjoy the

consolation of bringing them to perfection; none of
her sympathetic charm is lost upon me."[*] Unfortunately Madame Necker was not able to find these
joys in the same way as her friend; she guided her
daughter's education with the same painful conscientiousness with which she watched over her own
improvement and endeavoured to fulfil the most
trifling duties of her position. She exhausted all the
cares and anxieties of her motherly calling, but passed
its joys and compensations almost coldly by.

During the childhood of Anne Germaine, long-
winded treatises upon style, grammatical remarks
upon *Emile*, allusions to conversations with Buffon
or Thomas, are to be found among her mother's
writings; she hardly ever alludes to her daughter,
about whom it would have been infinitely more interesting to hear something beyond remarks as to the
perils of a Parisian atmosphere for young girls.

Under ordinary circumstances an education on the
system of Madame Necker would probably have come
to the desired result; in this instance, however, she
encountered an element which defied all her theories,
and this element was inborn genius. Madame Necker
started from the notion that everything could be learnt,
and that study was the principal thing. She held,
rightly enough, that where the first period in life is
not usefully filled up, the deficiency can never be
made up in after-years.[†]

[*] D'Haussonville, *Le Salon de Madame Necker*, ii. 28.
[†] Madame Necker, *Mélanges*, ii. 337

The daughter was, however, too original to follow the inspirations of others without the utmost difficulty; whilst she replaced perseverance and application by the most remarkably quick intelligence.

In default of information, we are unable rightly to estimate the positive amount of knowledge Mademoiselle Necker owed to her educational years; from later events and indications we may, however, deduce that she knew sufficient Latin to read Tacitus with her son, but it is further chronicled that it only needed a few words of the text, the meaning of which was in truth sometimes misunderstood, to start her on some clever dissertation which often led her far from the original subject.*

When in 1792 she went to England for the first time, she only spoke English very incorrectly; and, although she had diligently studied German before her arrival in Weimar, everything testifies that she understood it imperfectly; but in after-years she learnt it thoroughly.

A century earlier, educated women in France knew a great deal more; amongst others, Madame de Sévigné had thoroughly learnt Latin, she spoke Spanish and Italian fluently, and knew enough philosophy and theology to keep pace with the education of her day, and to form an opinion on the principal controversies of the moment. At least, an independent judgment in the times of Arnauld and

* Bonstetten, *Letters to Frederick Brun*, edited by F. Matthison, i. 181.

Pascal, Nicole and Bossuet—and the celebrated Marquise had hers—proves as much positive knowledge and intelligence as the fact of being able to form a more or less authoritative opinion upon Montesquieu and Rousseau in the days of Mademoiselle Necker. Neither at that time, nor at a subsequent period, did she pretend to be a learned woman in the real sense of the word, but she knew a great deal, read and taught herself incessantly, and in the course of time touched upon most of the problems which occupied the intellectual, artistic, and political circles of her generation. Madame Necker de Saussure does not fail to remark that the superiority of Madame de Staël was a great and natural phenomenon much more than it was the result of acquired knowledge.*

"The education of early youth," she remarks, "left very little trace in her case." She certainly offered no opposition to the efforts of her mother, but her health suddenly gave cause for serious anxiety; and the decision of Tronchin, called in by the parents in their distress, put a final veto on Madame Necker's system of education, as he prescribed a residence at St. Ouen, continuous exercise in the fresh air, and a complete cessation of all mental exertion. The poetical and imaginative capabilities, which had hitherto been repressed, now began to develope themselves. The two young girls, Anne Germaine and her friend Mademoiselle Huber, roamed all over the park and

* Madame Necker de Saussure, *Notice sur le Caractère et les Écrits de Madame de Staël.*

gardens at St. Ouen (sometimes dressed as nymphs), busied themselves with music and song, composed poetry, read poems to each other, and even acted dramas or plays of their own composition. But the Neckers' *salon* was in reality the training-school, which furnished an opportunity for the interchange of opinions with interesting and clever men, broadened the ideas of the young girl, formed her taste, and soon developed her knowledge of men and the world, without which her extraordinary gifts would never have been brought to fruition.

This change in her mode of life and in her occupations added in a decided and considerable degree to her intimacy with her father. His attention being no longer devoted to the affairs of the state, he could now turn to his daughter; he discovered a disposition in her which was already in sympathy with his own, and she put forth every effort to please him. She felt he understood her better than her mother, although he neither praised nor encouraged her. They had many traits of character and intellectual qualities in common, and particularly an exquisite sense of the ridiculous. Mademoiselle Necker owed it to him that straightforwardness and simplicity were essential to her.

He at once detected anything affected or studied, but was ever ready for a joke. One morning when Bonstetten was their guest, Mademoiselle Necker had tried in vain to attract her father's attention at breakfast. Her mother, who regarded all these pranks somewhat severely, was called out of the room on household matters: the instant she shut the door behind her, the daughter's table-napkin flew at her father, who until then had been sitting gravely opposite her. As if he had been expecting it, he caught it, bound it round his head, and began to dance round the table with Germaine until the sound of returning footsteps fell on their ears, when they both hastened back to their chairs like truant school-children, forgetting to observe that they were betrayed by the father's wig, which was put on back foremost.*

But Madame Necker could never prevent her daughter from breaking in upon serious conversation with witty sallies; after which the latter would take refuge under Necker's wing, if her overflowing vivacity got her into trouble.

The mother could not accustom herself to this new state of things; her interest in her daughter diminished from the moment she ceased to be able to direct her education on her own plan.

When Madame Necker de Saussure, later on, praised the extraordinary gifts of Madame de Staël, whose acquaintance she had just made, Madame Necker characteristically replied: "They are absolutely nothing in comparison to what I intended them to be."†

On one occasion Suard found Mademoiselle Necker

* Steinlen, *Bonstetten, Étude biographique et littéraire.*

† Madame Necker de Saussure, *Notice sur la Vie et les Écrits de Madame de Staël. Œuvres complètes,* i. xxxiv.

in tears, and, guessing a quarrel with her mother to
be the reason of these, he endeavoured to comfort her
by saying that her father would pet her and make up
for it. The little girl at once dried her tears and
told him that she knew her father thought more of
her present, and her mother of her future happiness.*

In after-life she made the surprising statement with
regard to her father, that she used to think of him
" as young, lovable, and alone "—at an age when if
they had been contemporaries Fate might have joined
them together — " but," she added, " my mother
needed a husband who was not to be compared with
other men ; she found him, spent her life with him,
and God preserved her from the misfortune of out-
living him. Peace and honour to her ashes—she
deserved happiness better than I did." †

The first public notice of Mademoiselle Necker's
literary productions occurs in Grimm's *Correspondence*, September 1778. " Whilst Necker," it says,
" gained fame by his administrative measures, and his
wife withdrew from society to devote her energies to
the organisation of another hospital, her daughter,
aged twelve and gifted beyond her years, amused
herself by writing little comedies in the style of the
dramas of M. de Saint Marc. She has just finished
one in two acts entitled *Les Inconvénients de la ville
de Paris*. It is not only marvellous for her years,

---

* Dumont, quoted in the *Edinburgh Review*, 1867, cxxvi. 487.

† Madame de Staël, *Du Caractère de M. Necker et sa Vie privée*,
1804. *Œuvres complètes*, xvii. 6 and 17.

but seems superior to all the productions of that description which have served as her models."

The first poetical efforts of the young girl, already showing promise and especially interesting as a sign of the direction her talent was taking, are romantic love-stories, the scene of which is chiefly laid in ancient forests or in parks shaded by cypresses with funereal urns in the distance.

With the true delight taken by youth in exaggerated situations and poetically glorified destinies, there is a lavish amount of unhappiness, the heroes of the piece never die a natural death ; even among the savages who frequently figure in her pieces *l'homme sensible*, the favourite type of the day, is to be found, as in *Mirza*, in *Sophie, Adèle et Théodore, Pauline*, and *Zulma*.

In all these creations of Mademoiselle Necker's fancy—amongst others, in a drama, *Jane Gray*, dedicated to her favourite heroine *—love-affairs play the principal part. The words in the drama of *Mirza* might have been taken for the motto of them all : " I would know the sentiment which influences a lifetime and which demands entire possession of every moment in it." †   Beside the furtherance of love, custom and duty play a very subordinate part. It is said of women that " the history of their hearts is also that of their lives." ‡   Mademoiselle Necker's

---

* Madame de Staël, *Œuvres complètes*, xvii.

† *Idem*, ii. 230.

‡ *Idem, Sophie*, act i. scene i.

verses read like prose, but a keen observation of the mind, an early knowledge of the motions and impulses in human actions, shine through these youthful attempts, and elucidate many of the characteristics of the authoress.

It would have been quite excusable had such an early talent induced Mademoiselle Necker's parents to submit her prematurely to public judgment; they did not, however, make this mistake; none of the attempts we have mentioned appeared before 1760, the novels only in 1795. A second tragedy, *Montmorency*, which came after *Jane Gray*, and therefore about 1787, was never published, although it was far in advance of the first, and the character of Richelieu therein described attracted the attention of the severest critics.

Amidst the approval of friends Necker did not, however, forget the ill-will and the attacks likely to be the portion of those who leave the beaten track for remoter and more ambitious paths.

This old experience was again confirmed. The tears Marmontel is said to have shed on the first dramatic effort of a young girl of twelve years old did not prevent his finding fault with the tricks of his "dear madcap." Madame de Genlis—who in those days was making her experiments as the "governess" of the Princes of Orleans, and who was destined to follow Madame de Staël with her pen through life —in her letters to Madame Necker certainly praised the unusual talent of her daughter, but did not scruple to speak on other occasions of the bad bringing-up of Mademoiselle Necker, who spent three-quarters of the day in the drawing-room, and there discussed the nature of love with all the clever men.

This recalls an anecdote which Necker loved to relate about his daughter, who, when quite a child, inquired of the old Maréchale de Mouchy what she really thought of love.

When he saw what an affection she had for writing and composing, Necker used to call her Madame de Sainte-Écritoire, and he restrained her so long from any idea of publishing that when she was nineteen years old she wrote in her journal, "My father is quite right. Women are not meant to choose the same path as men; why compete with them, why excite a jealousy in them which would differ so much from that excited by love? A woman should call nothing her own, and she shonld only find her life's happiness in that of the man she loves. I can imagine Madame de Montesson in tears because of the failure of her play;* and how different the influence of those tears would have been if they had been produced by a softer feeling. If our tears could be of different colours, blue or yellow, it would not signify if we shed them for ordinary reasons, but it is dreadful to

---

* Madame de Montesson had secretly confided a play of her own composition to the Duke of Orleans (father of Philippe-Égalité). It was entitled Le Comte de Chazelle, and was unsuccessfully given at the Théâtre Français, May 6, 1785.

think that exactly the same kind must flow for vanity as for love." *

The first of her writings which stepped over the line separating purely *dilettante* productions from serious literary work—the letters on J. J. Rousseau —were more or less complete at the moment when Mademoiselle Necker thought she had renounced publicity.

But she adhered to her resolution by never publishing anything in her maiden name. She is only known in literature under that of her husband.

Marriage—the turning-point in a woman's life— was made unusually difficult for Mademoiselle Necker by her surrounding circumstances. Although the private life of her parents was spent in the midst of the universal respect and admiring confidence her father inspired, and although foreign princes as in 1782, amongst others the Comte du Nord, afterwards the Emperor Paul, and his wife, never failed to seek out Necker before leaving Paris,† the position of the family was nevertheless unusual. The great French aristocracy never at any time despised an alliance among the foremost financial families, but the Neckers were Protestants, and this entirely prevented a French marriage, which in their daughter's eighteenth year would otherwise have been their choice.

We must remember that the Protestant religion, suppressed as a political faction by Richelieu and

* D'Haussonville, *Le Salon de Madame Necker*, ii. 49.
† Baronne Oberkirch, *Mémoires*, i. 315-316. English translation.

persecuted by Louis XIV., certainly since 1743 had again possessed the right to conduct its services outside the towns in the open air; but it was only on the eve of the Revolution, by a royal edict in January 1788, that civil rights were restored to the Protestants, and their children legitimised. Hitherto they had been bastards in the eyes of the law.

They could not as yet expect entire equality, and all the barriers against Protestant alliances were naturally enforced by the Church. There was, however, no nobility in France belonging to the so-called reformed Church; either executions or civil wars had thinned their ranks, or they had sought the right to exist in foreign lands. Under these circumstances it was no use trying to marry Mademoiselle Necker to a Frenchman. She was seventeen years old when a journey to Fontainebleau Necker was obliged to take with the Court brought him and his family, in October 1783, into contact with a foreigner, whose fame and position, personal talents and qualities, as well as his religion, made him an eligible suitor for the hand of the young girl. This was William Pitt, Lord Chatham's second son. He had spent some time during that summer in Paris and afterwards in Rheims with his friend Elliot and with William Wilberforce, who at that time was twenty-four years old, and had already been four years a member of the House of Commons. Their purpose was to devote themselves to acquiring the French language. Maurice de Talleyrand, known as the Abbé de Périgord, happened to be paying a visit to his uncle, the Archbishop of Rheims, which gave him the opportunity of becoming acquainted with William Pitt. They mutually taught each other French and English during nearly six weeks, after which the young Englishman betook himself to the Court of Louis XVI.* It is not known whether during this visit, which gave him the opportunity of making her acquaintance, he already seriously thought of marrying Mademoiselle Necker; but it is quite certain that such a marriage would have been after Madame Necker's own heart.†

The young man, scarcely twenty-four years old, and even then famous, had already announced in the English Parliament that he could take no place but the first in his own country, and a year later he was Prime Minister.

But Madame Necker, whilst nourishing these desires, thought more, as usual, of her husband than of her daughter. She wanted most to persuade the former of the powerful support and valuable connection that a marriage with Pitt would bring. We know from D'Haussonville that Pitt took preliminary steps in the matter and that he desired to bring it about; and we also know that the project came to nothing, owing to the rooted aversion expressed by Mademoiselle Necker to any plans that would separate her from France in the future. Whereas, like most of such assertions, the words

* *The Greville Memoirs*, edited by H. Reeve, ii. 345.
† D'Haussonville, *Le Salon de Madame Necker*, ii. 53, &c.

ascribed to the young Pitt, that he was already wedded to his country, were probably never uttered.*

According to the confessions in her journal, this incident was not without painful results. "Why," wrote she in those days, "should this unlucky England be the cause of coldness and reserve between me and my mother? Accursed island, cause of all my present cares and future self-accusations, why must these brilliant prospects rob me of my happiness as well as of the right to bemoan my fate? They force me to choose, to wish for what I would willingly have done had I been forced to do it: they plunge me into such uncertainty that all the reasons for my actions are turned upside down and put to confusion by each other.

"It was not because my heart was already given away that I have been outwardly unchanged, although frightened and agitated when alone . . . . No, it is over; I cannot go to England."† Thus ran the somewhat confused explanation of the young girl's decision. But she never again had the chance of becoming a great man's wife.

In contemporaneous accounts the affair is often mentioned: Wilberforce speaks of it in his memoirs and in a letter to his father.‡ Count Fersen mentions the name of the English statesman as that of a rival of Staël, who at that time was a friend of his.§

* Stanhope, *Life of Pitt*, i. 132.

† D'Haussonville, *Le Salon de Madame Necker*, ii. 60.

‡ Wilberforce, *Life*, *Letters*, *and Diary*, i. 39.

§ Klinkowström, *Le Comte de Fersen et la Cour de France*. Introduction, xxxiv.

Mademoiselle Necker never gave it another thought after her mother left off reproaching her about it, and for this she had not to wait long. In the winter of 1784 Madame Necker received such undoubted proofs of her daughter's affection at a time when her health became worse that she forgave her resistance under characteristic conditions. As she believed herself to be dying, she desired that Necker should be her daughter's chief care and object in life, as well as that of her husband and children in the future. "Tell them," wrote Madame Necker in a sort of last testament, "that your father must be the centre of their existence, that they must make him their chief thought. . . . . Follow him wherever he may go; never allow him to sleep under another roof than your own unless for some very weighty reason. Cultivate your cheerful disposition. You will only err when you try to be different from what you are. Give up the world, you will never rightly understand its ways; live for God, for your father, and your duty."

This was the price of Madame Necker's forgiveness of the behaviour which had deprived her husband of a son-in-law who would have been so worthy of him and who would have been of such advantage to him. As her mother's health improved, Mademoiselle Necker was spared the pain of such a communication. It is in fact uncertain whether it ever came into her hands,* and in the spring of 1784 the family removed

* D'Haussonville, *Le Salon de Madame Necker*, ii. 55-58.

for a time to Beaulieu near Lausanne for the sake of the invalid.

Thence Madame Necker wrote to Thomas that neither quiet, native air, nor the milk in the mountains, made her life anything but a struggle against her own nature, and that every victory was won with difficulty.*

Of her earlier friends, Bonstetten was now *bailli* of Nyon, and had married Mademoiselle de Watteville in 1776. He meanwhile had formed a brotherly friendship with John von Müller, travelled to Italy, admired the Countess of Albany in Rome, become a member of the High Council at Berne on his return, and governor, first in the small mountainous district of Gessenay, and then on the shores of Leman, where, with his family and Matthison the German poet, with whom he had recently made friends, he led an idyllic existence, into which the arrival of the Necker family introduced a welcome variety.†

When Thomas came to seek out Madame Necker in the Swiss mountains he found her already established at Coppet, the new home Necker had selected as a permanent abode for his family.‡ It is characteristic of those times that the château was, and is still, so situated that its surroundings entirely shut out the panorama of the Lake of Geneva, one of the finest in Europe.

* Madame Necker, *Mélanges*, iii. 202, to Thomas, June, 1784.

† A. Steinlen, *Charles Victor de Bonstetten, Étude biographique et littéraire*, 83.

‡ Madame Necker, *Mélanges*, iii. 205, to Thomas, Dec. 1784.

The past history of this property, situated close to Geneva in the Canton de Vaud, made it not altogether unworthy of the part it was to play in the literary and political history of the next thirty years.

Count Peter of Savoy built the château in 1257 when he took possession of the Canton de Vaud for his race.

Another prince of his house made Coppet into a barony, a title which Necker received with it, and which is mentioned in his marriage-contract, for the Canton de Vaud was just as aristocratic as Geneva was republican. After the sixteenth century Coppet frequently changed hands; it was burnt, restored, pulled down, and rebuilt, till, in the seventeenth century, it passed itno the hands of the Dohnas, a Saxon family. One of them, Count Frederick Dohna, then governor of the principality of Orange belonging to the house of Nassau, was highly thought of by the Genevese Government. Bayle was eighteen months at Coppet between 1673 and 1674 as secretary and tutor to his children, but he never mentions it in his writings. In 1713 the property passed out of the hands of one of his pupils, Count Alexander Dohna, into those of the Baron Sigismund von Erlach, who in his turn only kept it a short time. After many changes it came into the possession of Thelusson the banker, and he sold it to Necker, who engaged to become the good and true vassal of their excellencies of the high council at Berne, and never without their especial sanction to give up the property to any one who did not profess the Reformed faith. The maintenance of this clause, occasioned by the intolerance of the Bernese councillors, at one time prevented Voltaire from becoming a householder in Lausanne on account of his Catholic views.

Thus at a cost of 500,000 francs, and by the payment of a third of this sum to the Bernese Government, Necker became the possessor of the château of Coppet, after he had for a time thought of succeeding Voltaire at Ferney. We leave it to his grand-nephew the Vicomte d'Haussonville to give a description of Coppet which belongs to the history of the Necker family as the frame to a picture.

"Then as now," he writes, "the château was a big building without any particular ornament; it consists of the main body and two wings surrounding the courtyard. To get into the latter one has to pass under an arched gateway. An iron gate which formerly must have been connected with a drawbridge separates the park from the courtyard. This gateway ends in two towers; one of these is modern; but the thickness of its walls proves the antiquity of the other. One of the piers has an iron ring to which prisoners used to be secured."

From the windows of the long gallery which Necker chose for his study, and which later on was used for theatrical representations, nothing can be seen across the level ground in summer except the tops of the plantains hiding the houses of the neighbouring village; but from the balcony on the next floor there is a view that can never be forgotten by the beholder, and the charm of it brings him back to Coppet, just as, according to popular belief, the traveller who has once tasted of the waters of Trevi is irresistibly drawn to return to Rome.

To the right lies Geneva, almost invisible in the sheen of the midday sun, reflected in its zinc-adorned towers; but towards evening its rows of white houses stand out against the reddened horizon. The massive forms of the mountain chains in Savoy are to be seen opposite, varied by woods and meadows. To the left is the lake, the beautiful lake, stretching its smooth surface towards Lausanne. Any one leaving the house for the park might imagine himself a hundred miles from the lake and the mountains. Two long straight alleys, the last trace of a French fashion, would tell him that this park belonged to the times when people did not walk for the sake of the view, but principally to enjoy conversation in the shade. He will then understand why the tall trees, described by Madame de Staël as "the friends and dumb witnesses of her fate," shut out the view on all sides, only permitting an occasional glimpse of the distant blue of the Jura. Coppet is exactly as it was a hundred years ago. Not a stone has been altered. Lovely dwellings have been since erected on the hills surrounding the lake, and charming gardens lead to its shores; but when the enchanted eye is turned from them back into the somewhat sombre courtyard at Coppet, and above all when the visitor crosses the

threshold to find the house unchanged, and many of
the rooms ready as it were for the reception of their
former guests, he will readily admit the special charm
of melancholy grandeur linking it with its associations
in the past.*

Under its new possessors Coppet was more a busy
intellectual centre than a retreat from the turmoil of
life or for the enjoyment of nature.

Crassy being only at an hour's distance, all the
memories of her childhood were awakened in Madame
Necker.　She erected a monument in the village
church at Coppet in memory of her parents, worked
as much among the poor and the sick as she had
done in Paris and at St. Ouen, and was judicious in
the use of her time and in her expenditure.　As she
would take no money from her husband for her own
use, he made one of her friends represent to her that
a small sum of her own of 8,000 francs had increased
to 30,000, and this she devoted to charitable purposes.

If she could not sleep at night she liked some one
to read aloud to her, or else she wrote down her impressions; † her greatest consolation was to gather
old friends around her.　To her sorrow an early death
prevented Thomas from carrying out his plan of
settling permanently in the neighbourhood of Coppet,
but Moultou and his family lived an honoured and
active life as formerly in Geneva, and Gibbon was
much visited in Lausanne.

* D'Haussonville, *Le Salon de Madame Necker*, i. 235 and 282.

† Baronne de Gérando née de Rathsamhausen, *Lettres*, *Madame de
Gérando sur Madame Necker*, 1802.

To reassure his friends in England, who feared that he was being separated from the world by his residence in Switzerland, he tells one of them how on the same day he had visits from the celebrated doctor Tissot, the French author Mercier, the Abbé Raynal, Prince Henry of Prussia, the Abbé de Bourbon, a natural son of Louis XV., and from a natural son of the Empress Catherine. He does not mention his name, but it was the young Count Bobrinski.* Besides these, the Necker family, Servan, and perhaps a dozen remarkable counts and barons, met together on his terrace.†

Victor de Bonstetten frequently came over from Berne or Nyon to recover from the dreadfully dull society of his colleagues, and to be cheered up in his literary efforts, which alternately busied themselves with death, eternity, idylls in Gessner's style, or the question of the free export of home-made butter, which finally were all bound up peaceably together in one volume.‡ The historian John von Müller, who had met the Neckers at Bonstetten's, was afterwards taken by him to Coppet during the winter of 1783, at which period he was enlightening the minds of the rising generation in Berne with his lectures on ancient history.§

* J. Groth, *Letters from the Empress Catherine II. to Grimm,* 1774-1796.

† Gibbon to Lord Sheffield, Oct. 1784.

‡ K. Morell, *Charles Victor de Bonstetten: A contemporary Sketch of Swiss life.*

§ A. Steinlen, *Charles Victor de Bonstetten,* 141.

Only Madame Necker was entirely content with the quiet life they led; she had tasted the cup of worldly honour and joy, and found it bitter. The day she had sought for was over, and her celebrity now appeared to her as a fearful phantom.

Even during her husband's first administration she wrote to Thomas that she had hoped to live in the Golden Age under a model government, but she had only found the Iron Age. "Everything tends to show that all we can aspire to is to work as little harm as possible;"[*] and to this she adds a sentence as true as it is just, for it alludes to the danger incurred by even the best of people who meddle with public affairs: "What erroneous judgments one forms," she says, "even when one has spent one's life with distinguished men!"[†]

Her further share in the fortunes of her husband lay in the entire and unselfish devotion she had made her rule in life. "The best way is never to think of oneself if one wishes not to be forgotten."[‡]

His second administration, with its difficulties and responsibilities, not only impaired her physical strength, but her mental capacity for satisfying all the demands of such an entire change of position.

During that time at Coppet he was completely dominated by a longing to resume his public activity. This longing was at once painfully increased by the

[*] Madame Necker, *Mélanges*, iii. to Thomas, 1779.
[†] Madame Necker, *Mélanges*, i. 83.
[‡] *Idem*, ii. 298.

arrival of any old friends or colleagues. Mademoiselle Necker mentions this, on the occasion of a visit from de Lessart, afterwards minister under Louis XVI. and of a son of the Maréchal de Castries, who was among the independent deputies in 1789. He bore the reputation of a clever financier, and as such had energetically supported Necker's first minority. " The presence of ambitious men," she writes after the departure of their guests, "was unbearable to my father. The words ' Only those who will return shall receive shelter' ought to be written over our door. Must I confess it? Ah yes! my father cannot bear to be reminded of the loss he still mourns : how can it be otherwise when he knows so well what he can accomplish? . . . A splendid career in which public opinion would have encouraged him ; successes which must have flattered him, because they aimed at the present and future well-being of a nation, with France and Europe as the scene of action. I thought indeed that his work would compensate for all this. I used to tell him that after he had taught and shown mankind what might be accomplished he need neither distress nor reproach himself when condemned to inactivity ; but the development of his ideas, his increased knowledge of the resources of France, and of the nation's misery, give him a taste of the torments of Tantalus, although his differ in their nature. He sees a splendid building tottering, without being at hand to save it. He will not acknowledge this feeling, and I follow his example. His former position is to us like an unfaithful sweetheart : we do nothing but abuse it, but if it came back we should talk very differently. . . . . . My father was at his happiest at Coppet; there we breathed independence, and were happy. In presence of those mountains, soaring to heaven, all ambitious desires seemed so small. Between us and France there arose an enormous barrier. The people in Switzerland do not in any way remind my father of greatness and power, as these are quite foreign to them, whereas in France society values nothing so much. In society our present position suffers from what we were formerly; a minister out of office is like a woman who was once beautiful, and would prefer henceforward to live with those who had not known her in her youth."

The praises of Coppet are sounded with many variations at that period, but where Necker is in question they always end in one form or another with "How delightful it would be were he again called back to govern France."

This lovely idyl of the Swiss mountains, over which the fascination of the *Nouvelle Héloïse* spread like morning dew, represented a place of banishment whence not only Madame de Staël, but Mademoiselle Necker before her, longed to escape, and once again to mix in society and the stir of the great world. When she first expressed her disinclination for a country life she wrote as follows: "A terrible fear took hold of me that my father would choose to spend the rest of his days at Coppet; may he forgive me, but my store of memories will not suffice me for the rest of my life; I neither strive after illusions or pleasures, but, although I worship him, I would shrink from thinking that the door was shut behind us three for ever. Perhaps I only need a little time to become accustomed to solitude. Were he to be left without other ties I would at once give up everything and devote myself entirely to him; I should banish every other desire from my soul. To purchase a moment of happiness for him is worth the sacrifice of a life-time.* If only I might die first when the moment comes for our separation! It would be more than I could bear that I should be the survivor; I have given my whole life to those who in all probability have fewer years to live. Oh, God, hear the sincerest prayer my soul has ever uttered! Spare me a grief that I cannot name; and, if Thou sendest it, grant forgiveness if I lay hands on Thine Image, that I may go to thee."

These outpourings of an excited imagination bear the date of the 28th July. The following day these impressions had not calmed down, and in the midst of the beauties of summer these same dark visions recurred. "Last night," the young girl writes, "we had a dreadful storm; the great efforts of Nature make more impression on me than anything artificial could do. Nature was created for our use, and we feel this by its influence over us. I was alone, and

---

* D'Haussonville, *Le Salon de Madame Necker*, ii. 178.

only heard the sound of the storm; that of the surrounding inhabitants had ceased, and a quiet melancholy took possession of me. I heard the rain falling in torrents; the thunder made me feel God's might every moment and the danger I was incurring. A feeling of confidence drew me heavenwards, and, to still further reassure myself, I passed in review all that could make it indifferent to me to cease to exist; a fatal enumeration if death is not to follow. I was bathed in tears; I conjured up the thought that I was attacked by the small-pox,—a woman had died of that malady in the neighbourhood just at that time; this manner of death horrified me; all those we loved must be sent away from us; we must refuse the charm of death, the happiness of giving them the last tokens of tenderness, which are made so solemn and touching at that fatal moment; we may not speak to them, just when all we have to say is so full of weight. Ah! it seems as if the happiness of life were gathered into those moments, which we know to be the last. And how dreadful to feel that the illness could affect our minds and make us different to what we generally are!

"What! could we be capable of coldness to those we usually adore? They would never be able to detach their remembrance of us from that time of delirium. I know that it is a great mistake to allow a death-bed impression to dwell in one's mind, but this pain is inseparable from the last farewells . . . . and then I dread the disfiguring results of this unholy malady. Our features can no longer express our thoughts or our eyes behold those we most love; when our lips are closed our glance can no longer express what they could have said; we may not lay a beloved hand on our heart to count its last pulsations. And how dreadful it would be to die in the fear of having communicated the poison that has consumed us to those we love! We wish them to mourn, but we desire that they should live; we do not die when we leave those behind us whom we love, we escape from annihilation; and even in our last moments the thought that those we love must die presents itself in all its horror." *

We cannot be surprised if one whose mind and imagination were filled by such pictures should in thinking of her own youth break out in the words: " *Ce temps si faussement vanté, ce temps de passions et de larmes !* " "When nature strikes a chord," as Herder says, "the secret growth of talent produces scarcely understood or recognised storms and visions, which at the appointed hour take the form of ideals which then become *Werther, Posa, Réné, Delphine,* or *Corinne.*" We only find one allusion to another feeling aroused in the young girl's heart, and confided to a German friend. She deplores the fate of those who are not free to dispose of their own future, and mentions that her first and only love was a man who sued in vain for her hand.† He was

---

* D'Haussonville, *Le Salon de Madame Necker*, ii. 65-70.

† Varnhagen von Ense, *Denkwurdigkeiten und vermischte Schriften, Justus Erich Bollman*, i. 1-33.

destined to come across her later in life, as she here alludes to Comte Louis de Narbonne, whose betrothal to another lady was already decided in 1782, when she first met him in her sixteenth year.

The family spent part of the winter of 1785 at Montpellier, for Madame Necker's health. Its celebrated doctors attracted invalids from all parts of the world.

The only reminiscence of this visit is to be found in a Swiss correspondence, describing the Necker family as "*consummées de vapeurs et d'ennuis.*"* On her return with her parents to Paris, Mademoiselle Necker partly undertook the household supervision, corresponded with her mother's friends, and received the strangers and resident guests in Paris as well as at St. Ouen. One of these, Sir John Sinclair, gratefully records the pleasure she gave him by reciting some Scotch ballads; † while the Comtesse de Sabran, who was not easily amused and whose memory has been prolonged by the publication of some of the most charming letters of the eighteenth century, no less gratefully relates how she was unable to resist her overflowing merriment.‡ This return to Paris brought plans to maturity which for some time had been connected with Mademoiselle Necker's destiny.

Since the days of Louis XIV. and the Northern Alliance, the Swedes enjoyed a popularity in the

---

* Gaullieur, *Etudes sur l'Histoire de la Suisse-Français*, 300. M. de Salgas à Madame de Charrière.

† Sir John Sinclair, *Correspondance*, i. 153, 154.

‡ E. de Magnieu et H. Prat, *Correspondance de la Comtesse de Sabran*, 254.

French capital, to which politics had only given an incentive. It is true that they were still prized as the allies of Richelieu and the French crown, which in return gave the Swedish subsidies a more or less permanent place in its budget; but, independently of this, the Swedes were cordially received in Paris as refined and pleasant men of the world and gallant soldiers. The predecessors of Count Creutz in diplomacy had increased the dignity of their position by their personal qualities and diplomatic skill. Count Sparre was especially remembered as ambassador to the court of Louis XV., during the first half of his long reign, no less on account of his manly beauty than on account of his intellect. On the occasion of a great dinner to which all the ambassadors were invited, the king addressed him in these words : "Monsieur de Sparre, you are not of the same faith as I am ; this I regret, as I shall never meet you in heaven." Thereupon came the quick retort, "Pardon me, sire : my master the king has given me orders to follow your majesty wherever you go." *

In Sweden people affected Descartes' philosophy, French literature, art, and industry, and looked to Paris as another Mecca.

The good understanding between the two countries was first disturbed when the aristocratic party in Stockholm had taken the upper hand in 1720, and had injured the power of the crown under a weak

---

* Geffroy, *Gustave III. et la Cour de France*, ii. 83.

monarch of German origin, who used to say that he would rather be a drummer in Germany than a king in Sweden. The humiliations he endured only made his queen, Louise Ulrica (sister to the Great Frederick), all the more determined that her son, the Crown Prince, afterwards Gustavus III., should avenge all the injuries they had suffered at the hands of an insolent Swedish nobility. "Never forget," she wrote to the Crown Prince, when he wended his way to Paris across Germany in 1770, "never forget that we are the greatest beggars in Europe, and that there is no small prince in my country who would not have handsomer furniture, handsomer silver plate, and a better establishment; the small amount of fortune we still possess is in the hands of the clergy and the peasantry. The nobility, which ought to be insured against want all over the world, is ground down in this country, and stupid enough into the bargain to ignore its only means of help. What is worse, it accelerates its own ruin by accepting bribes of 2,000 or 3,000 thalers, and in every Reichstag sacrifices its privileges and its opinion to the majority.

"This is a terrible picture, verify it yourself. You will say, 'My mother is in a bad temper,' but who would not be, in this miserable country where people are dying of *ennui*, where politics are perpetually discussed, and after all the talking no results follow ?"*

The young man to whom these bitter words were

* Geijer, *Gustave III. Posthumous Papers*, ii. 5.

addressed was twenty-four years old, and was brought
up in the French style, but with the opinions of the
ruling party; when his education was completed his
heart was supposed to be as shallow as his brain,[*]
and he was forced into an unhappy marriage. Always
at dispeace with his mother and wife, mannerless,
superficial but clever, calculating, bold, and above all
things determined to sacrifice even his life to the
security of the throne and the independence of the
kingdom; such was the young prince, judging by
outward appearances, who came to Paris intending
to restore the disturbed relations with France, aided
by the influence of Choiseul. When he reached the
capital, Choiseul had been dismissed from office, and
the young prince's success seemed questionable. Just
then his father died suddenly, in February 1771, and
Gustavus was king. He did not leave Paris without
having come to an understanding with Louis XV.
and his new ministry, which led from that moment
to the renewal of the French subsidies to Sweden,
whereby he succeeded in restoring the power of the
crown against a predominating nobility, unfavourable
moreover to the French alliance. These conditions were
agreed to on the 19th August, 1772. Gustavus III.
carried out this stroke of policy without the loss of a
drop of blood, met his Estates with the outlines of
three constitutions in his pocket, and in a quarter-of-
an-hour the oath was taken to the one amongst them

* Geffroy, *Gustave III. et la Cour de France*, i. 97. Léouzon Le
Duc, *Gustave III., Roi de Suède*. Paris, 1861.

K 2

which seemed the most suitable. A recent historian
bestows the merit upon it of having saved Sweden
from the fate of Poland.* The young king continued
to govern in Stockholm, and to be admired at Ferney
as one of those enlightened beings who are "powerful
for good, and restrain their hands from evil." He
protected the freedom of the press and of education,
supported the physiocrats, allowed Dalekarlien to be
planted with potatoes in deference to the wishes of
his French lady friends, and his capital to be embellished by French artists,† and was quite pleased when
his young Swedish nobles were admitted into the
French regiments, only stipulating that they should
eventually return to his service. From a military
point of view, the most brilliant of these was Count
Stedingk, a contemporary of Gustavus III. Born in
1746, the same year as the king, he was destined to
outlive him until 1837. He fought in the American
War of Independence with his friends Lauzun, Coigny,
Talleyrand-Périgord, Vaudreuil, Noailles, Vauban,
Ségur, La Fayette, and distinguished himself so
immensely at the storming of the fortifications of
Savannah, that, on his return to France in 1780, in
consequence of a severe wound, he found his doughty
deeds celebrated in the Parisian theatres and himself
the hero of the day. It must also be observed that
Mademoiselle Necker celebrated this event in *vers
d'occasion.* He left the service of Louis XVI. in

* Albert Sorel, *L'Europe et la Révolution Française,* i. 65.

† Geffroy, *Gustave III. et la Cour de France,* i. 5.

1787 to join the royal Swedish regiment during the
campaign in Finland ; he left it as a field-marshal,
and at its termination went to Petersburg as Swedish
ambassador to the Empress Catharine. He remained
in this position with her successor, and during this
time * Count Joseph de Maistre learnt to know and
appreciate him.   In the year 1774 a young com‐
patriot of Stedingk's, Count John Axel Fersen, first
came to Paris, at the age of nineteen ; he was a son
of the senator, Count Joseph Axel, one of the most
influential and distinguished men in Sweden. His
mother was of French descent, and belonged to the
Protestant family of De la Gardie, which had taken
refuge in Sweden.   He only remained a short time,
but was presented to the king at Versailles, to Madame
du Barry, and the whole court, and from that time
was dubbed the "handsome Fersen." Count Creutz
wrote to the king that the young man's bearing was
most commendable, and that he united rare nobility
of thought to the most engaging appearance and to
considerable intelligence.†   Louis XV. granted an
officer's commission to Count Fersen in the royal
Bavarian regiment; he returned, however, in 1778
to Paris, and from that moment enjoyed the favour
of Queen Marie Antoinette, which later on gave rise
to much misinterpretation. It was imagined that on

* Graf Biörnstierna, *Mémoires du Feld-Maréchal Comte Stedingk.*
2 vols. Paris, 1844.

† Geffroy, *Gustave III. et la Cour de France*, i. 359. Reumont,
Kleine historische Schriften : König Gustav von Schweden in Aachen,
1780-1791, 319, &c.

one occasion when, she sang the lines out of the opera
Dido at the harpsichord,

"Ah que je fus bien inspirée
Quand je vous reçus dans ma cour,"

her glance was directed with scarcely concealed
emotion towards Fersen.   In a letter to the king
Graf Creutz relates how well he withstood this severe
ordeal, and the events to follow increased the value of
such weighty testimony in favour of these two victims,
so tragically sacrificed to the Revolution.   On the
10th of April, 1779, Creutz writes: "I must own to
your majesty that Count Fersen is in such favour
with the queen that many people take exception to
it : I myself cannot avoid seeing that she inclines
towards him, for I have seen such unmistakeable
signs of it that it is impossible to have any doubts on
the subject.   His behaviour under the circumstances
deserves   admiration ;   he has proved himself so
modest   and   reserved.   His   resolve   to   go   to
America puts all danger aside ; but a power of will
far in excess of his years was necessary to pull
through such a complication.   During the last few
days the queen never kept her eyes off him, and
they were filled with tears.   I implore your majesty
for the sake of the queen, and of Senator Fersen, to
preserve the strictest secrecy on this subject.   When
the news of his intended journey was spread abroad,
the Duchess of FitzJames said to him 'So you give
up your conquest?'   To this he replied, 'If I had

made one I would not give it up; I take my leave as a free man, and fortunately no one will regret me.' Your majesty will admit that an answer of this sort showed remarkable wisdom and self-control." *

The young man's appearance agreed with his old friend's description; it had something noble and distinguished about it; the handsome, and gentle, but melancholy features, would have suited the hero of a romance, but not a French one,† as a contemporary says, for he had neither the boldness nor *entrain* of that nation. When Dumouriez met him in Belgium in 1792, Fersen himself relates that the general, who had only bowed to him slightly, apologized, with the remark that he might have remembered him by his good looks.‡ Many years after, Herder used to quote him as the handsomest man he had ever seen, only he thought his appearance lacked animation.§ Fersen fought with renown in America, and was appointed colonel, travelled with King Gustavus on his return, and only revisited Paris in 1784, when Louis XVI. gave him the command of the royal Swedish regiment.

Meanwhile another Swede, Baron Erich Magnus von Staël - Holstein, had become domesticated in Parisian society, and had been secretary to the Swedish embassy under Count Creutz since 1776.

* Geffroy, *Gustave III. et la Cour de France*, i. 361.

† Duc de Lévis, *Souvenirs*.

‡ Klinkowström, *Le Comte Fersen et la Cour de France*, ii. 69. Fersen, *Journal*. April, 1792.

§ Böttiger, *Literarische Zustände und Zeitgenossen*.

Born in 1749 the young man came of an old Swedish race, and was intended for the army, in which he served until he joined the diplomatic service : at one time Staël had thought of sharing in the American war, but on the English side.*　He was pleasant in society, clever, persevering, and careful of his appearance, although not as brilliant as Stedingk or as winning as Fersen.　On the other hand he perfectly understood how to ingratiate himself with the older French ladies, the friends of his sovereign.　King Gustavus used to correspond with several of those after his residence in France, and to allow them to keep him informed in all the news and political incidents of the day.　The most attractive among these ladies, the beautiful, enthusiastic, and clever Comtesse d'Egmont (one of the first to whom Rousseau read his *Confessions*), tried even on her deathbed to inspire Gustavus with political ideals concerning freedom and the happiness of mankind.　Very different from this poetic and original creature was the old Comtesse de la Marck, whose existence dated from the days of Louis XIV. and who was derided by Palissot as the pedantic authoress of a quarto volume, treating,

> " de l'esprit, du bon sens,
> Des passions, des lois, et des gouvernements,
> De la vertu, des mœurs, du climat, des usages
> Des peuples policés, et des peuples sauvages,
> Du désordre apparent, de l'ordre universel,
> Du bonheur idéal, et du bonheur réel."

---

* Léouzon Le Duc, *Correspondance Diplomatique du Baron de Staël-Holstein.*　Introduction, v.

More influential and practical than Madame de la
Marck was Madame de Boufflers, but equally full of
a political ideal which she imagined was to be found
in the British constitution. She was the friend of
Hume, Jean Jacques, and Gustavus III., whom she
hospitably entertained at Auteuil; she was also the
only woman of her day who had acquired a thorough
personal knowledge of other countries. A long-
established friendship with the Prince of Conti, who
lived in the neighbourhood of the Temple, earned
for her the name of "*Idole du Temple*"; she had the
reputation of being as amiable as she was clever, and
was not offended when Voltaire's sound sense took
exception to "all those ladies who occupied themselves with the French constitution," in the following
squib:

> "Mais, monsieur, des Capets les lois fondementales,
> Et le grenier à sel, et les lois féodales,
> Et le gouvernement du Chancelier Duprat." *

Young Staël was so successful in pleasing the
Comtesse Boufflers that Creutz wrote to the king that
she was as fond of him as if he were her own son;
he added jestingly that all the pretty women, like
Madame de la Marck and the Maréchale de Luxembourg (both over sixty), had sworn to work his ruin
if he did not take Staël. The sort of protection the
latter required may be gathered from Creutz's last
remarks about him, mentioning that he had run

* Voltaire's *Satire: Les Cabales.* 1772.

through all his fortune and was without a farthing.*
The first indication of the ways and means whereby
Staël sought to escape his difficulties is found in a
letter addressed to the king on the 27th of June, 1779,
in which he reminded him of having spoken to him
before as to his intention of seeking Mademoiselle
Necker's hand. Staël knew later on, from a conversation on the subject between Comtesse Boufflers and
Madame Necker, that the affair would be favourably
entertained, but Madame Necker had emphatically
said that only a man in a completely assured position,
and that in France, could have any chance of becoming her son-in-law, as neither she nor Necker
could bring themselves to consent to a permanent
separation from their daughter. Mademoiselle Necker
was then in her fourteenth and Staël in his thirtieth
year, but, notwithstanding all the considerations and
difficulties which were opposed to him, he never from
this moment dropped his matrimonial projects. In
a series of letters, the tone of which became more
and more pressing, he implored the king to assure
him of the reversion of the post of ambassador to the
French court as the goal of his desires, and he enlisted all the influence of his friends to attain this
object. When Gustavus III. showed signs of indecision, although his answers were friendly, Creutz
wrote to him in April 1782 that the outcome of this
appointment would be to secure one of the most con-

---

* Léonzon Le Duc, *Correspondance Diplomatique du Baron de Staël-
Holstein.* Introduction. Geffroy, *Gustave III. et la Cour de France.*

siderable fortunes in France to Baron de Staël, and
that with an income of 500,000 francs his family
would occupy a brilliant and influential position,
equal perhaps to that possessed by the Duc de Soubise,
only no time should be lost, as Mademoiselle Necker's
parents would soon decide about her. His efforts,
and the repeated prayers of Madame de Boufflers and
her *protégé*, seemed at last to have obtained the
desired hearing. Gustavus III. gave his lady-friend
the assurance that, in case of any change in his
diplomatic representation in Paris, he would appoint
a minister-plenipotentiary, and give this post to
Baron de Staël only, who tendered his most grateful
thanks in July 1782. In the following year the
anticipated change came to pass, as Creutz was appointed Chancellor and Minister of Foreign Affairs,
and returned to Sweden. But Staël suffered a new
and bitter disappointment, when, unmindful of his
promise, the king appeared to be determined to name
Baron Taube for Paris. " My position is too dreadful," wrote the distracted Staël; "nothing can save
me from ruin if your majesty is not pleased to alter
the determination which seals my misfortune. If it
remains unaltered nothing is left me except to hide
myself in the remotest corner of the world, whence
my prayers and complaints can be heard no longer,
and where I can upbraid the fate that has destined
me to be the only one born to misfortune of all your
majesty's subjects." Things did not turn out quite
so badly as this letter represents them, for there was

one means of obtaining favour still left,—and this
decided the question,—namely, the queen. In 1771,
when still dauphiness, the king of Sweden had
earned her disapprobation, as he had not been too
proud to appear at Madame du Barri's, and to present
a valuable collar to her lap-dog, in pursuit of his own
purposes. Since that date, however, their relations
had become very friendly, and Marie Antoinette was
always glad to see the Swedish nobles about her
court. It was she who notified her wish to bring
about a marriage between Count Stedingk and Mademoiselle Necker; nothing, however, came of it, as
Stedingk cared too much for his liberty to give it
up.* But Baron Staël was also a favourite of hers,
and even in 1781 she expressed her hope, in a note
to King Gustavus, that they should keep him permanently in Paris. In March 1783 she again returned
to the subject,† and Creutz wrote to his sovereign
that he ventured in his own interests earnestly to
remind him that a serious misunderstanding with the
French court was to be feared if this suggestion,
already once offered by the queen, was not carried
out. Meanwhile Gustavus had gone to Italy, and,
as his own revenues could not satisfy his love of
magnificence, he could afford less than ever to do
without the French subsidies. However little Staël's
appointment might suit his own intentions he never-

* Geffroy, *Gustave III. et la Cour de France*, i. 355.
† Geffroy, i. 373, 376, 573. Léouzon Le Duc, *Correspondance du
Baron de Staël*. Introduction, viii.

theless granted it to the queen, and before the end of the year 1783 Staël was *chargé d'affaires*, then minister-plenipotentiary, and afterwards, according to the mistaken custom of the day, ambassador for six years, and stood so high in the royal graces at Versailles that Creutz declared that during his long term of office he never had received such marks of favour either from Louis XVI. or his queen.*

From Florence Gustavus wrote to his new ambassador, " If you marry Mademoiselle Necker you will be the richest noble in your own country, and like Caesar you will be able to say, ' Better to be first there than second in Rome ! ' " and later on he says, " Try and bring the affair to a satisfactory conclusion, and then I will myself come to Paris for the signature of your marriage-contract.†   In other words, the king had done his best and all the more impatiently awaited the fulfilment of the conditions advanced by the other side.

Staël had not, however, come to an end of his trials.

When his sovereign actually came to Paris, in 1784, no marriage-contract was ready for signature.   The Necker family was in Switzerland, and no longer seemed to set the same value on what had been accomplished after such prolonged uncertainty.   The king's visit cost his ambassador the round sum of 200,000 francs.   On this distressing   occasion the

---

* Léouzon Le Duc, *Correspondance Diplomatique du Baron de Staël-Holstein.*   Introduction.

† Geffroy, *Gustave III. et la Cour de France,* i. 379, and ii. 412.

Comtesse Boufflers came, however, to the rescue and saved the situation for her friend Staël. She again addressed herself to Coppet, and at last received the final conditions on which the Necker family expressed themselves willing once again to entertain the Staël project of marriage. These conditions, dated May 21st, 1784, were :—

(1) A life appointment of Staël to the French embassy.

(2) A pension of 20,000 francs, should unforeseen events deprive him of this post.

(3) The title of Count, especially to obviate any confusion between Baronne de Staël and another lady of the same name who bore a doubtful reputation.

(4) A solemn promise on Staël's part only to take his wife to Sweden for a short time, and then only with their consent.

(5) Investiture of the Order of the Polar Star for the ambassador.

(6) An explicit declaration from Marie Antoinette in favour of this marriage.

Whilst these conditions depending on King Gustavus reached their destination and awaited their despatch, an untoward fate prepared fresh dangers for Staël. In the course of the year 1785 no less a suitor than a German prince, George Augustus of Mecklenburg, brother of the reigning duke, appeared on the scene, a man of forty, whose suit was no less businesslike than were Necker's conditions in the Staël project. He describes himself as "a posthumous son, and as having amassed a considerable amount of debt as a simple major in the emperor's service." He could add in his favour that by a union with him Mademoiselle Necker would be related by marriage to the king of England. Necker added that he had already entered into engagements for his daughter's marriage, the result of which he was bound by loyalty and affection to await, and there was no further mention of the German prince.* Meanwhile, as no marriage with Staël seemed to be coming about, Fersen again casually thought of becoming a suitor for Mademoiselle Necker's hand; since the king's return he was again living in Paris, as colonel of his French regiment, and was, as he had always been, the darling of society and of the Court. Gustavus III. was at Malins when news of this project reached him. However much he might have wished for the consummation, he says in a letter to Fersen, written June 1785: "If I am to believe the newspapers," he writes, "you are on the point of making a great marriage, and poor Staël seems to have been unsuccessful. I cannot be surprised; there are a hundred reasons why M. Necker should prefer you to any one else for his daughter, and your prospects of a settled income are of no small importance in the eyes of a banker. Still, I have my doubts about it all, as your small inclination for matrimony and your preference for English women is known to me."†

* D'Haussonville, *Le Salon de Madame Necker*, ii. 75, 76.

† Léouzon Le Duc, *Correspondance du Baron de Staël*. Introduction, xiv.

We know the reason of this allusion. Before he
went to America there was a talk of a marriage
between Fersen and a very rich girl, Mademoiselle de
Beijol, whose father was a naturalised Englishman.*
But the king was quite right, and Fersen never
married. "You will already have seen," he writes
to his father, "why the idea I once entertained
about Mademoiselle Necker could never have been
fulfilled, even although you had consented to it, and
that because of my friend Staël, whom it suits exactly,
and far better than it would suit me. To please you,
my dear father, I had thought of it, and am not in
the least annoyed that I did not succeed."† Even to
the king nothing was left but to give his consent.

In the peace of Versailles he had also made his conditions, and in return for giving Staël the post of ambassador he demanded the island of Tobago in the Antilles,
which Sweden had long coveted. By the Versailles convention of July 1, 1784, he received the island of Saint
Bartholomew instead, which had hitherto belonged to
France, and he now assured to his ambassador all that
Necker desired, except indeed the title of Count and
the promise that he should hold his post for life. The
king engaged that after six years Staël's appointment should again be secured to him for another six
years. Who could guess that his appointment would
last much longer than the French monarchy itself ? ‡

* Klinkowström, *Le Compte Fersen et la Cour de France.* Introduction, xxxix.

† *Idem.*

‡ Geffroy, *Gustave III. et la Cour de France,* i. 377, ii. 41.

Madame de Boufflers wrote in great delight to her royal friend that she must confess the affair had not only taken up her attention for a long time but that it also had often very much fatigued her. "The first proposals," she says, "I made five years ago, and for the last three years I have never ceased to repeat them both verbally and in writing, so that I hope this rich marriage may be of advantage to Sweden."* On the 16th October, 1785, Fersen wrote again to his father that at last the affair was decided, and he himself delighted with the brilliant piece of business Staël had accomplished. In this letter he mentions that Mademoiselle Necker had preferred the latter to Pitt, and ends by saying, "I saw her a few days ago; she is the reverse of beautiful, but she is very clever, cheerful, and amiable, and she is very well brought up and full of talent. The wedding is to be either on the 10th or the 15th of this month." So much for Fersen. What love had not done was accomplished by politics, and they separated the chivalrous worshipper of the queen of France from the friend of his youth and his friend's wife. The marriage suffered fresh delay owing to Mademoiselle Necker's illness in the autumn, and the last difficulty in this matter, which was treated as an affair of state, arose on the part of the ever-scrupulous Necker, who desired that the certificate of Staël's birth should be

Léouzon Le Duc, *Correspondance Diplomatique du Baron Staël.* D'Haussonville, *Le Salon de Madame Necker*, ii. 70-75.

* Geffroy, *Gustave III. et la Cour de France*, i. 378.

produced. "I knew, my dear fellow," wrote Gustavus when he heard of this, "that a man had to be
good-looking and amiable, and an ambassador, if he
were to be a fit husband for Mademoiselle Necker, but
I was not aware that he was obliged to be signed and
sealed a good Christian. If you had said a word to
me on this subject I could have given you as good a
certificate as your parish priest, as I am Pope in my
Church. You were unaware that had you and Mademoiselle Necker seen the light only ten or twenty
years sooner you could never have married at all,
for at that date there were no certificates anywhere
in Sweden. The practice has only come in of late."*
A marriage, so entirely in accordance with the prevailing ideas and usages, ought to have gained the
approval of the Paris of that day. This, however, was
not the case, if the Empress Catherine, who was kept
informed by innumerable letters, is to be believed.
On the contrary, "every one thought that Mademoiselle Necker had made a very bad marriage."†
Marmontel asserts that he was the first to whom the
Staël project of marriage was confided, and Necker
set aside 650,000 francs as his daughter's portion, an
enormous sum for those days.‡

Count Guibert, their intimate friend, and, amongst
the older generation, one of Mademoiselle Necker's

* Geffroy, i. 378.

† Grimm and Catherine II., *Correspondance.* *Recueil de la Société
Impériale de Russie*, xxiii. 370.

‡ D'Haussonville, *Le Salon de Madame Necker*, ii. 74.

warmest admirers, wrote a sketch of her in the taste of that day, calling her by the mythical name of Zulmé. He gave out that he had borrowed his glowing colours from a Greek poet, and amongst other things he says of her: "Zulmé is about twenty years old, but already one of the most honoured priestesses of Apollo, whose incense is pleasant to him, and whose voice he prefers to any other . . . . . Her large black eyes sparkle with the fire of genius, and her ebon locks fall in rich profusion on her shoulders. Her features are more marked than gentle, there is something in them which promises more than the usual fate of her sex."

Sainte-Beuve speaks of a portrait of her in her youth which confirms this description, and says she was in the fullness of her bloom, and had wavy hair, a clear and honest expression, a high forehead, and lips apart as if about to speak. The whole description of her features spoke of amiability and cleverness, the blushing cheeks betrayed quick and lively feelings, her arms and neck were bare, her clothing gathered together in loose folds by a sash. We have seen the picture from which his description is taken; it is that of Rehberg, and was painted about that time. The great French critic ended by saying that "the bride led to the altar by Baron de Staël might recall the Sophie in *Emile*."*

The marriage of the young couple took place with

---

* Sainte-Beuve, *Portraits de Femmes: Madame de Staël.*

all the splendour of their rank and position in society in the Reformed Lutheran chapel attached to the Swedish legation, one Saturday, the 14th of January, 1786, a few days after the king and queen of France had witnessed and signed the marriage-contract.

CHAPTER IV.

THE Official Gazette dated Feb. 3, 1786, chronicles
the appearance of Madame de Staël in Parisian society
and her presentation at Court. It sets forth that "the
Baronne de Staël-Holstein, wife of the envoy-extra-
ordinary of the king of Sweden, was presented on
the 31st of January to their majesties and the rest of
the royal family by M. de Tolozan, introducer of ambassadors, and M. de Sequeville, the king's first secretary for the presentation of the said ambassadors." *

On the same day the ambassadress was invited to
a dinner of forty-eight people presided over by the
Marquis de Talaru, the queen's high chamberlain.
The queen's lady-in-waiting, the Princesse de Chimay,
did the honours.

* Geffroy, *Gustave III. et la Cour de France*, i. 392, note,

The eventful day was not to come to an end without some excitement, for in making the last of the three customary curtsies to the queen, during which the lady who is presented has to take hold of the queen's skirt, and appear to kiss it, some lace on Madame de Staël's train was torn, and she was reduced to the most pitiful state of embarrassment.

It would appear that her movements were a good deal hampered by her short sight.* The king, who was also present, said laughingly to her, "If you have not confidence in us you can have it in no one." And no less graciously Marie Antoinette summoned one of her women to repair the disaster.†

Although the circumstance was insignificant, it gave occasion to a flattering *quatrain* which found its way into Grimm's *Correspondance :*

> " Le timide embarras qui nait de la pudeur
>   Bien loin d'être un defaut est un belle grâce,
> . La modeste vertu ne connait pas l'audace,
>   Ni le vice effronté l'innocente rougeur,"

and to various unfriendly remarks on the part of the Baroness Oberkirch, the first of the many detractors Madame de Staël was destined to encounter among her own sex. Her criticisms culminated somewhat curiously in reproaching Necker's daughter for the stiff manners and prudery of a Genevese woman, although she undoubtedly possessed genius ; and she

* Simond, *Voyage en Suisse*, i. 295.

† Lescure, *Correspondance Secrète*, &c. 1777-1792, ii. 13. Baronne d'Oberkirch, *Mémoires*, ii. 206, the English translation.

was further accused by those competent to judge in those matters of being frequently ill-dressed.* Madame de Boufflers was the next who had a good deal of fault to find. Although she had principally brought the marriage about, she anticipated wonderfully little satisfaction from its accomplishment. She gave the young wife no time, but wrote to King Gustavus immediately after the wedding: " I wish I could think that Staël will be happy, although I cannot believe that he will be. His wife has certainly been brought up with a strong sense of duty and rectitude, but she lacks all knowledge of the world and its ways. She is so persuaded of her own superiority that it will be difficult to draw her attention to what she lacks. She is obstinate and domineering, and possesses an assurance such as I have never come across in any society, or in any woman of her age. She passes thoughtless judgment upon everything, and, although she is very clever, she often says twenty things she had better have left unsaid before she says the right one. The ambassador does not venture to draw her attention to this, as he fears to alienate her at the outset; I recommend him, however, to show firmness, as very often all future relations depend on the line first taken in these matters. Her father's friends extol her to the skies; his enemies cover her with ridicule ; those who are neutral give full justice to her understanding, but they accuse her

---

* Caro, *La fin de la dix-huitième siècle. Études et Portraits,* ii. 186. *La Jeunesse de Madame de Staël.*

of talking too much, and of having more cleverness.
than tact or common sense. If her head were not
turned by so much incense I should try to advise her
a little."[*]

If we consider that at the very outset this was the
judgment of so-called friends, what must antagonists
such as Rivarol and Madame de Genlis have had to
say ? Good-will was never freely granted to Madame
de Staël; she had to work for it, and always in the
first instance to overcome prejudice and even dislike.

According to the prevalent custom, the newly-married
pair had to remain for some weeks under the paternal
roof before taking possession of the Swedish embassy
in the Rue de Bac. Since Necker's return, the family
had lived in a house in the Rue Bergère from 1781
to 1788, as they had let the Hôtel Leblanc somewhat
prematurely, for a term of years, on his accession to
office.

The letter in which the young wife took leave of
her paternal home has been preserved, and was
addressed to Madame Necker: "This evening," she
writes, "I shall not return. This is the last day I
shall spend as I have spent all the rest of my life.
How much this change costs me! I know not if
another mode of life be possible, as I have never tried
another, and the unknown adds to my sorrow. I
know only too well, my mother, that I have failed in
my conduct towards you. My actions rise up against

* Geffroy, *Gustave III. et la Cour de France*, i. 384.

me at this moment as they would on my death-bed, and I fear my departure may not cause you the regret I would fain arouse. But pray believe that imaginary shadows have often come between us and have put me in an unfavourable light. Nevertheless, I feel that the love brought to the surface on this occasion has always been equally deep. It is a part of my life, and the thought of our separation crushes me.

"To-morrow I may return, but to-night I have to sleep under another roof! I shall no longer have my guardian angel by my side. She who would support me in the hour of death, and cover me with the rays of her beautiful spirit in God's presence, will no longer be with me. I shall be unable to hear how you are at any moment of the day, and in many other respects I see how I shall miss you at every instant. I cannot describe, dearest mother, how I am strengthened by my love for you. You are so pure and innocent that every thought connected with you must be derived from Heaven. I pray God to make me worthy of you. Happiness may come later on, by degrees, or it may not come at all; everything in this world must have an end, and you are so sure of a future life that neither can I have doubts on the subject. I might write for ever without exhausting my theme. Accept, my dear mother, my deep respect and unalterable love.

"Thursday morning. Still at home." *

* D'Haussonville, *Le Salon de Madame Necker*, ii. 78.

The marriage ties might be privately or publicly despised in the society of that day, wherein the Staël couple first made their appearance, but the question still remains whether the new life brought inward happiness to the young wife from the standpoint then in vogue.

Madame de Staël has only alluded to this herself in a negative way, and that by unceasingly representing married bliss as the highest although the most unattainable object of her desires.

A first indication on this subject occurs a short time after her marriage; her last words on it is the celebrated chapter at the close of her book on Germany, on which she lavished her highest efforts and most persuasive eloquence. An allusion to the situation between herself and her husband will have been found, where Corinne, speaking of her lovers, mentions a distinguished German nobleman who had at first won her esteem, but who on further acquaintance had betrayed such a lack of intellectual distinction that he could not retain this esteem. Some remarks in her *Letters on Jean Jacques Rousseau*, published in 1788 shortly after her marriage, are still of closer import: " Rousseau may have intended to attack all other social institutions, but marriage he never attacked. How highly he valued the bond to which we were destined by nature ! How could he give us more clearly to understand that he awaited our salvation by this means than by proving to us that even to hearts that have known other joys it brings con-

tent ? Who can assert that such sacrifice is unknown
when Julie, the most luckless of women, was capable
of it ?"

But she nevertheless feels the danger threatened by
Rousseau's theories when she speaks of his system for
female education in the following terms : " Rousseau
would bring up women in the same way as men—by
the laws of nature; only definitely cultivating the
difference which nature has herself established between them. I do not know whether he is right thus
to uphold and, as it were, strengthen women in their
weakness. They require great self-control; their
passions and their impulses are always in opposition
to the customs of a country where they are, as a rule,
forbidden to give expression to their affections."

And, passing on to the infidelity imputed by the
author to Emile's wife, Madame de Staël exclaims,
" Ah, Rousseau ! that is a very false judgment of
women. Her heart may deceive her, but it will also
protect her. Not even the weakest of women would
allow herself to be drawn from the earthly paradise
and break loose from the chains of a marriage that
was grounded on love." *

So spoke Madame de Staël in those letters which
it has been rightly observed "were written before
the storm broke." When this occurred she was naturally defenceless. Of what avail was this poetical
analysis of married love which neither recognised a

* Madame de Staël, Œuvres complètes. Lettres sur J. J. Rousseau,
i. 1. Letter ii. Héloïse.

definite duty nor ethical motives independent of a
personal desire for happiness when it ceased, as
Rousseau describes, " to find its duty in inclination,
and to be virtuous from a natural impulse "?

Thus it happened, as under similar conditions it
was bound to happen, that the Staël marriage, after
a very few years, was virtually dissolved. Although
the innate uprightness of her inner nature could not
keep off actual shipwreck, at least it prevented
Madame de Staël from making unwarrantable complaints as to her fate ; she admitted that she had not
herself risked a sufficient stake to justify her in ex·
pecting to draw a prize.

Her husband, on the other hand, seemed at first
to have made the mistake—by no means unusual—
of supposing that after he had provided for all
worldly emergencies his wife's heart would likewise
fall to his share. When disenchantment on this
subject ensued he was the more disappointed. All
his friends testified that this woman had not only
inspired him with a passing fancy but with a feeling
of sincere affection.

One of these friends, Reuterholm, wrote even in
1793 to the chancellor of the duke-regent in Sweden :
" It is greatly to Staël's credit that he has never
ceased to be sincerely attached to his charming wife,
although she shows entire indifference to him." *
An indirect confirmation of this is certainly found in

* Léonzon Le Duc, *Correspondance Diplomatique du Baron de Staël-
Holstein*. Introduction, xii.

Staël's correspondence with Reuterholm, which is by no means uninteresting in other respects.

A characteristic trait of the waning eighteenth century was its preference for everything dark and secret, which in some took the form of enthusiastic sentimental religious views, and in others that of secret societies and superstitious practices of every sort. Under the pretence of a thoroughly religious education the pious beliefs of childhood were repudiated.

The much-abused craving for the supernatural and eternal, so contemned by the materialists, took its revenge in the culture of secret knowledge, in introducing new prophets, invocations of spirits, and visions of every kind. Serious and even distinguished men joined in these practices, but clever impostors were much oftener mixed up in them. There was no essential difference between material philosophy and this kind of mysticism, which, under Mesmer and Puységur, imagined it had found a universal panacea in animal magnetism for all physical suffering and the natural key to miracles : but at the same time it struggled against the introduction of the supernatural by means of somnambulism and second-sight, and even formed a separate sect.

When Mesmer left Paris in 1781, the Sicilian, Cagliostro, made his entry into that city ; and later on, during his Roman imprisonment, he gave himself out as one of the messengers of the German sect of

Illuminati,[*] whose founder, Weishaupt the Bavarian, with the assistance of adepts, such as Knigge, attempted to imbue the political and secret masonic societies in France with his own teaching, which in its last expression was nothing more than the views held by Rousseau as to property and society, and hitherto followed out in their logical sequence.

In the opinion of Louis Blanc, Weishaupt was one of the most remarkable impostors who ever lived, but his plan fell to the ground. French freemasonry preferred the more definite plan, and one moreover started by Mirabeau, their own countryman—that of a steady opposition to despotism or spoliation of civil and religious liberty—to Weishaupt's ideal in the far distance, which was however revived in part by Fauchet and Babeuf.[†] Cagliostro subsequently was known in another way; his notorious name is connected with the affair of the necklace and with the Cardinal Louis de Rohan, the best known and most guilty of all its victims; whilst La Fayette may be numbered amongst the most enthusiastic of Mesmer's adherents.[‡]

The religious mysticism of that date was directed to quite different regions of thought and feeling than those of politics and materialism as represented by

[*] Henri Martin, *Histoire de France*, xvi. 531, 4th edition.

[†] Mirabeau, *Mémoires*, ii. livre vi. *Lettre sur Cagliostro et Lavater*, 1786.

[‡] La Fayette, *Mémoires*, ii. 98, and his *Correspondence with George Washington*.

Martinez, Pasqualis, St. Martin, Swedenborg, and
Lavater ; through the pious and noble St. Martin it
may be traced back to Joseph Böhme, and in this way
is as much of German origin as the discoveries of
Mesmer and the plans of Weishaupt.

These religious and mystical tendencies had a
disciple in Baron de Staël, if not in his wife, and they
attracted him by their seductive resemblance to the
tone of thought in his own country.   As always was
the case in the north, Sweden was specially favourable to them.   " Your majesty is aware that Sweden
is the land of spirits, apparitions, and miracles,"
wrote Joseph de Maistre to his sovereign from St.
Petersburg,* where he saw a great deal of Count
Stedingk and his compatriots.   Without going further
back than the eighteenth century a marvellous example is furnished in this respect by the great Lin-
næus.   Almost simultaneously with the appearance
of the first highly significant writings of the theo-
sophist St. Martin, which even attracted men holding
the same opinions as the Count J. de Maistre by
their profoundly Christian tenets, a first translation
of Swedenborg's *Wonders of Heaven and Hell*
appeared in Paris in 1783, Gustave III. showed
himself a true child of the times when, instead of
referring to this source of earnest religious thought, he
preferred to seek for comfort and instruction in the
muddy waters of the supernatural.   He questioned

* A. Blanc, *Mémoires et Correspondance Politique du Comte J. de
Maistre*, 329.

adventuresses upon the future, believed in every sort
of apparition and prophecy, in the mysteries of the
lodge, and seriously busied himself during his stay in
Rome with the building of the Temple at Jerusalem.
Even the manly sympathy he lent to the Pretender
Charles Edward Stuart during his stay in Italy was
mingled with the design of being invested by him as
by the rightful king of Scotland in the succession to
the grand mastership of the freemasons held by him
at that time.   The legend which pointed to the
Scottish king as being also the hereditary descendant
of the knights templar has been poetized in the *Sons
of the Valley* by Zacharias Werner.*

Whilst Gustavus III. was lost in these thoughts and
dreams, Charles, his brother, Duke of Sudermania,
invoked the spirits of darkness to find out how he
should supplant his brother and nephews on the
Swedish throne; a dangerous experiment, in which
exorcism more and more took the appearance of a
conspiracy.   His confidant in this was Baron Reuterholm, his most intimate friend, who knew so well
how to use this disposition on the part of his princely
patron that he soon had him completely in his power.
Reuterholm, a zealous freemason, was the friend of
Baron de Staël and thoroughly shared his taste for
mystic ceremonies.   Amongst the *personnel* of his
embassy a certain Halldin was specially appointed to
arrange all these rites and exorcisms.†

* Reumont, *Die Gräfinn von Albany*, i. 239-240.
† Geffroy, *Gustave III. et la Cour de France*, ii. 247, &c.

A letter from Staël to Reuterholm, after the long stay of the latter in Paris, Avignon, and Rome, from 1789 to 1790, in the interest of the *Illuminati* and freemasons, gives us a closer insight into the extraordinary state of mind he was in. "My dear friend," he writes to Reuterholm, "I have spent many bitter hours since your departure. If I knew how to bear my cross my fate would be more endurable, but the old Adam prevails. I cannot sincerely follow the guidance of God, whose power and mercy are infinite. When I think of all the evil I have done and all the good I have left undone, I feel that I deserve to be a thousand times more tried than I have been. Pray for me, my friend, that my feeble faith may be strengthened. My heart is heavy and tears choke my utterance. Pray, ah pray, that my trial may teach me and turn me towards the right path. Oh to attain that faith which leads to the arms of the Comforter! May God keep you and bless you! . . . . . I have deserved my present suffering. I am punished in my innermost feelings, but I still dare to think that notwithstanding all my faults my heart has remained steadfast. Pray for my wife. May she never suffer from the torment I endure."* Thus ran many pages, and it is easy to guess what manner of trial induced Baron de Staël to pray for higher consolation.

* Geffroy, *Gustave IV. et la Cour de France*, ii. 271; and more fully in, Léouzon Le Duc, *Correspondance Diplomatique du Baron de Staël-Holstein*. Introduction, xxi.-xxiii.

Although, judging by letters like this, he might occasionally be discouraged and weighed down, this did not prevent his outwardly leading a brilliant existence and one highly satisfactory to his ambition. The letters of the day repeatedly mention the ambassador as devoted to gambling.* On the occasion of a ball given by him at Versailles no provision was made for the servants, who, wearied with hunger and with waiting in the cold, gave such loud expression to their discontent that it was with the utmost difficulty they could be silenced.† The luxury of Baron de Staël's table was accounted so great that the queen requested Necker to make friendly representations to the young wife that they should not exceed their income. In allusion to this the Baronne de Staël wrote to her husband from St. Ouen to Paris, "I beg you, my dear, to invite Madame de Simiane to our dinner on Thursday; one extra person makes no difference, and whatever they may say we shall not be ruined. 'They,' however, are not altogether to be disregarded. It was the queen herself who begged M. de Castries to say to my father that she feared we might get into difficulties and that he must look after us. This made my father give me a lecture, as he was much struck by the warning, and above all much touched by the queen's kindness. He is sure to tell you about it, but I do not think he will say as much

* Lescure, *Correspondance Secrète Inédite*, 1777-1792.   Goncourt, *Histoire de la Société Française pendant la Révolution*, 24.

† Lescure, *Idem*, ii. 221.

to you as he has to me, for I feel, just as he does, that it is difficult to express affection for people in that rank; there are so many who only feign it. As a fact I have always observed, that, in a special way of his own, he praised her intelligence, her nobility, her kindness; always took her part if she were attacked in any way in his presence; and, above all, I noticed how sad he became whenever he heard that she still kept up her interest in him.

" Women's talent lies in their instinct, and I guess every thought in those I love. As you are going to Versailles, be sure you remember me to M. de Vergennes—it will please him.

"Be so good as to order the dinner. Sixteen courses should be enough I think—you see the queen's precepts are taking effect! Good-bye, my dear friend."*

The chief literary effort of Madame de Staël during those years was her correspondence with Gustavus III. giving him all the Parisian news that could be of interest to him.

The first of these bulletins, which she begged her royal correspondent to burn when read,† is dated March 11, 1786, and is an answer to an autograph letter from the king, whose acquaintance she was never to make.

Meanwhile Cagliostro and his wife had been thrown into the Bastille, and "he aroused universal sympathy.

* D'Haussonville, *Le Salon de Madame Necker*, ii. 187.

† Letters of Madame de Staël in the University Library at Upsala. To King Gustavus from Madame de Staël, undated, 1787.

In this country the victims of the law have the public always on their side, and for a short time an effort was made to arouse it in favour of the cardinal. The cardinal is Prince Louis de Rohan, the hero of the necklace affair, by whose deadly snares the queen had been calumniated. The contempt he is held in," continues Madame de Staël, "is so thorough, that no strong feeling can be aroused for or against him. We shall have no *nuncio* in France till the cardinal's trial is over . . . .

" Madame de Genlis lately inherited 200,000 francs from the Maréchale d'Estrées: she owes us an account of this sum, as the public generally knows all about her private affairs.

" The queen and king both received me most graciously ; she told me that she had long wished to make my acquaintance : the dinner was more splendid than any that had ever been given for an ambassadress. A week after I dined with the Spanish ambassadress at M. de Vergennes : he led us both to table, so that there should be no difficulty about precedence. I notice these marks of politeness as they are no longer personal to me. The queen's balls were especially brilliant this winter. The ball-rooms were like a fairy palace. They were like the gardens of the Trianon, and the fountains played all the while. The pleasures and attractions of all this courtly splendour recalled the open-air delights of the summer time. Close by, in another room, the less ideal occupation of card-playing was carried on to an unlimited extent. A young M. de Castellane has left the paternal roof, having lost everything he possessed. The queen, however, sets the example of moderation, and it is not to please her that people ruin themselves; but gamblers care for no other occupation, as they have accustomed themselves to this great excitement and its dangers . . . . . The Maréchal de Duras was waited on the other day by a young *débutante.* The Comédie Française is under his control as first chamberlain. 'Well, my young lady,' said he 'what parts do you wish to appear in first?' 'It is quite the same to me; I can take either comedy or tragedy, anything that is wanted.' 'And who taught you elocution?' 'Ah! that was an abbé who took great interest in me. He took an extraordinary amount of trouble, but he was not the most useful of all to me.' 'And who, my young lady, may that have been?' 'A vicar-general, of whom I may say that he really loved me and improved my talent in the most remarkable degree.' 'Well,' said the maréchal, 'this gets better and better. Is that all, mademoiselle?' 'No, sir; a bishop is my chief benefactor; he gives me lessons, and if necessary he will recommend me.'

" The names connected with this perfectly authentic anecdote are those of the Abbé Délille, the Abbé d'Espagnac, and Jarente the coadjutor at Orleans. This I think may be called a thoroughly French story. . . . . .

" The public has busied itself greatly with the *agiotage* of the Abbé d'Espagnac and the fortunes he helped the Duke of Orleans and others to make by this means. It seems the king has expressed his displeasure that an abbé should follow such an occupation. The abbé has been dismissed by his chapter, all because he had not the wisdom to hold his tongue. If he had kept silence his reputation would have been smaller, but his fortune would have increased. Taking it altogether, money is preferable to this kind of notoriety. The controller-general, under whose administration it could be possible to amass a considerable fortune by such means, certainly may be reckoned among those who do not get angry about what they see themselves, but only about what others force them to see."

This finance minister was Calonne, of whom Madame de Staël does not hesitate to tell the following anecdote in another place: " Not long ago a discussion arose at table when Calonne was present concerning the finance ministers of the reign of Louis XIV. A friend of the minister's mentioned the immense fortune made by his predecessors in office, and, recalling Mazarin and Richelieu, regretted that such fortunes could no longer be amassed. ' Excuse me,' interrupted Calonne, 'the business is not yet destroyed.' It would be better," says Madame de Staël, " not to say such things, at any rate at table."

Further on she says, " The Cardinal de Rohan is having a sad time at his abbey in Auvergne. The beautiful Countess de Brionne, who upholds the cardinal, ought to meet with sympathy, but she is so theatrical in her grief, that although it is quite genuine it seems like acting."

Madame de Staël has not a word to say in favour of the most injured queen, although the necklace trial, which lasted nine months, almost entirely engrossed public attention during that year, but we gather from Baron de Staël's despatches what was thought in the Neckers' house upon the subject. "It seems certain," he writes, "that M. de Vergennes and M. de Calonne have gone against the queen, and that instead of trying to diminish the feeling against her they do all they can to increase it. It is much to be deplored that the queen has no one upon whom she can rely to advise her, and that, with her other amiable qualities, the strength necessary to assert her innocence is absent,—but she needs guidance and support.

"Those around her seem to show her no consideration at the present moment; for instance, the Polignacs and the Vaudreuils are most zealous in the cardinal's cause, and even the Comte d'Artois has testified warm sympathy towards him. I cannot discover that the queen altogether enlists the sympathy that she deserves. She has succeeded less in her wish to please than any one in a private position would have done. This is, perhaps, a proof that notwithstanding the frivolity of the nation it expects prominent merit from its sovereigns, and only accepts them in proportion to what they have accomplished

. . . . . The celebrated sculptor Houdon has brought back a bust of Washington from America. It has the coldest features I have ever seen in my life, and it is amusing to compare them with those of Cagliostro. One might almost think it impossible for Washington to interest himself warmly in anything, and certainly one would imagine that he was indifferent to renown. He is like those doctors who do not believe in their profession. . . . . Figaro has reached its ninety-second representation. Beaumarchais said lately that the success of the piece would only be decided after the hundred and fiftieth. . . ."

Madame de Staël's account of the visit of the Archduchess Christina and her husband, Duke Albert of Saxony, closes with the words, " The Parisian society becomes daily more uninteresting ; no one cares nowadays to shine in it, and if it were not for cards no excitement could be had."

The next bulletin is written the same year, and dated November 1786. It busies itself with details about the court, which King Gustavus wanted to know. This time the journey to Fontainebleau, undertaken every autumn by the king and queen, gave her material. "Dinners and suppers," the young ambassadress relates, " are the only events of the day. Three times a week people sup with Madame de Polignac, three times with Madame de Lamballe, and once in the queen's intimate circle. She generally appears at eleven o'clock in the evening, and plays a game of billiards, which are much in fashion.

At midnight this circle disperses and betakes itself elsewhere.

" Games of chance are absolutely forbidden, but other games are all the more sought after.

" The sole pleasure of a hostess appears to consist in settling her guests as quickly as possible at *tric-trac* or at a *quinze* table.

" There was, moreover, such a crowd at Fontaine-bleau that people could only amuse themselves with the two or three others seated at the same table. The chief pleasure consisted in allowing oneself to be nearly crushed to death. The crowd around the queen was especially dreadful. It is not possible to lend greater charm and amiability to politeness than she does. Without letting others forget that she is queen she appears never to think of it herself. The expression and bearing of those who await notice from her is worth study. Some seek to attract attention by laughing loudly at the remarks of those at the same table with them, although under other circumstances they would hardly smile; others endeavour to look absent, and thus to hide the thought that is uppermost with them; they resolutely turn their heads the other way, but cannot prevent their eyes following every step the queen takes; others, if she makes a remark to them about the weather, consider this a chance not to be despised, and pour out a flood of conversation. There were some, however, who showed respect without servility, and a wish to please without unseemly effort. . . . . The king of

France does not appear in this society. He is only
seen in the morning and the evening at the customary
ceremonies, and on Sunday in solemn state. He is
never present at the queen's card-playing. He hunts
or reads. If he is doing neither it is funnily remarked that 'his majesty is doing nothing to-day,'
which means that he is busy with his ministers.
During this year's journey he gave various individuals of doubtful reputation convincing proofs of
his disapproval, and this raised the impression that
both the king and queen desired their surroundings
should be distinguished for their uprightness and
thorough respectability.

"Baron de Breteuil has a project of introducing an
edict to increase the security of Protestant marriages
and to settle their civil rights, and this has been much
talked about in Fontainebleau. It certainly is very
dishonourable now-a-days for one of the interested
parties to find an excuse for divorce in the religious
creed; nevertheless, such a law continues to exist,
and only custom prevents its being put into shameful
operation. . . . .

"The Chevalier de Boufflers gave a notable example
of self-sacrifice at the end of this year when he went
to Senegal for the second time to arrange about
sugar-plantations for the negro population, and thus
to encourage voluntary cultivation in place of the
forced labour, which was at the bottom of all the
miseries of the poor blacks.

"What an honour to the country would be the

emancipation of the slaves," remarks Madame de
Staël. "The man who could accomplish it would
have done more good than any one had ever done
before. But it is dreadful to have to confess that
the negroes, if left to themselves, are idle and hate
work, and this is the argument against granting them
freedom.

"The Chevalier de Boufflers told me some heart-
rending facts. Thus the Europeans have a plan of
seizing old men and women. As the negroes are
patterns of filial piety, as soon as they hear of their
parents' capture they give themselves up in their
place. In this way the barbarous European merchants
often obtain two strong young men instead of an old
man, and draw profit from the virtues of these negroes,
whose natural gifts they are quite right in considering
to be very different from their own."

At the time Madame de Staël wrote, her friends
Wilberforce and Romilly were proposing to lead the
great crusade against the slave-trade. Romilly relates
how in April 1789, shortly before the discussion in the
House of Commons, he wrote, in the name of his
supporters, to Necker, to invite the co-operation of
France. M. Necker's answer was very flattering to
them, but gave them so little reason to hope for the
concurrence of France that they thought it advisable
not to publish it, and so his name does not appear in
the list of the liberators of the human race.

In his book upon financial administration Necker
shows that the greatest difficulty in the abolition of

slavery lay in replacing that trade by another equally advantageous.   Wilberforce profited by the situation to express his conviction that France, at least, would not be the country to enrich itself by this means at the expense of England.*

Later on, Madame de Staël took up the thread in this matter which had slipped from her father's hands, for in 1814 she appealed to the allied sovereigns in favour of the abolition of slavery. . . . .   The fourth and last bulletin written for King Gustavus by Madame de Staël already bears signs of the growing excitement, and is dated 1787.

" Paris has been so occupied for the last six months with public affairs that not only do private affairs excite no interest but they have come to a deadlock, as people recognise how useless all individual attempts are to excite attention.   I am tempted to be angry with my friends and acquaintances for their inactivity, as it deprives me of anything to tell your majesty about them."

The political event of the day was the banishment of the Duke of Orleans, who, in a public sitting of the Parisian Parlement on the 19th November, 1787, replied to the king's request for a supplemental tax amounting to 440 millions that the Estates-General alone had the right to settle this and all other taxation.

Only the necessary social relations existed between

* *Memoirs of the Life of Sir Samuel Romilly*, 1840, i. 343, 345, April, 1789.

Madame de Staël and the duke. She never took him seriously, and, when his instructions for the elections of 1789 required that he should take up the divorce question, Madame de Staël thanked him in the name of the ladies at a ball given by the Duke of Dorset. " Oh," replied the duke, " I always try to do what may be agreeable to them."*

She shows a certain amount of contempt in her opinion of him which may be seen in the following : " The duke is so bored in his exile that he has written to the king to allow him, at least, to live at his château of Raincy, in the neighbourhood of Paris. The duke has done himself a great deal of harm by this request. If a man wishes to uphold his actions he ought not to own himself in the wrong, which he does by seeking to have his punishment lightened, It was remarked to the archbishop of Toulouse that his banishment would give him an opportunity of rehabilitating himself. ' Oh, I know him.' was the reply, ' he will miss his opportunity.' As a matter of fact the Government would be ill-advised to aggravate the exile, as it would not be popular with the public.

" It is the habit of the Duke of Orleans to fill the places at his disposal with people who do not suit them at all. Thus he has appointed a naval officer as the chancellor of his household. Monsieur de la Touche, the officer in question, thought that he was being made fun of, and went in his naval uniform to

* Lord Auckland, *Memoirs and Correspondence*, ii. 305.

the duke; 'Monseigneur,' he said, 'I present myself in uniform to remind you, in case it has been forgotten, that I am a sailor, and that I am incapable of adding up a sum, and therefore am quite unsuitable for the situation.' 'That is exactly what I want,' replied the duke. After de la Touche had asserted his incapacity he no longer hesitated to accept an income of 100,000 francs, as the duke wished it.

" The latter is of such a merry turn of mind that I am often tempted to think that his chief desire is to do whatever will give himself and others the most to laugh at. Nothing amuses him more than to hold himself up to derision. . . . ."

A remark on the religious dissensions of that period may not be thought out of place, as it again testifies how strongly Madame de Staël felt the injustice of the French laws from a Protestant point of view. She writes: "Madame de Noailles is the craziest of all pious Catholics and at the same time the most superstitious. She keeps up an incessant correspondence with the Pope and is a pillar of the Church, whilst she preaches intolerance like any of the Fathers. No sooner had she discovered that the king had proposed an edict for the amelioration of the civil rights of Protestants, than she went into such a state of desperation that she will certainly fall a victim to the warmth of her feelings if the edict is made law; which it probably will be.

"In a book of hers, which shall reach your majesty by the next courier, she has put together all the his-

torical occasions on which Protestants were in the
wrong, so as to awaken a dread of toleration. The
book is not bad, once we admit its object; and it is
well put together, if we could forget that it is un-
reasonable. What surprises me, however, is that it
should influence any one. We are so apt to imagine
that the century is enlightened because those immediately around us are free from prejudice—and yet
half France is probably under the shadow of super-
stition. Those especially who do not read make no
advance : the people change their opinions but never
moderate them. I further send the memorial started
by the maréchale which she sent to all the members
of parliament along with the following note :—' The
Maréchale de Noailles presents herself to M. N. that
she may recommend the interests of religion and law
confided to the care of Parliament.'

" I further add the excellent work of the equally
learned and sensible Malesherbes. He is one of the
most enlightened men in France, and would be an
excellent minister without a portfolio. But he himself confesses that his capacity is not backed by corresponding energy. What he initiates should be
carried out by others."*

It is not altogether uninteresting to compare these
remarks of Madame de Staël with the impressions simultaneously formed on the same subject by the Genevan

---

* Geffroy, *Gustave III. et la Cour de France*, i. 388-412, ii.
Appendix, 430-437, and 439-444. *Bulletin des Nouvelles de Madame
de Staël.*

Protestant Mallet du Pan. He writes :—" The edict in favour of the Protestants always meets with fresh delay. It is curious to find the public divided in its opinions on such a subject, and all the antiquated fears and silly ideas of the dark ages brought to life again.

" It shows that we are still a long way off from enlightenment. The Maréchale de Noailles sells and distributes a libel written by the Abbé Beauregard at her request. The monks in the cloisters elevate the host and implore Heaven to enlighten the king and avert the misfortune of toleration. Malesherbes has written a thick book in favour of the Protestants, as if there were anything left to say on the subject. The majority of the Parisians are opposed to the Toleration Edict. On all hands remarks upon it are to be heard as at the time of the League. The people and the Government are equally despondent on this subject, so that it is already held to be a great concession to legalise Calvinist baptism and marriage . . . . . The Protestants are endured although scarcely tolerated." *

The year 1788 found the Swedish king on the borders of Finland, leading the war against Russia, which was above all to serve as a means towards freeing himself from family and public relations which had become unbearable.

Whilst this went on in the north the prologue to the drama was being enacted in France, which left

* Mallet du Pan, *Analecte sur l'Histoire du Temps. Unpublished family papers*, 1787.

no time for the interchange of harmless literary and social news. From this date the epistolary intercourse between the young ambassadress and her sovereign was limited to a few letters, which could no longer prevent the ever-increasing misunderstanding between him and her husband or allay the dissatisfaction of the king. The relations between him and his representative in Paris, although binding in appearance, had never from the first been quite sincere and confidential in their nature. The prince held all kingly prerogatives to be unassailable, whilst his minister at the court of Versailles had long been of opinion that the rights of kings should be limited. The breach was unavoidable when these doctrines were put to the proof by the course of events.

The first indication of a change was the delay in granting the decoration promised in the marriage-contract to Baron de Staël, and of which his wife had in vain made mention in 1788 on the occasion of an especial mark of favour,* when the king assented to giving his name to her first child, which was a daughter. It died almost directly after its birth, and is not mentioned in any biography of Madame de Staël, although Saint Lambert thought it necessary to comfort Madame Necker on being now a grandmother, and the latter wished that her grandchild should grow up in the fear of God, as the thing most to be desired.

* Letters from Madame de Staël in the possession of the Library of the University of Upsala. Madame de Staël to Nils Rosenstein.

From this time the Neckers' *salon* in the Rue Bergère or at St. Ouen became more and more that of Madame de Staël, who oftener received there, for her invalid mother, than at the Swedish embassy, her own home in the Rue de Bac: or she received at Versailles when the residence of the court at that place required her to do so.* The old friends, Diderot, d'Alembert, Lord Stormont, Galiani, Creutz, Thomas, were dead or had left Paris. Buffon was to follow in 1788, and, according to Grimm's considerably exaggerated and not unbiassed words, "they close the lists of the greatest period France has ever known."

Of the friends and guests of early days Marmontel, Grimm, Suard, Morellet, Saint Lambert, Chastellux, Guibert, the Duchess of Lauzun, Madame d'Houdedot, led the way for an entirely different generation, which the new days had already brought to the front. Side by side with the old names those of the future started up.

The *Journey of the Young Anacharsis* appeared in 1788. A year earlier Volney had published his travels in Syria and Egypt. The *Studies* of Bernardin de St. Pierre bear the date of 1784; the idyl of *Paul and Virginia* had been written long before, but only appeared in the year 1787.

* Geffroy, *Gustave III. et la Cour de France*, Appendix, ii. 447. *Madame de Staël à Gustave III.* Juin, 1787. Madame de Créquy, *Lettres Inédites à Sénac de Meilhan*, Juillet 25, 1787. Baronne de Gérando, *Lettres Inédites de Madame de Staël, &c.* 55. *Madame de Staël à Gérando*, 1803.

Unknown to the public — Greek by birth and genius — André Chénier, the greatest lyric poet of the eighteenth century, which hitherto had been so prosaic in France, was steadily developing fruits that could never fully ripen, "because poetry was slain by the Revolution, and the poet by the Terrorists;" * because, in the words of Ducis, another poet, "when tragedies were being enacted day by day in the streets there was no use in writing them."

The 27th of April, 1784, is memorable in theatrical history. On that day Figaro was played for the first time, and Beaumarchais experienced an unequalled triumph when he induced the leaders of French society joyously to applaud their own death-warrant. The court, the nobility, the high officials, the princes of the blood, with the queen at their head, listened to the undying words: " J'étais né pour être courtisan. On dit que c'est un métier si difficile. Recevoir, prendre, et demander, c'est le secret en trois mots. La place demandait un administrateur—ce fut un danseur qui l'obtint." . . . . . And the monologue, " Non, monsieur le comte, vous ne l'aurez pas—vous ne l'aurez pas. Parce que vous êtes un grand seigneur vous vous croyez un grand génie ! Noblesse, fortune, un rang, des places, tout cela rend si fier. Qu'avez-vous fait pour tant de biens ? Vous vous êtes donné la peine de naître et rien de plus."

One individual only, usually ready for any joke,

* Nisard, *Histoire de la Littérature Française*, iv. 158.

laughed not on this occasion. "Never have I been in worse company than at this celebrated marriage," wrote the Empress Catherine,* shaking her head over the sort of entertainment that was appreciated in Paris. With the dramatic poet Beaumarchais, the most distinguished authors in these years immediately preceding the Revolution were Mirabeau and Rivarol; and it is said of them that Beaumarchais issued the manifesto of the Revolution, Mirabeau brought it about, and Rivarol fought it.†

Rivarol, surrounded by a small group of true friends and ill-natured tongues, employed the dreadful weapons of mockery and satire incessantly in society, and he was soon to direct them against Madame de Staël as he had done against Necker. Eventually his real fighting weapon became the political pamphlet. But Mirabeau, in whose spirit rebellion blazed into a clear flame, was as yet personally almost unknown in Paris, although his political ideas had already been expressed in numerous pamphlets. People at that time were only busied with his immense reputation and his family history, his law-suits, his imprisonment at Vincennes; the scandal with his father, who, by means of *lettres de cachet*, had all his belongings put in prison; with his mother, who fired a pistol at her son one day because he spoke of reconciliation with her husband.

* Grimm and Catherine II., *Correspondance, Recueil de la Société Impériale de l'Histoire de Russie*, 1878, xxiii. 334.

† Chênedollé in Sainte Beuve, *Chateaubriand et son Groupe Littéraire*, ii. 177.

Charles Maurice de Talleyrand, abbé de Périgord, born in 1754, had, on the contrary, filled a brilliant position for some years in Parisian society. Talley-rand, who, on account of a deformed foot, had been destined by his parents for the Church, filled the responsible position in the capital, of agent-general for the clergy, although his thoughts were already full of other and more important subjects. A cardinal's hat was coveted for the abbé, then scarcely thirty years old; and in the autumn of 1784 the beautiful Madame de Brienne had already asked the king of Sweden, who was then in Rome, to use his influence with Pius VI. in his favour. Whether he ever did so we have no means of knowing. This hat belonged, however, to the very few things Talleyrand did not receive in the course of his life. As bishop of Autun, the year 1789 already found him at the head of a group of elegant and distinguished men, such as Narbonne, Jaucourt, Lauzun, and many others of the same sort, who boasted of having carried the art of refined enjoyment, intellectual taste, and familiar intercourse, to the highest perfection.

Personal identities and social circumstances had, however, sensibly changed during the last twenty years. The comparatively few *salons*, by means of which social centres an entrance into the great world could be achieved, had for the most part ceased to exist, and their influence was never resumed.

Existence had become more complicated, the houses in which celebrated men were to be met were now far more numerous; literature began to be oppressed by politics. In the same way as tea had taken the place of coffee in the English fashion, it was said that the old customs of French life had vanished before other habits.

Horse-racing began to be the fashion, whist was played, and boston after the American war, dress became simpler, and the heavy embroidered damasks with gold and silver brocade were replaced by muslin and simple stuffs; powder, feathers, and laces gave way to plain ribbons and simple hair-dressing. Men no longer wore their daggers. Clothes were worn à la J. J. Rousseau, coats à la Franklin, and the portrait of the beloved object was worn as an ornament in the hair, were it that of a husband, child, friend, cat, or dog. It became the fashion to make a long stay in the country. In the same way as Marie Antoinette went from Versailles to the Trianon, the nobility and rich financial set left Paris for their properties and country-houses, where Florian's pastoral poems and Berquin's pedantic sketches of family life were realised in poetical fêtes. A whole quantity of poems—The Seasons by St. Lambert, The Months by Roucher, The Garden by Delille, and the prose of the Prince de Ligne entitled Coup d'Oeil sur Bel Oeil, taking his own park for his subject—testified to the taste for woods, fields, and meadows that had been awakened in these satiated beings.

The Duc de Broglie gave the word "Love your wives and your homes." Although spent in the country, the life was not any more serious or more natural, and it continued to be equally costly and corrupt, although outwardly blameless. With an income of 600,000 francs people felt themselves to be the slaves of their rank.

"I really only feel my riches by the burden they impose," said the Duchesse d'Estissac to Bonstetten; "and ah! what delicious milk is to be had in your mountains."[*]

But in the parks and in the pastorals no less than in the splendour of the Parisian hotels people alike aimed at unclouded gaiety, covering all the pitfalls of existence with flowers, and turning away from grief and self-denial as from what not only was painful, but was contrary to all the true philosophy of life. Manners even among the lower classes were apparently so refined, that Jefferson, who was by no means partial to the French, remarked in 1785 that here one might pass a life without encountering a single rudeness. He had never met a drunken man.[†]   In the same year, 1785, an English traveller, Andrews, also took away the impression that in France the highest object of existence was to spend it in unclouded merriment.[‡]

Such perfection was attained in this respect that sociability and cheerfulness followed this light-hearted race from palace to prison, to the law-court and the

[*] Karl Morell, *K. V. von Bonstetten ein Lebensbild*, 68.
[†] Jefferson, *Complete Works, Correspondence*, i. 443.
[‡] Taine, *Les Origines de la France Contemporaine. L'Ancien Régime*, i. 191.

scaffold, and, almost without exception, death **was**
heroically and often smilingly encountered. This
epicurean art of existence would have wanted spice
if it had not punished everything that opposed it, **cast**
aside all experience and authority which had at **any**
time undervalued the state of things it advocated.

"Sire," said the Maréchal de Richelieu to Louis
XVI., "under Louis XIV. people did not dare to
speak; under Louis XV. people talked in whispers;
under your Majesty's Government they speak out."
The first clubs were instituted and soon became
political centres. Galiani had already said that
" Paris was no longer the *salon* but the *café* for all
Europe." Diderot's *Neveu de Rameau* gave point to
this criticism, which soon became a truism. Members
of the House of France led the opposition. The Duke
of Orleans contributed no mean sum towards the publication of pamphlets which educated public opinion,
as newspapers did not then exist, or at least were
only represented by a few official organs such as the
Gazette and the *Mercure de France*. When the
Revolution broke out it was headed by noblemen
who were ready to speak and to fight, priests who
could organize, bishops who could bless, princes who
could pay for it, and a king who could allow it to
happen. Nothing was too venturesome for this race.
Everything might be said or done if only the manner
of doing it were correct, pleasing, and *piquant*.

" Truth does not excite me, only novelty." Countless contemporaries shared these sentiments of Sénac

de Meilhan, who was considered to be a supporter of what already existed.* They never for an instant doubted that the Reign of Reason had set in, overcoming all traditions, and that they themselves were destined to renew the golden age.

It is of these years that Talleyrand said that no one who had not lived previous to 1789 could form any idea of the seductive charm of existence.

If the men had this impression how could the women resist the overpowering seduction of all that unfolded itself before them like a *fête?* It was for them that the darkest problems of philosophy strove for clearness of expression, that learning became epigrammatic and eloquent, and that the driest theories hid themselves under attractive forms.

All observers of the social conditions of that time in Paris and France have testified to the overwhelming influence of the women. Scarcely any one has described it better than Roederer, who in 1787 was in his prime, and subsequently alludes to it in these terms :—" Who can tell how much the learning in France owes to social intercourse and to the desire of clever men to make women understand what they meant? Serious study is so difficult for women that their teachers are obliged to be clear in their meaning. Fontenelle wrote his *Celestial Bodies* for the Marquise de Lambert ; Voltaire *Newton's Philosophy* for the Marquise de Châtelet ; Madame Lavoisier was

* Nisard, *Histoire de la Littérature Française,* iv. 126.

initiated in her husband's chemical discoveries before any one else . . . . . I myself saw the equally beautiful and charming Madame de Fourcroy mix with her husband's colleagues with intelligent interest.

" Madame de Condorcet was introduced to the study of the deepest philosophical subjects by her family; the book written by this unusually clever and fascinating woman on Adam Smith's theory of moral sentiments is a witness of this.

" Need I remark how much the presence of eight or nine of the most celebrated women of the capital and the court, and by their presence and their discussions before and after the debate, contributed to the eloquence of our greatest orators during the sitting of the *Constituante.* May I be allowed to say that the Revolution of 1789 was accomplished by public opinion; that this public opinion was formed and ripened in assemblies where woman's voice was heard, and that her share in the Revolution largely contributed to its permanence.

" The interests, rights, desires, fears of the mothers of families, sisters, wives, were in sympathy with the law-givers, and it was unnecessary for them to procure a hearing to be understood." *

Strangers were all of the same opinion, such as Mallet du Pan the Genevan, and the Americans Jefferson and Morris. It is true that Mallet complains that Parisian women are characteristically

---

* Roederer, *Fragments de divers Mémoires concernant la Société Polie en France.* Paris, 1834.

devoid of any trace of real deep womanly feeling and
innocent charm, but he admits their unequalled
intellectual vitality.

Jefferson, the stiff republican, makes fun of the way
these women spend their day, beginning with visits
at 11 o'clock, paid at the ladies' bedside, and barely
allowing for a turn through the Palais Royale
between their forenoon toilette and the hairdresser;
and a further half-hour's stroll through the streets
after dinner as their only exercise; in the evening,
visits and the theatre; supper and card-playing
prolonged far into the night.   But, however much he
may have to find fault, he confesses in the end that
the opinion of the young and beautiful women who all
favour the *Tiers* is more powerful than all the king's
200,000 men.   He goes even further, and considers
that by the women's influence the fate of France will
be decided.   No system of reformation had hitherto
included such an influence, and happily nothing of
the kind existed in his country.   If such were the
influence and position of the fair sex it is certainly
worth while to ask what use it had made of them, and
on which side of the scales, history, the great judge of
all human events, has found the weight of its share in
events, and the measure of its tremendous responsibility ?

The question can only be solved by recalling the
line taken by the women in reference to the intellectual supremacy — contemporaneous with the

American war, which at that time encountered
fierce opposition, although almost unrivalled in
regard to thought, imagination, and politics, between
1780 and 1790. This was the supremacy of Rousseau.
All are agreed on this point. Grimm, of whom
Rousseau wrote that he was the only man he hated,
and who on his side had no reason to stand up for
him, nevertheless bears witness in his *Correspondence*
to his ever-increasing influence. In February 1775
he does not hesitate to say that Voltaire's *Don Pedro*
shows signs of advancing years—*sent la décrépitude ;*
but, although he judges Rousseau's system most
severely, he never for a moment casts doubt on the
extent of his talent. . . . . About this time the
Genevan Dumont came to Paris to his friend Mirabeau, from London. "Except on the stage, Voltaire's
reign is at an end," he wrote to Romilly in England.
"Rousseau rises in proportion as the other sinks.
Posterity will wonder why they were ever considered
rivals."

Oelsner, the German friend and fellow-worker of
Sièyes, says in a letter to a compatriot at the beginning of 1791, and in the midst of the Revolution :—
"Jean Jacques Rousseau is to have a statue as the
author of the *Contrat Social*, and a pension of 1200
livres is granted to his widow. The worshippers of
this divinity are to make a pilgrimage on the first fine
spring day to Ermenonville. Voltaire's followers
exclaim against all this idolatry, and sigh that their

prophet is forgotten; and truly the last part of their grievance is not groundless." *

In Germany there was hardly a dissentient voice on the subject.

According to Lessing, J. J. Rousseau was "the bold philosopher who having no prejudices went straight to the truth." †

We learn that Kant twice gave up his daily walk to read *Emile*.‡

The young Schiller was inspired to write the lines,

> " Sokrates ging unter durch sophisten,
> Rousseau leidet, Rousseau fällt durch Christen
> Rousseau—der aus Christen, Menschen wirbt,"

and he sent his robber *Moor* away from civilisation into the woods. Rousseau was the starting-point— but certainly that only—to another. With *Götz* in his hand and *Werther* in his mind, young Goethe exclaimed, " *Tais-toi, Jean Jacques, ils ne te comprendront pas.*" §

Herder, Jacobi, Klinger, Campe, Heinse, down to Lenz, testify to the power of Rousseau's ideas over them, and this may be said of every civilised land in

---

* Oelsner, formerly councillor of the Prussian legation, *Letters from Paris*, 1790-1792, *to the Councillor von Halem*, 36.

† H. Hettner, *Geschichte der französischen Literatur in achtzehnten Jahrhundert*, 448, 456.

‡ J. Honegger, *Kritische Geschichte der französischen Kulturein-flüsse in den letzen Jahrhunderten*, 359.

§ M. Bernays, *Der junge Goethe*, iii. 53. *Goethe an Sophie Laroche.*

Europe. Everywhere, except perhaps in England, where political opinions were too wide-awake, and where intellectual independence was moreover too firmly established to care much for this mere paper-felicity.

For if ever there was an anti-English mind and disposition it was that of Rousseau. His rhetoric, his universality, and his love of foregone conclusions, his lack of principle in fixing and representing facts, his perpetual self-deception and deception of others, the absence of all the attributes of a *gentleman* in him, as well as the want of method in his life, made it especially difficult for English people to be just towards him.*

Curiously enough J. J. Rousseau has now become a text for English politics. Formerly considered one of the most dangerous enemies of liberty by the great Liberal party, he is now, a hundred years after his death, adopted by the rising Radical school. Their cleverest author, Mr. John Morley, has put forth an apology for J. J. Rousseau, in which he is startled by nothing—neither by the consequences of the *Contrat Social* nor the horrors of *Les Confessions;* nor does he withold his admiration for the Mountain.† He admits all the principal points of Rousseau's theories so unconditionally that an important critic like Karl Hillebrand brings forward what

* K. Hillebrand, *Aus und über England.* John Morley, *Studies in the Eighteenth Century,* 338.

† John Morley, *Rousseau,* 1873.

is really a terrible excuse for the "noble error" of his English friend, and shields it under the pretext of extraordinary simplicity and a want of acquaintance with Continental thought.*

Mercier, on the other hand, the critic, publicist, delegate in the Convention, who, like many others, at the eleventh hour repented his share in the work, might well publish a complete volume in 1791 upon J. J. Rousseau, considered as one of the first instigators of the Revolution.†

Bernardin de St. Pierre, his enthusiastic follower, went a step further. He not only denied the Patriarch of Ferney, but emphatically called him "the evil genius of the century, which found its good genius in Rousseau."

It is also noticeable that the first actual apology for Rousseau proceeded from Barrère, "the Anacreon of the guillotine." It appeared in 1787.

Napoleon's remark to Stanilaus Girardin is well-known—that "without Rousseau there would have been no revolution in France."

Madame de Staël repeats it, as well as his further remark that he did not regret it, " *car j'y ai attrapé le trône.*" ‡

---

* Karl Hillebrand, *Aus und über England*, 339.

† Sebastien Mercier, *Jean Jacques Rousseau considéré comme l'un des premiers Auteurs de la Révolution.* Paris, 1791.

‡ Jobez, *La France sous Louis XV.* v. 640. Madame de Staël, *Considérations sur la Révolution Française*, partie iv. chap. xxi. Edition 1838.

Finally, Madame de Staël herself, who on entering the path of literature emphatically placed herself under Rousseau's banner, seldom spoke of Voltaire, and then only very casually.

The views of her most intimate friends, as well as the powerful current of public opinion, influenced her in his favour as far as her personal feelings were concerned.

It has repeatedly been mentioned that Madame Necker did all she could to keep Rousseau's tone of thought away from her daughter in her youth—not because she blamed his ideas, but because they had taken such a powerful hold upon herself. This irreproachably virtuous woman writes to Moultou, after reading part of the *Confessions* in manuscript, " I confess that as long as Rousseau gives us *Héloïse*, *Emile*, and all these heavenly and human elements, I can only regard the author's mode of life as a weak adjunct, and it appears to me that a veil should be drawn over the faults of this Father of Virtue." *

And Moultou, the former preacher of the Gospel, who gave up his position and renounced theology because he thought he had discovered that the Apostle Paul and St. Augustine had destroyed the teaching of Christ, now outstripped his friend's enthusiasm. In 1763 he writes to Jean Jacques, who had sought refuge in the Val de Travers, which was in Swiss territory, but under Frederic's sceptre, " Oh,

* Madame Necker, *Mélanges*, i. 147.

my friend, you are great, but I am sufficiently great to feel the grandeur of your mind." . . . . He thankfully and calmly took Rousseau's advice and gave up his priestly appointment, "which had become a disgrace to him," and in 1769 assured him that he remained "strong in the faith."[*]

Villemain is of opinion that "Rousseau's writings were the Bible of their times." It made very little difference that Grimm, Diderot, St. Lambert, should have become violent opponents.

They had all paid homage to the thinker before they quarrelled with the man. Malesherbes, the royal censor, took care that *Emile* should be circulated; and, although officially forbidden, it wandered about from house to house under the seal of that great deputy. He was not merely an adherent of Rousseau, but belonged to his sect.[†]

When *Emile* and the *Contrat Social* appeared in 1762 Bachaumont wrote: "Rousseau only says aloud what every one else is thinking." [‡] Raynal, Thomas, Marmontel, Mably, Bernardin de Saint Pierre, Dupaty Florian, Bouchier, Mercier, Berquin, were under the direct influence of Rousseau.

In Lyons the churches were filled to hear a preacher who took *Emile* for his text.[§]

---

[*] Berthoud, *Rousseau au Val de Travers*, 109, 140, 142, 147. Gaullieur, *Etudes sur l'Histoire Littéraire de la Suisse française.*

[†] Saint-Marc-Girardin, *J. J. Rousseau, sa Vie et ses Ouvrages,* ii. 364.

[‡] Bachaumont, *Mémoires*, 137, quoted from Rocquain, *L'Esprit Révolutionnaire avant la Révolution,* 235.

[§] Costa de Beauregard, *Un Homme d'autrefois*, 25.

It is related that Christophe de Beaumont, the
archbishop of Paris, whose pastoral letters against
the book were the cause of one of Rousseau's greatest
successes, never spoke of him in private otherwise
than to praise his disposition, his virtues, his genius,
his voluntary poverty, and his sincerity.*

When Madame de Staël left these distinguished
social and literary circles she found the same view
again in the simpler middle classes, held amongst
others by Coindet, the cashier of the firm of Thelus-
son-Necker. Coindet, whose name in common with that
of many others is so unnecessarily slandered in the
Confessions, remained her true friend until his death
in 1808. He admired Rousseau intellectually, and
was besides this a clever observant man, who had no
reason for flattering the great, as Rousseau charged
him with doing.† If Madame de Staël passed from
the men to the women-kind frequenting the Necker
salon she found but one or two who had escaped
Rousseau's influence. Among his friends and pro-
tectors might be counted the Comtesse Boufflers, the
Comtesse d'Egmont, the Maréchale de Luxembourg,
and Madame d'Houdetot, if we merely mention those
who played a part in his life. In this atmosphere
Mademoiselle Necker grew up. Her *Letters on
Rousseau* without any positive dates show that she
had read him with interest in her early years.

* Berthoud, *Rousseau au Val de Travers,* 85, note.
† Rousseau, *Confessions,* "Séjour à l'Hermitage." Saint-Marc-
Girardin, *J. J. Rousseau, sa Vie et ses Ouvrages,* ii. 261.

His fascination took hold of her as it took hold of the whole generation belonging to the last decade before the Revolution, and for the same reasons. These reasons owed their force to the double fact that his system was at once a novelty and a reaction for her.

New were his paradoxes in favour of a state of nature and against civilization and culture in the treatise of 1750 and 1755, " On the Influence of Progress in Science and Arts upon Manners," and " On the Origin of Inequality amongst Men," this manifesto against society which none of Rousseau's later works surpassed in regard to the extent of its revolutionary programme.

New to the modern European world was the teaching of the *Contrat Social*, of the incontestable sovereignty of the people, the proclamation of the unrestricted, unconditional will of every individual as the only foundation of the State and of authority. New the consequent doctrine, not so much of civil equality and the equal rights of each individual in sight of the law, as of the right of every one to have a share in the Government, the sole claim to the existence of which lies in the ever-changing and contradictory will of the multitude. New also was the educational system in *Emile*, the return to nature which was not to be opposed or restrained but merely supported and developed.

After the explanation of the rights of men in the *Contrat Social* followed the explanation of children's rights, described by Goethe as the " gospel of education according to Nature"; an impossible Utopia, taken as a whole, as every system was that Rousseau built up, but taken in detail, full of fruitful, although often contradictory, suggestions and useful truths like everything originated by his genius.

Every one who has even casually studied Rousseau knows that these ideas of his, although new to his readers, are not for the most part original. A hundred years earlier the Englishman Hobbes had lived through a revolution, but Rousseau contributed to bring one about. Hobbes ascribed the political anarchy he so much disliked to the working of religious influences. To counteract them both he met the difficulty by favouring despotism as centered in one man. His prince is invested with unlimited power over Church and State, as every subject by virtue of contract has permanently and freely given up all individual rights to his direction; and the will of the multitude cannot err. As this power is only the will of each individual in the great mass represented by the prince, he need not be restricted, and the people require no guarantees.

How could a prince ever be tempted to undertake anything against those whose advantage and interests he represents and of whose will he is the mouthpiece? This is the point where the doctrines of *The Leviathan* and *De Cive* come into contact with the theories of Rousseau.

Uncontrolled princely authority granted by universal suffrage is just as false and historically impossible as Rousseau's teaching concerning the original liberty and equality of individuals and their inalienable rights.. Hobbes's system culminates in absolute monarchy—Rousseau overthrows it and sets the sovereignty of the people in its place. Both come to the same result. The last word of the political teaching and of the philosophy according to natural law, advocated by the adherent of the Stuarts or by the citizen of Geneva, is in favour of the throne in the one case and in favour of democracy in the other; but both destroy the lawful independence of individuals and the right of the minority., they both ignore historical development and the true nature of the State; both end in despotism. Even in *Emile,* his most enduring monument and his greatest creation, Rousseau had a pattern before him, and predecessors to point out the way. The *Essays* of Montaigne, the works of Locke, the political opponent of Hobbes, not only stirred his soul but excited him to opposition. It is easily understood that the first principles of those intellectual teachers who up till now had held all but exclusive sway were likewise pressed into his service.* Grimm, however, spoke in all good faith when he asked, from whom Rousseau had stolen his style, his eloquence, and his word-painting. The real kernel of the question was that the most self-evident truths had been forgotten or laid aside until Rousseau appeared and breathed new life into them. He obtained supremacy not so much because he had a new message to convey

* Brockerhoff, *Jean Jacques Rousseau, his Life and Works,* iii. 48 and 155.

as because he partly restored knowledge and invested it with new brilliancy. The secret of his power is to be attributed less to himself than to the weakness of his opponents and to the development of the Church, of the State, and of society since the death of Louis XIV.

Louis, who did not possess the talent of ruling to any great extent, thought in part to condone the sins of his private life by fulfilling his conception of orthodoxy in persecuting the Calvinists outside and the Jansenists in the bosom of his own creed. To the second half of his reign belong many sombre pictures; none is more tragic than that of the expulsion of his own subjects, hungry, cold, and needy, and the desecration of the graves of those nuns of Port Royal who had died in the faith, whose bones were given to the dogs just outside the confines of Versailles because they held different opinions to those of the king. Such deeds cannot be excused, but they can be explained. Not only on the part of the victims, but on that of their opponents, there existed strong and sincere convictions.

Courtiers might flatter to gain the favour of the king in his advancing years. Bossuet, however, and the theologists of the Gallican Church, were no less in earnest than Pascal and the Port Royalists. Intolerance closely resembles strongly-developed religious belief, and is always to be deprecated; but it was all the more despicable that persecution should continue to exist after convictions had been shaken and when they had ceased to be deeply-rooted.

" The court exhales hypocrisy," says Saint Simon in the latter years of the old king's reign. The regent, proud of his infidelity, no longer demanded this tribute, but quietly allowed men's belief to be forced, although he himself so greatly despised all religion as to desire the Roman purple for a Dubois; and this in no small degree assists us to understand Voltaire.* Fleury did no less harm, although in another way. He placed the teaching of the Church at the disposal of the crown, and forced the Roman see to take all manner of unworthy steps.

The struggle between the ultramontane views of the Government and the Jansenist views of the members of Parliament and their followers fills the first half of the later histories of the eighteenth century.

The Jansenist views were dominant in Paris when the Bull Unigenitus was forced upon France. It demanded submission from the conscience even without conviction. In 1731 one of the greatest speakers in the Parisian Parliament, the Abbé Pucelle, speaks in the following terms of the working of the bull: " Since this bull has come into operation in France we are surrounded by mischief. All the sources of good are stopped, all the schools are poisoned. What has become of the Sorbonne, whence at one stroke a hundred of the most learned and loyal professors

* Voltaire, *Lettres Anglaises, Œuvres*, xxvi. 29. Quoted in Buckle's *History of Civilisation in England*, i. 692 note.

have been ejected ? What has become of the celebrated school of Sainte-Barbe, which educated such
excellent servants for Church and State ? Are not all
our national customs, all our established institutions,
changed and upset ? " *

The Catholic Church in France never recovered
from the purifying process undertaken by Cardinal
Fleury. It is true that by far the greater portion of
the nation lived and died moderate in its creed,
otherwise the existing order of things would have
ceased even then. But the power of religious ideas
over the intellect and education of the day was lost.
Their strength was exhausted in the long party strife.
Banished theologians, professors dismissed from their
chair, suspended priests, were to be found in every
town in France. Even nuns were forced to wander
roofless for conscience'-sake, and good Catholics to
die without the last sacraments.

A noteworthy instance of this occurred, amongst
many others, when the Emperor Joseph visited Paris
in 1778.

The emperor expressed a wish to make the acquaintance of the Abbé de l'Epée, the benefactor of the
deaf and dumb, who not only enabled these unfortunate beings to communicate by signs with their
fellow-creatures, but also spent his whole fortune to the
utmost farthing on their behalf. Neither Louis XVI.
nor his sister could gratify the emperor's request. They

* Abbé Pucelle, *Les Parlementaires Jansénistes du xviii siècle,
Revue des Deux Mondes,* 1881.

had never even heard of this excellent priest, for he
had been suspended in consequence of his Jansenist
views in the reign of Louis XV.* The whole literature
of the day testifies to what was suffered, and shows
how the leaders of the French Church had verified
the saying, " *Desertum faciunt pacem appellant.*"

Christianity survives crises such as these, but the
state is shattered. Injured convictions fled to the
shelter of parliamentary freedom. In rising against
the misuse of ecclesiastical authority, a disciplined
opposition formed itself against the extension of royal
prerogative.

As monarchical absolutism had joined itself to the
highest authorities in the Church, the reaction now
followed on political grounds against what was considered unfair pressure in religious matters.

The first newspaper published by the opposition in
France was the *Nouvelles ecclésiastiques*, and was
read by every one because it was prohibited.

But oppressors and oppressed alike worked into the
hands of a common foe.

" Jansenists and Jesuits tear each other," wrote
Voltaire in 1762 ; " the one must be destroyed by
means of the other and the collected fragments must
serve as a footstool for the truth." † The truth ?
What indeed did Voltaire and his contemporaries
call the truth ? He himself considered it to be
secured by a dreadful disturbance, a struggle against

* Droz, *Histoire de Louis XVI.* i. 233.
† Rocquain, *L'Esprit Révolutionnaire avant la Révolution*, 236.

all positive religion, an epicurean Deism, the best side of which is an optimist humane tone of mind, and is typified in these words: "Let things be good or bad; let be it our care to make everything better."

His share in the Revolution was not sympathy for the people, for whom he neither had much respect nor sympathy; it consisted far more in the fact that he changed the views of the reigning powers. His blind fanaticism against Christianity, which his marvellous intellect makes still more inexcusable, was not the way to such reform; he gave the lie to his doctrine of toleration. When the " System of Nature," this " Code of Atheism," appeared, Voltaire tried too late to counteract the spirits he had evoked.

Holbach's work, which considers every religious impulse to be an hallucination, was only the most complete of a long list of similar works.* After a while Rousseau appeared on the scene, bringing a reaction which could only be possible or understood by the light of what had gone before. His first declaration of war is levelled at the preponderance and over-estimation of the intellect. " The thinking man is an animal spoilt." "Come into the woods and become men."† The appeal to Nature, " *Remonter à l'état de la nature*," as Rousseau expresses it in *Emile;* ‡ the theory that Nature made man happy

---

* Barante, *Tableau de la Littérature Française au xviii siècle*, 94.

† J. J. Rousseau, *Discours: Le rétablissement des arts et des sciences a-t-il contribué à épurer ou a corrompre les mœurs?*

‡ Barni, *Etudes sur le xviii siècle. J. J. Rousseau*, ii. 213.

and good, society had made him depraved and wretched,* may be traced like a red thread through all his writings. Upon this follows the postulate that education be carried out according to the direction and development of nature; that society return to its original conditions, or rather to what Rousseau considers them to have been; that property be divided according to the more natural rights; † that religion be founded on feeling, to the exclusion of all dogma and in indifference to all forms of worship; making Christianity itself nothing else than "the more enlightened natural religion."‡

Among the spiritual followers of Rousseau were two celebrated women: Madame Roland and Madame de Staël. They are reciprocally necessary to each other. Neither can be fully understood without taking Rousseau into account, and, on the other hand, they complete our idea of Rousseau's intellect.

Madame Roland, the elder of the two, comes first in reference to this. Born on the 18th March, 1754, Marie Jeanne Phlipon was, like Rousseau, the child of simple middle-class people. Her father was an engraver. Her solitary childhood and blameless dreamy youth were spent more amongst books than

* Rousseau, beginning of *Emile.* Rousseau, *Juge de Jean Jacques.* 3 *Dialogue.*

† Rousseau, *Discours sur l'Economie Politique.* Barni, loc. cit. on the subject, ii. 236.

‡ Berthoud, *Rousseau au Val de Travers. Rousseau a J. Jequiers, Motiers, Decembre,* 1762, 135.

amongst men, in her parents' quiet home and near her father's work-room.

Amongst her books Plutarch was one of her favourites; "this poetical rather than historical source," writes one of her biographers, "whence it is well known that Rousseau borrowed his images from the republican characters of olden days and his brilliant pictures of ancient republics, and whence he conceived an idea of conditions of government which never existed and never could exist, but which would all the more delight a woman's mind." *

And Rousseau himself? "I read him very late," she says in her *Memoirs*, "and perhaps it was as well; he would have driven me crazy; I should never have wished to read any other books; and as things turn out he might only have intensified my weak points." †

Dauban, another of her biographers, dates her knowledge of Rousseau's works from the year 1777, when she was 23 years old.‡ She says herself that her education, her first impressions, her intercourse with the world, all contributed to imbue her with a republican perception of the absurdity or injustice of a crowd of social differences and distinctions.§

To this intercourse with the world belongs a visit in 1771 to a relation at Versailles, who was a wait-

---

* F. C. Schlosser, *Madame von Staël and Madame Roland.*
† Madame Roland, *Mémoires*, Edition Dauban, 101.
‡ C. A. Dauban, *Étude sur Madame Roland.* Introduction, liv.
§ Madame Roland, *Mémoires*, Edition Dauban, 92.

ing-woman to Marie Antoinette, then dauphiness. Mademoiselle Phlipon spent a week in an attic in the royal palace and watched the doings there with a mixture of philosophy, fancy, sentiment, and judgment, which, as she remarks, had been alike cultivated in her, but which did not prevent her liking to see the great display. Only she was annoyed that such personally insignificant and otherwise contemptible men should reap the benefit of it all, and when her mother asked her what impression her stay had made upon her she replied, that if she had stayed a few days longer she would have hated the people to such a degree that she would not have known how to contain her hatred. "But what did they do to you?" asked her mother again. " They let me feel injustice and see absurdity." It filled her with astonishment and indignant contempt to see this simple crowd greeting their self-created idol with acclamation on state occasions.* Her youth was otherwise uneventful. In 1780, at the age of six-and-twenty, she married Roland de la Platière, aged forty-six, and at that time inspector of the Lyons manufactories. An only child, a daughter, was born of this union. In the year 1780 Roland took his wife to England for a short time, where he had business, and then to Paris, to which town he repaired that he might put in a claim for elevation to the rank of nobility, in which fruitless attempts he was supported by his wife. Otherwise the couple lived in the country in the neighbourhood of Lyons. The husband wrote treatises and

---

* *Idem*, Introduction, xxxix. and pp. 75 and 93.

learned disquisitions, amongst others one in 1787 proposing that oil and phosphorus should be extracted from human remains for the benefit of farming.

In imitation of the ancient Egyptians, he proposed in 1788 that the Villefranche Academy should organize a tribunal for judging the dead.*

Meanwhile Madame Roland busied herself with her household, hospitably received her husband's friends (who respectfully admired the enthusiastic and beautiful woman), and looked after her husband and child, regarding matrimony as an institution which "confides the happiness of two human beings to a woman." †

During which her imagination worked on, restless : and this imagination was filled and dominated by Rousseau. How could this have been otherwise ? She had nothing to set in his place, no knowledge of men and the world, no experience, nothing to compensate in her affections. Like a true woman she took him by the letter, and endeavoured with one great exception to realise his theories. This exception was to be found in the purity of her nature, which kept her from any false step although perhaps not from experiments. There was one dangerous moment in the life of the Queen Marie Antoinette, namely, when she spoke of Louis XVI. as *le pauvre homme*.‡ There

* Baron de Girardot, *Roland et Madame Roland*, i. 83, 185, quoted by Taine, *Les Origines de la France contemporaine. La Révolution*, ii. 109.

† Dauban, *Mémoires de Madame Roland*. Introduction.

‡ Arneth, *Maria Theresa and Marie Antoinette. Correspondance*,

came a moment when Madame Roland called her dull, pedantic husband *le malheureux Roland*, and this in a letter to Buzot, whom she loved.* Fate was merciful and the infidelity was only ideal.

Her farewell to the man she loved, beginning, "Oh, thou whose name I may not utter,"† is to be compared with all that is most beautiful in prose, and not merely that of Rousseau. In it she extols the prison-walls which guard her affections, and certainly greets death as the only way out of an unbearable dilemma.‡ But in other respects Madame Roland only gave herself up all the more willingly to Rousseau.

Her style, as Saint-Beuve rightly remarks, is by no means original; when true passion takes hold of her, in the highest exaltation, and with the prospect of death before her, she rises to real eloquence. But under ordinary conditions her letters and reminiscences are full of affected, laboured, and inelegant sentences, and leave no doubt that they are imitations, and not the natural result of her own impulse. We know the original. Rousseau's over-weening self-esteem almost leads to the threshold of madness—he expects altars to be dedicated to him. Madame Roland is not more modest. "There is only one

Marie Antoinette to Graf Rosenberg, 1775. Geffroy et Arneth, *Correspondance Secrète entre Marie Antoinette et Mercy*, ii. 359. July, 1775.

* Sainte-Beuve, *Nouveaux Lundis*, vii. 248.

† Madame Roland, *Mémoires, Dernières Pensées*, 390.

‡ Dauban, *Étude sur Madame Roland*, 39. The wonderful, last letter to Buzot. July 7, 1793.

position in the world that would suit me," she says, "it is that of Providence." She not only describes herself as intellectual, she further describes herself physically; and as she has nothing dishonourable, none of the defects of her master to relate of herself, she falls back on an episode that is quite outside the matter, and writes an inexcusable page to lower herself to him.

The hatred of all tradition and a corresponding disinclination for all history is another feature in Rousseau, and is shared by Sièyes and Condorcet and many of the revolutionary party.[*] "Thoroughly unhistorical" he is termed by one of his best German biographers.

The great historian Hume could not resist saying, " He has read very little during the course of his life, and (in 1764) has now totally renounced all reading; he has seen very little, and has no curiosity to see or remark; he has reflected, properly speaking, and studied very little; and has not, indeed, much knowledge; he has only *felt* during the whole course of his life." [†]

And Rousseau himself feeling his deficiency gives the word to Hume: " I still dread that my writings are good for nothing at bottom, and that all my theories are full of extravagance.[‡] The perusal of

[*] Hettner, *Geschichte der französischen literatur im achtzehnten Jahrhundert*, 3 auflage, 441.

[†] Hume, quoted by Sainte-Beuve, *Causeries de Lundi*, ii. 78.

[‡] Sainte-Beuve, *Causeries de Lundi*, ii. 79. Rousseau to Hume, 1766.

novels gave me romantic, quaint conceptions of real life, and no substantial experience or reflection freed me from these."

Madame Roland knew as little of these thoughts as of the historical past of her own or any other country, with the exception of a few ordinary conceptions and broad effects borrowed from Athens or Sparta.

Knowledge is necessary to a correct comprehension of the past, although sound judgment is generally all that is needed when recent events are in question. But what was Madame Roland's conception of the history of the times?

After going through many vicissitudes and struggles in common with her people with whom she always maintained motherly relations, the Empress Maria Theresa had gone to the grave, honoured in her private relations and beloved by the nation as well as by all Europe, Frederick alone excepted. No difference of opinion appeared possible on the point until Madame Roland advanced hers.

Speaking of the Queen Marie Antoinette in her *Memoirs*, she says that "Frivolity, the confidence of power and of youth, the Austrian insolence and illusions of the senses, first led her astray, and the king after her." She adds, "Marie Antoinette was herself led astray by all the vices of an Asiatic court, and her mother's example made this only too easy." *

This explains how Mallet du Pan, who knew her, could say of Madame Roland that she was quite in-

* Madame Roland, *Mémoires*, Edition Dauban, 350.

capable of describing the scenes of horror which she did not hesitate to instigate.* In this condition the Revolution found her: and to her who thought the most enthusiastic too lukewarm, the most excitable too moderate, it brought bitter disappointment even in its dawn.

On the 26th of July, 1789, she wrote to her friend Bosc, the future editor of her *Memoirs* :—" You busy yourselves with forming a municipality and you shield the heads who continue to mischief. You are mere children, your enthusiasm is a short-lived flame, and if the National Assembly does not arraign two illustrious personages, or fails to find a nobly inclined Decius to cut them off you will all be . . ."†

Thus runs the invitation to regicide, the bloody shadow of which falls even on the scaffold prepared for Madame Roland. From that time forward she fires the courage of her friends and contemporaries, Lanthenas and Bancal des Issarts, of Brissot and Camille Desmoulins. In September 1791 she preaches " Insurrection, this holiest of duties if the Fatherland be in danger." She appeals in Paris against the luke-warmness of the inactive provinces : " even a father should not be deterred by any feeling of mercy when the public good is in question." ‡

These contributions to the free-republican *Courier*

* Mallet du Pan, *Mercure Britannique*, 10 Dec. 1798, 533.

† Madame Roland, *Correspondance.* Printed with the *Memoirs.*

‡ Madame Roland, *Correspondance. Lettres du 20 Decembre,* 1790, *et* 24 *Janvier,* 1791.

de Lyon, edited by Champagneux, a friend of Roland's, prepared her for the political *rôle* she was to fill. This began with her arrival in Paris on the 20th February, 1791, made her the life and soul of the Gironde, and came to a tragic conclusion November[r] 8th, 1793.

To what extent is J. J. Rousseau even responsible for this short but decisive period of her life? He himself was a man of impulse, and had very lucid intervals.

The whole creed of the radical demagogue, even to definite communism, can be adduced from his writings: [*] but, on the other hand, each separate article of this creed can be set aside by a contradictory assertion of Rousseau's own.

The *Contrat Social* sets up to teach the fundamental liberty and equality of every individual, and declares this liberty to be eternal and unchangeable. The state, in his judgment, is nothing more than the expression of the general choice, and at any moment its borrowed power may be limited, altered, or taken away. At the same time the *Contrat Social* exacts as an unavoidable condition on the part of each individual that it shall possess a complete control over all his rights in favour of the state, or of that unity represented by the state.

On these grounds the state is omnipotent and must settle everything that it considers necessary to the

---

[*] H. Hettner, *Geschichte der französische literatur im achtzehnten Jahrhundert* 483.

general good, even to the foundations of religion,* upon which the *Contrat Social* ends with the notorious sentence: "If any one, after solemnly receiving the dogmas of this religion, behaves as if he did not believe in them, he is to be punished with death."

In other words, the abstract unconditional offer of freedom for the individual leads to his absorption in the state : absolute democracy resolves itself into uncontrolled despotism !

In this same *Contrat Social* Rousseau in vain explains " that even the most successful revolution would be too dearly bought with the blood of a single citizen ; † in vain does he declare that the constitution he had thought out was not for society as it now exists, but for an ideal republic of about ten thousand men ; in vain did he consult the Poles, not so much to verify his system as to remove the ban on liberty and to choose a king from the national aristocracy.

The question is not how he wished to be understood, but how he has been understood. The real interpreter of the *Contrat Social* in this instance was not J. J. Rousseau, who devised the work, but Maximilian Robespierre, who executed it.

The way to the Mountain led through the midst of the Gironde, and Madame Roland had given her-

---

* J. J. Rousseau, *Le Contrat Social.* Barni, *La Philosophie du dix-huitième siècle,* ii. 207, 222, 227. Lanfrey, *Éssai sur la Révolution Française,* 62-63.

† *De l'Économie politique,* quoted by Barni. J. J. Rousseau in the *Philosophie du dix-huitième siècle,* ii. 323.

self heart and soul to the Gironde. She wished to upset the present state of things because they not only offended her sense of justice but they had offended her vanity. Social conditions in which she had no place must be destroyed,* to be replaced by an ideal republic—the chimera of her solitary dreams. Rousseau might reflect when he had reached the threshold of the truth, but Madame Roland remained unmoved.

The turning-point was the king's flight, the return from Varennes. "To bring Louis XVI. back to the throne," writes Madame Roland to her friends, "is mad, even abominable. The best and wisest course would be to put him on his trial. But you are incapable of doing this. Therefore you should suspend his powers." †

This was written on the 24th of June, 1791. Even after Mirabeau's death in April she longs for civil war, the most fearful of all calamities, as the great school for public virtue. Eight months later Roland was minister. He proved himself as incapable as he was honourable. Brought into contact with the king, he was on the point of showing him mercy and proving that he also was an honourable man. Here Madame Roland interferes with the remark that "Louis has been nurtured in all the prejudices of

* See Fontanes on this subject. Sainte-Beuve, *Nouvelles Causeries de Lundi*, viii. 190.

† C. A. Dauban, *Étude sur Madame Roland, Notice biographique*, 6.

despotism and in the pursuit of pleasure, and there-fore cannot love the constitution." *

It was certainly difficult for him to love the con-stitution, as it was the noose that strangled him.

His last attempt to save himself was the dismissal of the Girondin ministers who imposed the perse-cution of the non-jurors upon him.   Madame Roland and her friends retorted by an open accusation of the king, by the invasion of the Tuileries on the 20th June, 1792, by setting up the Paris Commune, by a plan for federation of the departments, and by their last sin-laden victory, the overthrow of the throne on the 10th of August.

In vain did the instigator of the murder of the Swiss guards protest against the slaughter three weeks later in September.   From that moment Danton ruled, and the duel between Madame Roland and Robespierre began.   The latter, more consequent than she, included wholesale murder in his logic, and sent his former ally to the scaffold.

" I knew not," writes the unhappy heroine of the Gironde, speaking of the *ancien régime*, "that there could exist a still more dreadful form of govern-ment, a more horrible system of corruption.   Indeed who could have supposed such a thing?   All the philosophers have been mistaken as well as I."†   Not all; but certainly he of whose work Benjamin Con-stant writes that he knows of "no system of servitude

* Madame Roland, *Mémoires*, Edition Dauban, 350.

† *Idem.*

which has sanctioned more pernicious error than the aimless metaphysics of the *Contrat Social*." *

And now to Madame de Staël and her *Letters upon Rousseau*. When they appeared in 1788 she had, as she herself says, "as yet no notion of what constituted a government." † She had however none of the misconceptions of Madame Roland and so many others, for she had grown up in an official atmosphere, and was perfectly aware that people did not build houses over powder-mines. The few allusions she makes to the subject of Rousseau's political ideas leave no doubt that in this essential point she is not in accordance with the object of her admiration. " He wished," she writes, " to lead mankind back to social conditions of which the fables of the Golden Age can alone give any idea. Such a project is of course a mere flight of imagination. But in their search for the philosopher's stone the alchemists made many useful discoveries." ‡ " I venture," she continues, "to reproach Rousseau for refusing to consider that a nation governed by its own representatives is free, and for insisting on a general assembly of every individual. Enthusiasm is all very well in sentiment, but it is out of place in practical schemes. The defenders of liberty should beware of exaggeration. Montesquieu is more useful to society

* Benjamin Constant, *Cours de Politique Constitutionelle*, i. 329.

† D'Haussonville, *Le Salon de Madame Necker*, ii. 191.

‡ Madame de Staël, *Œuvres complètes*, i. *Lettres sur Rousseau : Lettre* i. *Du style de Rousseau*.

as it now exists; Rousseau would be more useful to
those combining together for the first time: most of
the truths he developes are speculative . . . . . but
perhaps we must ourselves have governed in order to
relinquish an ideal prosperity, and to take the bad
and the good together." *

Madame de Staël's opinion of him is in accordance
with that of her father, who in 1775 had spoken
against the longing for a return to a primitive state
of existence, as even then, men had to put restraint
on their desires and had to employ force to keep what
they had earned by their skill.†

Her approval of Emile was equally conditional.
There could be no objection, she says, to his system
of physical education and training, and his eloquence
had restored motherly feeling in a certain class of
society. He caused mothers to realize this happiness
and this duty. He even reinstated childhood in its
kingdom, and it is quite right that his portraits
represent him crowned by children; but to the
question whether she would bring up a child on
Rousseau's system she replies in the negative.
" For," she says, " mere vanity would lead me to
choose a settled calling for the young man to enable
him to make his way in the world." ‡

That is precisely what Emile could not do, and

* *Idem*, Lettre iv. *Les Idées Politiques de Rousseau.*
† Necker, *Œuvres complètes*, i. *Sur le Commerce des Grains*, 13.
‡ Madame de Staël, *Œuvres complètes*, i. *Lettres sur Rousseau:*
Lettre iii. *Emile.*

thus Rousseau's system of education is relegated in the most polite manner possible to the region of chimera, to which Madame de Staël had already consigned the *Contrat Social.*

This kind of free and independent judgment betrays an astonishing capacity for political questions. Had Rousseau been satisfied to suggest theories of natural rights he would have made very little impression upon Madame de Staël. But she soon found Rousseau's republican ideas more approachable under the double influence of events and personal inclinations. It is the task of this biography to mention that Madame de Staël was not prevented by her admiration for her father from deserting his political standpoint during many years, and that her opinions influenced him later on, to so great an extent that even in 1802, in his will, he pledged the authority of his name in favour of a republican form of government as the only possible form for France, although personally he retained his preference for a constitutional monarchy.*

A taste of despotism was needed to bring the great constitutional theories to perfection which are inseparably connected with her name as authoress of *Les Considérations.*

But we have only reached 1788. She is two-and-twenty, and her passionate nature dominates her intellect. The former accepts teaching that the

* Necker, *Œuvres complètes*, xi. *Dernières Vues de Politique et de Finance,* 222, 226, 240.

latter would repudiate. The opening words of her *Letters upon Rousseau*—" We must be moderate if we wish to convince . . . . I will try to write impartially of *La Nouvelle Héloïse* as if Time had already robbed me of the enthusiasm of youth "—at once prove that she feels herself to be prejudiced in his favour. In her opinion *La Nouvelle Héloïse* is a great moral idea dramatised and put into practice. The aim of the author is to lead to repentance. She acknowledges that his chosen object is by no means moral. " I could wish," she writes, " that the author had described Julie as the victim of her kind heart. It further seems to me that indulgence for certain shortcomings is the only virtue which it is dangerous to preach, although it is so useful to practise it.

" The real use of a novel is to be sought in its effect much more than in its plot. If, as it were, men must be driven to be virtuous, if, by reason of their imperfections, all the eloquence of a great passion must be employed to interest them—can Rousseau be blamed for having chosen love as his medium ? Perhaps in the first days men knew no other virtue than that which sprang from similar feelings. Love can sometimes call forth all the qualities that religion and morality prescribe. We are virtuous when we love that which deserves to be loved. We then involuntarily fulfil all that our duty requires of us. Once we have given up all selfish aims it is impossible to turn back, and piety takes the place of love. This is the truest definition of our heart."

She goes on to say that she knew that people blamed Rousseau for describing a tutor who had seduced the pupil confided to him, but she owns that this hardly occurred to her when she read it, as it was evidently borrowed from the Héloïse of olden times. A romance of this kind might lead a man like Saint Preux astray, but Saint Preux was entirely imbued with the notions of equality which may still be found in Switzerland. No, the example of Saint Preux was not immoral, although Julie's might be, or might have been if her remorse and her subsequent conduct had not condoned her fault. Madame de Staël further excuses Julie's silence towards Wolmar, but she adds, "how much she would have appreciated the impulse that might have led her to confess everything to him."

She rightly feels that the only admissible excuse for Julie d'Etanges was to be found—not in the reflections and sermons Rousseau puts into her mouth, but in the irresistible force of her overmastering passion. "If the charm of virtue is renounced, all those qualities must at least be retained which have brought about such renunciation. Rousseau was mistaken in thinking that Julie would gain by seeming less passionate." *

And now to the crucial test of the *Confessions* published in the years immediately preceding the Revolution, but not completed when she wrote: "This book is not written in the noble strain one

* Madame de Staël, *Œuvres complètes*, i. *Lettres sur Rousseau : Lettre* ii. *La Nouvelle Héloïse.*

might expect of a man telling his own history. But
Rousseau had a sentiment of pride that guaranteed
his sincerity. He considered himself to be the best
of men. He would have blushed to conceal a single
fault in describing himself to others . . . . I imagine
that he wrote his memoirs far more with the desire
to shine as an historian than as a hero . . . Rousseau
was not out of his mind, but one of his attributes,
that of imagination, had exceeded all bounds. His
intellectual superiority came very near madness. He
was born to enjoy nature but not society. He was
like an Indian on the shores of the Orinoco, who
would be content to sit all day on the banks and
watch the water flowing past.

"We can scarcely say that Rousseau was virtuous,
as a man's actions and their results must justify such
commendation. . . . .

"His proud disposition did not alienate me from
Rousseau. I drew the conclusion that he knew himself to be good. He was perhaps the only man who
was base at intervals; as a rule it is a fault that
becomes more and more habitual. . . . . His faults
were follies. His writings breathe the noblest, most
virtuous thoughts."

And now to *Les Charmettes* and Madame de
Warens. "Rousseau thought less of her than of his
love, which required some object. . . . . He was
naturally good, sensitive, and confiding. It may be
remembered how much he cared for his fellow-creatures when he was young. If later on he altered in

this respect it was because he was, less than other
people, prepared for disappointment. Madame de
Staël is the first who puts the report of Rousseau's
suicide into words; the letter in which he condemns
suicide is much less important than that in which he
justifies it. She adds that perhaps he feared to
deprive himself of this means of escape.* This sup-
position,† which made no small commotion amongst
those connected with Jean Jacques, led to a controversy between Madame de Staël and Madame de
Vassy, the daughter of that Monsieur de Girardin in
whose summer residence at Ermenonville it is well
known that Rousseau died. The question is undecided to this day, although mostly answered in the
negative.‡ Madame de Staël's criticism of Rousseau
would be incomplete if she did not mention the
"creed" of the Savoyard vicar. She calls it a
master-piece of eloquence in the matter of sentiment,
and of metaphysics in argumentation. She writes:
"Rousseau is the only genius of his time who main-
tains his respect for the pious beliefs we so much
require. He consults natural instinct, and then lends all

* Madame de Staël, *Lettres sur Rousseau* : Lettre i. *Caractère de
Jean Jacques.*

† Madame de Charrière, *Lettres, Mémoires. Revue Suisse*, 1857.
798.

‡ Brockerhof and Barni amongst his later biographers doubt his
suicide. Bougeault, *L'État moral de Jean Jacques*, 1883, is against
it, as likewise Corancez, a contemporary of Rousseau, and in this
century Saint-Marc-Girardin. L. Blanc and Sainte-Beuve, *Chateaubriand et son Groupe Littéraire*, i. 107.

the power of his superior mind to testify to the truth of this instinct.* Combining warmth and moderation, Rousseau has the undying merit of influencing the conscience and of soaring to eloquence by the force of passion. He believes in love, therefore he may be forgiven." † Sixteen years later, in 1814, in a second preface to these *Letters*, Madame de Staël tells us that their circulation, which had not been desired by her, had decided her literary vocation. "I do not regret the circumstances," she ends by saying, "as this calling has given me more pleasure than pain. Everything in woman's destiny points to decline, except thought, which by its nature tends ever upwards. Intellectual pleasures help to calm a tempestuous nature."

On the occasion of her first real connection with the public Madame de Staël found herself in harmony with public opinion. She received ample recognition, and this success never deserted her. Grimm, although he had written a bitter satire on the *Confessions* not long before, confirms this fact, and calls her *Letters* "*un charmant ouvrage.*" ‡

And now we must put the question whether Rousseau's influence on thought left any lasting trace in the life of Madame de Staël. Most certainly it did.

The characteristic traits of his political system were brought into prominence. Even his system of

---

* Madame de Staël, *Lettres sur Rousseau.* Lettre iii. *Emile.*
† *Idem :* Lettre i. *Style de Rousseau.*
‡ Grimm, *Correspondance Littéraire.* xiii. 243, and xiv. 472.

morals had its peculiar stamp.   More than any previous moralist, he confused the hitherto-undisputed
theories of right and wrong by his seductive rhetoric.
All who would not lower themselves to base so-
phistries agree in this.   " The *Nouvelle Héloïse*,"
writes Madame Necker, "is a monument erected to
virtue on the foundations of vice."

To confound former sinfulness with enthusiasm in
the cause of righteousness means spiritual chaos and
a loss of the capacity for ever disentangling them.
This is the danger of the book,* and Mallet du Pan
is of the same opinion.   He says in his decided way,
going straight to the point, " Rousseau tempted even
honour." †   Villemain says, " His morality was an
appeal to passion against duty." ‡   Bersot speaks of
his moral teaching as of a sample of his heart,
"searching his feelings for a rule of conduct, and
only considering himself bound by duty when these
feelings are interested." §   Nisard accuses him of
professing what he did not practise.‖

Those who think such comments too severe should
remember the spiritual offspring of Rousseau,
Werther, Delphine, and a few of the favourite

---

* Madame Necker, *Mélanges*, i. 30, and iii. 67.

† Mallet du Pan, *Mercure Britannique*, ii. 342, *Du degré d'influence qu'a eu la Philosophie sur la Révolution.*

‡ Villemain, *Tableau de la Littérature Française au dix-huitième siècle*, iii. 442.

§ Saint-Marc-Girardin, *J. J. Rousseau, sa Vie, ses Œuvres.* Preface de Bersot.

‖ Nisard, *De la Littérature Française*, iv. 489.

creations of George Sand, who terminate an unsuccessful existence in suicide because they all believe in the doctrine that passion justifies everything, and in the original perfection of human nature. "There is not much good in men," said the dying Kant. *Homo homini non Deus, sed diabolus.* "Let every one search his own conscience."* "I know not how the life of a worthless man is ordered," says Joseph de Maistre. "I never was one. I know however that the life of a respectable man is distracting enough."

Rousseau and all his followers hold that "man is good, and that the only constraint laid on his instincts is ordained for his own happiness."

What is this otherwise than antagonism to Christianity? The whole basis of a Christian conception of this world is destroyed by it, and with it all the defensive weapons it has provided for weak human nature. Madame de Staël herself was to experience this. Not only on the outward circumstances of her life, but in her inner development, she had to live through the Revolution before she obtained freedom by submission to law.

* Hasse, *Letzte Æusserungen Kant's. Von einem Tischgenossen.* Königsberg, 1804.

CHAPTER V.

BETWEEN Necker's first resignation, on the 19th May,
1781, and his return to office in August, 1787, four different personages succeeded each other in the financial
administration, and practically in most of the home
administration, as the former included public works,
trade, and a great part of the responsibility of Government.* These were Joly de Fleury, d'Ormesson,
Calonne, and Loménie de Brienne.

Joly de Fleury was chosen by Maurepas because he
was of a reactionary turn of mind, insignificant in
character, and agreeable to the Parlement.

His short administration is marked by one of the
most mischievous measures of the reign of Louis XVI.
the edict promulgated three days after Necker's retirement on the 22nd May, 1781, debarring not only

* Chérest, *La chute de l'Ancien Régime*, i. 80.

the middle classes from serving as officers in the army, but even the sons of the nobility if unable to trace back their descent for four generations.

Madame Campan rightly alludes to the "despair" occasioned by this edict. It divided the army into two camps, and in the words of a German historian it fostered Catilines who had nothing to lose by a revolution.*

To infer from this measure that the whole of the nobility united in favour of reaction and the maintenance of former conditions would be to come to one of those misleading conclusions frequently drawn from isolated facts in revolutionary development, and generally to be disproved by their own evidence when taken in connection with each other. It was not the aristocracy, as such, who obtained this Pyrrhic victory, but the courtiers and a part of the lesser nobility, who needed class privileges to prevent their sinking back into the masses.

From copious contemporaneous evidence, such as the letters and notes of the elder Marquis de Mirabeau, we gather the amount of hatred and contempt cherished by the independent nobility living on its own property towards the courtiers at Versailles and their attendant camp of intriguers, who sapped the nation for their support and for the gratification of their boundless avarice.

The old families who had been robbed of their privileges, and yet felt themselves strong enough to do without the support of the court, now showed them-

* Oncken, *Das Zeitalter der Revolution,* i. 34-35.

selves most eager for reform, giving an impetus to agitation and furnishing leaders to the *Tiers État*.

The alliance was both natural and essential. In one point at least the interests of the nobility were identical with those of the *Tiers*. The latter strove to attain political power, the former desired to recover it in the new order of things, as well as a position similar to that of the English aristocracy, even were great and material sacrifices to be necessary.

The position of the clergy was entirely different.

According to a saying of Heinrich von Sybel, there never was a revolution that did not originate in religious or social causes: in this case both of these influenced the sixty thousand members of the French clerical body.

We have already alluded to their reasons for demanding a reform in religious matters during the second half of the eighteenth century.* But the social question also concerned them.

Whilst the high dignitaries of the Church (numbering about 2,800 persons, according to Taine) disposed of incomes derived from the rich convents and monasteries, in some cases amounting to 400,000 livres or a million, the parish priests lived in the utmost poverty, even in want.† The immense Church property, with a capital of four milliards and an income of 200 millions, was quite unequally divided amongst its servants. Whilst some disposed of colossal for-

* Chapter IV.
† Taine, *Les Origines de la France Contemporaine*, i. 17-20, 54, 58.

tunes and enjoyed several benefices at one time, and in utter opposition to ecclesiastical law—others suffered not merely from want, but had often to draw their scanty income from communities no less poor and oppressed than themselves.

In the year 1768 the French parish priest had an income averaging 500 livres, the curate only 250 livres, which in 1785 were respectively raised to 700 and 350 livres, whilst the Abbé de Vermont, reader to the queen, received a salary of 80,000 livres, and Loménie de Brienne, archbishop of Sens, enjoyed a yearly income of 678,000 livres. The numerous pamphlets which showed up this state of things in the years immediately preceding the Revolution also described the feelings that it must engender in the parish clergy. One of them says, "There is much abuse in the Church; those who serve the altar do not live by the altar, but on the contrary those who do not serve it."* The archbishop of Toulouse himself admitted in 1775 that an old or infirm priest had no refuge against the stress of poverty except in the charity of his bishop.†

Many of these bishops, who had never gone through the trouble and experiences of parish work, only despised those they were wont to designate as *prétraille*.‡ Yet these were just the men who preserved

* *Les Droits des Curés et des Paroisses considérée dans leur rapports temporals et spirituels*, 172.

† *Essai sur la Réforme du Clergé*, 12, *par un Vicaire du Campagne, docteur en Sorbonne*, Paris, 1789.

‡ *Idem.* Taine, *Les Origines de la France Contemporaine: l'Ancien Régime*, i. 382.

the honour of their calling by keeping religious convictions intact in the great majority of the people, and nurturing those modest virtues which protect civilisation and preserve a nation from decay against the destructive tendencies of the upper classes and literary circles of the capital.

In the ranks of these priests were to be found learned theologians, and amongst their fellow-thinkers the devout laymen, to whom Church doctrine and strict practice had been handed down by the old French catholicism, and who held to it with a tenacity which provoked the admiration of Voltaire and even enlisted the sympathy of a philosopher like Taine.[*]

This class, if any, had a right to expect justice from the devout tendencies of the king.

Necker recognised this fact, and later on endeavoured to draw the king's attention to these deserving and natural allies in the struggle against privilege.[†]

But, as has been already said, it was decreed that the old monarchy was to burn the Sybilline books, one after the other, that fate had reserved for it.

During the latter days of the *ancien régime* there was an increasing tendency to appropriate the ecclesiastical benefices exclusively as a provision for the descendants of the nobility; and the fifty thousand French parish priests, wrongfully described as the "lower clergy," and still more wrongfully consigned

---

[*] Voltaire, in Taine, *Les Origines de la France Contemporaine*, i. 95.

[†] Necker, *De la Révolution Française. Œuvres complètes*, ix. 99 and 162.

to hopeless poverty by the policy of the day, gave their vote in 1789 in favour of the *Tiers*.*

Hand in hand with these measures in favour of the privileged classes went an increase of taxation, burdens, and debts, under the short administration of Joly de Fleury. He fell in March 1783 without having even attempted reform in any direction whatsoever.

After the death of Maurepas the king had announced his intention of reigning alone.

There was nominally no prime minister, but Count Vergennes at the head of foreign affairs was very influential and showed undoubted ability in his department, although at the same time his home policy was reactionary. After Joly de Fleury came the honourable and conscientious d'Ormesson, who in vain begged the king to relieve him of the unaccustomed burden.

The attempt to substitute the system of the *ferme général* by a royal direction is associated with his short administration. This, for the time being, was a pure loss, as Necker had considerably increased the contracts with the *ferme*. At the end of seven months d'Ormesson gave up his post without any remuneration, upon which, in a private memorandum, the Maréchal de Castries ventured to remind the king of Necker's popularity. But it was quite in vain. Louis let his personal dislike retain the upper hand, although

* Oncken, *Das Zeitalter der Revolution*, i. 41, note.

the loans had reached the sum of 345 millions since his retirement, and the king, who had bought Rambouillet for fourteen millions, had only 300,000 livres left in his treasury.

Thanks to the influence of Maria Theresa and Mercy the queen favoured the candidature of Loménie de Brienne, archbishop of Toulouse, a follower of the Economists and a friend of Turgot's. But on this occasion Louis was mindful of Maurepas' advice, never to let a priest be prime minister, and moreover felt a personal antipathy to the prelate, whom he knew to be both infidel and immoral.

Vergennes next proposed Calonne, the intendant of Lille, who was backed by the queen's adherents, the Polignacs, and above all by the Comte d'Artois. He was hated alike by the king and the public, and it required a series of intrigues to set him up.*

Niebuhr, who formed his impressions of the French Revolution mostly by direct intercourse with those immediately concerned, compares the brilliantly endowed, frivolous untrustworthy Calonne to Egmont.†

The court had no restraint to encounter from him. He encouraged expenditure; promised inexhaustible resources; bought St. Cloud for the queen, who for years had wished to possess it; ‡ increased pensions, and reconciled the financial world to his monetary operations by permitting it to profit by the need of

---

* A. Chérest, *La chute de l'Ancien Régime*, i. 32-37.

† Niebuhr, *Geschichte des Zeitalters der Revolution*, i. 152.

‡ Augeard, *Mémoires*, 134.

the state. As amiable as he was pleasure-seeking, he still could on occasion show an astonishing capacity for work and imperturbable good humour under the most adverse circumstances.

Although 1784 proved a disastrous year he enforced the taxes with a severity which exceeded all precedent, but without curtailing the expenditure. It was at that time that he bought over Mirabeau, the people's future tribune, to write up his various financial operations, and this in the further course of events led to Mirabeau's secret mission to Berlin; * but Calonne himself came into collision with the Parlements, and these refused to ratify the royal edicts.

Necessity now accomplished what foresight, reason, and honour ought to have brought about in a man who "had fostered all manner of abuses and now wished suddenly to abolish them."†

The "financial orgie" he had introduced was now at an end, and with it the ruinous method whereby the remains of the national property were diverted into an exhausted treasury.

Without any circumspection or preparation Calonne next drew a despairing picture of the state of affairs which he had himself brought about and which had become unendurable. In a memorial to the king he required "the reform of everything that was bad in the constitution of the state," but he also added the celebrated sentence, "Abuses are what support the

* Droz, *Histoire de Louis XVI.* i. 345, note.
† Malouet, *Mémoires,* i. 287.

monarchy." In his mouth this signified that they smoothed the way for necessary changes. The plan for taxing the privileged classes, attempted by Machault under Louis XV. in his temporary taxation of the clergy, appeared again in the project of a universal land-tax.

Homage was done to Turgot's ideas in calling together the people's assemblies and those of the districts; in the reform of personal taxation; in the abolition of guilds, and of the obligations imposed by corporate bodies. In deference to their favourite theory, free trade in corn was conceded to the Economists. The imposts between the provinces were to cease, the hated *gabelle*, the salt-tax, was to disappear: Necker's project for an assembly in all the provinces, which had been rejected by each successive government, was to be put into practice.

By promising a share in the future local government to the landowners, the minister hoped to reconcile the nobility and clergy to the sacrifice his proposal imposed upon them. One of the greatest evils of the *ancien régime*, the insurmountable difficulty of unravelling the tangled threads of its rule, finds utterance in Calonne's desire for a uniform system of administration. *

" What you now require of me," answered Louis XVI., in reply to Calonne's last note, " is Necker's recipe." " Sire," was Calonne's reply, " we possess

* A. Chérest, *La chute de l'Ancien Régime*, Introduction, xix. and 82-85.

no better."* The thought seemed to imply that such being the case it would be better to employ the remedy first-hand.

The Parlements could not of course be counted on, to carry out this programme. For a short time Calonne thought of calling together the *États Généraux*, but he was aware that his accounts would not bear examination.† A way out of the difficulty offered itself in summoning together the notables; and Mirabeau took pride in having been the first to propose this line of action.

They had last been summoned by Henry IV. to take counsel on the affairs of the state, and this circumstance contributed to win the king's consent, after that of Vergennes and Miromesnil, the keeper of the seals, had been obtained. The king was unaware of the entire extent of the financial ruin, but the mere thought that he was to be relieved of a part of his responsibility led him to remark that " his happiness deprived him of sleep." The queen never forgave the fact that she was left out of the secret.

On the 22nd February, 1787, a hundred and forty notables and about six or seven non-privileged members of the *Tiers* assembled together in presence of the king, and took council regarding the reforms to be undertaken. Vergennes had died a few days before. He was replaced as minister for foreign

---

* Pontécoulant, *Mémoires*, i. 80.

† Jefferson, *Complete Works, Autobiography*, i. 70. Droz, *Histoire de Louis XVI*. i. 350.

affairs by an honourable, rightminded, but weak man, Armand Comte de Montmorin, once the king's playmate, and afterwards his confidant.

The notables divided themselves into seven bureaux, declared themselves of one mind as to the principles of reform, refused however to discuss them singly before they were furnished with accurate information on the state of the finances, and gave it clearly to be understood that they had no intention of being guided by a Calonne in these reforms.

In the course of affairs the Archbishop Dillon of Narbonne and Dulau of Arles, along with La Fayette and Castillon, the procurator-general of the Aix parlement, announced that the right to impose taxation evidently belonged, not to the king, but to the *États Généraux*, which they desired at once to summon together.*

Calonne had lost the game, as he could not grant what was required of him without contributing to his own ruin, whilst, without bringing the odium of the refusal upon themselves, the privileged classes had found a means of granting nothing. Calonne next achieved a change of front, allowed his six memorials to the notables to be publicly disseminated, and declared himself ready to sacrifice the privileged classes, and "in the name of justice to raise the money from those who hitherto had not paid enough." † The notables now found themselves respected and recog-

---

* Droz, *Histoire de Louis XVI.* i. 482.

† Henri Martin, *Histoire de France*, xvi. 580.

nised as the representatives of liberty and the rights of the people; and deserved this quite as little as the parlement had deserved it before them,

The coalition against Calonne, in which, influenced by the Abbé Vermont who was the friend of Loménie de Brienne, the queen as well as the notables, the court and most of the ministers, took part, was considerably strengthened by the conflict between him and Necker. Not long before the assemblage of the notables, Necker had heard that Calonne intended to cast doubt on the accuracy of the *Compte Rendu* in his opening speech, and he appealed to him in writing not to carry out this intention without giving him an opportunity of defending himself. Calonne in his frivolous way had assured him that he had no idea of doing anything of the kind. To be sure he refrained in his speech from any direct attack; but it nevertheless led to the conclusion that Necker's statement had been incorrect. The latter begged the king to allow him to exonerate himself, either in his presence or before a committee of notables.

Louis XVI. notified that he was satisfied with his services, but that he imposed silence upon him. Necker had already taken a step which did not incline the monarch more favourably towards him. In the year 1784 he had published a book on financial administration; 80,000 copies of it were spread over Europe, and it met with almost unparalleled success.

In this book experiences were confirmed and failures exposed, of which Necker alone as minister could be cognisant,* and in it he further advanced the leading thought of the *Compte Rendu*, the principle of publicity and control in financial affairs, which at the time had met with the king's approval, but later on had ceased to do so.

Any allusion to this was taken as a reproach and a reminder, and the king, who had been prejudiced against Necker by all his successors, authorised one of those mild official protests which were more to the credit than to the disadvantage both of the books and of the authors of that day.† After Calonne's attack the question was no longer one of system or mere difference of opinion, but of Necker's personal honour.

More than his popularity might depend on the refusal to permit him to defend himself. He had never renounced the idea of prosecuting the work of reform begun in 1780, and had never lost sight of the prospect of once again taking office.

Calonne was not the man who might venture with impunity to question the integrity of one in whom all the hopes of the nation were centred, unless he had the most crushing proofs. But he could bring forward none, he had even failed to point out the self-evident mistakes in the *Compte Rendu*. Necker had now to choose between obeying the king (and thus closing his public career) and the probability of a

---

* Niebuhr, *Geschichte des Zeitalters der Revolution*, i. 169.

† Auguste de Staël, *Notice sur Monsieur Necker*. *Œuvres complètes*, i. 188.

recall to the ministry, should he pay no heed to the royal command.

He chose the latter course—now the less dangerous of the two—and circulated a justification of his administration amongst the notables which soon became public property.

Joly de Fleury, the former minister, who was made umpire in the quarrel, decided emphatically for Necker and against Calonne.

Louis XVI. took the thing seriously to heart. At first he was so annoyed that he told the queen he should banish Necker from the land. She reminded him of his deserts, his upright and disinterested conduct, but could not prevent the banishment of Necker by *lettre de cachet* to forty miles distant from Paris.*

In one of the few letters known to have been written by Necker to Madame de Staël he tells her the news in a tone which gives a notion of the impression caused by the king's displeasure in those days. He writes: "My dear Minette—After mature consideration, and with due respect for your last advice, we are to start early to-morrow morning for Château Renard if nothing prevent. I imagine that the château is of considerable size, as the d'Outremonts and De Fougerets lived in it every autumn. I have no idea what the surrounding country is like. I rather dread your dear mother's judgment, favourable or unfavourable

* Auguste de Staël, *Notice sur M. Necker*, i. 199-209. Wertheimer, *Documents Inédits relatifs à Marie Antoinette. Revue Historique*, 1884, ii. 326. *Mercy to Kaunitz*, Paris, April 17, 1787.

it is always outspoken, but she is meanwhile in the best possible frame of mind. At the end of the week you must collect all the news; Germany's * letters, and still more your own, which appear to have been written during a rapid journey, have hitherto supplied us with it.

"But that does not make up for my good Minette, from whom I feel I have been separated for ages, and whom I long to see again. Your dear mother will give herself up to the complete rest she so much needs. Sometimes I cannot help feeling that we have been hardly dealt with in this forced change of abode. Not on my own account, but on that of my wife, who is known to be a great invalid, and on account of my daughter's condition. All this adds to the severity of my banishment, and I feel it more since I have been left to myself and have tasted the evils of a residence under a strange roof, added to which, the expression 'temporary' that I used in my letter to Baron de Breteuil seems to have made no impression. But we all have plenty of time to moralise over the whole thing. We have great compensation in the universal sympathy, otherwise . . . . but I can only hear from you what follows."†

Failing Madame de Staël, our informant as to the feeling in Paris on this occasion is Mallet du Pan, who, although no partisan of Necker's, definitely and truthfully writes: "Grief and dissatisfaction are loud and universal; the crowd surrounded Necker's door

* Necker's brother.
† D'Haussonville, *Le Salon de Madame Necker*, ii. 189.

until the very instant of his departure . . . . . The archbishop of Toulouse, supported by the abbé de Vermont, is to administer the finances. He has apparently turned against Necker whose adherent he was. Montmorin is supposed to be the minister most in the king's confidence. Necker's party has tried hitherto to serve the archbishop of Toulouse and has done itself no good by it. It was asserted that he had advised that Necker's pamphlet should be published, that he might get rid of him, and thus free himself both from Necker and Calonne." *

Family documents, especially Madame Necker's *Mélanges*, mention the friendship for the archbishop of Toulouse, who, with the Maréchal and Madame de Beauvan, the Dukes of Duras, Nivernois, du Châtelet, De Castries, the archbishop of Narbonne, Tours, and the bishop of Arras, belonged to their intimate circle since Necker's retirement.

As far back as 1785, Baron de Staël had pointed out the archbishop of Toulouse in a despatch to Gustavus III. as one upon whom attention was centred and as likely to be a future minister.†

In the Revolution, accelerated by Calonne, Madame de Staël would never recognise the work of separate individuals. But, as far as it could be laid to the blame of one man, Calonne was answerable for it in the eyes of Necker's daughter. Two of his colleagues,

* Mallet du Pan, *Analecta sur l'Histoire du Temps*. Unpublished family papers, April, 1787.

† Baron A. de Staël, *Notice sur M. Necker. Œuvres complètes*, i. 221. A. Chérest, *La chute de l'Ancien Régime*, i. 198.

friends of Necker's, Ségur and de Castries, who owed
their appointments to him, now considered that the
moment had come for recommending his recall to the
monarch. The king hesitated, but was on the
point of giving his consent, although unwillingly.
At this juncture Breteuil, trading upon the king's
well-known dislike to Necker, remarked, that, if he
were recalled from banishment to take the head of
affairs, his pride and arrogance would be unbearable.

Alluding to the past discussion, in a work he published in 1796 on the subject of the French Revolution,
Necker certainly gives strong proof of his self-confidence when he says, " The king's choice was moment-
arily directed towards me. Had it remained steadfast, all that has happened would have been avoided;"
and he adds pointedly, " There would still have been
time to make another treaty with public opinion . . .
I have no doubts on the subject : a thoroughly wise
Government would have appeased the disquietude
that was now turning the thoughts of the nation to
the summoning of the *États Généraux*."

Louis XVI. had become accustomed to the adroit
Calonne, who saved him the trouble of ruling, and
had approved of the minister's policy in the Assembly
of the Notables two months before ; but the notables
now raised such complaints against the prime minister
that he was obliged to take refuge in England.

To avoid the trouble of a definite resolve, the king
next chose Fourqueux, who had " the most incapable
head," says Madame de Staël, " ever surmounted by

the wig of a councillor of state, and who now took
his official position like a man sent to keep a place
in a box before the piece begins." *

But the need was pressing, and as the king would
not have Necker he had now to resign himself to the
choice of Loménie de Brienne. He was only appointed finance minister at the outset, but the king
subsequently became possessed of a dull indifference,
only increased by the activity of this, the most fate-
ful of his councillors.

The queen was not the only one to be mistaken
in Brienne. He had won favour by his great success
in the administration of Languedoc, which, owing to
its special conditions, was the best-governed province
in France.

The democratic Jefferson, who went the length of
saying that had it not been for the queen there
would have been no Revolution, and did not hesitate
to say that he would have shut her up in a convent,
lavished even greater praise on the Archbishop of
Toulouse than she did; he called him "a virtuous,
patriotic, and able character;" preferred him for the
moment to Necker; and for years after the Revolution still held him to be a "capable statesman, eager
for reform, doing all that he could at such a court." †

La Fayette was of the same opinion when he spoke

---

* Madame de Staël, *Considérations sur la Révolution Française.*
Œuvres complètes, xii. 127.

† Jefferson, *Works*, i. *Autobiography*, 70, 101-102; ii. 258 and 310.
Lettres of August 31st and November 3rd, 1787; iii. 52, *Lettre*,
June 14, 1789.

of Loménie de Brienne as the most capable and
honourable man who could be appointed prime
minister.* On this head Baron de Staël was better
informed when he wrote to King Gustavus III. that
Louis XVI. had taken Brienne because he could
not help himself. "The fright," he says, "was so
universal, the need of some ruling power was so
much felt, that he was received with open arms.
The ministers themselves were so disquieted that
they could offer no opposition to his appointment.
But he is unstable and changeable," adds Baron de
Staël in July, "and this absence of decision is very
general in the nation. Patriotism is nearly extinct,
and there is an inclination to suppose that great aims
can be accomplished without great sacrifices." †

The last mention we find of Loménie de Brienne
by the Necker family is in Madame de Staël's
Considérations. She calls him a clever man, who in
ordinary times would have possessed the necessary
capacity for his office. He had not, however, shown
himself to be more earnest in tone than his predecessor Calonne.‡

In April 1787 Madame de Staël had hastened to
join her father in his banishment. "I was very

---

* La Fayette, *Mémoires et Correspondance,* ii. 195 and 199. Letters
to John Jay and Washington.

† Léouzon Le Duc, *Correspondance Diplomatique du Baron de Staël-
Holstein,* 58 and 60. Despatches No. 61, 63, and 65, of May 31 and
July 8, 1787.

‡ Madame de Staël, *Considérations sur la Révolution Française.*
Œuvres complètes, xii. 120, 129, and 135.

young at the time," she mentions later on ; "a *lettre de cachet* seemed a terrible fate to me. I screamed aloud when I heard of it, and could conceive no more dreadful disaster." *

This feeling soon gave way before a feeling of pride in all the proofs of sympathy which were bestowed on Necker. But she never overcame her bitterness with regard to the behaviour of the court, and specially that of the queen, of whose mediation on her father's behalf she had no knowledge, and towards the end of the short exile it finds expression in writing to Baron de Staël, who had remained in Paris : "I thank you, my dear friend," she says, "for the letter you sent me by Madame de Beauvau. I had been rather vexed that M. de Crillon had brought me none. You see that the queen has treated you no better on this occasion than she did on a former, for nothing would have been easier than to let you know that the *lettre de cachet* was withdrawn. It is only an ordinary attention which she shows to every one to whom she wishes to be gracious.

"I consider therefore that it is more than ever important to maintain great reserve; but, if she shows any wish to see you, then speak to her as we agreed you should do, in a manner worthy of my father.

"Let it be felt that the termination of this exile is much more important for the king and queen than for my father ; that the coldness and indifference you

* Madame de Staël, *Notice sur le Caractère de M. Necker et sur sa Vie privee. Œuvres complètes*, xviii. 35.

have personally experienced have given you a great deal of pain; and lastly, bring the fact to notice that you have never spoken about my father to the queen.

"I feel that everything I am now writing can be said perfectly well if you manage with your wonted carefulness, and speak firmly and respectfully, especially if it is the queen who summons you.

"You have not answered my letter concerning the journey to Fontainebleau. If your position and due regard to your king's dignity permitted, I confess to you that I would never again set foot in Versailles. It would have delighted me to solace my offended pride by this voluntary banishment. But as our position does not allow of such a decided step I think that a few audiences with the queen and a few days' stay during the hunting and theatricals will give no ground at my age for suspecting me of intrigues or of wishing to obtain special favour with the queen.

"The fact that M. de Montmorin is your foreign minister will make my visit to Fontainebleau a great deal more agreeable than those we paid in the days of Vergennes." *

These lines were written shortly before the birth of her first son.

Necker's banishment had not lasted altogether more than a couple of months, and was thought by Madame Necker to have passed all too quickly, for she preferred the happiness of spending her days in peace and quiet, alone with her husband, to any other.†

* D'Haussonville, *Le Salon de Madame Necker,* ii. 191.

† Madame Necker, *Mélanges. Letter to Saint Lambert,* Aug. 19, 1787.

On his return to Paris Necker found the assembly of notables dissolved.

The king had been bitterly disappointed in his hope of receiving counsel and help from them in matters of political economy. Loménie de Brienne had certainly laid a statement of affairs before them in his capacity of minister, as he had so urgently required of his predecessor in office when he himself was merely a notable. But these could make nothing of the unintelligible and insufficient information ;* they were content to take average figures, to recommend economy with a warning against contracting new debts, and to propose that a yearly statement of accounts should be submitted to a special commission. They certainly instilled the principle of equally divided imposts and burdens as before, but they ended up with the announcement that they were not disposed to suggest or consent to any fresh taxation.

When the assembly broke up on the 25th of May they had, as a matter of fact, achieved nothing except a change of ministry, and a public statement of the "terrible beginning of the approaching evil." †

Thus a merely negative result in the chain of events had been achieved by summoning the notables. The actual outcome of Calonne's administration lay in his adoption of the plan of provincial assemblies formulated by Necker, approved of by the notables, and now

---

* Droz, *Histoire de Louis XVI.*, i. 387.

† Speech of the first President of the Parisian Parlement in the final sitting of the notables, May 25, 1787.

frankly adopted by Brienne.   The economist Dupont
de Nemours developed it still further under Calonne,
without encountering the same difficulties as Necker
and Turgot had to overcome.   Calonne and Brienne
took a step still further in advance, which Necker had
shrunk from doing, when they fell back on Turgot's
plan of popular and departmental representation.

In the former the parish priests and proprietors had
seats and votes: the rest of the members, always
consisting of three, six, or nine, according to the
extent of the community, were to be the free choice
of all those who paid a tax of ten livres on their
property or their personalty, and this came to much
the same thing as universal suffrage.*

This first assembly had to choose another, the district
assembly,—and this again had to select the provincial
assembly, the organization of which remained very
much the same as Necker had left it

All the members took council together without class
distinction, and the *Tiers* supplied as many deputies
as the nobility and the clergy together.   The
presidents were chosen out of the two first orders, and
pending the complete organization of the whole,
(which did not take place before the outbreak of the
Revolution) the king chose half the members, and
those again chose the other half.   Votes were taken
by head and not by order.   On the prorogation of
the notables, Brienne specially pledged himself to the
latter measure as a compensation to the *Tiers* for the

* Lavergne, *Les Assemblées Provinciales*, 107, 109.

advantages derived by the privileged classes from their property and rank.*

During the year 1787 nineteen of these provincial assemblies began a career which, even under the unfavourable circumstances then predominating, would have borne good fruit if their work had not been prematurely put to an end. None of these assemblies met more than once before the Revolution.† Whilst an effort was being made to pave the way in the country towards establishing these institutions the task of the Government was rendered abortive in the midst of its activity. It had been expected that, immediately on consent of the king, Brienne would carry forward the measures instituted by his predecessors and approved of by the notables, by summoning together a special *séance royale*, and thus securing their acceptance by the Parlement.

He contented himself instead with ordinances concerning the calling together of the provincial assemblies, with freeing the corn trade, and abolishing public burdens.

The Parlement offered no opposition. It waited for a better opportunity to revenge itself for the summoning of the notables and to reinstate its overshadowed authority without losing the people's favour by doing it. This opportunity soon arose. Brienne had two financial edicts ready; the one proposed a territorial subvention, that is, a ground-tax, which was

* Lavergne, *Les Assemblées Provinciales*, 107 and 389.
  Idem, 128.

to meet the requirements of the Treasury and to be shared by every one alike and without exception in favour of the privileged classes; the other was a stamp-tax, and the ill-advised minister laid this first before the Parlement.   The latter began, as the notables had done, by demanding exact information as to the finances, but it soon found that this was over-stepping its prerogative; and chose a better point of attack against Brienne, when, using the Abbé Sabatier de Cabre as its mouthpiece, it announced for the first time that it had no right to dispose of the finances as it hitherto had done, and that the *États Généraux* alone could grant subsidies and raise taxes at indeterminate times.   It was added, that monarchs must be reminded of the old traditions of the kingdom·

It is true that this extreme step was only taken with a full grasp of its consequences by men like Duval d'Espréménil, an enthusiast for the rights of the body to which he belonged, a few earnest supporters of the theories of reform in the tone of the old Jansenist Parlementeers, or by younger men like Duport and Fréteau, who shared the admiration entertained by La Fayette and his followers for American institutions and for the results of the Revolution in America.

The rest, and they represented by far the greater number, reckoned that the Government would consent to any proposal advanced by their Parlement rather than summon the *États Généraux*.

When however the Parisian Parlement, without

consideration for the king, pronounced the *finance edicts* he had wished to pass to be " illegal, null, and void," he forthwith banished it to Troyes.

Brienne made use of the serious disturbance in Paris to have himself named prime minister, upon which Necker's friends Ségur and de Castries were recalled. During the exile to Troyes it was soon seen what a small number of the Parlementeers had been in earnest as to the step they had ventured to take. This assembly, which had not retired into banishment " because it had defended their privileges, but because it had sacrificed them,"* felt incapable of enduring the dullness of a provincial town in September, and notwithstanding the protestations of d'Espréménil and his adherents voted financial concessions, upon which Brienne also gave in, and withdrew his two edicts, although he had described them as indispensable. The Parisian populace celebrated the return of the Parlement by burning the Duchesse de Polignac and Breteuil in effigy. A similar demonstration against the queen was only just stopped in time. Two months later Brienne saw he could only procure money by proposing another edict which required 420 millions; the total to be paid off in five years; and promised that the *États Généraux* should be summoned to assemble in the year 1792 after this time had elapsed. At the *séance royale* which was held on

* Léouzon Le Duc, *Correspondance Diplomatique du Baron de Staël-Holstein,* 64. Despatch of the 16th August, 1787.

the 19th of November for this purpose, the minister
caused all the attributes of absolute power to be re-
capitulated to the king and to the keeper of the great
seal, and declared the king to possess sole power, without restraint or interference.

Supported by various adherents d'Espréménil replied
with the request that the estates should be called together not later than 1789.

The assembly seemed on the whole willing to meet
the king's wishes, when the keeper of the seal, suddenly and without heeding the general dissent, procured the command for the promulgation of the edicts
from the king. No sooner was this command made
known than the Duke of Orleans rose to protest
against it.

In one of the edicts, Malesherbes, who had meanwhile joined the ministry, had given the Protestants
their rights as citizens which they had so long coveted.
After it was read the king left the assembly, which
Malesherbes and the Duke of Nivernais tried in vain to
appease. Thus began the political rôle of the Duke of
Orleans, who, on account of his extraordinary conduct,
had hitherto been the object of universal contempt.

Madame de Staël has related in her letters to Gustavus III. how Louis XVI. had banished the duke;
that, although he had long been at enmity with the
queen, he preferred demeaning himself to ask her to
intercede for him rather than to remain at one of his
country seats.

But the Parisian Parlement continued to enjoy

popularity, and all who opposed the Government from any cause whatsoever turned to it without exception. The same d'Esprémenil who had required the king to grant liberty to the people desperately opposed the edict in favour of the Protestants, whilst a short time afterwards the Archbishop Dillon of Narbonne solemnly thanked the king for it in the assembly of the clergy.*

Madame de Staël describes the scene as one never to be forgotten; she then says of d'Esprémenil, with whom she was personally acquainted, " He was certainly an energetic, noble creature, this unhappy and eloquent tribune of the magistracy. But he was also easily influenced and of an uncertain temperament, and his leanings to Martini's doctrines bore curious fruit.

" In 1788 he imagined that he had seen the Holy Virgin, and that she had recommended him to protest in Parlement against Malesherbes' edict which relieved the legitimate children of Protestants from the stain of illegitimacy. He obeyed her commands, and, pointing to the picture of the Crucified One, exclaimed in the pathetic tone of a Capuchin, 'See you not that his wounds bleed afresh?' " †

The situation between the ministers and Parlement was no longer tenable, and everything pointed to a speedy catastrophe, which Brienne in vain tried to avert.

* Lavergne, *Les Assemblées Provinciales*, 409.
† Lacretelle, *Testament Politique et Littéraire*, ii. 70.

To prepare against emergencies the Parisian Parlement met together on the 3rd May, 1788, in solemn conclave. D'Espréménil read the celebrated declaration freely granting subsidies by means of the *Étais Généraux*, as the mouthpiece of the nation; also the establishment of the rights and capitulation-grants of the provinces, the institution of permanent judges, the introduction of royal edicts into Parlement only where they agreed with the fundamental laws of the province and of the state; and further, the inviolable right of every individual to be judged by the law only, the king and every class in the kingdom being bound to respect law and justice.

The Government answered by repudiating these resolutions and by the issue of a warrant to arrest Duval d'Espréménil and Goislard.

The Parlement now met in solemn assembly; troops appeared before the Palace of Justice; and at midnight the Marquis d'Agoult demanded that a major of the *garde française* should be admitted into the chamber where the deliberations were taking place, and delivered the royal letter issuing the warrant for the apprehension of these two members.

D'Agoult, who was unacquainted with them, invited the assembly to point them out to him, upon which there was a unanimous cry, "We are all d'Espréménil and Goislard!"

D'Agoult retired to take further orders regarding a situation that had been unforeseen, and only on the following day a sitting which had lasted thirty hours came to an end and procured a moral triumph, although the two members were arrested.

The Parlement was now summoned to Versailles on the 8th of May, and new edicts were proposed, which, under other circumstances, would have earned the thanks of the nation.

One of these was for the abolition of torture; another guaranteed weighty reform in the transaction of justice, which had been partly carried out by Malesherbes at the cost of the judicial power hitherto exercised by the Parlement. But the salutary working of these measures disappeared before the consequences of others to follow, for every one was aware that these only served as their prelude.

A further royal edict ordered the establishment or the restoration of a high court of justice, the *Cour Plénière*. No one had hitherto thought of the existence of such an arrangement, but it was endeavoured to assimilate this suddenly-awakened revival of the customs of the past with imaginary and historical tradition.* All the royal edicts and commands were in future to come before this court of justice. It was to be composed of the high officers of the realm and a certain number of the members of all the parlements, and the king himself was to preside.

Nothing was left to the parlements but the introduction of measures relating to purely local matters, and for the time being they were not to re-assemble.

* Henri Martin, *Histoire de France*, xvi. 664, note.

The weightiest questions, the answers to which were awaited with the greatest anxiety by all classes, were left undetermined by Brienne, or set aside with contradictory statements, which on the whole aimed at maintaining the integrity of absolute power for the monarchy. His sole concession was an indefinite allusion to the summoning of the *États Généraux*, and until that assembled the *Cour Plénière* was to settle all taxation.

The beginning of the French Revolution may be dated from the 8th of May, 1788, if this comprehensive and often misunderstood term expresses the moment when, as Mounier says, the Government capriciously and unlawfully employs force, and those who are governed take to armed resistance and yet remain unpunished.*

In Madame de Staël's opinion the Revolution began when the Parlement, represented by the Abbé Sabatier, asserted the right of the people to possess those full powers which they had so obstinately refused to the crown.† The first proofs of open opposition to the king's ill-advised command were given by those parlementeers and nobles who were appointed to compose the *Cour Plénière*. They hesitated to obey, and thus prepared a sudden termination to Brienne's stroke of policy.

A close bond of union was established between the

---

* Mounier, *Les Assemblées Provinciales*, 382.

† Madame de Staël, *Considérations sur la Révolution Française. Œuvres*, xii. 131.

deputies and the aristocracy by his unwise proceedings, and this fostered a spirit of opposition in the army—now almost entirely officered by the nobility.

No less dangerous was the satisfaction derived by the parlementary party from the approval of the masses, and the support which the representatives of the law did not hesitate to accept from the street population.

The first scene of this sort in honour of d'Esprémenil rapidly awoke the spirit of uproar in the provinces.

During the early summer of 1788 the inhabitants of Brittany imagined that they were on the eve of civil war. The governor, Comte de Thiard, weakly prevented the troops from interfering with the tumult.*

The intendant of the province, Bertrand de Molleville, was obliged to fly, and those who were subsequently to fight in the Vendée found their way for the present into the Bastille.‡

In Pau and Béarn the populace hastened down from the mountains to insist that their parlement should be reinstated. But the most important of these scenes of disorder began in Dauphiné.

When first united to the French crown this province

---

* Baron Grimm, quoted by Smith in his *Lectures on the French Revolution*, i. 184. Thiers, *Histoire de la Révolution Française*, i. 14.

† Lavergne, *Les Assemblées Provinciales*, 421, 426. Droz, *Histoire de Louis XVI.* ii. 69, 71.

‡ A. de Tocqueville, *Coup d'œil sur le règne de Louis XVI.* 280 and 283.

had retained its representative assembly, and after its suspension under Louis XIII. it had never ceased to claim its restoration. In 1779 Necker's attempt to substitute it by a provincial assembly proved unsuccessful.

When Brienne repeated the attempt in 1787 and banished the contumacious parlementary party the peasantry rang the alarm-bells, forcibly prevented the measure from being carried out, and threatened to hang the Duke of Clermont Tonnerre to the chandelier of his reception-rooms if the keys of the Palace of Justice were not delivered into their hands.

There, after a short encounter, in which two regiments unwillingly allowed themselves to be led against the victorious populace, the deputies chosen by the three orders met together and decided that the old system of representation should be revived in Dauphiné, without further ratification from the king, on the 21st of July, and afterwards they declared that the law had to be very carefully observed if a monarch's legitimate rights were to be distinguished from despotism, and that the safety of individuals could in no case be attacked without endangering the whole nation.

Any upholder and supporter of the May edict was accused of treachery to the king, the nation, and the constitution. In this the nobility and clergy took the lead, whilst the *Tiers*, which at first resisted these

extreme steps, was only influenced in their favour
by Mounier, one of the royal judges in Grenoble,
who, although only thirty years old, had already
acquired extraordinary respect on the part of his
fellow-citizens.

The Government replaced Clermont Tonnerre by
the Maréchal de Vaux, and placed twenty thousand
men at his disposal, and this new governor, who had
a reputation for energy, could do nothing further
than conform to what he could no longer prevent.
The only concession he obtained was that the representatives of the estates should assemble at the neighbouring castle of Vizille, instead of at Grenoble as
first arranged.

Under the probable leadership of Mounier, who
was supported by his young friend Barnave, it was
here determined that the king should be requested to
grant the *États Généraux* for the whole nation, and
the regular calling together of the estates for all the
provinces, and for both that the *Tiers* should be
equally represented with the privileged orders, and
that the votes should be taken in one assembly, and
by persons; upon which the six hundred deputies at
Vizille took an oath not to forget the rights of the
nation whilst endeavouring to re-acquire those of
their own province.

The representations to the king, which were drawn
up by Mounier, already closed with the favourite
formula of the Revolution, borrowed from the *Con-*

trat Social : "That the rights of men are derived from Nature alone, and are independent of all contracts." *

This was the origin—and it was of wide and historical importance—of what Madame de Staël calls "the peaceful, well-thought-out, insurrection in the Dauphiné," † and it was in point of fact the prologue to the Revolution.

This example inspired others. Most of the provinces supplied protests from the parlements and estates, and information concerning the existing disorder, the constant confusion and ferment, which the minister met by repressive measures, all the more exasperating because inadequate. A storm of ill-will was especially directed against the *lettres de cachet.* Lavergne in vain recalled the fact that they had been less employed in the reign of Louis XVI. than in that of any other monarch. Once aroused, the consciousness of the unlawful tyranny of this mode of procedure could no longer be appeased by ordinary methods. ‡

In the *Generalités* of Bordeaux and Besançon, in La Rochelle and Limoges, the introduction of provincial assemblies had meanwhile been unsuccessful, and it now became a question how far the Government was able to enforce its authority in the rebellious provinces.

* Lanzac de Laborie, *Jean Joseph Mounier*, 13-20. Lavergne, *Les Monarchien de la Constituante. Revue des Deux Mondes*, 1842, ii. 551.

† Madame de Staël, *Considérations. Œuvres*, xii. 208.

‡ Lavergne, *Les Assemblées Provinciales*, 378-379.

The necessity for raising money had now become so pressing that as a last resource Brienne determined on applying to the clergy, and to that end he summoned them to Paris in extraordinary conclave.

He brought the idea of confiscating the conventual property before his colleagues, and reckoned principally on his intimate knowledge of all the circumstances and individuals to win over the assembly to his views and make it possible to carry them out. But even here he found opinion so altered that he was obliged to reduce his demands to a modest sum, and was unable to pass the May edict or obtain approval of his past policy.

Although the clergy refused all pecuniary sacrifice in the same way as the nobility and magistracy had done, they were just as popular by reason of their opposition to the Government. They too invited the monarch rather to be king of the French than lord over France, and to call together the *États Généraux* as soon as possible.

The answer of the Government was about as momentous as these resolutions of the Assembly. It now granted to the clergy what it had refused to the parlements, and, forced by the universal excitement, pledged itself in definite words to the principle that the sovereign could only levy grants by consent of the *États Généraux*.[*] By the 8th of August they were summoned to appear on the 1st of May, 1789,

---

[*] Leser, *Necker's Second Administration*, 58-60. "Réponse du roi aux remontrances du clergé, 15 Juin, 1788."

by royal decree, and the sittings of the *Cour plenière* were for the time suspended. A few days later, on the 16th August, 1788, the alarming announcement was published by edict that the payments of the royal treasury must be partly suspended and partly curtailed; only three-fifths of the necessary payments were to be in specie, the rest were to be settled in promissory notes. In other words, this was an acknowledgment of state bankruptcy with assets of only sixty per cent., whilst to keep the machinery of the Government in working order nearly a million livres were required daily.*

Madame de Staël was quite right when she wrote to King Gustavus that the history of France might be told in epigrams. Brienne added one to the number. He is said to have remarked that "there were so many chances and yet it only needed one to save the State." †

As this chance did not turn up he had no hesitation in laying hands upon the funds of the *Invalides* and the proceeds of a lottery for the poor. Then, when he had tried everything, he entered into negociations with Necker, whom he sought to associate with his financial administration, by the queen's wish made known through Mercy-d'Argenteau on the 20th August.

What would have been possible a year sooner was however no longer possible; Necker answered Mercy's

---

* Jefferson, *Works, Correspondence*, iii. 40.

† Darest, *Histoire de France*, vii. 132.

overtures with the demand that Brienne should be dismissed, that he himself should be placed at the head of affairs, and that the promise of the assemblage of the estates should be fulfilled.*

Under the extraordinary pressure of the universal wish of the nation, his point of view on the latter subject had also undergone a change. He, who on the dismissal of Calonne had declared that it should be the first act of a wise minister to refuse to call the *États Généraux* together, now made it an essential condition, and "awaited the moment," as he says himself, "with indescribable joy, in which the elevating and splendid spectacle of the assemblage of the representatives of six and twenty million men was to take place, and the justice of the monarchs of the French nation to resume its former influence over the course of public affairs." †

There remained no further doubt that Necker would decline to accept the unlucky legacy of Brienne and Calonne unless he was promised the support and the control of the nation. "No time should be lost," he writes on the controversy that had then arisen, against Calonne. "Public opinion, this moral and political force, must wipe out the past and bind the present to the future." ‡ Necker had held similar opinions

* Auguste de Staël, *Notice sur M. Necker. Œuvres complètes,* 225. Leser, *Necker's Second Administration,* 21, 22.

† Necker, *Nouveaux éclaircissement sur le compte-rendu au Roi. De l'Administration,* etc. *Œuvres,* ii. 599, vi. 59. *De la Révolution Française,* ix. 53.

‡ *Idem,* ii. 467.

during his first term of office, and they equally held good under new conditions.

He consulted public opinion as he had done formerly; whether he was to guide it time alone could tell. Mercy again returned to the charge, officially authorised by the king. Brienne's dismissal was silently conceded. He received it on the 25th of August, not before he had exchanged his archbishopric of Toulouse for that of Sens, which was considerably more profitable; increased his income to eight times a hundred thousand *livres;* and obtained the queen's promise to intercede for a cardinal's hat for him.

History only once mentions his name again, and that is to chronicle how the last unworthy adviser of an absolute monarchy put an end to his own life by taking poison on the 16th February, 1794. On the evening previous to his retirement Necker's appointment as director of finance was confirmed. Two days later he was minister and member of the council. The rank of premier was not again conferred, but Necker possessed all its prerogatives.

Moral ruin went side by side with this financial ruin, even exceeding the latter in its far-reaching effects. Confidence in the Government was as exhausted as the treasury. Since Louis XVI. had ascended the throne, more abuses had been abolished, more improvements introduced, than had been the case during the whole of the preceding century. Adam Smith bears witness that the French Government

under this monarch was more humane than any other
on the Continent after the abolition of the *lettres de
cachet* and of abuses in the taxation, especially in the
matter of the *Taille*.*

Almost a hundred years after him, Tocqueville
draws attention to the share that the reforms instituted
by the *ancien régime* had in its fall. Not merely
had the Government assented to just demands, but it
had shown itself more enlightened in important
questions than the great national corporations. Thus
the institution of provincial assemblies was incomparably more favourable to a free development and
participation in public affairs than the old-fashioned
assemblies were. It was the king who abolished
torture and who employed Malesherbes to offer legal
reforms to the parlements, only to be rejected by them.

The edict in favour of non-Catholics was enforced
by Government notwithstanding the opposition of the
clergy and the magistracy. The censorship existed
only in name. Brienne demanded freedom for the
press on the eve of his overthrow.

Many of the most detested privileges of the nobility
and clergy had fallen into disuse; the imposts in the
interior had lapsed; the ideas of the economists with
regard to the corn-laws, especially in connection with
trade and industry, had been for the most part
carried out.

The score of guilt attached to the *ancien régime*,

* Adam Smith, *Wealth of Nations, Collected Works*, xviii. 296,
note.

as drawn up by Jefferson amongst others, was already
wiped out, or on the point of being so.* But, in
proportion as the evil diminished, the want of confidence appeared to increase, for the king's will was
the only guarantee for reform, and he hesitated between his natural impulses, which were always good,
and the surrounding influences, which went constantly from one extreme to another.

People had not forgotten that Louis XVI. had
passed over Machault, impeached Turgot, tolerated
Calonne, and reposed confidence in Brienne. He
now accepted Necker's ministry as an experiment
forced upon him, with the honourable intention
of upholding it, and at the same time cherishing a
secret hope that it might wear itself out.

What was to happen next no one knew.

Necker rightly characterizes the old French rule as
having all the necessary means at its disposal for maintaining the laws of property, order, and liberty, but as
having also the power of setting all these laws at
defiance.

"Without any inconvenient inquiries," he says,
"the king's decision could reduce the interest on the
national debt or suspend the repayment of the principal; by means of a royal sitting, or *lit de justice*,
it could prescribe taxes or extend them, and by a
lettre de cachet it could deprive whomsoever it
pleased of his freedom." †

---

* Jefferson, *Complete Works, Autobiography*, i. 86.

† Necker, *Du pouvoir exécutif dans les Grands États. Œuvres*,
viii. 592.

An observation made at that time by Marie Antoinette testifies to the existence of the predominating feeling that the fate of a whole nation practically depended on a caprice. Not only were the *États Généraux* promised, but the date of their assembly was fixed, when she wrote to the Emperor Joseph that she hoped that the expected French intervention would be avoided in the Dutch disturbances, " for in the event of a war it would be no longer possible to avert the summoning of the states." *

So, with the exception of the courtiers whose opinions the queen expressed, there was scarcely any one left in France who thought it possible to continue in the old paths and to depend on the king's good intentions alone.

By far the greater number said with La Fayette: " We will have the *États Généraux* or nothing." †

The *ancien régime* had reached this point when Necker undertook the conduct of affairs, and pledged his word that for the future government should be carried on in the full light of day and with the entire consent of the nation. The people received him with acclamation. Paris overflowed with pamphlets, pictures, and allegories in his honour. Demonstrations in his favour took place in the theatres, and his name was shouted enthusiastically when the verses in Collin

---

* Arneth, *Marie Antoinette, Joseph II. and Leopold II.* Letters, 118. Marie Antoinette to the Emperor Joseph, 16th July, 1788.

† La Fayette, *Mémoires*, ii. 229. Letter of the 25th May, 1788.

d'Harleville's comedy, *Les Chateaux en Espagne,* were spoken : " Je choisirais d'abord un ministre honnête homme. Le choix est bientôt fait quand le public le nomme." *

"Wonders are expected of Necker," wrote his son-in-law to King Gustavus, " and no one doubts that in a few years, if it is confided to his charge, France will be born again. The confidence reposed in him is unbounded. It would be difficult to over-estimate the love and respect that his genius, his moderation, his disposition, the purity of his private life, have inspired." †

Although not without a struggle, even the opposing nobility resigned themselves—at any rate, outwardly—to the minister they were obliged to endure. In the first days of his administration the general in command in Lorraine, Comte Clairon d'Haussonville, and the Maréchal Duc de Broglie, met in his ante-chamber. "Let us go in together," said the latter to the count ; "I am not acquainted with Necker : you can introduce me." "So you think that I know him ?" replied the other. "In that case we can introduce each other," said the marshal, and this was what they ended by doing. The descendants of both married Necker's grand-daughters. D'Haussonville, who was one of them, tells the anecdote.‡

* Grimm, *Correspondance Littéraire,* xiv. 825.

† Léouzon Le Duc, *Correspondance Diplomatique du Baron de Staël-Holstein,* 88. Despatch No. 100, August 31, 1788.

‡ Comte D'Haussonville, *Souvenirs et Mélanges: Vie de mon Père,* 9.

Baron Staël mentions that the preliminary steps towards Necker's recall proceeded from the queen. The opposition at court seemed so far overcome that no further intrigues complicated the first months of his administration.*

Even the discreet Malouet, who passed severe judgment on Necker as a statesman, testifies that he was superior to most of his opponents both in talent and in personal merit, and that all the disorder and mistakes leading to the *États Généraux* were to be reckoned from his first retirement.†

Dumont, Mirabeau's friend, confesses that Necker was *la divinité du moment*.‡ Even Rivarol, who attacked his religious philosophy, gave unstinting praise to Necker as minister.§

This being the public tone of mind, Necker's own family could scarcely show greater sobriety of judgment. Even Madame Necker looked to the future with confidence and hope, as everything now seemed to satisfy the wish of her life and to play into her husband's hands.‖

And Madame de Staël? Her state of excitement

---

* Léouzon Le Duc, *Correspondance Diplomatique du Baron de Staël-Holstein*, 116. 1788.

† Malouet, *Mémoires*, i. 199.

‡ Dumont, *Souvenirs sur Mirabeau*, 44.

§ Lescure, *Rivarol et la Société française pendant la Révolution et l'Emigration*, 147.

‖ *Lettres Inédites de la Marquise de Créqui à Sénac de Meilhan*, 210. Letter of September, 1788.

was such that the Marquise de Créqui (the friend and correspondent of Sénac de Meilhan, Necker's systematic opponent) took occasion to doubt her sanity. Sainte-Beuve on the contrary remarks that cooler heads should excuse her enthusiasm just because of her intellect.*

When Necker, to whom she was the first to bring the news to St. Ouen of his nomination, saw the manifest pride and joy shining out of her eyes, he felt that the daughter of a minister only saw the advantages without the terrible responsibilities of his position.

The following day, the 25th of August, being the feast of St. Louis, Madame de Staël was obliged to go to Versailles. She was so excited that in returning through the Bois de Boulogne she fancied she should be attacked by robbers. It seemed as if Fate must punish her for being so happy. "It is true that no robbers appeared," she writes in the *Considérations*, "but the future fully justified my fears."

The following day had a sobering influence. She was received by the queen at the same time as a niece of Brienne's, and clearly saw by the difference made between them that, although Necker had become necessary, the queen's personal sympathies remained with his predecessor. Madame de Staël made no mistake as to the extent of this feeling, and she adds that Necker's efforts at conciliation made no differ-

* *Idem*, 28. Sainte-Beuve, *Causeries de Lundi*, xii. 386.

euce, and that it remained one of the great difficulties of his second administration.*

There are several assertions as to his own grasp of the situation. When the nomination of the archbishop of Toulouse was announced to him he said to his daughter that the situation which was then sufficiently difficult would soon become unbearable. After he had taken Brienne's place he could not refrain from exclaiming that it was now too late, why had he not been granted the fifteen months the archbishop of Toulouse had had? † But he comforted the king with the assurance that, although the evil was certainly great, the resources of the nation were still greater. Before he had been three days in office the first disturbance took place in Paris, and Brienne was burnt in effigy by the people. The commanding officer of the watch interfered, and, unable to secure obedience, he allowed the crowd to be bayoneted. Two or three men were killed and many wounded before the crowd could be dispersed.

Filled with anger and bitterness the populace again assembled on the following day, attacked the watch at several different points, burnt down ten or twelve dwelling-houses, and killed several soldiers. The tumult had to be quelled by the troops and Paris was in a state of siege.‡

* Madame de Staël, *Considérations sur la Révolution Française,* xii. 164, 166.

† *Idem,* ii. 160.

‡ Jefferson, *Works and Correspondance,* ii. 471.

For the first time in his administration the streets of the capital were dyed with blood. Meanwhile the money-market greeted Necker's return to office with a rise, which, although it did not reach the 30 per cent. given by Madame de Staël,* was nevertheless sufficiently considerable to restore confidence, to enable the minister to cancel the conditions of the edict of August 16th, and to make it possible again to pay all demands in cash. Great financial houses made overtures; one province (Languedoc) started a loan of 12 millions; every means employed in banking transactions were set in motion. In his history of Necker's second financial administration, Leser comes to the conclusion that the former certainly employed means of a doubtful sort to bring money into the treasury, but that he never endangered the public confidence which lent him the support so necessary to him.† He directed every effort to carry on the business of the State by a series of financial operations until the "General Estates" should assemble, and to shield the Government from the dangerous humiliation of having to appear before them in a state of financial depression.

Droz, the historian of Louis XVI., considers it wonderful that Necker should have been able to resume payment and to refill the treasury, which at

* Madame de Staël, *Considérations*, etc. *Œuvres*, xii. 158. Leser, *Necker's Second Administration*, 33, and note.

† Leser, *Necker's Second Administration*, 33-41.

the time of Brienne's retirement only contained five
hundred thousand *livres ;* * and this notwithstanding
the fact that the struggle against famine and the sale
of corn had alone swallowed up seventy millions in
the winter of 1789.   He not only considers Necker's
second administration to have been of far more importance than the first, but adds, that it was free from
any trace of the charlatanism that was sometimes
apparent in the former.†

A thorough alteration of the whole system would
be impossible once the *États Généraux* were re-
established unless these gave their co-operation, and
until that happened it was necessary to keep France
from dissolution.‡   When the *États Généraux* assembled he found that they would give no heed to questions of administration, but gave themselves up
entirely to politics.   He writes, *Il fallut continuer
la manœuvre.*§

Necker set greater store on the fact that he was
able to avert famine during the winter and spring of
1789 in the capital and in various provinces than on
his activity in financial matters, and he called the
provisioning of Paris his greatest work.‖

After ten years of bad harvests there now followed
catastrophes of every kind ; prices went up, and the.

* Necker, *De l'Administration de M. Necker.   Œuvres,* vi. 25.
† Droz, *Histoire de Louis XVI.* ii. 94, 95.
‡ Henri Martin, *Histoire de France,* xvi. 615.
§ Necker, *De l'Administration de Monsieur Necker,* vi. 25.
‖ *Idem,* vi. 298, etc.

coldest winter that could be recollected in France since 1709 set in. As a consequence of this 40,000 labourers in Normandy alone were without food and occupation.*

From every quarter of France impoverished homeless wanderers came to Paris, in vain seeking relief from the misery that had overtaken them, and steadily adding to the crowd of malcontents who only awaited a sign to become more desperate.

The Government, on its side, had, beyond everything, to import a supply of corn to nourish these famished crowds; for bread had become so costly that even those invited to dine in wealthy houses were obliged to bring it in their pockets with them, and finally all festivities were given up that the poor might be warmed and nourished, and fires kept burning for them at every point in the capital where the streets crossed.†

Necker's earlier views upon free trade in corn had gone through no alteration: according to his own saying "they were of the simplest, and yet restricted by the necessity of accommodating them to circumstances." ‡ When he ascertained that there had been a failure of the crops for that year he stopped the free export of corn (on the 7th September, 1788) that had been granted since June, 1788, for an inde-

* Jefferson, *Autobiography, Complete Works,* i. *Correspondence,* iii. 40.
† *Idem,* ii. 591. Letter of March 11, 1789.
‡ *De l'Administration de M. Necker, par lui-même. Œuvres,* vi. 298.

finite period, and strenuously endeavoured to import grain, especially from America.

He next organised the purchase of corn on a large scale in foreign lands, which resulted in crippling the activity of private firms. These knew to their cost that they could not rival the State without severe loss, as the latter brought its corn direct to the market, and in the worst times could sell it cheaper than it had bought it. Still more severely felt was the prohibition to buy corn except in the market. Necker hoped by this means to put a stop to usury.

His regulations in this direction had not merely an economical but a far-reaching moral effect, as the people now saw themselves as it were officially strengthened in the distrust with which they had habitually viewed the corn-dealers in bad times.

Deeds of violence were perpetrated in every part of the country, which accustomed the masses to uproar and encouraged the spread of anarchy.*

The winter of 1788-1789 witnessed the first *Jacquerie* in Provence, when the Government practically allowed the people to go unpunished for freeing the prisoners, refusing to pay the taxes, settling the price of food, and declining to receive the king's envoys.

But even such toleration, almost reaching self-effacement, could not secure peace or provisions for France. To meet the growing distress, Necker, as

---

* Taine, *Les Origines de la France Contemporaine*, ii. *La Révolution*, chapter i. : " L'anarchie spontanée."

on a former occasion, again renounced the 220,000 francs to which he was entitled for his salary, and lent the sum of 2,400,000 livres out of his private fortune, at five per cent. interest, to buy corn, remarking that when peace and comfort were in question it was worth risking a fortune.*

The responsibility he had undertaken nevertheless exceeded his strength; he certainly provided for the population of Paris, numbering six hundred thousand souls, but only by artificially occupying for twelve thousand of the unemployed and by neglecting the provinces, whose cry for help only too often obtruded itself in vain upon the ear of the overburdened minister.†

The history of the Revolution tells us that it was hunger that taught the principles of the *Social Contract* to the masses.

This effort to replace the working of independent influences by the energy of the state was the last that Necker attempted as administrator under the old monarchy. A still more severe trial awaited the statesman.

Necker's endeavours as minister were in favour of a moderate and conciliatory policy. The Breton nobility were released from the bastille and d'Esprémésnil from his prison on the Isle of Sainte Marguerite. He reconciled the Parlements by inducing the king

* *De l'Administration de M. Necker, par lui-même. Œuvres complètes*, vi. Madame de Staël, *Considérations*, xii. 245, 313.

† Leser, *Necker's Second Administration*, 45, 54.

to replace Lamoignon by Barantin as keeper of the seals, and also by enforcing the reforms instituted by Malesherbes.   He then gave these assemblies their legal vacation before they could again raise the old subjects of quarrel, but promised that the estates should reassemble in the following January.

By this means he intended promptly to allay the excitement in every part of the nation, which excitement had been brought to the highest pitch through a last mistake committed by his predecessor.   For, on realizing that none of the existing parties were to be won over by his promise to summon the *Etats Généraux*, Brienne had conceived the notion of once again securing his position by means of the existing discord.   A decree issued on the 5th of July declared that it had not been possible for the Government to find out the general opinion as to the mode of election and the composition of the " States," and that therefore by the king's desire not only every corporate body in the kingdom but every well-educated individual was invited to give an opinion and to discuss the matter.   The minister hoped amidst all the opposing opinions and interests he might easily obtain support from the strongest party.

What would have been the wisest course of statesmanship, with certain fixed instructions, became in this way a subject of quarrel and the sport of chance. Throughout the land, high and low, young and old, the wise and the ignorant, statesmen and women, sincere enthusiasts and bold intriguers, true patriots and greedy adventurers, started, like the Argonauts of old, in search of the fleece, or of this lost constitution, which grew in importance in proportion to the impossibility of finding it, for like all the institutions of the old monarchy it had been altered in some particulars, whilst in others it had never been submitted to definite rules. Thus, deputies had never been elected in the early days, but the entire nobility and clergy appeared at the assemblies of the nation; and towards the end of the fifteenth century the clergy, nobility, and citizens in each official circle, under a *bailli* or a seneschal, elected their deputies.

In the same way the number of representatives allowed to the *Tiers Etat* was quite indefinite.* The first to be sent forth by Brienne to explore this wide ocean was the Abbé Maury; he returned, owning to having seen no land. But Malesherbes, on the other hand, who had been one of the first to demand the *Etats Généraux*, at a time when authority seemed still to repose in the hands of the Government, renounced popularity to warn the king in a memorial, dated July 1788, of the danger of bringing the three orders together under altered conditions with sympathies so opposed to each other.

He went back rather to the project, formed by his friend Turgot, of one assembly only, similar to the provincial assemblies, and composed of elected members belonging to the proprietary classes.

* Leser, *Necker's Second Administration*, 64.

He specially implored the king to permit no equivocation on the part of his minister and to allow no diminution of confidence in the sincerity of his intentions; "for," he ended, "the results of general discontent are incalculable." Dufresne Saint Léon expressed himself in a similar sense to Brienne. The advice was excellent, but it came years too late, and only gained the useless support of a few sensible men for whom there was no place or hearing in the Revolution. "It is no question of what *was* but of what is *to be*," said Mirabeau.*

The Parlements answered characteristically. They demanded the calling together of the *Etats Généraux* according to the laws set down in 1614, and that the vote should be taken by orders in direct opposition to the wish of the *Tiers*.

This was the last blow to the claim of these bodies to represent the national wishes, and they vanished from the political scene of action beneath a storm of attacks on the part of the press and of literature.

Whilst the storm Brienne had provoked continued unabated in the provincial assemblies, pamphlets and periodicals, reckoned at three thousand in the ten months between July 1788 and 1789, occupied themselves with the solution of the same problem.†

When the Comte de Ségur returned to Paris, after fulfilling a diplomatic mission of some years' duration,

---

* Henri Martin, *Histoire de France*, xvi. 617, note.
† Lacy, *Louis XVI. et les Successeurs de Turgot*, xxxi. 650.

he could not restrain his astonishment at the social change he perceived. The polished wit, the familiar intercourse, and the thoughtful moderation of olden days, were no longer to be found. Political passion had changed the *salon* into the arena, everyone tried to speak louder than his neighbour, and no one listened.

He adds, " The women did the same, and among the remarkable and attractive members of the young generation the Baronne de Staël in particular betrayed such especial pungency of argument and eloquence that very few could enter the lists against her, as she not only surprised but convinced and carried away her hearers."* The want felt by Ségur did not exist for Madame de Staël, who was too young to feel the difference which even in social relations marked the change from the domain of theory to the region of fact. Whatever might happen in the future, the present fulfilled her wildest dreams. Her father was at the head of the State, and the whole nation shared her enthusiastic love for him. Everywhere his name fell on her ear, and his picture met her gaze; the highest aims of existence, the happiness of the people, aspirations for liberty and for the future, were mingled with her deepest and holiest affections. All this came to her at the right moment, in the spring-time of her life and in the full strength of her four-and-twenty years. The muses beckoned to her, and crowned her youth-

* Comte de Ségur.

ful tresses with those garlands so often reserved for brows grown cold.

As we have already mentioned, in Talleyrand's opinion the highest point of social enjoyment was reached during the years immediately preceding the Revolution. The year 1789 represented this for Madame de Staël; she says that never had so many clever intellectual people come to the front. Society had never been more brilliant or more earnest in tone than it was during the three or four years from 1788 to 1791, and in no country or period had the art of conversation come to greater perfection.*

Active and eager to join in the fray, she thus stepped into the place she had long been destined to fill. Circumstances had modified the political doctrines of Madame de Staël; the time we now speak of had nothing or very little to do with the great constitutional theories of *Les Considérations*. The woman who lived through the Revolution was not the same as she who related its story, and the mature experience of 1816 spoke a different language to that of the youthful enthusiasm of 1789. But, however much her experiences might and did influence her tone of thought, her sympathies remained the same. They belonged at that time and subsequently to that group of the nobility for whom she invariably claimed the honour and glory of having initiated the Revolution.†
To her high conception of liberty Madame de Staël

---

* Madame de Staël, *Considérations*. *Œuvres complètes*, xii. 385.
† *Idem*, xii. 54, 132.

linked the conviction that a revolution in its favour could only succeed if the impulse came from above, and if the noblest and best came. to its assistance. The great aspiration of all those inclined to reform, from Vauban and Fénélon to Turgot, had always been to make the crown responsible for reform, and not to call the national assembly together until a monarchy freed from the shackles of despotic power could be brought to meet it. The younger generation, and among them Madame de Staël, tried to solve the problem of the future by applying to the next grade in the social hierarchy. If the king could not be won over then the nobility must take the lead, that liberal youth of 1789, who, as Rénan says, created the conception of a Fatherland — the Clermont-Tonnerres, Lally-Tollendals, Crillons, Castellanes, La Rouchefoucaulds, Toulongeons, La Fayettes, Montmorencies, whose unselfish devotion could never be outstripped by the men belonging to the *Tiers*, as Madame de Staël, agreeing with Sièyes, wrote at a later date.* Her whole conception of French history and her preference for English institutions is formed on her appreciation of the importance and the responsibilities of a strong, independent, intellectual, and politically-powerful aristocracy. In her eyes Richelieu was the evil spirit of the nation, as he lowered the aristocracy and turned the greatest vassals of the crown into mere courtiers.

* Madame de Staël, *Considérations*. *Œuvres complètes*, xii. 351. Sièyes in A. Chérest, ii. 255.

She made his despotism answerable for the destruction of originality and loyalty in the French character, and went the length of calling the great minister a foreigner in France.* It is almost comical to see her defending her father from the imputation of resembling Richelieu as if it were the most serious reproach.† Whilst the only statesman of the first phase of the Revolution invited the minister to undertake the general salvation,‡ Necker almost simultaneously and in the full consciousness of moral superiority explained to the king, during a conversation regarding the situation, that if ever the course of events required a Richelieu or a Mazarin he would no longer be suitable as minister.§ Madame de Staël's opinion of Louis XVI. and the French monarchy betrays the same views. She answered the great question of the day—whether a constitution really existed — by asserting that the Government was carried on partly according to old customs and usages, partly according to fancy, but never by fixed laws. The nominal constitution of the nation only reposed in the hereditary power of the king, its history was made up of the incessant struggles of the

* Madame de Staël, *Œuvres complètes*, xii. 36-38.

† Madame de Staël, *Du Caractère de M. Necker, et de sa Vie Privée. Œuvres complètes*, xvii. 40.

‡ *Correspondance entre Mirabeau et de la Marck*, i. 350. Letter of May, 1780.

§ *De l'Administration de M. Necker, par lui-même. Œuvres complètes*, vi. 183.

nation to secure its rights and of the nobles to secure their privileges, whilst their kings introduced absolute powers.*

The dreadful danger to which an order is exposed whilst occupying a prominent position, and the amount of jealousy it excites after all power has forsaken it, had not escaped Madame de Staël. She never doubted that the French nobility must sacrifice some privileges, but considered that this should be equalised by a revival of political power; to attain it she reckoned not on the lesser nobility, which had obtained its titles, patents, pensions, and tithes, by gold or servility, and thereby had lost its whole significance, but on the ancient historical races possessing the old vitality necessary to the patricians of a great nation, on the lines of the English aristocracy, independent of empty class prejudices and injurious prerogatives, and willingly opening its ranks to merit of every description.† The same sentiment which induced her to glorify resistance to the despotism of the throne in the seventeenth century, induced her to excuse what she would otherwise never have forgiven, and what she more than once forgot when Mirabeau was in question—the fact that she was speaking of her father's most energetic opponent.‡ There can be no doubt that if Madame de Staël had not been Necker's daughter she would have

* Madame de Staël, *Considérations. Œuvres complètes*, xii. 147-151.
† *Idem*, xii. 171, 190, 201.
‡ *Idem*.

associated herself with one who, more than any other, represented the genius of the Revolution, as it was understood by Madame de Staël in 1789. So long as Mirabeau lived her eyes remained upraised upon his Titan form, and her every nerve receptive for his electric words. She explained her admiring approval of her father's political attitude by the sophism that, as far as a statesman could, he desired the same thing as the aristocratic tribune of the people. And what did Necker really desire? In neither of the books he wrote during the long period of rest between his two administrations is there any information to be gained on this point. The book on financial administration showed an early admiration and preference for English institutions, without contributing anything new on the subject or adapting these institutions to French requirements.* The work on the importance of religious belief bore witness to the frightful social danger of an advance of irreligion, and received the Academy prize at the very time when its author was recalled to office.† But however honourable it may have been to the thinker and the Christian to have occupied himself with these questions at such a time, as a statesman he could not have done so had the question of reconstructing the monarchy entirely absorbed him. Only his later writings are taken up by the political system which, as minister, he ought to have carried out. His will-.

* Necker, *Œuvres complètes*, v. 598.
† *Idem.*

ingness to give up his former opposition to calling together the states did not originate from any alteration in his convictions. Later on he repeated that the commotion which led to the promise given by the Government to assemble the states, and the impatience with which the nation demanded the fulfilment of obligations, were the cause of all the subsequent troubles. " The deputies," he says, " met together without having had time to prepare themselves for such an important step." *   " Why should I conceal the fact that from first to last I was in favour of a government which resembled neither the *Etats Généraux* represented by the three orders, nor any other institution of the old monarchy." †   His favourite system of government was the constitutional, according to the English model, and supported by a strong, powerful, and influential aristocracy, without which even Necker thought a moderate monarchy impossible. A military aristocracy seemed dangerous to him, a financial aristocracy too liable to variations ; he desired to see an hereditary nobility and the country represented by two chambers, predicting that from the moment this did not succeed the demand for equality would exceed the conception of liberty.‡

Later events have entirely justified these anticipations. Unfortunately Necker did nothing to carry

* Necker, *De la Révolution Française*, 1796. *Œuvres complètes*, ix. 126, 128, 145.

† *Idem*, ix. 131.

‡ Necker, *Dernières vues de Politique et de Finance*, 1802. *Œuvres complètes*, xi. 240.

them out, although he indicates the moment when if
there had been an energetic king, before the assem-
bling of the States-General, the question might have
been decided in this sense.*

The king emphatically shared the antipathy felt
by his whole family for English institutions,† although
he did not carry it to such a pitch as his brother
the Comte d'Artois, who even after the restoration
declared that he would prefer to chop wood rather
than reign subject to the conditions of an English
monarchy. But there were other means such as the
Etats Généraux themselves, or Necker's own rein-
statement, to which Louis XVI. had assented much
against his will; certainly a minister who undertook
a bankrupt state had good right to bring forward
a programme and have an opinion. That he did
not so much as attempt this may be attributed
more to Necker's own disposition than to outward
circumstances. He himself says he was undecided
and prone to reflection.‡ Madame de Staël had the
same opinion of him, and says his character and tone
of mind led him to await events instead of precipi-
tating them by any decision of his own. Reflection
had the same power over him as passion had over
others; the working of his intellect, and his lively
imagination, sometimes placed him in a state of piti-

* Necker, *Dernières vues de Politique et de Finance,* 1802. *Œuvres
complètes,* xi. 132.

† Necker, *De la Révolution Française,* 1796, ix. 132.

‡ *De l'Administration de M. Necker, par lui-même. Œuvres complètes,* vi. 88.

able indecision. He often reproached himself bitterly
and unjustifiably on this account. Madame de Staël is
quite consistent when she adds that "only against his
own will, and when forced by circumstances, had
Necker lent a hand to any alteration in the political
organization of France." * Her description of his ✕
mode of operation is perfectly accurate. When he
took office he lost no opportunity of recalling the fact
that he had found the king and his advisers pledged to
fulfil the promises and the hopes they had awakened,†
but he also indicated the responsibility he had himself incurred, as it was now his duty not only to
consult the wish of the nation but to guard the king's
authority. The questions which pressed for discussion
concerned the total number of deputies to be elected
both in the whole assembly as well as in each of the
three orders ; the extent of the districts into which
the electors were to be divided, the mode and style
whereby the elections should be conducted, the right
and privilege of voting for dismissing that assembly,
in which according to ancient custom the electors
made known their wishes to the deputies.‡ On one
of these points Necker's personal views were quite
decided. He desired a double representation of the
Tiers, and, as Madame de Staël expresses it, he could

---

* Madame de Staël, *Considérations. Œuvres complètes*, xii. 66-67,
69-70. *Du Caractère de M. Necker. Œuvres complètes*, xvii. 89.

† Necker, *De la Révolution Française*, 1796. *Œuvres complètes*,
x. 58. Madame de Staël, *Du Caractère de M. Necker*, etc. xvii. 41.

‡ Leser, *Necker's Second Ministry*, 71. After the *Procès verbal
de l'assemblée des notables tenue a Versailles en l'année* 1788, 74-79.

not see "how the king was to avoid the imputation of injustice and the danger of unpopularity if he refused it."*

He had not so entirely made up his mind as to whether the right of election should (as Turgot desired) be decided by settled conditions of property and income. When he first left office he declared this to be absolutely necessary,† but in a later pamphlet he concluded that it was not possible to carry it out in France owing to the existing mode of taxation; that it would moreover exclude the poor clergy who possessed nothing, and many of the most capable members of the *Tiers*, who by the humiliating condition of paying the *Taille* were prevented from acquiring land.‡ Neither as minister did he bring French conditions more into accord with his political ideal of the English constitution, but he fell upon the unlucky expedient of calling together an assembly of notables a second time and left them to fix all the laws of election. Even Madame de Staël could not defend this step of her father's, and according to Thiers it was calculated to destroy all regard for the throne as far as the two 'first orders were concerned,§ an accusation which the Extreme Right

* Madame de Staël, *Du Caractère de M. Necker. Œuvres complètes*, xviii. 41.

† Necker, *Du pouvoir executif dans les grands Etats*, 1792. *Œuvres complètes*, viii. 578.

‡ Necker, *De la Révolution Française*, 1796. *Œuvres complètes*, ix. 87-89.

§ Madame de Staël, *Considérations. Œuvres complètes*, xii. 178. Thiers, *Histoire de la Révolution Française*, i. 17. Edition de Bruxelles, 1838.

has never ceased to bring against Necker. The accusation is not justified even by the fact that the calculation of the minister proved fallacious. The king, indeed, in giving his consent to summoning the notables, had stipulated that their councils should in no way be influenced. " This recommendation on the part of the monarch," says Necker, "seemed quite favourable to his interests." It gave time to study the progress of public opinion, and whilst the king's advisers let the notables set independently to work, they gave the king a chance of doing a little more than these latter would have done in favour of the *Tiers.** In other words, Necker wished to gain time and secure his popularity without alienating the two first orders who were essential to the foundation of the political structure he had in view.

Under these conditions the notables assembled together for the second time on the 6th Nov. 1788; and instead of Barentin, the keeper of the Seal, Necker, who had emphatically reserved this right to himself,† laid before them the result of the investigations instituted by the Government on the constitution of the States-General, and invited them to consider whether they would maintain the old traditions unaltered, or take the requirements of the situation into account in pursuance of the king's wish. They were to use discretionary authority on the whole

* Necker, *De la Révolution Française,* 1796. *Œuvres,* ix. 87.
† Leser, *Necker's Second Administration,* 63. Barentin, *Mémoire Autographes,* 48.

subject of the laws of election. The notables were as much pledged as Necker to the important question of double representation for the Third Estate, as they had already conceded it in the previous year to the provincial assemblies. Since that date the question had, however, been treated by numberless pamphlets and disquisitions of every kind, as an unqualified demand on the part of the *Tiers*, and as a weapon of attack against the two other orders. In the face of this growing danger, all the notables in their several bureaux (with the exception of that presided over by the Comte de Provence) declared against the double representation of the *Tiers*, and in this way denied their moral support to Necker as they had denied pecuniary assistance to Brienne. Thus their sittings came to an end on the 12th Dec. 1787. They had already been popularly and wittily designated as the "*Not-ables*" by the English.* Necker himself admits that he both expected, and was glad to have, the decision left in his own hands. He was indeed still very undecided, and, according to Malouet, he yielded reluctantly and only under the influence of the public opinion, which never failed to move him.† In the end he decided in the king's name on all that the notables had left unaccomplished. The double representation of the *Tiers* was now assured, but it did not occur to Necker that he thoroughly discredited

* Lord Auckland, *Journal and Correspondence*, i. 249.

† Malouet, *Mémoires*, i. 249. Necker, *De la Révolution Française. Œuvres*, ix. 97.

the two superior orders, which were already attacked from every quarter, when he called them together, consulted them, and then dismissed them, with the determination to do exactly the reverse of what they had counselled in their overwhelming majority. Meanwhile much time was lost, and the assembly of the States, promised for January, had again to be put off. Necker took the whole responsibility of deciding the conditions of voting, and of the numbers to represent the *Tiers*. His projects were first laid before the king, and then ratified by the ministerial council Dec. 27, 1788. Mercy tells us that Madame Necker assured him, " as the confidant of her husband's inmost thoughts," that he had decided on resigning should the king not yield ; for, in the event of the *Tiers* being sacrificed, he saw no further chance of avoiding civil war. Should his wishes be gratified it might be possible for him later on to assure the importance and splendour of the other two orders.[*] Later on Necker characteristically agreed that it would be inaccurate to call this arrangement a double representation, *un doublement du Tiers ;* he explained that noblemen and priests could be elected in the third order, whereas the unprivileged could represent no other order than their own ; added to this the number of votes in the States-General were not nearly so important to the Government as the number of followers

---

[*] Wertheimer, *Documents Inédits relatifs à Marie Antoinette. Revue Historique*, 1884, ii. 327. *Mercy au Kaunitz*, 6 Jan. 1789.

it possessed throughout the nation.* The parish priests had been the most trustworthy and faithful of its adherents, and Necker had distinguished them as the chosen representatives of the poor. With the consent of the notables he had called upon them as electors to join in the assembly of the clergy, and had expected their support.† But on this most weighty point in the history of the Revolution, Necker's expectations were again to be deceived. The parochial clergy, so long neglected and debarred from filling any responsible position, declined to lend its interest to the high dignitaries of the Church, who had hitherto been deaf to their prayers and representations. The one hundred and eighty-seven vicars who joined the *Tiers* on the 9th of June, 1789, turned the scale in its favour ; contrary therefore to Necker's anticipation the first two orders did not acquire adherents from the *Tiers*, but the latter attracted the opposition element to swell its ranks.‡ To this mistaken calculation was added another portentous mistake. In virtue of the decisions of the 27th Dec. Necker believed that he had granted all the conditions of constitutional freedom, § whilst in reality the most important

---

* Necker, *De la Révolution Française*, 1796. *Œuvres*, ix. 64, 97, and 99.

† *Idem*, ix. 97 and 162.

‡ Malouet, *Mémoires*, i. 279. Niebuhr, *Geschichte des Zeitalters der Révolution*, i. 170-171. Bernhardi, *Geschichte Russlands*, ii. 173. Taine, *Origines de la France Contemporaine. La Révolution*, i. 11. Chérest, *La chute de l'Ancien Régime*, ii. 255.

§ *De l'Administration de M. Necker, par lui-même*, 1791. *Œuvres complètes*, vi. 207.

questions were left to be decided by the States-
General. As Madame de Staël rightly observes, the
double representation of the third order should have
resulted in a division of the national representatives
into two Chambers, and all her father's later works
proved that he had this end in view when he instituted it.* The decision of the ministerial council,
on the 27th December, was only a first step
towards this. The *Tiers* could not remain satisfied
with the concession offered; if the votes were to be
taken by orders there could be no real concession,
for it would thus return to the old position of one
vote against two. If the *Tiers* were to obtain any
political mastery it must, as it did in fact later on,
establish voting by head. If, in fulfilment of Necker's
aspirations, the political balance were on the contrary to be established in a moderate monarchy, the
national representatives must necessarily sit in two
Chambers. This could only be accomplished were
the minister to succeed in finding supporters, prepared to carry the measure at the right moment.
There was no time to lose. The demand for representation in one single assembly daily acquired force,†
and there could remain no further doubt as to the
answer to be given by the great majority of the

* Madame de Staël, *Considérations. Œuvres complètes,* xii. 179.
Necker, *De la Révolution Française. Œuvres,* xi. 73. Malouet,
Mémoires, i. 279.

† Leser, *Necker's Second Administration,* 107, note. *Considérations
intéressantes sur les affaires présentes.* Août, 1788.

national representatives when the minister came to put the question before them. There was, moreover, no lack of men such as Necker required to carry out his ideas. Mallet du Pan, Malouet, the archbishop of Bordeaux, and the bishop of Langres, Mounier, the young Barnave, Lally de Tollendal, were among the most distinguished of Necker's adherents. However much their views might differ on weighty matters or might still remain undecided, they were all convinced that it was no longer possible to restore the old system, and that reform must be carried out by means of the monarchy. They would have formed Necker's party if he had at all recognised the necessity of governing with the support of party. The chagrin of finding that he was incapable of being their leader first turned such men as Rivarol and Mallet du Pan into his personal opponents. The year which he had allowed to slip by was drawing to a close when a last offer of this kind was made to him by the numerous followers of the Comte Mirabeau. The memorable letter written by the latter to Montmorin bears the date of Dec. 28, 1788, and contains the following sentences: "As a citizen, I tremble for the royal power, which never was more essential than it is at this moment, when it is approaching its ruin . . . . Has the ministry (which is hastening into a most serious position, by putting off the Estates-General, instead of preparing for them) · has it thought of a means of counteracting their power, or still more of gaining their support? Has

it a definitely determined line of action, which can
only be approved of by the nation? I hold that it
is to be found in a constitution that would save us
from the plots of the aristocracy, the encroachments
of the democracy, and from boundless anarchy.
Anarchy, into which authority has fallen in our land,
because it claimed to be unrestricted." *

The extraordinary strength felt by the writer in
itself explained his words, and guaranteed a hearing
for them. Mirabeau was then forty years old; all
France talked of his youthful irregularities; the
terrible quarrels with his father in early manhood,
with his wife, and with his sisters; his year's imprisonment in Vincennes, whence he returned to society
with undiminished energy, but in open hostility to
all the ties he had outraged.

Then followed the stay in England, the publication of political pamphlets, their condemnation by the
parlement, a first journey to Germany, the meeting
with the great Frederick. The year 1785 saw his
first connection with Calonne. The works on finance,
which terminated in 1787 with the attack on Necker
and Calonne, because the latter had not prevented
the condemnation of his political works by the parlement.† During that time the mission to Berlin
suggested by Talleyrand took place. It combined

---

* *Correspondance entre Mirabeau et de la Marck*, i. 340, 341.

† Mirabeau, *Essai sur le Despotisme*, 1776. *Considérations sur
l'ordre de Cincinnatus*, 1784. *Essai sur les lettres de cachet et les
prisons d'Etat*, 1782.

the purpose of sending Mirabeau away from Paris, and of watching King Frederick in his last moments; under those circumstances the work on the Prussian monarchy * was written, and the secret correspond· ence with Vergennes most unjustifiably published to relieve himself from pressing monetary embarrass· ment.†

From 1788 Mirabeau could not longer remain away from Paris. He felt that his hour had come. Although he was still an object of suspicion and curiosity to the public, an outcast from society, in politics an adventurer, he was part of that element which stirs up and constitutes revolution when nothing more can be gained from social order. As he first appeared, "great but tarnished in reputa- tion," Madame de Staël describes him as one who knew everything, and foresaw everything; calculated on his eloquence to obtain that foremost position of which his want of principle had deprived him; one who possessed a far reaching mind and restless energy; ready to force his way into the Parisian *salons* by setting a whole section of society on fire.

Before accomplishing this Herostratus-like‡ feat, Mirabeau sought rehabilitation.

His letter to Montmorin announced at what price

* Mirabeau, *De la Monarchie Prussienne*, 1788.

† Mirabeau, *Histoire secrète de la Cour de Berlin*, 1788, and Bacourt on the subject, *Correspondance entre Mirabeau et de la Marck*, i. 343-346.

‡ Translator's note : Herostratus set fire to the Temple of Diana at Ephesus in order to get his name talked about.

his writings previous to the Revolution favoured the principles of a moderate monarchy, and amidst the general disorder he alone kept them clearly in view.* Necker's friends in vain looked for a similar manifestation from him ; it came too late when four years afterwards he published his best work—called by Madame de Staël, his " Social Gospel." †

It would thwart the aims of democracy were it unable to prove that Mirabeau represented its doctrines : its historians therefore make light of Montesquieu's influence upon him, and emphasise that of Rousseau ; they cast doubts upon his preference for English institutions ; and as he never deviated from his outspoken monarchical sympathies, they endeavour to describe a *démocratie royale* as his principal object. This assertion is based upon Mirabeau's hatred for the nobility of the *ancien régime*, with whom a personal reconciliation was no longer possible. He soon saw that it could never as an order adapt itself to a constitutional monarchy. But the testimony of all Mirabeau's most intimate contemporaries, and his own calmer statements, refute this, as well as his plans and his mode of conduct in the latter days of his life. According to Dumont he wished for a constitution similar to the English, but adapted to French requirements. When, on the contrary, the *Tiers* constituted itself a national assembly he

* Lanfrey, *Essai sur la Révolution Française*, 126.

† Madame de Staël, *Considérations. Œuvres*, xiii. 18. Necker, *Du pouvoir exécutif dans les Grands États. Œuvres*, viii.

indicated this step as the cause of every subsequent
disaster, and spoke the well-known words, "They
wanted to rule the king instead of ruling through
him." *   De la Marck emphatically points to his
exclusion by the Provençal nobility as the turning
point explaining his subsequent action, " for," he
adds, " his disposition and principles showed him to
be an aristocrat, an admirer of the existing state of
things in England, where a powerful, wise, and
moderate aristocracy is a link between the monarchy
and the people, and combines all the important
elements to be found in either." †

Madame de Staël held the same opinion of him.
" He was too superior not to be aware of the impossibility of a democracy for France. But even had
such been possible he would have had no taste for
it." ‡

"Aristocrat by inclination; tribune by calculation," Necker says of him.

In one of the first and most uncompromising of his
writings, Mirabeau would not even allow that the
burdens of feudalism should be removed without
equivalent compensation. He had no notion of
giving in to the general outcry. He required the
guarantees afforded by property in return for any

* Dumont, *Souvenirs sur Mirabeau*, 218, 219, and 268. Mirabeau,
Lettres à Mauvillon, 468.

† *Correspondance entre Mirabeau et le Comte de la Marck*, i. 109,
110. Malouet, *Mémoires*, ii. 13.

‡ Madame de Staël, *Considérations. Œuvres complètes*, xii. 262, 263.

participation in public affairs,* and rejected the appeal to the people " which would reduce the law-givers to slaves," as well as Rousseau's idea that the people should rule for themselves. On the other hand, Mirabeau held fast to Montesquieu's notion of the division of power, and sacrificed the system of the two Chambers only when the *Tiers* became the sole alternative to no government at all.† Thiers owns that Mirabeau did not act from conviction in this matter, but on compulsion, ‡ and Henri Martin reproaches him for the indecision he showed in this change of front. §

These views lay at the root of Mirabeau's plans at the beginning of 1789; Necker coincided with them all, but could not reconcile himself to their originator. He had always held that it was, if possi-ble, more important to follow the moral laws in public than in private life.|| Faith in the triumph of reason and justice, and purity of intention, were worth more to him than cleverness or foresight.¶

" Morality is essential in all things," he used to say.

---

* Mirabeau, *Essai sur le Despotisme. Essai sur les lettres de cachet et les prisons d'État*, 1782. Henri Martin, *Histoire de France*, xvi. 535, &c.

† Decrue, *Les Idées Politiques de Mirabeau. Revue Historique*, Mai, Juin, 1883, 43, 337, 383.

‡ Thiers, *Histoire de la Révolution*, i. 189.

§ Henri Martin, *Histoire de France depuis* 1789, i. 49.

|| Madame de Staël, *Considérations. Œuvres complètes*, xii. 72.

¶ Necker, *Discours à l'ouverture de l'Assemblée des Notables. Œuvres complètes*, vi. 429.

It suited both his upright character and his vanity to uphold it as a statesman ; this in itself made reconcilia- tion impossible with the man bearing the worst repu- tation in the kingdom, even had Necker ignored his personal attacks. Mirabeau himself complained that his early irregularities were remembered against him, but he need not, and ought not, on this account to have been allowed to become an opponent. His ambition and above all his monetary embarrassments presented means for securing him. Necker did not seize the advantage. As already remarked, he was a keen observer of human weakness and perversity but he did not possess that sympathy which lies at the root of all true knowledge of human nature. Indi- viduals are hardly ever mentioned in his numerous writings with the exception of Montmorin, whom he calls his friend ; the chief participators in the Revolu- tion are almost unnoticed by him ; a passing allusion to Mirabeau, Danton, or Robespierre barely recalls the epoch in which he lived. Thus he missed the first chance of coming to an understanding with Mirabeau. Montmorin, who seriously entertained the idea of waylaying Mirabeau on his road to Provence and deporting him, wrote him an offensive letter threaten- ing to prosecute the man who had published the *Secret History of the Court of Berlin*. This letter found the "Hercules of the Revolution," as Goethe calls him, fighting for election in Provence, on which occasion he proved himself to be the greatest orator in France, and was chosen as the leader of the *Tiers* as a constitutional monarchist. On the 24th of January Necker issued the regulations for election to the States-General, which at first were to meet on the 27th of April, but eventually were postponed to the 5th of May. It was useless to persuade the Government to influence the elections. Louis XVI. had forbidden his ministers to interfere with the counsels of the notables; Necker also considered it to be immoral to do so, and subsequently viewed the attempt to gain over a party in the National Assembly in the same light.

Whilst nought but the constitution was talked of, the king and Necker alone acted constitutionally. Thus it came to pass for the first and last time that the entire nation—the women, including abbesses,* as well as the men belonging to the privileged orders, representing property—had full liberty to elect their deputies during three months, and in hundreds of assemblies, and further to compile the far-famed *Cahiers*, in which it was formerly the custom to collect all the grievances and wishes of the electors of each order for their representatives.

In most of the important points, such as the cessation of all despotism, division of power in legislation between the king and the nation, ministerial responsibility, regular assemblage of the States-General, and the provincial assemblies and reform of judicial pro-

* Laboulaye, *Cours de Législation comparée. L'Assemblée constituante. Revue des Cours Littéraire*, vi. Année 1868-1869, 322.

cedure,* there was no special difference to be found
between the wishes of the various orders—none that
would have prevented their coming to an understanding if the establishment of liberty had really been the
general aim.†   But the *Tiers* wanted not merely
political but social equality, and the peasants who
coveted the land were not to be satisfied by any of
the above concessions.

The Government had ample warning of what
might be expected if it did not come between the
parties as mediator, and with a settled programme.
In three provinces—Provence, Franche Comté, and
Brittany—the various orders came to open violence.
Mirabeau helped to restore order in Marseilles and
Aix, for, as Necker put it, "the Government feared
to employ force without due consideration." ‡

Franche Comté led the way in attacking the châteaux,
and the nobles of Brittany hesitated to choose deputies
from their midst.   During the four months preceding
the taking of the Bastille three hundred risings took
place in France.   The first broke out in Paris on the
28th of April, when the populace, suspecting a reduction
of wages, set fire to Reveillon's paper-factory, and in
all probability was bribed by the Duke of Orleans

---

* Larcy, *Louis XVI. et les États Généraux. Correspondance*, 1868,
505.

† Dareste, *Histoire de France*, vii. 149.   Henri Martin, *Histoire de
France*, xvi. 648, 649.

‡ *De l'Administration de M. Necker, par lui-même. Œuvres complètes*, vi. 183.

to do the deed.* The gardens of his Palais Royal had become a club, where seditious speeches daily inflamed the people, and where owing to an ancient prerogative the police might not enter. Even in February Necker acknowledged that obedience could no longer be reckoned on, and that he was by no means sure of the troops. He repeated this to the king a fortnight before the opening of the States-General, and his fears that the king might be mistaken as to the disposition of the army.† Madame de Staël must have forgotten this when in one of the most erroneous statements contained in her *Considérations* she asserts that confidence in the Government was so strong that notwithstanding the prevailing distress there were no disturbances in France during the winter of 1788-1789. One of her letters, dated Jan. 21, 1789, expresses the hope that, notwithstanding the divisions among the existing forces, constitutional reform may be accomplished. "France," she writes to her Swedish correspondent—personally unknown to her, "is on the brink of presenting a tremendous spectacle to Europe. This in itself should awaken ambition, but I tremble for the steersman surrounded by such rocks." ‡

The place of meeting for the States-General was

* Taine, *Origines de la France Contemporaine. La Révolution*, i. 13, 17, 18, 40. Jefferson, *Complete Works. Autobiography*, i. 100.

† Malouet, *Mémoires*, i. 287.

‡ Unpublished Letters, Madame de Staël, in the Library at Upsala. *Madame de Staël to Nils von Rosenstein.* Paris, Jan. 21, 1789.

still to be decided. It has often been brought up against Necker that in his subsequent writings he never acknowledged himself to have been in the wrong in any of his public transactions; he made one exception however.* "A mistake," he writes, in 1791, "was never known. It lay in my advice to the king that he should assemble the States-General in Paris, and not at Versailles; my proposal was set aside by his majesty himself on very sufficient grounds." The monarch feared the Palais Royal and the uproar in the streets, whilst the minister feared the cabals at Versailles more than the ascendancy of the capital, which, according to Madame de Staël, he hoped to counteract by the provincial assemblies.† In this way Louis XVI. made room for the deputies under his own roof; the meeting-place for the *Tiers* was however left to the last moment; and this led to the allotment of a hall called the Salle des Etats, surrounded by galleries. Malouet relates that when the populace took advantage of these galleries Necker conceived the notion of pulling down the building in one night, under pretext that it was unsafe.‡ The walls stand to this day; it was the monarchy of Louis XVI. that fell.

---

* *De l'Administration de M. Necker, par lui-même. Œuvres complètes*, vi. 88.

† Madame de Staël, *Considérations. Œuvres complètes*, xii. 88.

‡ Malouet, *Mémoires*, i. 295.

CHAPTER VI.

The États Généraux—Mirabeau and Necker—The king begs Necker to remain in office—The Estates unite—Gouverneur Morris—Thomas Jefferson—The Court against Necker—The king dismisses Necker, July 11, 1789—Impression created in Paris—14th July—Necker returns to Paris—Letter from Madame de Staël to Gustavus III.—La Fayette and the National Guard—Talleyrand—The Rights of Man—The Veto—Mounier—Plans of flight for the Royal Family—Banquet of the Gardes du Corps at Versailles—October days.

"Those who imagine the French Revolution to have been a chance occurrence can have taken neither the past nor the future into consideration. They have confused the players and play, and ascribed the work of centuries to the passion of men of the moment." * With these words Madame de Staël begins her memorial of the Revolution.

Madame de Staël was at the same window with Madame de Montmorin, wife of the Minister for Foreign Affairs, to see the procession of deputies on the 4th of May, the day previous to the opening of the *Etats Généraux*. A solemn service was to be held, and half Paris had streamed out to Versailles.

* Madame de Staël, *Considérations. Œuvres complètes*, xii. 1.

"I gave myself up to the most sanguine anticipations," she writes, "when for the first time in France I beheld the representatives of the nation. Madame de Montmorin, who was by no means specially clever, made a considerable impression upon me by emphatically remarking that I had no reason to rejoice: 'All this will bring great catastrophes both to France and to us.'"

Madame de Staël further adds; "This unfortunate woman died on the scaffold, with one of her sons. The other was drowned. Her husband was massacred on the 2nd of September. Her eldest daughter died in a prison hospital; her younger daughter, a clever, noble creature, sank beneath the weight of her grief before completing her thirtieth year. The story of Niobe was not more tragic than that of this unfortunate mother." *

In the ranks of the nobles she saw "brilliant nullities"; amidst the high dignitaries of the prelacy many of notorious reputation. These were separated from the numberless parish priests by a band of music. Then came the *Tiers*, advocates, notaries, a few doctors, thirty-eight small proprietors, about sixty tradesmen, and amongst five hundred and seventy-seven deputies perhaps ten men who had held high offices in the State.†

Madame de Staël could not take her eyes off Mira-

---

* Madame de Staël, *Considérations*, xii. 194.

† Taine, *Origines de la France contemporaine. La Révolution*, i. 155.

beau's broad shoulders and shaggy head of curly hair. He, as it were, fascinated her gaze.

On the following day, the 5th of May, she was in her place in the tribune for the opening ceremony.

Another eye-witness, Grimm, describes it even more minutely than she does. A platform for the king, princes, and high officials, was arranged at the end of the provisionally erected chamber, which was supported by Ionic columns, draped like a tent, with white silk to shade the skylight, and adorned with exquisite carpets. The throne stood beneath a splendid canopy; on its left was an armchair for the queen, and chairs beyond for the princesses; those of the princes were to the right.

The Keeper of the Seal, and the Lord High Controller of the Household, took their places at the foot of the throne, and, further down, the Secretaries of State at a long table, covered with a purple velvet cloth embroidered with golden lilies; right and left were councillors of state, *maîtres de requêtes,* the provincial governors, and military commanders. The whole of the right side was filled by the deputies of the clergy, the cardinals, and episcopacy in full canonicals. Opposite them sat the nobles in black cloak and tunic embroidered with gold, turned-up hat, lace cravat, and white stockings.

In the middle sat the *Tiers,* facing the throne, in the black costume so often depicted in pictures and in books, with the short mantle and three-cornered hat without any distinguishing ornament.

The ambassadors and onlookers, numbering, perhaps, two thousand—chiefly ladies in the first row—
occupied boxes separated by the pillars.

Amongst the ministers Necker alone appeared in
the simple garb of a citizen, "*pluie d'or, sur fond
canelle,*" richly embroidered, in place of the aristocratic dress and accompanying sword, or the official
attire of the members of parlement.   Loud cheers
greeted his entry, and were renewed for the Duke of
Orleans when he alone of the princes of the blood
appeared as a representative of the *Tiers* for Crepy
in Valois, and gave precedence to a parish priest, his
colleague.

The deputies for Dauphiné received a certain
amount of recognition from the fact that their action
had led to the assemblage of the States, but the attempt
to cheer the deputy for Provence was received with
groans and hisses.   The Comte Mirabeau was the
first to comprehend that these were directed against
himself.   Heralds in splendid attire, and the royal
guards, were meanwhile distributed about the chamber
to keep order.

Two hours later, about eleven o'clock, the king
entered.   He was surrounded by his entire household
and the high officials of the crown, and wore a long
mantle and a hat adorned with plumes and splendid
diamonds, but it could not fail to be remarked that he
wore none of the insignia of royalty.*   The whole

---

* Droz, *Histoire de Louis XVI.* ii. 174.

assemblage rose to receive him, with enthusiastic cheers.

Some time elapsed before the queen made her appearance. She had been received with icy silence on the previous day, and her features now betrayed signs of unusual emotion.

For the first time Madame de Staël felt anxious and uneasy. She felt that the weight of the situation might be read in the expression of the deputies, and wondered within herself "what would be the end of an assembly which had nothing to do but to talk."

The king read his speech, greeting his estates with much dignity. It expressed the most fatherly feelings, and hopes that better times might be in store, but contained nothing of any political importance. The king was nevertheless twice interrupted by cheers. It was expected that his councillors' speeches would contain what his own had omitted.

Barentin, the Keeper of the Seal, took up the word after him, but said even less. He touched but slightly on the great question of the manner in which the elections should be conducted, and only mentioned that the States-General would decide on the subject, with the consent of his majesty. He then returned to commonplaces, as to the necessity of peace and harmony, and the blessing of sweeping reforms.

Next followed Necker with a three hours' speech. At the end of the first half hour, Broussonet, who represented the farming interest, continued to read for the minister, but the latter finished his own speech, that the bad impression might be removed which it seemed to create.* It was principally financial, and as such reiterated the tactics of the compte rendu. It contained nothing that was false, but by ignoring various important points it gave a false impression of the situation. The yearly deficit, reduced since the days of Brienne by about fifteen millions, was given at fifty-six millions, but the alarming fact that the floating debt amounted to five hundred and fifty-one and a half millions was left in the back-ground,† whilst the steps towards balancing the yearly budget were entered into so minutely that the advisability of selling the Government tobacco as snuff was even discussed.‡

The style of handling the subject was moreover intentional. Necker not only firmly believed that the monetary difficulties of the State might be got over by quiet, order, and wise economy; he desired beyond everything to avoid every acknowledgment of an embarrassment which could lower the king's dignity in the eyes of the national representatives.

After endless phrases, the minister at length reached the principal point—the great constitutional question, whether votes were to be taken by head or by order. Without doubt the king had the right to

---

* Chérest, La chute de l'Ancien Régime, iii. 22.

† Sybel, Geschichte der Revolutionszeit, i. 45, 46.   Leser, Necker's Zweite Ministerium, 123.

‡ Droz, Histoire de Louis XVI. ii. 176, note.

decide. It would have been useless jealously to guard his position with reference to the financial question if his authority were to be of no weight in the constitution of the States, which had been reminded very shortly before that they had to thank the king alone for a renewal of their existence. Next, amidst breathless silence, came the mere expression of a wish on the part of the Government, instead of the expected decision. Necker proposed that the States should at first take counsel separately, that the nobility and clergy might of their own free will accomplish the sacrifice of their pecuniary privileges, upon which each order might appoint special commissioners to decide on the questions to be discussed separately or collectively. He had something to say in favour of either mode of voting, and ended by inviting the assembly to assist the sovereign with wise counsel, to initiate the welfare of the State, and not to be outdone by the beneficent tendency of the age.*

The minister's personal sympathies were to a certain extent betrayed in the remark that it would be easier for the monarch to impress his influence on one assembly than to make it felt if there were two Chambers. Necker did not venture more emphatically to recommend his favourite system of govern-

* Lord Auckland, *Correspondence*, i. 320. The correspondent is Huber, a relation of the Necker family. Madame de Staël, xii. 196, 197. Léouzon Le Duc, *Correspondance du Baron de Staël-Holstein*, 99, 100. Dépêche No. 113 of the 10th May, 1789.

ment.* When late in the afternoon the sitting and
its solemnity came to an end, the king rose and left
the assembly, amidst enthusiastic cheers.

Whilst the queen prepares to follow him, " a voice
imbued by the milk of human kindness originates a
faint *vive la reine;* she makes a deep curtsey, and earns
an ovation." † A joyous multitude then accompanied
the court back to the royal palace. Necker was again
cheered.

The very next day the crisis was reached with the
formal question of verifying the votes.

The nobles did not hesitate to verify their mandates. The clergy seemed ready to do the same;
when the *Tiers* demanded that the verification should
be carried out by all the three orders, and referred
to the precedent of 1483, whereas the nobles took up
their position from the opposite mode of proceeding
in 1614.

On the suggestion of the clergy, commissioners
were appointed to negotiate between the orders, but
no understanding was achieved. Whilst the opposition of the nobles was considered as punishable
defiance, the peace-loving moderation of the clergy
was quite as severely criticised. Lally Tollendal
accused them of waiting to give their adhesion to the
victorious side.

---

* Necker, *Discours à l'Ouverture des États Généraux. Œuvres
complètes,* vi. 611.

† Jared Sparks, *Life of Gouverneur Morris, with selections from his
Correspondence,* i. 304, 308.

At the end of May, shortly before these events took place, Mirabeau attempted for the second time to come to an understanding with Necker. Undeterred by hatred and enmity, only too ready to attain leadership at the price of revolution, although not entirely as the instrument of democracy, Mirabeau had on the 18th of May frustrated Sièyes' first indirect attempt, inspired by his friend Chapelier, to unite the two first orders to the *Tiers*, and in event of failure to constitute the *Tiers* a national assembly. Mirabeau himself wished to unite the orders, but not to give the *Tiers* the sole mastery.

The more he got to know and to despise the elements around him the more he disapproved of the conduct of the Government.

" Did Necker but possess a shadow of talent," he wrote in May, " he would have secured taxes returning sixty millions, a loan of one hundred and fifty millions, and would have sent us all home on the ninth day. With a particle of character he would be unassailable, he would side with us who would fight his battles, would rule the court, as Richelieu did, and we should be born again."*

Mirabeau did what Necker left undone. He became a journalist, attacked the ministry, saw his first paper suppressed,† organized a second paper for

---

* *Correspondance entre Mirabeau et de la Marck*, i. 350.

† Mirabeau's *Les États Généraux*, which only appeared for a short time.

himself, and with it a party throughout the land,[*] took possession of the tribunes; earned first a hearing, and then applause, and on the 27th of May had nearly gained his point, with the help of the clergy, when the king interposed on the 28th with a compromise. In a special despatch to the orders he invited them to verify their powers singly, and then to exchange the results, and in cases of doubt to refer to ministerial decision. When the king's message was to be read to the *Tiers*, Malouet demanded that the galleries should be cleared, and was accused of cowardly perfidy by no other than Volney. " The deputies," he said, only too prophetically, "must deliberate in the presence of their masters." [†]

From these galleries, in the principal clubs of the capital, especially in the Breton club (to become the Jacobin club later on), and in the *cafés* of the Palais Royal, people were already making experiments in the art of governing, and were now unwilling to be disturbed in their occupation. The king's invitation was answered with reservations on the part of the nobles, which made it possible for the *Tiers* to decline it, on their part.

The clergy announced themselves undecided, but the majority were well known to have favoured the interests of the *Tiers*. On the 9th of June the renewed discussions again came to nothing, and the

---

* Mirabeau, *Lettres à ses Commettants.*
† Droz, *Histoire de Louis XVI.* ii. 191, 192.

next day Sièyes proposed that the two other orders should be invited to join the *Tiers*, and thus to "cut the only cable which held the ship to the shore." He had not long to fear that the king would succeed in obtaining peace. Victory was secured to the third estate by the alliance of the parish priests amongst the clerical deputies, and that of the liberal minority among the nobles. If a higher power did not consent willingly it would be compelled to do so.

In the tension of the moment the statesman got the upper hand in Mirabeau. He alone amongst all his colleagues asked himself what was to happen after victory, and whether it were advisable to leave an order which had already been proved, for another which apparently meant to start with usurpation. This perplexity brought about his second attempt at a fusion with Necker. The loyal, thoughtful attitude of Malouet had so impressed him in the *Tiers* that he allowed his Genevese friend Duroveray to arrange an interview with him, to which Malouet rather un-willingly assented. He met the deputy for Aix at the house of a third party, and with some surprise heard him declare that he shared his opinions. Never, Mirabeau declared, would he sell himself to despotism; what he really desired was a free constitutional monarchy. The monarchy was not to be disturbed. Amongst his colleagues, dangerous and seditious in-dividuals were to be found. Those amongst the aris-tocracy who had any intellect had no common sense. It was of small importance whether sympathy or liking existed between himself and the ministers. It was much more important to know whether they had any plan to recommend. "If such exist and it repose on a reasonable basis," ended Mirabeau, "I engage to support it with all the influence I possess, and to lend my whole strength to check the democratic invasion with which we are threatened." Malouet, whose long cherished wishes were thus realised in another, hastened in highest spirits to communicate with the ministry, and to effect the meeting desired by Mirabeau. He had a long interview with Montmorin and Necker, but could not impress upon them the importance of Mirabeau's co-operation. "They hated Mirabeau and did not as yet fear him." Necker said nothing, and gazed at the ceiling, a proceeding which always betokened extreme indecision on his part. He showed himself, however, more accessible than Montmorin, and an evening was fixed for the meeting with Mirabeau.

Unfortunately, Mirabeau arrived without Malouet, and had to meet the stiff, reserved man by himself. Necker adopted the coldest tone, and said: "M. Malouet tells me, sir, that you have propositions to make to me. Of what nature are they?" Mirabeau recoiled at this reception, measured the man who could thus address him with a contemptuous glance, and replied, "My proposition is that I wish you good day," and so departed. He found Malouet in the hall appropriated to the *Tiers*, climbed over several benches to reach him, and said to him wrathfully:

" *Votre homme est un sot, il aura de mes nouvelles.*"*
It was at the same period that he uttered the historical words to de la Marck: "The Government
ship is lashed by the storm, and no one is at the
helm. " †

Necker always remained in his opinion "the watch
that was always slow." They met for the future as
opponents in the National Assembly.

Madame de Staël defends her father from the reproach of failing to secure Mirabeau at the critical
moment by saying that he was not the right man for
such work; others would have done it better; and
further, that Mirabeau would never have been satisfied till he had become a leader of the people.‡

She may excuse the mistake, which was one of the
greatest perpetrated during the Revolution, but she
would never have committed it herself.

What followed is well known. On the 12th of June
began the verifying of the powers by the *balliages* in
the *Tiers;* on the 13th the three first parish priests
appeared in its midst, and were received with cheers.
Seven or eight others followed next day, upon which
the assembly announced itself constituted, and on the
15th Sièyes declared it to represent the nation's will.
On that day Mirabeau spoke thrice.   He demanded

---

* Malouet, *Mémoires*, i. 311, and ii. 471.   Mallet du Pan, *Mercure
Britannique*, 2 Janvier, 1800.   Dumont, *Souvenirs sur Mirabeau*, 56.
Chérest, *La chute de l'Ancien Régime*, iii. 76.

† Sainte-Beuve, *Camille Desmoulins.   Causeries de Lundi,* iv. 97.

‡ Madame de Staël, *Considérations*, xii. 262.

the king's sanction as a necessary condition, without which he could not recognise the resolutions of his colleagues as valid, and thundered out that he would rather live in Constantinople than in France if the sanction were not obtained. For nothing appeared more dreadful to him than a sovereign aristocracy of six hundred persons, who could to-day announce themselves to be permanent and to-morrow hereditary, and thus end like every aristocratic government by assuming uncontrolled mastery. A vision of the convention floated through his mind, and an excited opposition hurled the accusation against him of having sold himself to the crown. *

But Mirabeau's warnings were in vain. On the 17th June, incited by Sièyes, the *Tiers* declared by four hundred and ninety-one votes against ninety in favour of a national assembly. It accomplished its first act of sovereignty by declaring that all taxes raised without consent of the representatives of the nation were invalid, but added that they should continue to be paid provisionally until the assembly was prorogued, and guaranteed the rights of the state creditors.

Mirabeau did not approve of that day's work: in the midst of his colleagues, triumphant, rejoicing, he uttered the sombre prophecy that the first step towards civil war had been taken. Even Malouet

---

* Mirabeau, *Lettres au Major Maurillon,* 467, 17 June, 1789, and *Onzième Lettre à mes Commettants,* 222, 235. Laboulaye, *Cours de Législation comparée. L'Assemblée constituante.*

owned that the *Tiers* had overstepped its powers.[*]
"The decree," says Madame de Staël, "was in itself
the Revolution."

At last, when the decision had been taken, Necker
made up his mind to interfere. Incessantly, but
vainly, had he hitherto tried to persuade the king to
introduce a constitution on the English pattern. As
far back as the middle of May he had drawn attention to the alarming news from the provinces, and
expressed his fear that under certain circumstances
it might not be possible to rely upon the army. The
real situation was not as yet realised. The king might
employ the time to guarantee that which to-morrow
he might be forced to concede. "Never," added
Necker, with true insight into Louis XVI.th's character, "would laws be a greater restraint upon him
than the promptings of his own conscience." [†]

The only mistake the minister committed on this
occasion was that he did not speak out sufficiently.

Not only were the majority of the officers forced
into the opposition by the laws of 1781, which
debarred all the lesser nobility from filling the higher
ranks in the army, but the troops were themselves
disorganised and undisciplined. This was chiefly
attributable to an attempt made to introduce the
Prussian system, set on foot by a committee organised by Brienne, and presided over by Comte Guibert,
a great admirer of Frederick the Great.

---

[*] Malouet, *Mémoires*, i. 319.
[†] Madame de Staël, *Considérations*, xii. 218, 219

Corporal punishment was introduced, and the rule that only officers holding the rank of colonel could serve on the staff. Deprived in this way of the last chance of filling the higher ranks, the middle classes, the smaller nobility (and the soldiery for other reasons), were so incensed, that suicide, mutiny, and desertion increased daily, and two camps of exercise at St. Omer and Metz had in 1788 suddenly to be discontinued.

Internal affairs were equally unsatisfactory. Tocqueville had already set forth how and why the cumbrous, irregular machinery of French policy had come to a standstill, as its leaders could no longer control it. Years before the Revolution, each new attempt at reform had only made things worse, and the authorities had fallen into such discredit that they could no longer command obedience or enforce the new institutions.

When the Revolution subsequently broke out, it was a singular fact that tradespeople and merchants, proprietors and financiers, all turned against the existing state of matters, and the latter in particular are supposed to have promised their pecuniary support, if necessary, to encourage insurrection. *

This was not often necessary, for in every quarter of France during the summer and autumn of 1788, in Burgundy, Provence, Normandy, Languedoc, raged sedition and revolt, under pretext of restoring ancient

---

* Tocqueville, *L'Ancien Régime*, 286. Rivarol, *Mémoires*, 185, 186. Chérest, *La chute de l'Ancien Régime*, ii. 100, 101.

provincial rights and institutions, and Necker had to smooth things over and give in to every faction, if only to secure the loans without which it was impossible to carry on the government.   That he was still able to prolong his financial administration was considered even by Mirabeau to be " nothing short of a miracle." *

If Necker turned from the hopeless condition of the country to the individuals sent to represent the States, he, in common with many others, could have no great opinion of the political insight and capacity of an assembly which included the Cardinal de Rohan, chosen by the clergy belonging to the *bailliages* of Hagenau and Weissenburg, or Pêtion, and Brissot, the candidates brought forward by Lubersac, bishop of Chartres.† Shortly after the first days of intercourse with the deputies, Necker gave his undisguised opinion that it would be much more practical to allow the first man available amongst his followers, who possessed a stentorian voice, to read aloud the text of the British constitution from the tribune than to allow so many political visionaries and entire novices to speak on Government affairs without aim or object.‡

This text was looked for in vain, both then and later.

The king was to be brought to no decision, and the

---

* Chérest, *La chute de l'Ancien Régime,* ii. 136-140

† *Idem,* ii. 566, 575.

‡ Necker, *De la Révolution Française,* ix. 299.

representatives of the French nation in their immense majority regarded the mere suggestion of a constitution, after the pattern of their English neighbours, as an unbearable humiliation.[*]

The weeks uselessly squandered by the court and states helped on the revolt in the provinces. Proofs multiplied to justify Fréteau, the parlementeer, in begging his colleagues, as far back as the beginning of May, to occupy themselves less with political doctrine, seeing that war between the poor and the rich was declared.[†] From the days of Fénélon and Vauban down to those of Turgot and the Economists, the agrarian question had in vain claimed solution at the hands of the monarchy.

This subject, now so prominent, is thus noticed by Madame de Staël: "The younger generations and strangers, who knew France before the Revolution, and who now see the people enriched by division of the landed property and the suppression of the feudal dues, can form no idea of what this country was when still oppressed by all the former privileges.

"The partisans of slavery in the colonies have often said that a French peasant was more wretched than a negro. This argument was used for the consolation of the whites, and not intended to harden us against the blacks."[‡]

Now that most of these privileges were either

---

[*] Necker, *Du pouvoir exécutif dans les grands États*, viii. 42.
[†] Laboulaye, *Revue des Cours Littéraires*. May, 1869, 379.
[‡] Madame de Staël, *Considérations*, xii. 86, 87.

abolished, or else on the point of being so, the peasants engraved their interpretation of liberty, in letters of flame, by reducing country-seats to ashes and destroying archives. In the Palais Royal, in the centre of the town, Camille Desmoulins encouraged all the brutal instincts of the masses with prospects of plunder. "Forty thousand palaces, castles, and country-places, two-fifths of the possessions of France, were to be the reward of bravery; the nation must be cleansed," preached Robespierre's schoolfellow, the author of the ode :—

> "Necker descend de la montagne,
>   La raison seule l'accompagne,
>   En lui le peuple espère encore. . . ." *

Necker dared not admit that not only the third order, the commons in Versailles, but the fourth order, the peasants, had already risen in open rebellion against the Government.

The opposition to the Court, among the nobility and clergy, only awaited a similar sign to bring about a reaction, to which Necker himself would be the first to fall a sacrifice.

The excitement reached such a pitch that the Marquis de Montesquieu could scarcely obtain a hearing, when he, along with La Luzerne, bishop of Langres, proposed to meet the resolve of the *Tiers* with a plan to organise a higher chamber taken from the nobility

---

* Sainte-Beuve, *Camille Desmoulins. Causeries de Lundi*, iii. 80.

and clergy,* and L'Espremenil loudly observed that
if the procurator-general did his duty he would prosecute the members of the *Tiers* for high treason.

But Necker might still hope to persuade the king
to uphold his policy, just because it took a middle
course between the extreme parties.   He hoped to
prevent the return to the former state of things his
opponents wished to achieve by overthrowing the
Tiers, and to avert the destruction of every species
of government by means of an unconditional recognition of the declaration of the 17th of June.

This coincided with his proposal that the king
should now use his prerogative to summon the Estates
to meet together as the *Tiers* had just done in defiance
of it.

The clergy and nobility were only to deliberate
separately upon their own special business; the constitution to be drawn up by the Estates was to repose
on the system of two chambers, a strong executive
was to be assured to the king, beyond everything the
command of armed power; all the decrees of the
assembly to enforce the law were to require his sanction, and the public was for the future to be excluded
from the deliberations.†   The king on the other hand
promised to abolish all the existing privileges of taxa-

---

* Madame de Staël, *Considérations*, xii. 198.

† Bertrand de Molleville, *Mémoires*, Appendix. Barentin, *Mémoire
Autographe*, 182, 183.   Necker, *De la Révolution Française*, ix. 182,
196. Necker burnt the original project, with many other papers, when
Coppet was threatened by the Revolution.

tion, to recognise the right of the Estates to have a voice in the taxation and their share in making the laws; beyond all things, civil and criminal law was to be reformed and freedom to be secured both to individuals and to the press. The king was to declare his royal will in solemn assemblage, and Necker indentified his policy in the most emphatic words with these proposals. He says, " My resolution was born of the conviction that my plan would be supported by the great majority of the nation. To declare war against this majority and make light of public opinion, another than I must have been found." *
The court was at Marly, in deepest mourning for the little dauphin who had just died, aged seven years, when Necker tried to persuade the monarch on the 19th of June, two days after the *Tiers* had been constituted, to summon a cabinet council at that place. At first the king appeared willing to fall in with his projects, but on the following day, when the whole extent of the concessions to the *Tiers* began to be realised, grave doubts arose : so that only three ministers remained on Necker's side, Montmorin, St. Priest, and La Luzerne. During the sitting when a definitive resolution was to be taken, both Necker and St. Priest relate that the king was suddenly sent for by the queen, and when he returned he put off the matter till the following day, the 21st of June, upon which for the first time the king's brothers joined the

* Necker, *De la Révolution Française*, ix. 217.

Council of State. Louis, Comte de Provence, spoke
moderately, but left the great question of the fusion
of the Estates undecided. Charles, Comte d'Artois,
was in favour of their continuing to sit separately, but
allowed that the pecuniary privileges and the burdens
on the people should be abolished. The ministers
Barentin, de Puységur, and Villedeuil, along with
four other councillors of state, were of the same
opinion.* The king then announced that he was of
the same mind as this majority, and on the following
day, the fourth of their deliberations, allowed the new
plan to be registered.

A biographer of Necker's recalls the fact that he had
means at his disposal for overcoming the opposition
of his adversaries. The treasury was empty. He
had only to make this fact public and to add that
without the consent of the *Tiers* there was no possibility of carrying on affairs.† But such an admission
would have been out of keeping with his official
statement of the financial situation, and his political
triumph would have been at the expense of his reputation for obtaining credit. He therefore resolved to
keep silence, and, when he had explained that any
modification of his plan would make it useless, refrained from further discussing what course he should
pursue were he to be dismissed.

* Barante, *Notice sur Saint-Priest.* Necker, *De la Révolution
Française,* ix. 198, 199. Lesor, *Necker's Second Administration,* 146.
Larcy, *Louis and the États Généraux. Correspondant,* Mai, 1868,
516-518.

† Lesor, *Necker's Second Administration,* 146, 147.

Whilst all this was taking place in Marly, a report was spread abroad at Versailles of an approaching *coup d'état*. The excitement increased when the master of the ceremonies ordered the chamber appropriated to the *Tiers* to be closed, that it might be prepared for the *séance royale*. According to Madame de Staël this was entirely due to a misunderstanding. "The deputies thought," she says, "or pretended to believe, that they were forbidden to assemble," * upon which they adjourned to the tennis-court, and the well-known scene occurred during which Mounier summoned his colleagues to take a solemn oath not to separate before the national constitution was agreed upon. He claimed that the right of voting the taxation and a share in making the laws for the Estates, regular sittings, and ministerial responsibility, should be the foundation of that constitution.

Hardly a year elapsed before Mounier himself wrote that this unfortunate oath had been an attempt to resist the royal authority; he could not sufficiently deplore having proposed it.† "It was the signal for insurrection," said Malouet,‡ who, moreover, already seriously intended to give up his post, so thoroughly sobered was he by the daily and unusual spectacle of the crowds of small people, advocates, tradesmen, country doctors taking the

* Madame de Staël, *Considérations*, xii. 211.

† Mounier, *Recherches sur les causes qui ont empêché les Français de devenir libres.* Lanzac de Laborie, *Jean Joseph Mounier*, 89-93.

‡ Malouet, *Mémoires*, i. 278, 323.

field without any knowledge of affairs or any preparation, quoting the *Contrat Social* and suggesting
plans.

The oath had been taken in the tennis court on
the 20th of June. On the 22nd of June the clergy
placed the church of St. Louis at Versailles at the
disposal of the *Tiers*. The lengthy deliberations of
the latter were at an end ; 149 members of the
clerical body, headed by archbishops and bishops,
joined the *Tiers*, and were received with loud cheers.
On the following day, the 23rd of June, the king
appeared in solemn assembly without Necker. His
speech, delivered in a commanding tone, held to
Necker's programme in all essential points with one
decided exception—the three orders were still to
deliberate separately.

All that the *Tiers* had decided in opposition to this
was declared null and void, and the deputies were
commanded to separate that they might assemble
the following day in their separate orders.

Louis XVI. ended with the assurance of his impartial anxiety for the good of the realm.

If he could not obtain support he must carry it
out unaided. The majority heard him in icy silence,
under the over-mastering impression that the Crown
had taken the side of the nobility. When the king
had departed the Marquis de Brézé invited the
deputies to separate, on which Mirabeau made the
historical reply that "they were there by the will
of the nation, and would only yield at the point of the

bayonet."* Sièyes expounded what had happened in these words: "We are the same to-day as we were yesterday, let us deliberate," upon which the assembly declared the inviolability of its members. When the king was informed of the refusal to obey his commands he paced thoughtfully up and down for a few minutes and then said: "Well, if they will not vacate the hall they must stay there."

In the course of the day which had decided against him Necker tendered his resignation. Baron de Staël relates that at the council at Marly the Comte d'Artois met the first hint of his intention by exclaiming: "No, sir, you must remain with us as hostage: we hold you responsible for all the harm you have done." †

Necker says that he did not wish to take the consequences of the effect his resignation would have had upon the king, had he tendered it before the *séance royale*. But if he had attended it his popularity with the ministry would have suffered. Lally Tollendal is probably mistaken when he says that it was all that Necker's wife and daughter could do to persuade him to absent himself from the sitting of June 23rd. Bailly knew about it the evening before.‡ Whilst the monarch was compelled to retire from the *séance royale* amidst murmurs and insults to his

* Chérest, *La chute de l'Ancien Régime*, iii. 256-259.

† Léouzon Le Duc, *Correspondance Diplomatique du Baron de Staël-Holstein.*

‡ Necker, *De la Révolution Française*, ix. 215. Lally Tollendal. Necker, *Biographie Michaud*. Chérest, *La chute de l'Ancien Régime*, iii. 249.

own apartments, Madame de Staël witnessed the crowd which surrounded her father's residence cheering vociferously.

Deputations from the nobles, the clergy, and the *Tiers* were there. They shed tears when he invited their moderation, and assured him of their confidence. On which the king sent for Necker. The queen was present. She had heard the uproar for the first time from her own apartments, and tremblingly promised to offer no further opposition to the minister's policy. Louis XVI. implored Necker to remain in office, but refused to allow him to dismiss the ministers who had shipwrecked his plans. The excitement was so great in Versailles that Necker felt he would have to yield although he would not conceal from himself what a dreadful mistake he would be committing.[*] He only insisted that the troops should be withdrawn, chiefly because he was by no means sure that they could be relied upon.

The Treasury, *le contrôle général,* as it was called, was under the same roof as the royal palace at Versailles.

The minister could return to it without showing himself to the assembled multitude in the courtyard, and Madame de Staël specially says that nothing seemed more dangerous to him than a personal triumph at the expense of the royal authority.[†]

---

[*] *De l'Administration de M. Necker, par lui-même,* vi. 95. *De la Révolution Française,* ix. 214.

[†] Madame de Staël, *Considérations,* xii. 236.

Nevertheless he showed himself to the populace to quiet the excitement. The crowd conducted him to his house amidst stormy ovations, and thus the same day the monarch was insulted and his minister glorified. Madame de Staël thought that all these voices repeating her father's name were those of friends, and that their affection for her father bound them to her. She received him with the conviction that for the second time he had restored the supremacy of the king.* Necker did not thus deceive himself. When his friends surrounded him and drew his attention to the fact that the crowd called him the saviour of France, he replied that perhaps before a fortnight had elapsed they might pelt him with stones.† But he still agreed with his daughter in the opinion that the monarchy although tottering might again be restored.

An independent judgment could only be obtained from those who were not carried away in the whirl of passion let loose and who could observe the ferment from afar.

Amongst these witnesses of the Revolution, the two Americans we have already frequently mentioned, Gouverneur Morris and Thomas Jefferson, were two of the most prominent. The latter, who was Ambassador from the United States, always measured people

---

* Madame de Staël, *Considérations*, xii. 234. Léouzon Le Duc, *Correspondance Diplomatique du Baron de Staël-Holstein*, 104, 10th June, 1789.

† *De l'Administration de M. Necker, par lui-même*, vi. 96.

according as they agreed or disagreed with his republican ideal of liberty. He was not intentionally unjust, but was quite aware that he had brought with him "all the prejudices of country, habit, and age."

To these prejudices belonged an irreconcilable hatred against monarchy, which he put on a par with the greatest misfortunes that could happen to mankind. He considered that "if all the evils which can arise among us from the Republican form of government from this day to the Day of Judgment could be put into a scale against what this country suffers from its monarchical form, in a week, or England in a month, the latter would preponderate." This did not prevent his holding that Louis XVI. was "capable of great sacrifices," and that all that was wanted to induce him to do a thing was to be assured that it would be for the good of the nation. In August 1788 he calls him "the honestest man in his kingdom, and the most regular and economical," and says that he had "given repeated proofs of a readiness to sacrifice his opinion to the wish of the nation." *
"He had not a wish but for the good of the nation," testifies the old man of seventy-eight concerning Louis XVI. But the latter was a king, and as such, an irremediable evil. "Rather than see the Republican cause fail," Jefferson would not merely have consented to his overthrow, but "would have seen half the world desolated." †

---

* Jefferson, *Complete Works. Correspondence*, i. 400, ii. 221, 253, 439, 490.

† *Idem*, iii. 502.

It is all the more surprising that on that 23rd of June even such a fanatic as he should have earnestly recommended his friends belonging to the *Tiers* not to allow matters to come to an open rupture, but to effect a compromise and to content themselves with the concessions to which, in accordance with Necker's programme, the king had on the whole consented. " But," says Jefferson, " my friends thought otherwise, and time has proved how bitterly deceived they were. After so many wars, the loss of millions, the undermining of the happiness of many thousands, and the final dominion of the foreigner, they have not accomplished much more than what was offered them on that day, and then not without the fear of losing it again."

Amongst these friends of Jefferson who did not allow himself to be convinced was La Fayette, who according to the express instructions of his electors was obliged to vote for the decision by orders and not by persons. " I have not hesitated to press on him to burn his instructions and follow his conscience as the only sure clue . . . . . If he cannot effect a conciliatory plan he will surely take his stand manfully at once with the *Tiers* ; for," writes Jefferson, " his principles are clearly with the people." *

On the evening of that 23rd of June, Gouverneur Morris dined with La Fayette. Like Jefferson, Morris was a personal friend of George Washington,

---

* Jefferson, *Complete Works:* To G. Washington, iii. 29. Jared Sparks, *Gouverneur Morris*, i. 314.

president at that time of the United States ; for he,
too, had been a member of the congress which had
fought for their independence. He was well-acquainted
with Jefferson, although he had little in common with
the originator of the *Rights of Man.* Clever, accomplished, and inclined to irony, a man of the world and
with a thorough knowledge of his fellow-creatures,
his noble features so much resembled those of Washington that he sat to the sculptor Houdon to help him
to complete Washington's bust.

He had had his leg amputated in Philadelphia in
consequence of a fall in 1780. During the Revolution
in 1792 the populace on one occasion pursued his
carriage, shouting " Down with the aristocrat," when
Morris suddenly bethought himself of his wooden leg,
and thrusting it out of the carriage window, cried,
" What do you want with an aristocrat who has
lost a limb in the American struggle for Independence ? " Whereupon he was allowed to continue on
his way amidst shouts of applause.* To be satisfied
with mere words or to believe in the infallible superiority of any form of government was almost impossible to such a man. He judged France as it actually
lay before him, and not by the abstract chimeras
held by those around him.

When Jefferson spoke of the abolition of all difference of classes, Morris replied that it was problematic

* J. Chanut, *G. Morris, Nouvelle Biographie Générale,* xxxvi. 654.
Taine, *Origines de la France Contemporaine. La Révolution,* ii. *Psychologie du Jacobin.*

whether and to what extent man would profit by it, but he was quite certain that the French would not be able to maintain it.   In allusion to these views La Fayette, who sat next to him at dinner, remarked that he injured the cause as his sentiments were continually quoted against the good party.   " I seized the opportunity," says the American, "to tell him that I am opposed to the democracy from regard to liberty; that I see them going headlong to destruction and that I would fain stop them if I could; that their views respecting this nation are totally inconsistent with the materials of which it is composed, and that the worst thing which could happen would be to grant them their wishes.   He tells me that he is sensible that his party are mad, and tells them so; but is not the less determined to die with them.   I tell him I think it would be quite as well to bring them to their senses and live with them." *

Concerning Necker, Morris gave an equally decided opinion.   Shortly after his arrival in France, in February 1789, he had become acquainted with the minister and his wife, and afterwards with Madame de Staël.   He found Madame Necker stiff and devoid of charm, but always busy with the welfare of others, and felt real respect for her.   Necker, he considered, thoroughly upright, well-meaning and disinterested, but not of distinguished intellect.   In his own sphere, that of finance, he was insufficiently informed, although it would sound like a heresy to say so.

* Jared Sparks, *Gouverneur Morris*, i. 314.

"He is utterly ignorant of politics, by which I mean politics in the great sense, or that sublime science which embraces for its object the happiness of mankind. Consequently, he neither knows what constitution to form nor how to obtain the consent of others to such as he wishes. From the moment of convening the States-General he has been afloat upon the wide ocean of incidents." *

The plan which came to nothing on the 23rd of June was virtually Necker's last effort to direct the course of affairs. From that moment things took their own course. On the 24th of June the clergy then appeared in their full numbers in the hall set apart for the *Tiers.* Next day came forty-seven members of the nobility, with the Duke of Orleans at their head, under the leadership of Clermont-Tonnere and Lally Tollendal. The deputies who still held out were already insulted by the people.† A threatening multitude in the streets of Versailles forced the arch-bishop of Paris to conform to the decrees of his order. Bailly, the provisional president of the National Assembly, opened its doors to the first of these deputations from the people of Paris which were soon to govern it.

The royal guards were seen to assemble in the public places and to openly announce that they would defend the king's life, but would refuse to

---

* Jared Sparks, *Gouverneur Morris,* ii. 93, 94.

† Necker, *De la Révolution Française,* ix. 219. Droz, *Histoire de Louis XVI.* ii. 191.

murder their fellow-citizens, for they were the soldiers of the nation.*

In May Madame de Staël had called the army a troop of citizens. Camille Desmoulins called them "a legion of philosophers." Under his eyes hundreds of Parisian soldiers were entertained in the Palais Royal, and he well knew how to take advantage of their increasing insubordination.† The impression made by all this was so overmastering that the king, influenced by the queen, who had been won over by Mercy,‡ came back on Necker's proposition, and on the 29th of June, when there was no further chance that his decision could be considered voluntary, he commanded the Estates to unite. This time the minister felt that the sword had slipped from "the king's hands . . . . . that fear was his adviser."§

Versailles was illuminated that evening, but a feeling of irreconcilable bitterness prevailed. The victors had now no further cause to be thankful for a compulsory gift. The conquered only made a pretence of yielding.

In the course of five days, the king had twice given totally contradictory commands, and already believed his life to be in danger. The nobles could now make it apparent that it was no longer their own

* Jefferson, *Complete Works*, i. 93.

† Sybel, *Geschichte der Revolutionszeit*, i. 53.

‡ Wertheimer, *Documents Inédits relatifs à Marie Antoinette. Revue Historique*, 1884, ii. 328, 329. Mercy to Kaunitz, July 4, 1789.

§ Necker, *De la Révolution Française*, ix. 220, 277, 278. Jared Sparks, *Gouverneur Morris*, ii. 70.

affair that they had to defend ; and informed the king, by the Duke of Luxemburg, that they were mindful of their duty, and ready to sacrifice their lives for him ; whereupon Louis XVI. replied that no lives should be sacrificed on his account.* His surroundings did not share his resignation. If they were to be made an end of, it should not be without a struggle.

The court circles of Versailles found it impossible suddenly to abandon a situation which had lasted so long. Instead of tracing their destruction to a fatal sequence of events, mistakes, and responsibilities, it seemed more practical to make one man answerable for it, and to be able to say that if only he were removed the mischief of the last six months could be undone.

Mercy, who had day by day followed events for so many years, wrote anxiously to the Viennese Imperial Court that an effort was on foot in Versailles to make it appear that Necker was trying to use the enormous popularity he had acquired to become the dictator of the monarchy, and to induce the most Christian king to do anything he might suggest.

He writes: " The Princes of Condé and Conti, and Madame Adelaide, are at the head of this dreadful cabal, and amongst other distinguished persons they have drawn the Comte d'Artois, who is not very far-

---

* Laboulaye, *Cours de Législation comparée. L'Assemblée Constituante. Revue des Cours Littéraires*, June, 1869, 445. Chérest, *La chute de l'Ancien Régime*, iii. 285, 286.

seeing, into their toils, and they have selected this prince to carry their damaging insinuations against the above-named minister to the king's ear." *

Thus far Mercy, who does not omit to mention that, considering his avarice, the suddenly awakened generosity and popularity of the Duc d'Orléans could only be explained by a hidden intention of filling a place at the head of the *Tiers* very damaging to that of the king.† The situation in Paris justified this alarm. On the 30th of June the populace freed eleven soldiers who had been confined in the Abbaye prison for insubordination, without encountering any opposition from the watch. These incidents necessitated reinforcing the troops in the neighbourhood of Paris and Versailles by distant, therefore more trustworthy, regiments, under the command of the old Marshal de Broglie, whose son belonged to the liberal minority amongst the nobles, whilst the opposition looked to the father, the hero of the seven years' war, to defend their cause.

During this period a sense of victory caused a conciliatory spirit to reign for the last time in the assembly. On the 27th of June, two days before the introduction of the king's decree commanding the nobility and the clergy to unite the orders, Mirabeau had delivered a memorable speech.

He dreaded that the ill-will of the court party,

---

* Wertheimer, *Documents Inédits relatifs à Marie Antoinette. Revue Historique*, 1881, ii. 327. Mercy to Kaunitz, 4 July, 1789.

† *Idem.* Mercy to Kaunitz, 4 July, 1789.

and the excitement of the populace, might result in
deeds of bloodshed that could never be undone, and
he therefore issued a manifesto to the nation, in hopes
of appeasing the irritation, as a reminder of all that
had been guaranteed by the king even on that 23rd
of June, and as an expression of his conviction that
by strict moderation he would complete the work he
had begun. The king's subsequent resolve brought
this plan to nothing. It was not the last attempt to
come to an understanding.

On the 9th of July, Mounier laid the first draft of
a constitution before the assembly. In it he emphatically pointed out that it was much less necessary to
make new laws than to enforce those already in
existence. The fact must be remembered that the
French were not a recently civilised people, but a
nation composed of five and twenty million men, who
wished to strengthen their internal relations without
however weakening the foundations of the monarchy.
They were sworn to inviolable fidelity; the struggle
was only against despotism.*

But as usual there was no co-operation with the
minister at the head of affairs. Mounier states that
even he never saw the minister, and could only act
on general propositions.† "There were secrets and

---

* Larcy, *Louis XVI. et les États Généraux. Correspondant*, May,
1868, 522. Lavergne, *Les Monarchiens de la Constituante. Revue
des Deux Mondes*, 1842, 555, 556.

† Mounier, *Recherches sur les causes qui ont empêché les Français
de devenir libres*, i. 240.

pretended secrets," said Necker, "and I think that the king himself did not know everything." *

Madame de Staël states that no one had informed her father of the true reason of the concentration of the troops, but he continually received advice and information from outside sources which made it impossible to mistake what was going to happen. He returned home from the king, convinced each day that he should find a warrant for his arrest awaiting him.†

He again tendered his resignation, were his services no longer welcome, and added that in that case he would leave France as quickly and as quietly as possible.

" I take you at your word," said the king, " but wish you to remain."‡

Meanwhile, on the 7th of July, the number of the troops had increased under Broglie to thirty thousand; fifteen thousand more were expected. No one was further from expecting a *coup d'état* than the monarch himself, who was against all violent measures. About this time the project arose of making the Duc d'Orléans lieutenant-general of the kingdom by the side of the incapable king.

Mirabeau, who, notwithstanding the subsequent denial given by his friends, agreed to a certain extent

* Necker, *De la Révolution Française*, ix. 225.

† Madame de Staël, *Considérations*, xii. 236, 239.

‡ Laboulaye, *Cours de Législation comparée. L'Assemblée con-stituante. Revue des Cours Littéraires*, June, 1869, 459.

in the plan, did not by any means regard it as a plot,
but as an eventuality which circumstances might
bring about; he consulted with men of quite opposite
opinions, with the royalists Bergasse and Mounier as
well as with Turgot and Robespierre.* He now considered Necker to be merely a " pigmy," and he did
not think it necessary to take him into consideration
in any further plans.

A feudal reaction however must and should be
prevented. On the 8th of July, Mirabeau spoke
earnestly, wisely, and even moderately. His speech
led to the petition presented by four and twenty
members of the assembly on the 11th of July to the
king, praying him to withdraw the troops. Louis
XVI. replied that he was responsible for the public
peace. It demanded unusual precautions, and he
expected confidence. If the Assembly were uneasy he
would consent to its removing to Noyons or Soissons.
In that case he would himself go to Compiègne,—
therefore into the midst of the camp.

Comte Crillon quieted the malcontents amongst
his colleagues by pointing out that the word of Louis
XVI. was that of an honourable man. Mirabeau
nevertheless spoke warningly against sentimental
politics, and vainly pleaded that the petition should
be renewed for the removal of the troops.

On this 11th of July, Luzerne, the minister of
Marine, brought a note at three o'clock from the

* Droz, *Histoire de Louis XVI.* ii. 284, 286.

king to Necker, reminding him of his promise that if
necessary he would leave the country, and proposing
that he should do it at once and as secretly as
possible. The minister received his dismissal with
so much presence of mind that the assembled guests,
amongst whom were his brother, his cousin Huber,
de Cicé, archbishop of Bordeaux, and Madame de
Staël herself, had no suspicion of what had occurred.
It was only remarked that from time to time he
affectionately pressed his daughter's hand.* After
dinner he proposed to Madame Necker, who alone
knew what had occurred, that they should take the
air, and they went out in the carriage as if for an
ordinary drive. After going a few hundred paces he
ordered his servants at half-past five to drive towards
the first post-house, and there asked them whether
they would be willing to accompany him out of the
country. Madame Necker would not allow him to
consider her feeble state of health, so they travelled
straight to Brussels.†

The king repelled the alarm felt by Breteuil,
Necker's successor in the ministry, that the latter
would excite a rising in his favour in Paris, and that,
therefore, it would be well to arrest him. This was
based upon as great a mistake as the whole *coup
d'état*, the full purport of which was never fully ex-

* Lord Auckland, *Correspondance*, i. 331. Letter from Huber,
Paris, 14 July, 1789.

† Necker, *De la Révolution Française*, i. 226, &c. *De l'Administration de M. Necker, par lui-même*, vi. 97.

plained.   It is enough that it was universally believed
that it was intended to reduce Paris by famine, to
take two hundred of the States-General prisoners, to
dissolve that Assembly, and to govern in the old-
fashioned way.*

Notwithstanding every warning Necker was unpre-
pared for this turn of affairs, for he thought himself
indispensable to the public prosperity at a moment
when he alone protected the nation from bankruptcy
and starvation.†   When the news of his fall became
known in Paris enthusiasm reached a higher pitch in
his favour than it had ever done before.   Green
cockades were worn, because green was the colour of
his liveries and because Camille Desmoulins had for
that reason first decorated himself with a leaf from a
tree in the Palais Royal, whilst, before an innumerable crowd of people, he called Necker's banishment
"the sign for a St. Bartholomew's Eve for patriots,"
and pistol in hand called the citizens of Paris to arms.
The theatres were closed, the storm had burst: and
busts of Necker decorated with crape were paraded in
the streets with that of the Duke of Orleans who was
also thought to have been unjustly banished.

When Necker's brother prepared to follow him, he
and those accompanying him were stopped in the Rue
de Clichy and forced to return, "for," cried the

* Jared Sparks, *Gouverneur Morris*, ii. 78. Morris to Washington,
31 July, 1789.

† *De l'Administration de M. Necker, par lui-même*, vi. 97.

people, "if he leaves us there will be no one left to give us news of our father."[*]

Madame de Staël had returned to Paris on the 10th July, in the evening. She only heard by letter of her father's departure on the following morning, and even then he did not tell her where he had gone. He, however, ordered her to betake herself to the country that she might not become the object of demonstrations in the capital. But it was already too late for that. One deputation after another besought her to receive it, and demanded her father's return in the most extravagant terms. At last she got away and went to St. Ouen. There she received another missive from Necker with the news that her parents were on their way to Brussels, and by the 13th of July she had started to join them with Baron de Staël. It was not without some difficulty that she found them out—in this strange town, under an assumed name in a strange inn—and sank weeping at her father's feet. He and her mother wore the same clothes in which they had left Versailles.

Without any preparation for the journey, and without so much as a passport, they had had great difficulty in reaching the frontier. Necker employed his short stay in Brussels to renew his security for two million livres with the Hopes' bank in Amsterdam for a consignment of corn to Paris, that there might be no hitch in provisioning the capital. He then left

* Lord Auckland, *Correspondence*, i. 335. Letter from Huber, Paris, 16 July, 1789.

with Baron de Staël for Basle, and reached it on the 20th July.*

Madame de Staël followed with her mother in shorter stages, and thus for the first time saw the German Rhineland. A courier sent off by La Fayette on the 16th July missed her at Brussels. It conveyed the news of her father's recall : † but when the two ladies reached Frankfort they found a royal courier awaiting them from France with open letters from Louis XVI. and the Assembly, recalling Necker for the third time to take the head of affairs.‡ They got to Basle again one day later than these couriers, and there they at last heard all that had happened in Paris in the meantime : the desertion of the army, which had so long been feared, with the exception of a few foreign regiments; the struggle between the latter and the rebellious Gardes Françaises; the revolt in Paris; the plundering, the organisation and arming of the National Guard ; in one word, everything that had put an end, by the 13th July, to any species of government.

Next, the deeds of the 14th July, the taking of the Bastille, the murder of De Launay and Flesselles ; the unconditional capitulation of the king § before

---

* Madame de Staël, *Du Caractère de M. Necker et de sa Vie privée,* xvii. 52.   Necker to his brother Germany, Basle, 24 July, 1789.

† Lord Auckland, *Correspondence,* i. 336. Letter from Huber, Paris, 16 July, 1789.

‡ Madame de Staël, *Du Caractère de M. Necker et de sa Vie privée,* xvii. 44-51. *Considérations,* xii. 246.

§ Jefferson, *Complete Works,* i. 99. Lord Auckland, *Correspondence,* i. 328, 333, as an eye-witness.

the Assembly; the persuasive speech made in honour of Necker by Lally Tollendal, as ambassador from the Assembly in the Hotel de Ville; the end of Bréteuil's administration, after three days' duration; the failure of the plans in favour of the Duke of Orleans through the appearance of the king in the capital and at the Hotel de Ville, when he "thus concluded an *amende honorable* such as no sovereign ever made and no people ever received."* Mirabeau himself said when he heard of this step of the king's, "Whoever recommended him to take this step is a bold mortal; without it Paris would be lost to him. Two or three days more, and he could not have gone back."

No less extraordinary than the news were the messengers that brought it. On the evening of the 15th July the first emigration began. It included the Comte d'Artois, his friends Bréteuil and Montesson, the Duchesses de Polignac and de Guiche, the Comte Vaudreuil, the Abbé de Vermond; all intimate friends of the queen. Necker's informant was the Duchesse de Polignac. She sent to ask him to come and see her in her hotel at Basle, and after sympathising with him in his fall she described to him the events that had resulted from it, and those to which she had now fallen a sacrifice.

Madame de Staël tells us that Necker, who had never thought of the possibility of prescription, re-

* Jefferson, *Complete Works*, i. 101, 102. Dumont, *Souvenirs sur Mirabeau*, 114, 115.

quired a little time to realise the concatenation of circumstances imparted to him by the duchess. Then their paths separated never to meet again. She went to the native land of her friend the queen, and at Vienna distress at the tragic end of the companion of her happy days hurried her to an early grave.

Necker on his side made up his mind to return " to a court the temper of which he had experienced ; to an empty treasury, and to a people whose favour might very probably be quite as exhausted." Whilst still at Basle he wrote to his brother, Necker de Germany, that a precipice seemed to yawn beneath him.* Madame Necker sought in vain to dissuade him. His daughter does not mention what her own personal bias was—but everything leads us to think that she could not do otherwise than urge his return.

It was during this short stay in Switzerland that they formed acquaintance with Lavater. He was spending the summer of 1789 with his friend Sarasin, for change of air, when he met Necker. His letters describe Necker's characteristic countenance as possessed of the " gentlest, sweetest features." He says nothing of his "clever daughter " beyond mentioning that they spoke together of physiognomy.†

Madame de Staël's journey from Basle to Paris, by

* Necker, *De la Révolution Française*, ix. 237-240. Madame de Staël, *Du Caractère de M. Necker et de sa Vie privée*, xvii. 52.

† Gessner, *Life of Lavater*, iii. 123, Lavater, *Answers to Questions and Letters*, Berlin, 1790.

her father's side, resembled a triumphal progress; and she appreciated it to the utmost.

Crowds joyfully received Necker in the towns; on the roads the women went on their knees when they saw his carriage appear; the foremost citizens took the postilion's place; more than once the horses were unharnessed that the people might drag his carriage along. On one of these occasions, Junot, who was to become a marshal, very nearly lost his life in the crowd. Necker spoke frequently to the crowd, recommended calm and moderation, and procured passes for people who were threatened, to enable them to leave the country without hindrance. Ten miles from Paris he met Besenval, the commandant of the Swiss regiment, which had been brought into the capital on the 12th July, and which he led back from Paris to Versailles after the encounter with the rebellious soldiers of the nation, and without their having made common cause with the people. The king had permitted him to retire to Switzerland, but he was arrested on the road, to be delivered to the future Paris municipality, by order of the electors.

The horrible murders of Toulon and Berthier on the 22nd July left little doubt as to his probable fate. Necker in vain endeavoured to procure a free pass for him, and now resolved to do all he could in Paris to secure his release. He first betook himself with his belongings to Versailles, where the king gave him a gracious reception, and assured him of his entire confidence, and next proceeded to the assembly to express his thanks to it. *

The following morning he hurried to Paris, where every neck was craned to see and greet him, and to the Hotel de Ville to snatch their victim from the 'people. "I went on my knees, I humbled myself in every conceivable way," he himself relates, " to save Besenval." †

In a long touching speech he begged for pardon and amnesty; in the excitement of the moment he made the most dangerous admission; he told the victorious leaders of the rebellion that the Government no longer possessed any power, and that the salvation of the State lay in their hands—in that of the National Assembly. He, the minister, implored them to make an end of proscription and bloodshed.

This speech, made at first to a hundred and twenty members of the commune, had such effect that he was obliged to repeat in the public hall. There he was awaited by foreigners of distinction, members of the National Assembly, his wife and daughter. Adorned with the Parisian cockade, which the king had stuck in his hat a fortnight before, and amidst loud applause and cries of "pardon—amnesty," he was obliged to show himself on the balcony to the enthusiastic crowd. After the representatives of the commune had conceded Besenval's release, a resolu-

---

* Madame de Staël, *Du Caractère de M. Necker et de sa Vie privée*, xvii. 54, &c. Compare with Droz, ii. 389.

† *De l'Administration de M. Necker, par lui-même*, vi. 103. *Troisième Ministère de M. Necker*, vii. 5.

tion, granting amnesty, was drawn up by Lally Tollendal, in the name of the members of the assembly,
and their consent announced.

Necker was now revered as the saviour of the
state, and the people seemed nearly beside themselves
when he spoke to them of peace and reconciliation.
Madame de Staël remembered nothing more in that
hour, for, overpowered by her emotions, she sank
fainting to the ground.

She writes at the age of four-and-twenty, that this
was her last completely happy moment, and, although
she was in the full prime of life, she says that when
she recovered consciousness she felt as if she had
reached the limit of human happiness.*

A very remarkable letter of hers to king Gustavus,
dated August 1789, gives a clear impression of the
opinions held in the Necker family, both as to the
past and the immediate future. "Sir," she writes,
"accept the expression of my homage after so many
terrible, glorious, and incredible events. I ask myself whether a thousand years have elapsed during
the last year, the last month; I should think I had
been transplanted into another world if my glorious
king were not still in existence. Your majesty will
be informed about everything, and will have formed
an opinion, to which I should defer unconditionally
if you had formed it by personal observation."

"Any one who was not on the spot, and far from

* Madame de Staël, *Considérations*, xii. 258. *Du Caractère de M.
Necker et de sa Vie privée.*

the scene of action, might find it difficult to understand the origin of such weighty results, and might
be tempted to make other than the actual circumstances responsible for these dreadful occurrences.

" I who have been in the midst of it all, and know
that he whom I held most dear was at the helm
during the storm, can have little doubt as to the real
cause of what has taken place. It is evident to me
that it was owing to a court cabal, supported by the
extravagant demands of the nobility, to whom Versailles represented the whole nation, and who hoped
to annihilate the rights of the people, by an attack
upon their truest defender in the person of Necker.

" At their head was the Comte d'Artois, who succeeded in identifying his cause with that of the
nobility in the mind of the king. The example in
Sweden, where your majesty encountered difficulty
with the nobles only, was of no avail, nor the knowledge that the king's power must be grounded on his
popularity. My father vainly repeated in the ministerial council that millions of men were ready to
fight at the back of the six hundred members of the
Tiers. Things which required wise deliberation were
scornfully overlooked. My father's departure, the
concentration of the troops, the appointment of an
unpopular ministry, were like thunder-bolts from one
end of the realm to the other. I do not believe in
the report universally circulated of the intended bom-
bardment of Paris and imprisonment of the deputies;
but I think that people were mistaken in believing

that the king's authority would be restored if the Estates-General were dismissed, or that he could be persuaded that Necker was deceiving him when he insisted that it was no longer possible to dismiss the Estates.

"No sooner was my father's banishment made known than the nation rose up in arms, and I doubt not that both foreigners and Frenchmen took advantage of the situation for the furtherance of unworthy plans and to promote disturbances.

"But they could never have succeeded except through the mistakes of the Government and my father's dismissal.

"A cabal or isolated disturbance could be organised by means of gold and the dissemination of untruths, but a whole nation could not rise without some generally acknowledged and sufficient cause. During the short space of a fortnight the situation was entirely altered. My father, who had fled from France and his own glory as others flee before disgrace, returned as a sacrifice to the common weal, and not to satisfy his own ambition. He found every form of government disturbed or abolished. Violence had obtained the mastery as in the days of old. Instead of advancing, a nation possessing a great past seemed to have fallen into second childhood. A corrupted populace dreamt of liberty after the American pattern. This liberty was to be achieved without any preparation of the public mind. In one word, he found an alarming chaos of opinions, and an irreconcilable difference between the dispositions and the circumstances surrounding them. Time alone can efface the mischief done in a single day. My father's whole efforts must be consecrated to restoring the royal authority. It can no longer dispose of the executive if the troops will not obey, and in that case the country is lost as well.

"The very fact of the prolonged existence of this form of government proves that it is indispensable, just as a sum in addition can be proved by substraction. My father never dreamt of disturbing its foundations. He wished for reforms, which were as advisable as they were necessary. As the king and the nobility refused to grant them whilst there was yet time the nation was brought to confusion.

"My father constantly implored the king to grant freely what would eventually be taken by force.

"The defiant attitude of the people, the unpopularity of the monarch and of the nobles, may be attributed to the pursuance of the opposite course, which refused everything to reason, and was afterwards obliged to surrender to violence.

"If this state of things continue, France must come to an end, and its deliverance can only be effected by terrible means. I still hope that my father may be able to save it. Day by day he will encourage welldoing and avert evil, and time will remove the greatest difficulties.

"If these expectations be disappointed, flight is certainly the only alternative. In that case it would be preferable to take refuge in Constantinople rather than to remain in this country, if given over to boundless license and the despotism of the masses. Your majesty will pardon me for venturing to allude to things which so closely concern me, and for giving you an insight into events with which the glorious name of my father is so closely linked; and if the image which is ever before my eyes be calculated to inspire indifference for worldly honours and distinctions, it on the other hand increases respect for true greatness. In proportion as equality is insisted upon by despotism and anarchy, a monarch gains in worth by reigning without oppression and securing the permanence of monarchical constitutions by his own example.

" It is now my duty to inform your majesty as to my own personal action. I was the means of arranging that Baron de Staël took ten days' leave of absence to accompany my father at a moment when not only the liberty but the life of the latter were threatened; for the rage of his enemies grew in proportion to the homage that was offered to him. I do not hesitate to claim your majesty's indulgence in this matter, and I recommend my husband and myself to your favour, in the certainty that everything undertaken by Baron de Staël is in furtherance of the service of his king."

Only when the excitement was somewhat abated could the transformation, which three weeks had worked in the history of France, be realised.

In the country the populace raged with fire and

sword against property; in the towns anarchy reigned supreme.

The power wrested from the king had not remained in the hands of the Assembly. " It was not a Revolution but a dissolution; not the overthrow of one Government and the rise of another but the beginning of a despotism of the masses under the influence of fear, credulity, and misery." *

Hardly any one paid the taxes; the whole machinery of government stood still. The officials had mostly taken to flight; the archives were destroyed. " The democratic harangues which were applauded on the platforms," writes Madame de Staël, " were represented in the country by an equal number of crimes. The epigrams of the speakers in honour of the *constituante* burnt the *châteaux;* and the kingdom was plunged into mourning by means of phrases." †

When Necker unfolded a plan for a loan, on the 7th of August, to the National Assembly, he asked whether it would have been possible to foresee the unheard-of revolution which had taken place in a few weeks. The evil had increased to such dimensions that unfortunately no one could withstand it. Seen from the central standpoint of the king's minister, the picture was truly terrible. His sketch of the existing evil could not have been more clearly drawn,

* Taine, *Origines*, etc. *La Révolution*, i. 51.
† Madame de Staël, *Considérations*, xii. 270.

but Necker ceased to make any attempt to grapple
with it.   He declared his duty to consist in bowing
to the will of the Assembly and in endeavouring to
serve the king by means of the popularity he still
enjoyed. Just as he had implored the Parisian
municipality to spare the life of Besenval, in like
manner he now prayed the representatives of the
nation to rescue the State.*

Necker's third administration had only a passive
part to play in the further history of the Revolution.
The short triumph at the Hotel de Ville did not last
beyond that evening, for on it Mirabeau's *Revanche*
took place.

Shortly after the 14th of July he had proffered his
services through his friend de la Marck to the queen,
and received answer that it was to be hoped that the
king would never be sufficiently unfortunate to have
to take refuge in such means.†

Hereupon, passion obtained the mastery, and as he
was unable to govern with the reigning powers he
now turned against them.   His first thought had
been to get himself proclaimed mayor of Paris, in the
place of Bailly.‡   On hearing of the release of
Besenval he hastened to the capital, and excited the
public opinion against the resolutions of the Hotel
de Ville.   Influenced by him, the already terrified

* Necker, *Troisième Ministère*, vii. 132. *De la Révolution Française*, ix. 240.

† Droz, *Histoire de Louis XVI.* ii. 368.

‡ *Correspondance entre Mirabeau et de la Marck*, i. 94, 95.

National Assembly declared that Besenval should not
be allowed to escape the law.   Mirabeau's organ in
the press, the so-called *Letters to his Constituents,*
now openly said that the people had acted right-
eously and that the measure was full; the punishment of one vizier would be a wholesome warning
for others.   He himself said from the tribune,
speaking of the murders of the 22nd July, "one
should not let oneself be moved by the fate of individuals; only by this means could one be a true
citizen." *

That Besenval's life should have been spared was
the only gain of the day, which Necker had hoped
would be the first of peace restored, but which turned
out to be the last of his popularity.†

The way in which the events of the last few weeks
had influenced the opinions of her friends during her
short absence from Paris decided the future political
stand-point of Madame de Staël.   Amongst these
friends, Lally Tollendal was the first who, on the 20th
July, endeavoured to stem anarchy, by a proclamation to the French people.

On the 27th of July, Mounier presented the project
for a constitution, drawn up by the constitutional
committee, to the Assembly, which, taking the system
of two Chambers as its basis, had the restoration of a
moderate monarchy in view.

* Droz, *Histoire de Louis XVI.* ii. 396.   *Correspondance entre
Mirabeau et de la Marck,* i. 99.
† Ferrières, *Mémoires,* i. 78.

He, Malouet, Crillon, bishop of Chartres, the young Matthieu de Montmorency, Toulougeon, an independent nobleman and an intimate friend of La Fayette's, afterwards the historian of the Revolution, of whose impartial work Madame de Staël often made use,* all shared Lally de Tollendal's opinion, that the National Assembly was responsible for crime which it did not know how to punish.

But individuals who had recently sprung up, such as Buzot, the future Girondin, and Maximilian Robespierre, were of a different opinion. This was the first occasion upon which their names came before the public. They spoke of the want of faith towards the people, not of its wild conduct; called the Parisians heroic, because they had used their natural rights, and offered so much opposition that almost nothing was done. The chief thing was to keep up the panic. Mirabeau and Bailly name the amount paid out to the agitators in the capital.†

The eloquence of Lally and his friends failed in the end to secure the punishment of the murderers, owing to the equivocal attitude of the deputy for Provence.

The proposed proclamation was a meaningless invitation to peace and unity, and of the lengthy debate nothing remained but the undying memory of the words uttered by Barnave, after the murder of Foulon, when he gave his notorious answer to the

---

* Madame de Staël, *Considérations*, xiii. 102.

† Sybel, *Geschichte der Revolutionszeit*, i. 65, note. Droz, *Histoire de Louis XVI.* ii. 357, &c.

demand for justice; "Was the blood that was shed so pure?"

Whilst Madame de Staël's above-named friends could not rid themselves of the impression that the ground was already sinking from beneath their feet, another of those in her immediate circle was raised to a prominent position by these same events. Since July 15th, La Fayette had been commandant of the civic guard, which henceforward was to be called the National Guard.

We are told by the Baron de Staël that the idea, first started by Sièyes, was carried out by Necker himself.* Necker recommended the king, in the days when he insisted upon the withdrawal of the Duc de Broglie and his troops, to organise it as a species of defence against the growing disorder, and with the stipulation that he should himself appoint the officers. After the 14th of July the Parlementeer Dupont organised the arming of the people throughout France with marvellous adroitness and energy. He had long accepted every revolutionary doctrine. "Suddenly the regular army found itself as it were taken prisoner, by an army of from two to three million armed men, for the most part without work or bread, who were responsible to the municipality alone, whilst the king, since the 14th of July, could no longer dispose of any military authority." †

---

* Léouzon Le Duc, *Correspondance Diplomatique du Baron de Staël-Holstein*, 121, No. 127.

† Necker, *De la Révolution Française*, 377. Madame de Staël, *Considérations*, xii. 325.

Although the National Guard may not have been originated by La Fayette, he performed other no less important services.

He was the originator of the tricolor, which he took from the colours of the town of Paris, and added to the royal white, and which he prophesied would make its way over the whole world.[*]

Necker had to employ entreaties and representations to prevent his carrying this out by instigating revolutionary movements in Ireland and in Holland. The cap of freedom on the hilt of the sword, used by the National Guard, was originated by him : and no one is so closely identified with the naturalisation of the "Declaration of the Rights of Men" as he is. July the 11th, 1789, was the date of his first attempt to carry it through. It may be compared to an attempt to transplant green creepers, adorning the successfully planned gable of a new house, into the rubbish and dust of a demolished building. We cannot say whether La Fayette was ever able during any part of his term of command to enforce any other will than that of those he was supposed to command.

When Madame de Staël returned to find him in this position he had tendered his resignation, a week after he accepted it, that is on the 23rd of July, after the murder of Foulon and Berthier. But he withdrew it the same evening, without receiving any assurance that the murderers would be punished, a proceeding which was often to be repeated on similar occasions,

* La Fayette, *Mémoires*, ii. 267, note, iv. 82. Sybel, *Geschichte der Revolutionszeit*, i. 71.

without his ceasing to remain a popular hero of the day. The influence of this popularity may be traced in the chapter of the *Considérations*, dedicated to him by Madame de Staël.

She considers him as the type of a true Republican; and as he had sacrificed all class-interests, and proved himself indifferent to wealth, she believed him to be disinterested in friendship, and superior to the temptations of ambition and vanity.

It is related that a petitioner who wished to obtain a hearing from La Fayette brought forward his noble descent, upon which La Fayette replied: " Sir, that is no objection." Similar anecdotes were on every one's lips. There were, however, plenty others, which, under the form of a joke, often contained serious instruction. It had become the habit in the Parisian theatres to interrupt unpopular pieces with noisy demonstrations, which had never hitherto endangered life. A similar demonstration occurred on the representation of *Iphigenia*. Rotten apples were thrown into all the boxes which were supposed to contain " aristocrats."

One of these missiles struck the Duchesse de Biron, who sent it to La Fayette, with a note to the effect that the first fruits of the Revolution that had reached her should be his.*

La Fayette is still the type of the citizen-general of the National Guard, and that corps was called by him "his eldest daughter." His theories were formed

* Condorcet, *Mémoires*, ii. 65. Anonymously compiled.

on the "Rights of Man." He never departed from this great declamatory utterance, and Charles X. used to say that he and La Fayette were the only men who had never altered since 1789. Niebuhr, who knew him, confirms the correctness of this remark with regard to La Fayette, although he adds that personally he could not endure him, as he was so incapable of altering his attitude.

The saying, which is so often misapplied, was verified in him, " *Que l'homme de bien est extrême-ment peu de chose.*"*

No greater testimony to La Fayette's incredible want of political foresight exists than his own. He writes : " The profession of faith I issued on the 11th July was both a manifesto and an ultimatum . . . . It appeared three days before the national rising, the last that was necessary, and the last that I desired." †

But he himself led or permitted the insurrections he had not desired—those of October 6th, 1789, and April 18th, 1791,—because his power would have been sacrificed, and then his popularity, if he had opposed them, and he valued popularity more than life.

In the midst of the revolutionary storm he found heart to give himself up to the " delightful sensation caused by the smiles of the crowd," and to congrat-ulate himself that he possessed the favour of the

---

* Niebuhr, *History of the Revolution*, i. 201.

† La Fayette, *Mémoires*, iii. 219. Lettre à M. d'Hennings, Wittmold, 15th Jan. 1799.

people, without which "he could not exist." Public opinion, the abstract power so reverenced by Necker, had taken form in La Fayette, and now paraded the streets. He thought he was leading it when he placed himself at its head, decked out in the tri-coloured scarf.

Washington warned him in vain against "his unusual sensitiveness about everything that concerned his reputation."[*]

Jefferson spoke still more sharply, and showed his weak side to be "a canine appetite for fame." [†] Mirabeau quoted the Duc de Choiseul, who jokingly called La Fayette "Gilles-César" on his return from America.[‡] Mounier wrote to him after the 6th of October as follows: "If you have ceased to be the arch-promoter of the Revolution you still have remained its adherent." [§]

On the other hand he had the undeniable virtue of a spotless private life, brightened by the devoted admiring love of his wife, who belonged to the de Noailles family, and who was destined to give him heroic proofs of her devotion.

Madame de Staël, who remained ever constant to her admiration of La Fayette, nevertheless allowed herself to be influenced by the marvellous intellectual gifts of a man who could only be thought of in contrast to him.

* Thureau Dangin, *Le Parti libéral sous la Restoration*, 46.
† Jefferson, *Complete Works*, ii. 106.
‡ Thureau Dangin, *Le Parti libéral sous la Restoration*, 47, note.
§ Condorcet, *Mémoires*, ii. 329.

Charles Maurice de Talleyrand-Périgord, consecrated bishop of Autun, January 1789, laid early
stress upon the advantages of moderation, peace, and
temperate judgment, unwavering equanimity, and
the formation of wise views of life, which went side
by side with an insight that at times amounted to
genius. He never allowed himself to be carried
away by the optimism which led Napoleon to remark,
"*La Fayette est un niais.*"

Talleyrand was surprised at nothing; he spared
himself and others expressions of moral indignation
which he did not feel, and at a time when almost
every one lost his head he remained a calm and
collected spectator, never losing sight of his object,
and pursuing it if necessary by means of intrigue and
plots; unrestrained by moral reflections but never
misled by petty vanity or deceived by insignificant
results.

His inexorable judge, Sainte-Beuve, is not justified
in saying that Talleyrand's memory is stained by his
share in Mirabeau's death. It is enough to charge
him with complicity in the murder of the Duc
d'Enghien thirteen years later,[*] remembering the
words of the poet: "*Ainsi que la vertu, le crime a
ses degrés.*"

Talleyrand was aware of the accusation. In his
own way he had repudiated it : "Did a clever, wise
man ever need to commit crimes?" he said. "Those

---

[*] Saint-Beuve, *Talleyrand. Nouveaux Lundis*, xii. 12. Meneval,
Souvenirs, iii. 85.

are the means employed by political fools. Crime is like a flood. It returns and overflows. I have weaknesses, some people say vices—*mais des crimes? Fi donc !* " [*]

The shadow of crime clings nevertheless to the later Talleyrand, the Talleyrand of the Consulate and the Empire. In the year 1789 he had not reached that point, but he already worked broadly, and, caring not for the masses, he overawed the powers of the moment, and above all endeavoured to outlast them. He looked upon men as the pieces of the chess-board, but knew how to move them better than his colleague Sièyes, who only regarded them as lifeless forms.

In the great world La Fayette was clumsy and stiff; he was only at his ease in the clubs where he could possess himself of the ideas of others,[†] or sword in hand at the head of the people in arms.

Talleyrand on the other hand could be irresistibly charming, because daily accustomed to social inter-course, and skilled in the art of pleasing both men and women. Unrivalled in his social relations he gave Rivarol the impression at five-and-thirty that he could accomplish anything he pleased.[‡] As author of the *cahiers* for his diocese he was one of the few who only advanced practical propositions, and made

[*] Lamartine, *Chateaubriand et son Temps*, 145.
[†] Rivarol, *Galerie des Etats Généraux*. Philarète (La Fayette.)
[‡] *Idem.* Amène (Talleyrand).

no allusion to the favourite dreams of an approaching golden age.*

He belonged to the intimate circle of the Swedish embassy, having long been a friend of Necker's: relations of a different nature existed between him and the Comtesse Buffon, who in her turn was succeeded by the Comtesse de Flahault.

In the Assembly he was one of the closest adherents, amongst the clergy, of the *Tiers*. It acknowledged this by appointing him on the 14th July, along with Mounier, Cicé, Lally, Clermont Tonnerre, Chapelier, Bergasse, and Sièyes, to be a member of the committee appointed to draw up the Constitution.

When the weighty question had to be decided whether the mandates of the electors bound their representatives after the events that had meanwhile occurred, the bishop of Autun made his first speech in favour of full liberty of action for himself and his colleagues. The resolutions arrived at on that occasion decided nothing less important than the future course of the Revolution. For the mandates of 1789, the so-called *cahiers*, so far required revision, that those of the clergy and nobility, which in most cases required their representatives to vote separately in their order, had now become void. On the other hand almost all the *cahiers* without exception aimed, not at crippling or abolishing the monarchy but at reforming it. Moderate men like Malouet therefore recommended revision of the

* Sir Henry Lytton Bulwer, *Talleyrand*, 24. Tauchnitz edition.

mandates, inasmuch as this was necessary towards
securing the existence of the Estates-General.   Their
abolition seemed to him to entail the introduction of
despotism.*   But it was Talleyrand's motion, not
Malouet's, which was carried, and the now fully-
emancipated *constituante* was deputed to construct
the Republic.

What had taken place decided the line of action
for Madame de Staël's friends. The Duc d'Aiguillon,
Richelieu's heir, gave the first impulse to the incidents
of that memorable night when he proposed at the
Breton club to abolish feudal rights.   In the Assembly
itself the Vicomte de Noailles, La Fayette's brother-
in-law, introduced the triple motion of equal taxation,
of the abolition of all pecuniary rights, and of bondage;
at the same time inviting the nobles and clergy
solemnly to sanction the abolition of the feudal system.

There is no mention in the *Considérations* of this
circumstance—one of the best known in the Revolution—but there can be no doubt that Madame de
Staël shared in the glad and enthusiastic self-sacrifice
which during that night not only renounced that
which was already lost in point of fact, or still more
did not deserve to be prolonged—but which also
abandoned the established rights of property without
any definite compensation.

The economist Dupont de Nemours, once secretary
to Turgot, alone held to statesman-like ideas: spoke
against novelties leading to uncertain results and

---

* Malouet, *Mémoires*, i. 299.

recommended that the law should be respected and order restored. It is well known that the "electric current" which seemed to have attacked everybody was only resisted by two amongst the prominent members of the National Assembly.

Sièyes, supported by Lanjuinais, wished to see the tithes payable to the clergy redeemed, not suppressed; and moved by this open attack against property he uttered the celebrated words from the tribune—"You wish to be free and do not know how to be just."

Mirabeau remarked to his colleague that he must not be surprised if the bull gored him after he had let it loose, and being prepared for what was in store absented himself entirely from the sitting on the 4th of August. Meanwhile by overthrowing the propositions for abolishing the honours belonging to the nobility, he frustrated the latest attempt to establish equality and to remove all class distinctions.

The next motion for the pacification of the country, which had flung all restraint to the winds—in which laws were of no avail and judges had no authority, and where justice had become a mere phantom *— found so little favour that Necker was obliged to interrupt the debate on the resolutions of the 4th of August personally to instruct the Assembly upon the situation.

He expresses his opinion that this period of renunciation was initiated by an utter disregard for the

* Account of the Committee of the Reports to the Assembly, Aug. 13, 1789.

public advantage, and that the cession of so many rights, not only by classes but by provinces, towns, and corporations, without any settled indemnity, was the work of undue and useless haste.*

In public he limited himself, however, to speaking of the stagnation of all trade, the repudiation of taxation and arrears, of the empty treasury, and of the necessity for a loan of thirty millions to meet the most pressing requirements of the next two months, which Necker and many others with him imagined would suffice to bring the labours of the Assembly to a close.

In the debate on this motion the Marquis de la Coste and Alexander de Lameth for the first time let fall the threat, in their excitement, that the Church property shonld be appropriated, as belonging to the nation, to satisfy the State-creditors.

In consequence, however, of the reduction of taxation by the Assembly, Necker's loan was an entire failure. He became really ill when he saw that "not only his health and his peace, but his reputation was compromised. Confidence was lost and the credit of the nation destroyed: whilst never a day passed by without disorders and punishable revolt."† This disastrous result of their attack upon the financial administration soon induced the Assembly, with no further difficulty, to vote eighty millions: and thus

---

* Necker, *De la Révolution Française,* ix. 267. *Troisième Ministère,* vii. 68.

† Necker, *Troisième Ministère,* vii. 39.

leisure was ensured to return to abstractions, undisturbed by anything so prosaic as business.

Before the Constitution, "the Declaration of the Rights of Man," called by Rivarol the "*préface inutile d'un livre nécessaire*," was drawn up on the same model as that whereby Jefferson prefaced the Declaration of Independence at the Philadelphian Congress in 1776; and drawn up still more minutely by him for the slave-dealing State of Virginia when its constitution was established, so that as a German historian remarks: "A definition of mankind itself would have been necessary before supplying a definition of its rights." *

Jefferson had borrowed the leading idea of it from Locke, and from Locke's pupil, Jean Jacques Rousseau. Thus under a foreign garb the fundamental doctrine of the *Contrat Social*, teaching the sovereign rights of the people, once more returned to its native land. La Fayette ceded the honour to none of having introduced the Declaration of the Rights of Man, not only to his own compatriots, but to the whole human race.

"We desire," says his friend Duport, "an explanation of rights for all men, all times, all lands, to be an example for all mankind."

Whereupon Mallet du Pan is known to have referred him to the precepts of brotherly love in the Gospel; and Gneisenau, imploring moderation, is said to have replied: "Inspire the human race first with a

* Bernhardi, *Geschichte Russlands*, ii. 175.

love of duty, and then let it think about its rights."
On which Talleyrand himself paid tribute to the
phrase, and called the Rights of Man " the law of the
lawgiver." *

When the flood of speech was at last stemmed the
victory remained more or less on the side of Rousseau's
ideas uttered by La Fayette : the sole aim of the State
was to be the greatest possible happiness for each individual, as the expression of a union of which each
individual is a member but need obey no other than
himself and therefore remains as free as he was before.

In entire agreement with this, La Fayette started
from the theory of original liberty and equality for
all men, but immediately added that social differences
could only exist in as far as they benefited the common
good, by means of which he considered that institutions
similar to those in America might be obtained.

This idea was not realised.   The people sought for a
tangible, practical result in all these vague and for
the most part to them unintelligible definitions, and
found it in the theory of the right to rebel against
the Government whenever it considered the latter to
be in fault.

La Fayette's *Rights of Man*, disseminated all
over Paris as a pamphlet, was answerable for the
rising on the 13th of July and for the storming of
the Bastille.   The king was forced to give his sanction to the proposal on the 5th of October—on the last
morning that the monarch ever saw dawn in peace,
whilst under the roof of Versailles.   And, that the

* Lanfrey, *Essai sur la Révolution Française.*

right of the sovereign people to revolt should in no sense be restricted, Varlet, who was subsequently a member of the Jacobin Club, hid the pale face of murder under the protecting formula, that before a bloody necessity, " *Il faut jeter une voile sur la déclaration des droits de l'homme.*" *

Previous to this, and owing in· a measure to the butcheries in October, the great constitutional battle was fought in the Assembly.

The crisis was reached when the question of two Chambers or one only, and the definition of the king's prerogative, came under discussion. The constitutional committee was not united in itself. The majority, including Cicé, archbishop of Bordeaux, Lally Tollendal, Clermont Tonnerre, and Bergasse, all wished for a moderate monarchy even if they could not agree in detail. Talleyrand, Sièyes, Chapelier, equally desired a monarchy, but it was to be a royal democracy.

Mirabeau alone perceived that a monarchy of this sort lacked the conditions of vitality, although all parties approved of it. These included even Robespierre, who voted with the entire Left for the constitutional paragraphs, accepting the government of France as monarchical. Mirabeau had the courage to tell the Assembly that either it must renounce all idea of forming a constitution or else find means to restore some amount of power to the Executive. †

* Mortimer-Terneaux, *Histoire de la Terreur*, ii. 202.

† Droz, *Histoire de Louis XVI.* 427, 428.

A constitution on the English pattern, or an Upper Chamber, was no longer to be thought of. Not only had the order ceased to exist that it would represent, but the lesser nobility had joined the extreme left in overthrowing the peerage. Those even who desired this arrangement dared not so much as name it, but were obliged to limit themselves to the proposition of a Senate on Mounier's plan. It was to be composed of two hundred members taken from every grade of the people, chosen first by the Provincial Assemblies and then proposed by the deputations to the king, and by him nominated for life.

This Senate was in certain cases to appoint the ministers to settle disputes; to pass measures with the exception of financial laws and the budget; and to vote like the second Chamber.

True to his programme, Mounier led the way to the Constitutional Monarchy. He had already formulated his ideas in what is thought by the historians of the time of Louis XVI. to be the best political pamphlet written in 1789.[*]

Mounier endeavoured to counterbalance the undue power of the Assemby not only by means of the Senate, but he also required a strong Executive, as the crown was henceforward to be called. It was to secure to the monarch the right of proroguing the

---

[*] Mounier, *Considérations sur la Gouvernement, et particulièrement sur celui qui convient à la France.* Laboulaye, *Cours de Législation comparée. Revue des Cours Littéraires,* 1869, 632. Lavergne, *Les Monarchiens de la Constituante. Revue des Deux Mondes,* 1842.

National Assembly, and even of dissolving it under
the absolute condition of fresh elections : it gave him
the absolute veto, that royal sanction without which
no decision of the people's Assembly had any power.
In this he was upheld by Lally, who, supported by
Montesquieu and his Anglo-American school, and
especially by the Genevese Delolme, repeated the
axiom, "A single power in the State would swallow
up everything; two would rival each other; but three
would maintain the equilibrium."

On this question of the veto the storm broke loose.
Left to itself, the *constituante* would have assented
to Mounier's plan, for the secret votes always resulted
in his favour.* But the Assembly had long been
terrorized by the clubs, as they in their turn had been
by the streets. The danger menacing it always came
from above.

What had appeared a dream, impossible to realise
three months before, even to the boldest, was now no
longer sufficient. The unheard-of concessions to the
democracy—proposed by Mounier, partly against his
better judgment, and procured by excluding the king
from any active part in framing the laws and by
excluding the deputies from the ministry—no longer
sufficed.

When Mallet du Pan took up the cause in the
Mercure, and invited further discussion of this project
for a Constitution, four men armed with pistols ap-

* Lanzac de Laborie, *J. J. Mounier*, 173, etc.

peared at his house, and, as ambassadors from the Palais Royal patriots, announced that if he persisted in this course his life would be in danger. In Paris, proscription lists were circulated against the "traitors," as the adherents of a constitutional monarchy were described by the representatives of the sovereignty of the people. The constitutional monarchists received threatening letters in the Assembly warning them that they would lose their mandates and be pursued according to the law.

Anonymous pamphlets threatened to teach the adherents of the veto, amongst others the bishop of Langres, then President, "a better sense of their duty" by setting fire to their castles and country-seats.

The Breton club, with Barnave, Alexandre de Lameth, and La Fayette, declared against Mounier and his friends. He was invited to conferences, which mostly took place in Jefferson's house, and here the latter relates that "discussions in the style of Plato, Xenophon, and Cicero, were the order of the day."

"For peace' sake," and, as he immediately adds, "to frustrate the plans of the aristocracy," La Fayette declared himself ready to accept a compromise if a veto were instituted which might be suspensive instead of absolute, as Barnave and Pétion had suggested, and which the king might put into practice during two or three consecutive sessions.

On the other hand he was to have nothing to say to the composition of a council of ancients to be chosen by the people.*

The ultimatum tendered to Mounier by Adrien Duport in the name of his friends ran very differently. It was said of Duport that Barnave put his thoughts into words and Lameth put them into execution. He undertook to vote for the absolute veto and the dual representation of the people's assembly if Mounier would on his part promise that the king should have no power of dissolution, that the Senate should have a merely suspensive veto, and that the nation should have the power to summon conventions for the purpose of revising the Constitution. Mounier refused the proposal.

In his opinion the utmost limit of concession had been reached, and each further concession would merely confirm the despotism of the Assembly and the ruin of liberty.† He had still reason to hope that the majority of the *constituante* would support him. On the 8th September they had voted that the legal offices were to be permanent. But on the 10th September, when the vote was put whether there were to be one or two Chambers, 490 out of 1200 deputies were absent; 122 of those present declared themselves insufficiently acquainted with the question to give an

* Jefferson, *Complete Works*, i. 105. La Fayette, *Mémoires*, iii. 203.

† Mounier, *Rapport à ses Commettants*. Thiers, *Histoire de la Révolution Française*, i. 406-8, note 4.

opinion, and thus 87 men alone ventured to vote for the division of the National Assembly.

From the isolation his unsuccessful tactics had brought about, Necker could survey his political defeat and the vain struggles of his adherents. Faithful to their convictions, men like Malouet, Bergasse, and Virieu, supported Mounier to the very end.

But others—like a certain member of the Right, who said to Lally Tollendal "Are we to allow our women and children to be sacrificed?"—permitted terror to take the place of conviction under the impression created by the invectives of Camille Desmoulins, Loustalot, and Marat. Others again were influenced by ambition or the wish to take a middle course between the two parties. Barnave had long separated himself from Mounier; and young Matthieu de Montmorency followed La Fayette.

The greater portion who allowed themselves to be led by impulse or example might have been won over by either the one or the other when Necker's proposal that the king should be invited to enforce the absolute veto led them to a decision.

Later on, in writing to justify his action on this point after he knew it to be impossible of execution, he urged that he had at least wished to save the suspensive veto.* Experience has not justified any of the reasons he advanced in favour of it.

The minister thus lost the last opportunity he had

* Necker, *Troisième Ministère*, vii. 48.

of falling honourably. His intention of making the deputies acquainted with his memorial explaining his point of view to the king came to nothing, as they refused to give him the chance of speaking, and the absence of any understanding between the minister and the deputies was once more evident.

On the following day, the 11th September, when the votes were taken, there were only 325 for the absolute veto, whilst the suspensive veto numbered 675. Mirabeau had rejected the senate the day before, and now voted with the minority. Just as he had tried to prevent the Assembly on the 10th June from proclaiming itself a National Assembly, he now protested against the idea of turning the sovereign into the head official of a Republic, instead of seeking protection from him as defender and representative of the nation against the encroachments of an Assembly which at any moment might exceed that of an aristocracy it had only just abolished.

As he could not carry this, he prophecied anarchy with despotism in its train,* whilst Sièyes called any kind of veto a *lettre de cachet* directed against the nation, and endeavoured to protect the legislative body against itself by skilful reconstruction.

The plan was at that time unheeded, but it was again revised in the constitution of the year VIII.

During the period of voting Mounier hurried from place to place to encourage his adherents. He

---

* Mirabeau, *Courrier de Provence. Nouveau coup d'œil sur la sanction royale.* September, 1789.

tried to parry the blow dealt by Necker to his party, by refusing to acknowledge the king's legal right to interfere with the decisions of a constituant Assembly, and rightly regarded the situation which ensued as final.

On the same day he left the constitutional committee with Lally Tollendal, Bergasse, and Clermont Tonnerre.

"Thus," writes Rivarol in the *Acts of the Apostles*, with his invariable insight when things and not people were in question, " the French monarchy ceased to exist in September 1789 (whether permanently or only temporarily we cannot as yet say), after having existed since the year of grace 420, and survived the most varied experiences through fourteen hundred years. It began as a military aristocracy; it next became a more or less limited monarchy; and it is now a democracy with a crown surmounting its coat of arms."

Lally exclaimed in the Assembly that it was high time to raise the veil and to defend the imperilled throne.

According to the energetic words of Madame de Staël: "The king remained unarmed and alone against a nation of twenty-four millions, and was described to be their most dangerous enemy instead of the protector of their rights and liberties. . . . . The Assembly had combined a constitution similar to a plan for conducting a war. This one mistake is responsible for all the rest."* It was only in the

---

* Madame de Staël, *Considérations*, xii. 310, 311, 321.

THE FINANCIAL EMBARRASSMENT.   381

logic of facts that the enemy should be spared no humiliation.

It was Barnave who persuaded the Assembly only to grant the veto to the king after he had consented to the decree of the 4th of August. Then, when this was also secured, Necker brought the alarming message on the 24th September that the loans had failed one after another. The creditors of the French State, insensible to the oratorical utterances of the deputies, demanded guarantees which the minister could no longer promise, and the Assembly had more and more taken the guidance of the machinery of government into its own hands, so that nothing could occur without its consent. According to the irrefutable testimony of a Barère, France, *à coups de décrets*, was governed by an Assembly both deliberative and administrative; and, full of distrust of the ministry, he could only describe it as *un gouvernement plumitif.**

In this difficult situation Necker proposed that a quarter of the collected revenue should patriotically be placed at the disposal of the treasury. Credit being exhausted, the king wished that the whole truth should be told.†

The deputies hesitated between the alternative of bankruptcy and the necessity of requiring such a sacrifice of the people, to whom they had so frequently and solemnly promised a diminution of their burdens.

* Barère, *Mémoires*, i. 318, 319.
† Necker, *Troisième Ministère*, vii. 83.

Then Mirabeau arose, and in one of his most memorable and convincing speeches carried Necker's proposition.

Madame de Staël relates how she saw him ascend the tribune three times on that day, and how for two hours his marvellous eloquence held his hearers spellbound.

She attempts to describe it herself, but leaves off with a quotation from the *Journal de Paris:* "*Que seroit-ce si vous aviez vu le monstre?*" Again, referring to Mirabeau's description of the general ruin, she ends by saying: "No one yet realized the miserable state to which a nation could be reduced by bankruptcy, famine, wholesale murder, the scaffold, civil war, war with other countries, and tyranny. The mere picture Mirabeau sketched of it was then sufficiently startling."*

Morris relates that Madame de Staël was ready in those days not only to admire Mirabeau's attitude but also to render thanks to him for speaking of her father's extraordinary popularity as the reward of eminent merit, long experience, and an unusual knowledge of financial affairs.†

People asked each other at that time in the *constituante* whether Necker had at last won over his powerful opponent; or else they expressed the opinion, subsequently shared by Madame de Staël, that he

---

* Madame de Staël, *Considérations*, xii. 315.

† Jared Sparks, *Gouverneur Morris*, i. 326.

only desired to stifle him all the quicker by the weight of the responsibility he laid at his door.

She did not then think either idea had any foundation in fact. Mirabeau felt himself strong enough to be just to Necker, especially as he was aware that he was making his funeral oration.

The very fact that Mirabeau soon hoped to govern in person prevented his making all government impossible. His own special power over the Assembly dates from that day when, after long resistance, it at length yielded to the power of his word. He had no other rival in men's favour except La Fayette, who now stood at the head of that which was then the only real power in France, and who gave himself up all the more to the delusion that he commanded the situation, from the fact that Bailly, the mayor of Paris, had entrusted him with the actual leadership of the police, and thus with the care of the capital, Versailles, the Court, and the Assembly.

During these weeks he held the demagogues of the Palais Royal in check, with the help of the Common Council, and he apparently suppressed the Orleanist plots. At that time Danton acted on the right bank of the Seine as a paid agitator in the Orleanist cause.*

The momentary check was however no improvement on the situation, and was only to be ascribed to the chance intrigues of the conflict.

The Duke of Orleans, and still more the party which

* Sybel, *History of the Revolution*, i. 89.

had taken possession of this cowardly conspirator,[*]
reckoned on a crime to put themselves by some means
or other in possession of the vacant sovereignty.   La
Fayette did not go so far; he desired to bring the
king to Paris, there to dispose of him as a tool.[†]   But
this space of time was not lost to the Revolution.

La Fayette, who at the head of his city militia
dispersed crowds of rebels aiming at Versailles even in
the days of the discussion of the veto, invited the Paris
commune on the 8th September to obtain reform of the
criminal code from the Assembly, and, as this was not
carried out with sufficient alacrity, he proposed the suspension of all verdicts until it was done.[‡]   It was time
to think of the king's safety and those belonging to him.

"All is lost," Mirabeau even then said to his friend
de la Marck; "the king and the queen will be destroyed
after this and the populace will scourge their corpses."
"*Oui, on battra leurs cadavres!*" he repeated, realizing the impression his words created.[§]

The first project of flight was the queen's.   She
should go with her children to the Netherlands.[||]

In the middle of September several moderate
deputies, supported by the ministers Montmorin and
La Luzerne, recommended the king to withdraw with

[*] Madame de Staël, *Considérations*, xii. 308, 309.

[†] Necker, *De la Révolution Française*, ix. 275.   Sybel, *Geschichte
der Revolutionzeit*, 198.

[‡] La Fayette, *Memoirs*, ii. 294, 296.   Droz, *Histoire de Louis XVI.*
ii. 451.

[§] Bacourt, *Correspondance entre Mirabeau et de la Marck*, i. 112.

[||] Wertheimer, *Documents Inédits. Revue Historique*, ii. 1884.

the Assembly, to Soissons or Compiègne, so as to escape from the dangerous neighbourhood of Paris.[*] Louis XVI. had hardly any illusions as to his own personal situation. He had already made his will and settled his account with Heaven on the 17th July, before he went to Paris and repaired to the *Hotel de Ville*, for he believed that he should be butchered.[†] But in the face of danger he possessed that passive courage which would have saved him had it been united to strength of will. Necker relates that the king went to sleep, or pretended to be asleep, when this suggestion of flight was first made in the ministerial council. He himself could not answer for such a project, because, he said, in the whole land famine, uproar, and uncertainty prevailed; and moreover there was no money left in the king's treasury to dispose of. Bréteuil had already proposed in August that the royal family should take refuge in Metz, the head-quarters of Bouillé and his troops.

When La Fayette heard of it he remarked that patriots were to be found there in equal numbers; and that if the worst came to the worst it was better that one should die for all.[‡]

In this struggle of contending plans and intentions the court was satisfied to employ the Comte de Saint-Priest, the most energetic amongst Necker's

---

* Malouet, *Mémoires*, i. 339. Droz, *Histoire de Louis XVI.* ii. 470.

† Taine, *Origines*, etc. i. 69.

‡ Thiers, *Histoire de la Révolution Française*, i. 109. *Pièces justificatives*, 409, note 8.

colleagues, to request the town council to protect it from the threatened disturbances and to summon the Flemish regiment from Douai. It numbered about 1000 men, and even under the most favourable circumstances had it remained loyal it could have been of no real avail. Fate had however ordained that it should turn the scale in another direction.

The banquet in the theatre at Versailles in honour of the officers of the regiment was followed by the appearance of the queen and then of the king: the distribution of the white cockade instead of that adopted by the king on the 17th of June, the enthusiastic ovations for the royal family, and that whole incautious, but so easily explained scene, out of which a monarchy crushed to the dust found comfort in its unheard-of humiliation, and its adherents an opportunity for the expression of feelings ennobled by danger and oppression.

This demonstration of loyalty was even more welcome to the clubs than to the court. Such a proceeding might promote an uproar.

The harvest had again been a failure and had not as yet been brought to the market. Necker endeavoured to meet the rise in prices by the purchase of corn, more especially in England, and he succeeded in providing at any rate for Paris to such purpose that the price of bread remained moderate.*

He could not however do away with a crowd of about 40,000 homeless and unemployed vagabonds

---

* Sybel, *Geschichte der Revolutionszeit*, i. 95, note.

who lay in wait for a disturbance, nor could he hinder Marat from describing in the *Publiciste Parisien* how the Government exported the grain of the country that it might import poisoned bread to sell at its weight in gold.* When the news of the banquet at Versailles reached Paris, a report was spread abroad that the oath of the counter-revolution was in preparation. The long smouldering hatred against the queen burst into flames. Even amongst those who might be called educated people the shocking witticism went the rounds that it " needed a Marshal Turenne (tue Reine) to save France."† The patriotic cockade supposed to have been slighted was everywhere to be seen: reports of the king's intended flight with his family began freely to circulate. Meanwhile on the morning of the 5th October the king's consent to the decree of the 4th of August and to the Declaration of the Rights of Men reached the Assembly. But the king stipulated before giving his final consent that the constitution should first be completed and that the rights of the Executive should be amply secured.

At the same time he entreated the Assembly to desist from a sudden interruption of the course of justice at a moment when authority neither had sufficient power to impose taxation nor above all to maintain order and provide for the country. In the discussion which ensued upon these both moderate

---

* Hatin, *Histoire du Journal en France.*   Laboulaye, loc. cit. 653.
† Droz, *Histoire de Louis XVI.* iii. 19.

and reasonable remarks, Mirabeau had lifted up his voice against Robespierre on hearing that, represented by a crowd of bandits and furious women, " Paris was marching on Versailles."

There had been no bread in some of the bakers' shops in Paris on the morning of that day, and the rioters inaugurated the disturbance by taking possession of the Hotel de Ville.   That portion of the National Guard represented by the rebellious *Gardes Françaises* announced to La Fayette their general, that they could not fire on the famished populace. The latter himself prevented the unpaid city guard from carrying out its intention, and it is stated that the cry which summoned the king to Paris and settled the turn of affairs on the 6th of October, the following day, was raised by La Fayette's soldiers.*

Thus originated the procession to Versailles to free the king from the aristocracy and to demand bread for the hungry populace.   The ways and means adopted by La Fayette for following with his armed force is too characteristic to be overlooked.

It was about four o'clock on that 5th of October. Since sunrise the tocsin had sounded, and the crowds from the suburbs streamed past La Fayette, whose leadership they desired, shouting " To Versailles, to Versailles ! "

The general was on horseback on the *Quai de la Grève* at the head of his battalion.   For hours he contemplated the stream of men, taking apparently no

* Sybel, *Geschichte der Revolutionszeit*, i. 98, 99. 104, 105.

notice of the crowd and its stormy cries or else putting them aside with plausible reasons.

Then a young man stepped from the crowd and said, "General, you have hitherto led us, but it is now our turn to lead you." A moment later and the long and vainly expected order was given to go " Forward."*

Mirabeau had warned the president of the National Assembly at Versailles, who happened to be Mounier, of the intended approach of the Parisian multitudes, and had whispered to him that he should at once adjourn the sitting and send news of it to the palace.

On finding Mounier inclined to do nothing he insisted more urgently, and spoke of the great danger incurred even for the deputies. It was one of those hours in which character prevails over intellectual superiority. "So much the better," replied Mounier; " if they find us all here and kill us ; but All, it must be understood. The Republic will prosper all the better for it." † The Faust of the Revolution had nothing to reply, and the 6th of October dawned.

Madame de Staël witnessed this day. When she heard in the morning what was going on she hurried by quiet roads to join her parents at Versailles. On her way she met the king's hunt, recalled in breath-

---

* Sainte-Beuve, *La Fayette. Portraits Littéraires*, ii. 141. From the verbal account of a National Guardsman who was present.

† Droz, *Histoire de Louis XVI*. iii. 32. Dareste, *Histoire de France*, vii. 290. Lanzac de Laborie, *J. J. Mounier*, 212, 213.

less haste from the woods of Meudon to the palace. When she herself reached it Necker was with the king. She found her mother in one of the ante-rooms leading to the royal apartments, in deadly anxiety for her husband, but resolved to share his lot.

Others besides Madame de Staël resorted one after another in countless numbers to Versailles. Late in the afternoon, and much against his own convictions, Mounier came, on the part of the Assembly, to demand from the king an unconditional recognition of the Rights of Men. In relating the circumstance, Madame de Staël remarks that nothing excited the anger of the French so much as any attempt at resistance on the part of the weaker side, and that on the other hand they had become so accustomed to the necessity of the king's intervention that they were capable of asking his consent to the establishment of a Republic.

In the Versailles ante-rooms she heard discussions around her as to whether the king should fly or remain, whether he should offer resistance, or withdraw to one of the provinces. Later information and discoveries on this point have corroborated the assertion made by Madame de Staël, that amongst the ministers, Cicé, Montmorin, and Necker were inclined to assent to La Fayette's proposition that for the future the king should reside in the capital. Saint-Priest was alone in advising flight to Rambouillet, and declared that if Louis XVI. consented to being taken to Paris his crown was lost to him. "That is a piece of advice," Necker replied, "that may cost you your head." *

Those who were about the king said that he hesitated to fly, being certain that the National Assembly would replace him by the Duke of Orleans: a fear which Madame de Staël considered to be groundless both then and later.

Moreover she was convinced that even a military following could not avail to save the king, so overwhelming was the revolutionary spirit.

Thus nothing was decided in face of the approaching calamity, and those resident in the palace looked out upon the surrounding avenues with the full knowledge that the first shots would be directed thence towards the windows of the hall they were in. "But although the anxiety was universal not even a woman thought of leaving."

At three o'clock the first horde of women had reached the Assembly, and the well-known events took place in the courtyard at Versailles, when M. de Chinon, afterwards Duc de Richelieu, for once regardless of etiquette, rushed pale and dishevelled into the royal presence.

He had joined the surging populace in the capital to learn their plans, and half-way to Versailles had hurried on in front to bring news of them to the royal family. He gave a frightful description of what was to be expected. He described the women

* Sybel, *Geschichte der Revolutionszeit*, i. 98. Duchesse de Tourzel, *Mémoires*, i. 8.

to be more intoxicated with wine than with passion,
the men to be the dregs of the people, boasting of
the murders they had committed and still hoped to
commit.   Anxiety went on increasing as darkness
closed in, and the reports from without became more
and more contradictory, until at length at eleven at
night the news spread as a message of deliverance
that La Fayette with the National Guard had arrived.

Madame de Staël saw the general on his way to
the king, surrounded on every side and beset with
questions, as if he still were master of the situation
and not a leader taken possession of by the people.

" He seemed as composed as ever," she writes.
"When he returned from the king's rooms he restored
the courage of those present by such cheerful re-
assurances that towards midnight, everyone being exhausted to the uttermost, retired by degrees, imagin-
ing the danger to have passed.*

Thus began a night unsurpassed by any other
during the Revolution, the tragic history of which
has been summed up by an irreconcilable opponent
in these words: *" Monsieur de la Fayette a dormi
contre son roi."*   "General Morpheus," Rivarol called
him in jest, when the first horror had passed over.

Madame de Staël had also retired at last with her
parents and gone to rest.

Next morning she was awoke at early dawn by the
mother of the Comte Choiseul-Gouffier, an elderly

---

* Lanzac de Laborie, *J. J. Mounier*, 222, 223.   *Exposé de la Con-
duite de M. Mounier*, 69-92.

lady, who, although unknown to her, had come to implore her to save her. From her she first learnt that the hordes had made their way into the palace by an unprotected door, that the body-guard had been massacred, and that a mere chance had saved the queen from a similar fate.

Dressing hastily, Madame de Staël was told that Necker had already gone to the king, and that her mother was preparing to follow him. It has already been mentioned that the royal apartments were connected with the *Contrôle Général* by a long corridor. Madame de Staël could hear the report of firearms in the courtyard as she passed hurriedly along. There were signs of bloodshed all over the great gallery; in the neighbouring hall the body-guard were fraternising in great excitement with the *Gardes Françaises*, exchanging their cockades and shouting "Long live La Fayette!" whilst the latter was meanwhile endeavouring to save the life of those who had so narrowly escaped the carnage.

From the adjacent hall the howling, shrieking crowd might be seen letting off firearms and shouting the queen's name. Suddenly the door of a side-chamber opened and she appeared; her hair in disorder, pale as death, but dignified: "An apparition eminently calculated to take hold of the imagination." She heard how the people without, in the so-called marble-court, called for her. The men were all armed, most of them carried pistols or firearms. That which Marie Antoinette had to confront might be read in their faces. Nevertheless she stepped on to the balcony leading her two children by the hand.

The ensuing scene has been described a thousand times; it has inspired historians, poets, loyalists and republicans. Nothing can however surpass the impression made upon immediate eye-witnesses who, like Madame de Staël, saw the deadly fury of this crowd change first into silent astonishment and next into stormy admiration.

Just at that time the relations between Necker and La Fayette were of the friendliest, and both Madame de Staël and her father exert themselves to exonerate him from any blame in the occurrences of these October days,[*] whilst neither had any cause to be pleased with the queen's conduct towards them. The strength of character shown by the latter on that morning made, however, such an impression upon Madame de Staël that she never speaks of the part played on it by La Fayette. She only relates that the queen on returning into the hall went towards Madame Necker, and that, in a voice choked with tears, she said, "They want to force the king and me to go back to Paris, and to carry the heads of our faithful guards in front of us."

A few hours later, whilst the funeral procession of the monarchy wended its way to Paris, Madame de Staël and her family reached the capital by a shorter route through the Bois de Boulogne. She

---

* Necker, *De la Révolution Française*, ix. 273. Madame de Staël, *Considérations*, xii. 341.

says the weather was exquisite, there was not a breath of air, and the sight of everything tinged with golden sunshine only made the contrast more glaring between this smiling nature and all that had occurred.

Next day she again saw the queen, who received the diplomatic corps and the court circle at the Tuileries, which was so little prepared for her that camp-beds had to be put up in the reception room for the royal children. The queen could hardly speak for sobbing, and, says Madame de Staël, "none of us were in a condition to answer her. Her beautiful features expressed both grief and vexation. Those who saw her thus could never forget her."

Others besides the members of the royal family were made prisoners by the populace. A fortnight later the National Assembly followed them to Paris. "After it had triumphed by means of the people it neither had the right nor the power to restrain it, and nothing remained but to acknowledge its mastery."*

Only those formed an exception whose inward indignation at what had happened was stronger than their political cleverness. The leaders of the constitutional party—Mounier, Lally Tollendal, La Luzerne, and with him perhaps a hundred and twenty deputies, who in turn tendered their resignation and ceased to attend the sittings—gave up the game as lost. Mounier went to Grenoble, "firmly determined to protect his province from the decrees of the National

---

* Necker, *De la Révolution Française.*

Assembly, and rather to foster civil war and give a hand in the dismembering of France than to obey under such conditions."[*]

La Fayette acknowledged subsequently that he could not blame Burke, Mounier, J. Adams, and all the most enlightened public men with them, if they described France as a Republic after the October days.[†] But at that time he tried to divert Mounier from his intention, for he wrote to him that he was himself well aware of his own great responsibility. This did not however discourage him or prevent his devoting his whole heart to the people. He should continue to fight against the aristocracy, despotism, and the factions with equal zeal. The faults and mistakes of the National Assembly were well known to him; he hated tyranny represented by an individual; but he was convinced of the necessity of strengthening the Executive even to an extent beyond what Mounier could imagine.[‡]

The answer given by Mounier to this confession, so little in harmony with his correspondent's line of conduct, was an attempt to affect a rising in Dauphiné. What especially induced him to take this step, which has so often been called a tactical mistake, by Madame de Staël as well as by others,[§]

---

[*] Léouzon Le Duc, *Correspondance Diplomatique du Baron de Staël-Holstein*, 140, 141. Dépêche No. 136, Oct. 22, 1789. Madame de Staël, *Considérations*, xii. 249.

[†] La Fayette, *Mémoires*, iii. 193.

[‡] *Idem*, ii. 418.

[§] Madame de Staël, *Considérations*, xii. 349.

was his conviction, at that time loudly expressed, that Mirabeau was to blame for the October days, but this was not confirmed by subsequent testimony.* When at length Mounier realized how vain was his attempt to call a reaction to life against the capital in the provinces, in favour of liberty and order, he gave up his mandate, and retired into banishment, first to Switzerland and then to Weimar, where he earned his livelihood as a schoolmaster. The pamphlet he wrote in description of his share in events, and of his disappointments, is a valuable contribution to our knowledge of the Revolution.† Although they possessed no greater confidence in the future than Mounier, some of his friends and partisans, Clermont-Tonnerre and Malouet amongst the deputies, and Mallet du Pan in the press, took a different view of their duty.

They determined to stick to their posts although they considered the cause a lost one. Known at first by the name of *Les Impartiaux*, then during the latter times of the National Assembly as the Constitutionalists, these men redeemed their promise, until persecution again united them on foreign soil to those who had been their companions in arms in 1789, or until it in many cases exacted the sacrifice of their lives.

* Mounier, *Appel au tribunal de l'opinion publique*, directed aganist Mirabeau. Lanzac de Laborie, *Mounier*, 252, 253.

† Mounier, *Recherches sur les causes qui ont empêché les Français de devenir libres.* 1792.

The ideas they represented were however to outlive them, and the struggle of the constitutional
monarchists may thus be considered within the limits
of a biography of Madame de Staël. Five-and-
twenty years of mistakes, of terror, and civil war, the
seductive victory of imperialism and its fearful retribution, followed the shipwreck of the teaching they
represented.

Then after "catastrophes which had called the
interests of the human race into question"* there
was a return to the starting-point and to the theories
which the best intellects of the eighteenth century had
considered worthy of attainment.

The political importance of Madame de Staël rests
upon the circumstance that her experience in later
years cleared up the traditions in which she had been
brought up, and purified and freed them from many
illusions.

The woman, the authoress, has her own especial
story. Her chief historical merit lies in the fact that
she was a spiritual link in the chain of a great deliverance, and that, with masculine courage, she imparted
the liberal opinions she had preserved through twelve
years of persecution to a race bred up under despotic
pressure.

---

* Mounier, *Recherches*, etc., last chapter.

CHAPTER VII.

France after the October Days—Mirabeau—Ministerial Combinations
—Close of the year 1789—The three great Political Problems of
1790—Institution of the Clubs in 1789—Necker and the Financial
Situation—Appropriation of Church Property—The Court and
Mirabeau—Abolition of Titles—Civil Constitution of the Clergy
—Anniversary of the 14th of July—The Jacobins—New Issue
of *Assignats*—Death of Mirabeau, 1790—Necker's Book upon
the Executive.

AFTER those days in October, intrigue reigned supreme
in France. The first victim to the altered situation
was the Duke of Orleans, La Fayette having collected
sufficient proofs of his perfidy to get rid of the prince.
Huber, Necker's relative, writes to Morton Eden, the
English diplomatist, that the general went to the
duke on the 10th of October, and said to him: "Monseigneur, I fear that a personage of your name will
soon lose his head on the scaffold."

Then as the individual thus accosted stared at him
in astonishment, La Fayette added: " You intended
to have me murdered; be assured that one hour after,
you yourself would be overtaken by the same fate."
Upon this the duke protested innocence: the general
replied that he was of course obliged to accept his

word of honour, but that he possessed such proofs
against him that he must either leave France in four-
and-twenty hours or appear before the law-courts.
La Fayette next said : "The king has come down a
few of the steps of his throne, but I have taken up
my position on the last step. He cannot go further,
and any one wishing to reach him would have to pass
over my body. You have a grievance against the
queen, so have I, but at this moment we must forget
all injuries." * On the 14th October the duke received
his passport under the pretext of a political mission
on behalf of the king, and on the same day he started
on a journey to London, which removed him in the
meantime from the scene of action. He was accompanied by his confidential friend Choderlos de Laclos,
the author of many bad novels, one of which, *Les
liaisons dangereuses*, anticipates the style of Zola.
Years after the fate had befallen Philippe d'Orléans
that he himself had invoked, the most crushing
evidence against him was discovered in his own hand-
writing. This was the letter to his banker, so often
subsequently quoted, ordering him to refrain from
paying certain moneys as " *L'argent n'est point
gagné, le marmot vit encore.*" †

The same Duke of Orleans, speaking of Mirabeau,

* Lord Auckland, *Journal and Correspondence*, ii. 364. M. Huber
to Mr. Eden, Paris, Oct. 15, 1789. Bacourt, *Correspondance entre
Mirabeau et de la Marck*, i. 126.

† Sybel, *Geschichte der Revolutionszeit*, i. 105, note. Ducoin,
Philippe d'Orleans, 72.

had said that the latter had nothing to lose.*   A similar thought appeared to be at the root of the accusation brought against Mirabeau. not only by his opponents on the right, not only by Mounier or by Necker, but also by La Fayette, although he opened negociations with him a very few days afterwards.†

There were certainly sufficient grounds for suspicion against him in the past.   Without reference to the events of the 14th of July, it was only necessary to recall how in the first days of October he had engaged to denounce all the promoters of the "sacrilegious orgie" at Versailles on condition only that the king's person should be unharmed; all others compromised therein should however be answerable before the law; words which the queen was not singular in thinking were meant by Mirabeau as a threat against her life; although impartial research, which must decide between the statesmenlike thoughts and intentions, the passionate outbursts in his career, and the blameable concessions to the false idol of the day, has found nothing to prove his complicity or to increase the weight of his responsibility for those events in October.

His attitude afterwards was certainly not that of a man who feared publicity.   He did not conceal from himself the increase of power and influence La Fayette had acquired by the removal of the Duke of Orleans.

* *Correspondance entre Mirabeau et de la Marck*, i. 129.

† Droz, *Histoire de Louis XVI.* ii. 342, note.

To counterbalance this, although the public considered him to have been his accomplice, he boldly offered to defend the duke in the National Assembly, and this to La Fayette's cost. The proposal came to nothing, as it was refused by the Duke of Orleans, who preferred to withdraw himself to England, and by secret flight to escape the threats of the one party and the scarcely less dangerous offers of the other.* Soon afterwards the investigating committee established by the Parisian town council entrusted the law-courts of the Châtelet with the enquiry into events which it characteristically called the "misdemeanours of the 6th of October." The Paris commune was then entirely under the influence of La Fayette, and his name protected the operations of that day.† When, after an investigation of ten months, the Châtelet, in 1790, demanded the judicial prosecution, not only of the Duc d'Orléans but of Mirabeau, the testimony against the latter was so feeble that even Maury acknowledged the fact, ‡ and La Fayette as the best informed person on the subject promised Mirabeau that he would make the real state of matters known to the National Assembly. But when the day came La Fayette did not appear, and Mirabeau wrote to de la Marck, "I could have branded La Fayette irrevocably; I had hitherto intended to leave history to do it. I

---

* Droz, *Histoire de Louis XVI.* iii. 44, 127.

† Maxime de la Rochetrie, *Les Journées du 5-6 Octobre,* 1789. *Revue des Questions Historiques,* xiv. 1873.

‡ Droz, *Histoire de Louis XVI.* iii. 274.

did not do it, and contented myself with unsheath-
ing my sword without striking a blow. Time will do
it for me."

This prophecy was fulfilled. These very letters
between Mirabeau and de la Marck, and the accounts
written by the latter, justify him as much as they
condemn La Fayette. De la Marck has no less
convincingly established that La Fayette, with whom
he spent a part of the night between the 5th and 6th
of October, was perfectly aware of the fate awaiting
the *Gardes du Corps*, and that he nevertheless
treacherously assured the Count Montmorin that
nothing would disturb that night, and thereupon
went to bed, instead of taking measures to protect
them.* Supported by these documents the German
historian of the Revolution accuses La Fayette not
only of calling forth the cry " The King to Paris,"
on the 5th of October, but of encouraging the panic
by introducing it at Versailles, before it had actually
been raised in the capital.†

If any one still desires to believe in the chivalrous
loyalty of La Fayette they must find a better plea
for him than the ambiguous apology tendered by
Rivarol, who, although not fully aware of the part he

* *Correspondance entre Mirabeau et de la Marck*, i. 115-
119.

† Sybel, *Geschichte der Revolutionszeit*, i. 97-106, but we find that
Droz states it to have been raised several times in Paris. *Histoire de
Louis XVI.* ii. 344, and iii. 18.

had played during the October days, still remarked
that a lack of understanding in certain cases is often
accompanied by all the results of a vicious disposition.*   The royal family had hardly been twenty-
four hours in Paris when Mirabeau implored de la
Marck to convince Louis XVI. that he and his family,
and France into the bargain, were lost if they did not
leave the capital as soon as possible.   His memorial
of the 15th of October was written from this point of
view.   It is full of the idea that neither the king nor
the Assembly was safe or free in Paris, and that
incalculable danger lay in the future, seeing that the
capital, given up to *agiotage* and anarchy, was hurry-
ing both itself and the nation to its ruin.   A nation
was principally to be valued by the amount of work it
accomplished, and France had become unused to
work.   Thus ran a remarkable portion of the letter.
No help was to be expected from the irreconcilable
elements which composed the Assembly.   It had
itself closed the way back to daylight when it pronounced its decrees to be irrevocable.

Necker is the only minister mentioned. . . . . But
he too was " un seul qui toujours eut plutôt des
enthousiastes qu'un parti; . . . . et ce financier de-
structeur ne laisse un souffle à Paris qu'en ruinant le
royaume."

A return to the former state of things was impos-

---

* Lescure, *Rivarol*, 223.

sible. If the king went to the frontiers, to Metz, he would separate himself from the nation and might abdicate. No less dangerous would be an appeal to the nobility; the abolition of feudalism was the expiation of ten centuries of irregularities. The people did not however as yet know the difference between the nobles and the patriciate, and would mercilessly extirpate the nobility if its help were sought in any way to effect a reaction. The only means of salvation lay in the completion and establishment of the Revolution by the closest union between the king and the people. To this end the king, after establishing the necessary military organisation, should leave the capital in the full daylight, and betake himself to Rouen in the heart of Normandy, and from thence call upon the provinces to oppose the tyranny of the capital, summon the Assembly to join him, and appoint a national convention to complete the constitution, and to alter and improve anything in it which appeared impracticable.

The difficulty of the plan was thought no objection; some risk must be incurred to avoid a great danger; a crisis was inevitable.[*]

Recent events had so prejudiced the queen against Mirabeau that there could be no chance of her intervention on behalf of his propositions. Therefore his memorial was entrusted to the Duc de Provence, and it is by no means proved that it ever reached the

---

[*] *Correspondance entre Mirabeau et de la Marck,* i. 365.

king.   De la Marck emphatically speaks to the
contrary. Mirabeau did not even shrink from the
possibility of civil war. When Dumont pointed out
that the memorial would give the sign for it, he did
not know, Mirabeau said, how greatly France still
depended on the king's person, and how thoroughly
monarchical was the mind of the nation.   If La
Fayette (Cromwell Grandison, as he had derisively
named him since the 6th of October) wanted to play
the part of Washington, he deserved to come to grief.*
To de la Marck he also said that civil war renewed
the spirit and revived the energy that corrupt morals
had destroyed.   France could always be managed by
the prospect of gold or of place.   If one or the other
might be expected of the king his party would soon
have the upper hand, and Mirabeau likewise saw
that nothing could be done until a strong energetic
ministry was established at the head of affairs.

Each day brought new combinations.   As far back
as the beginning of September the deputy for Aix had
used the *Courier de Provence* to demand that the
Assembly should withdraw its resolution debarring
the ministers from attending deliberations.   The
affair then remained for some time in abeyance, but
in the course of October Mirabeau attacked the
ministry in a way that left no further doubt of its
weakness and incapacity.   At the same time he again
entered into negociations with Necker, and afterwards

---

*. Dumont, *Souvenir sur Mirabeau*, 164.

with Cicé, archbishop of Bordeaux, and allowed La Fayette to take him to Montmorin. Their views differed; enmity and mutual distrust complicated the negociations.

Talleyrand, the Staëls' friend, was of opinion that no administration could work well, in which M. Necker had a share. His removal was a *sine qua non;* as to La Fayette, he had no fixed plan.* Internal dissension had long reigned in the Government; Cicé had intrigued for months against Necker; Saint-Priest, the most energetic of the ministers, was not to be relied upon. Montmorin was well-intentioned but had no strength of will. Necker again tried to come to an understanding with Mirabeau without having to work with him. He made La Fayette offer him the post of ambassador to England or to Holland, and place a sum of fifty thousand francs at his disposal, to help him out of his most pressing pecuniary difficulties. But Mirabeau desired to see pecuniary offers justified by a great position. He refused everything except a sum of money, which was however returned immediately.† As far back as the middle of October Mirabeau was so exasperated by Necker's attitude that he now completely went over to La Fayette, and by his means the threads of intrigue reached the queen. He ministered to the vanity of the commandant by procuring the triumph of an ovation for

* Jared Sparks, *Gouverneur Morris*, i. 335.

† *Correspondance entre Mirabeau et de la Marck*, i. 353-387, 395, 396.

him and Bailly from the Assembly, on the occasion
of its first sitting being held in Paris.   He then forced
the dictator, as La Fayette was now called, to form
a ministry which would be quite under his control.
The note written by him, and noticed as early as the
12th of October by Morris, reconstructs the cabinet
with Necker as Prime Minister, " That he may thus
be as powerless as he is incapable, but that the
remains of his popularity may continue to be of
service to the king."

Cicé was selected as Chancellor, and Liancourt as
War Minister, being the king's personal friend.   De
la Marck was entrusted with the naval administration ;
Talleyrand with the Exchequer.   Mirabeau entered
the Government without a portfolio, and La Fayette
as Marshal of France and Generalissimo, with a commission to reorganise the army.   Nor was Mounier
forgotten.   The project was to unite every kind of
capacity.   In a second note Talleyrand was appointed
to the Foreign Office, Sièyes to the Educational
department.*

Always convinced that Paris was the great hot-bed
of anarchy, Mirabeau had tried to put the means for
a strong rule into the hands of the new Government
directly after the 6th of October by proposing a powerful military law for the capital only.   Talleyrand's
proposal to seize the Church property dated from the

---

* _Correspondance entre Mirabeau et de la Marck_, i. 411, 412.
Malouet, _Mémoires_, i. 373.

10th October, and a book written by Puységur further stirred up excitement on the same subject.*

Mirabeau was perfectly aware of the connection between this step and the current course of affairs, and had also most emphatically promised a portfolio as the reward of the promoter of it, so that were these transactions successful the four milliards, at which the property belonging to the Church was reckoned,† would become at the same time the forfeit that Talleyrand paid to the Revolution on entering its service. In Mirabeau's opinion the Church of France was lost, but he approved as little of this violent measure as he had approved of the deeds of the 4th of August or those of the October days; and after it had been carried out by the Assembly he called it the most deadly blow that had ever been dealt to the nation. After the impulse had been given by another, he supported the motion that the Church property should be placed at the disposal of the nation on condition that a totally separate administration should secure it to be hypothecated for the purpose of paying off some portion of the floating debt in bonds.‡ It was in the course of these financial discussions that Mirabeau thought the time had come for taking a decisive step. On the 6th of November he brought forward the

* Jules Simon, *Une Académie sous le Directoire*, after Bachaumont, *Mémoires secrètes* v. 148.

† Taine, *Origines*, etc. *L'Ancien Régime*, 18, 19.

‡ Mirabeau to Mauvillon. Sybel, *Geschichte der Revolutionszeit*, i. 114. *Correspondance entre Mirabeau et de la Marck*, i. 358.

triple proposal that peace should be secured to Paris by accumulating corn; that the national debt should in future be managed by a separate administration, and, before any debate arose on the subject, that a place and a voice in the Assembly should be allotted to the ministers.

He had reason to hope that, notwithstanding the opposition of the Right and of the Extreme Left, he should be able to win the votes of his other colleagues by the power of his word if the court, the ministry, and, above all, La Fayette, by his influence with the Moderate Left, would support him. In this expectation he was disappointed. In Mirabeau's proposal people only saw the danger of his own rise to power. The Left opposed the motion by an adjournment; and next day, the 7th of November, Lanjuinais, one of "the most honourable and at the same time one of the most foolish men in France," * brought forward the great name of Montesquieu in support of a theory which he entirely misunderstood, and completed the rejection of the motion. He did not for an instant try to conceal how little weight one of the most important constitutional questions had in bringing about this decision, when he addressed the Assembly in the following terms : " His persuasive genius carries you along with it, and governs you. What would he not venture to do, if he were minister ? "

In vain did Mirabeau retort with cutting irony

* Niebuhr, *Geschichte der Zeitalters der Revolution*, i. 226.

that the Assembly might pass the motion, and leave
him and his opponent Lanjuinais out of the question
if only it might be carried out. Maury and d'Espréménil, Sièyes and Montlosier, Dupont and Robespierre, Lameth and Barnave, all found themselves
suddenly in agreement. The battle was lost, and
with it the Monarchy.*

In indignant wrath, Mirabeau made Necker answerable, and next to him Cicé, for the change in the
opinions of the hitherto irresolute deputies between
the nights of the 6th and 7th of November. But he
was soon convinced that the individual really to
blame was no other than he, who had not kept his
engagements with him on a former occasion, namely,
General La Fayette.†

Even after the decision of the 7th November, Mirabeau did not give up the game as entirely lost; if he
really were necessary, he used to assert, he could and
would attain power. For the Assembly must withdraw the decree concerning the minister if the Revolution were to be established. To establish an enduring
union between the monarchy and the people after the
annihilation of the clergy and the banding together
of the nobility another disturbance must occur; the
parlements must be sacrificed. Enough would then

---

* Madame de Staël, *Considérations*, xii. 350. Bacourt, *Correspondance entre Mirabeau et de la Marck*, i. 130. Droz, *Histoire de Louis
XVI.* 64, etc.

† *Correspondance entre Mirabeau et de la Marck*, i. 428. Mirabeau
to La Fayette.

have been accomplished, and the regeneration of the king's authority must begin.

In so far as this programme was intended to be a work of destruction, it succeeded easily enough. On the 3rd of November A. de Lameth, although one of Mirabeau's most decided political antagonists, proposed to adjourn the parlements indefinitely, and, as he expressed it, "to bury them alive." Until the constitution had instituted a new mode of procedure, Mirabeau helped to stifle the last protestations of the condemned "aristocratic magistracy" in one of his forcible speeches on the 9th of January, 1790, and it was in the intermediate space of time that Mirabeau tried to bring La Fayette to an energetic decision. The idea arose of making the Comte de Provence the ministerial president, but this was soon given up as the prince showed that he could not be depended upon; moreover, in Mirabeau's opinion, he was quite unfit for it, whilst his friend Dumont declared himself of the opinion that the Marquis de Favras had heroically gone to the scaffold a victim to the personal plans of the prince. It proved just as difficult to bring La Fayette to the point. His self-confidence had increased in proportion as everything tottered around him. Not only did he speak of the advantage it was to know the king to be safe in the Tuileries, but he thought himself more than ever in a position to command the capital, since the murder of a baker had obliged the National Assembly to

decree a martial law for the whole of France similar
to that required by Mirabeau for Paris alone; as long
as he appeared to be able to govern the capital he
thought he could also give a direction to the Revolution.   It flattered his vanity to be courted by
Mirabeau and to work with him, but, failing to
recognise the extreme danger of the situation, he
rocked himself in treacherous safety and was all the
more unwilling to share with another the power he
imagined himself to possess.   The Duc de Orléans
was sent out of the way; Monsieur compromised;
Necker's influence at an end; the king in his power.
He did not fear Mirabeau because he utterly despised
him; he considered Lameth to be a schemer; Barnave
and Dupont to have no political capacity.*

In January 1790 he informed Morris, to his
no small astonishment, that, notwithstanding many
blunders, the National Assembly had completed a
constitution that was "beyond comparison superior
to the English."   The letter addressed to Mounier
dated October 23rd was only a gleam of a better
insight, the basis of his views remained revolutionary
throughout.†

On the eve of the 6th of November Mirabeau had
written to his friend de la Marck that he had seen
through La Fayette, and that he found him quite as

* La Fayette, *Mémoires*, ii. 448-458. Jared Sparks, *Gouverneur
Morris*, i. 338. Léouzon Le Duc, *Correspondance Diplomatique du
Baron de Staël-Holstein*, 154. Depêche No. 145.

† See Chapter VI.

incapable of breaking his promise as of keeping his word at the right moment. Hardly four weeks afterwards he wrote to La Fayette, whilst smarting under the bitterest disappointment, that he had vainly warned him against the rocks upon which he would be the first to be dashed to pieces. Blinded by his position, pursued by his irresolution, and his preference for useless half-measures as by a fate, he would drag himself and the State with him to destruction.*

During the next months Mirabeau was comparatively inactive. He was deeply discouraged. He might master his enemies, but he acutely felt that his own past could not be undone, and that he must bleed to death from the wounds he had inflicted upon himself.

Thus amidst mutual enmity, distrust, and plots, the year 1789 came to an end;—the Baron de Staël and his wife sharing all its excitement and chances to the last. The Swedish ambassador is constantly mentioned as one of those who frequented the conferences at La Fayette's house.†

In describing the life and movement in the French *salons*, and their influence on the questions of the day, Morris, who was ever an attentive observer, draws attention to the Swedish embassy. He had

---

* *Correspondance entre Mirabeau et de la Marck*, i. 417, 423, 424.

† Jared Sparks, *Gouverneur Morris*, i. 328.

made acquaintance with Madame de Staël in the autumn at the Countess Tessé's house. He ap- proached her with prejudices which were never alto- gether dissipated. He was not only displeased by the coquettish manners of the young ambassadress ; he thought her whole demeanour too self-conscious and decided. Morris was not likely to sympathise in her adoration of Necker, as he himself says. When he heard her say that wisdom was a rare quality, and that she knew of no one who possessed it in a superlative degree excepting her father, the assertion seemed to the American to proceed from the most exu- berant vanity.* But he was soon obliged to confess that she was a woman of wonderful wit, and above vulgar prejudices of every kind. " Her house," he writes in January 1790, to Washington, " is a kind of Temple of Apollo, where the men of wit and fashion are collected twice a week at supper, and once at dinner, and sometimes more frequently. The Count de Clermont-Tonnerre, one of their greatest orators, read us a very pathetic oration, and the object was to show that penalties are the legal compensations for injuries and crimes; the man who is hanged, having by that event paid his debt to society, ought not to be held in dishonour ; and in like manner he who has been condemned for seven years to be flogged in the gallies should, when he had served out his apprentice- ship, be received again into good company as if nothing had happened. You smile, but observe the

* Jared Sparks, *Gouverneur Morris*, i. 835.

extreme to which the matter was carried the other way. Dishonouring thousands for the guilt of one has so shocked the public sentiment as to render this extreme fashionable. The oration was very fine, very sentimental, very pathetic, and the style harmonious. Shouts of applause and full approbation. When this was pretty well over I told him that his speech was extremely eloquent but that his principles were not very solid. Universal surprise! A very few remarks changed the face of things. The position was universally condemned, and he left the room. I need not add, that, as yet, it has never been delivered in the Assembly. And yet it was of the kind that produces a decree by acclamation; for sometimes an orator gets up in the midst of another deliberation, makes a fine discourse, and closes with a good snug resolution which is carried with a huzza. Thus, in considering a plan for a national bank proposed by M. Necker, one of them took it into his head to move that every member should give his silver buckles, which was agreed to at once, and the honourable mover laid his upon the table."*

A more striking example was at his disposal had he remembered to quote the letter from a courtesan to the *constituante*, stating that she had been able to save sums of money which she now placed at the disposal of her country. Whereupon the Assembly decided to make honourable mention of the female in

* Jared Sparks, *Gouverneur Morris*, ii. 90. Morris to Washington, Paris, Jan. 21, 1790.

question, and Condorcet rejoiced over the destruction
of prejudice, which restored actors and individuals
like the letter-writer to the arms of their country.*
This apparently incredible tone of thought and this
excitable turn of mind led the witty Duc de Lévis
to remark that where soldiers ruled, and judges were
politicians, where literary men legislated, and abbés
administered finance, confusion had reached such a
pitch that no one was left to laugh at it.† Under
these circumstances it was by no means a matter of
indifference into which scale fell the weight of the
personal opinion and judgment of clever, lively
women.

Madame de Staël busied herself greatly with the
three great questions occupying the *constituante*
during the winter and spring of 1790—the re-division
of France into eighty-three departments, the abolition
of the parlements, and the seizure of Church property
by the State. She showed herself inclined to adopt
the opinions of her friend Talleyrand, whereas her
father belonged to the few who, with the Jansenist
advocate Camus, maintained and defended the rights
of the clergy.‡ Appealing to the argument used by
Thouret and Chapelier, she asks by what right man
can exact that his institutions shall endure perman-

* Condorcet, *Mémoires*, ii. 86. Paris, 1824.

† Duc de Lévis, *Souvenirs et Portraits*, 1780-1789, 99. Paris,
1819.

‡ *De l'Administration de M. Necker, par lui-même*, vi. 142, 276; and
his memorial to the king, May, 1790.

ently? and how it can be possible to search in the
obscurity of past ages for title-deeds which are no
longer authentic, and to expect them to be accepted?*
Sympathy with the injustice thus endured was the
point on which she—a Protestant—agreed with the
Revolution. That she was a member of a Church
which had long endured bitter persecution was not
the only reason for this. As she openly admitted at
a later period, she could not forget that the happiness
of her own life had been shipwrecked by the fact
that marriage with non-Catholics was forbidden by
the Church. Where Necker made personal motives
of this kind a reason for reserve, and thus came to a
fairer decision, his daughter seized on the history of
the religious persecutions, on that of the Cevennes
wars and of the revocation of the Edict of Nantes,
to make the foremost representative of the French
Church—to make Bossuet responsible for the combination of intolerance with despotism, and to deprive
the Church to which he belonged of her rights and
privileges in the State. Intolerant as this conclusion
was in itself, Madame de Staël nevertheless fully recognised that one of the chief causes for the diminution
of religion in France lay in " the union of dogma and
privilege," in the confusion of the articles of faith
with the political creed.† Her sincere love of liberty
drew her back to the right path when the attack on

---

* Madame de Staël, *Considérations*, xii. 355, 362. Jared Sparks,
Gouverneur Morris, i. 335.

† Madame de Staël, *Considérations*, xii. 299, 355, etc.

the clergy no longer concerned their property or worldly honours but their conscience.

In her later records, as in her personal attitude during the year 1790, although she may not herself have been aware of it, the withdrawal of the influence of Necker's views made itself gradually felt. Whilst he found himself more and more relegated to play the part of a passive spectator after filling the first place in the State, it was only natural that, although Madame de Staël continued to look up to her father with undiminished admiration, she should nevertheless be possessed by the current ideas arising from the pressing necessity for an independent effort towards the social salvation which an overthrown government could no longer accomplish.

For every administration was condemned to inaction by the decree of the 7th of November; on the one hand the Assembly refused to give the king ministers from its midst; and on the other hand it fancied it could govern, although unable to command obedience. That which followed was inevitable. A crowd of officials spread over France who virtually depended on the National Assembly alone. The right of election was worked upon every conceivable system during the whole period of the Revolution, and almost amounted to universal suffrage, as it embraced four million active citizens, although, by maintaining a small census on the wages of three working days, the Constitution of 1791 refused to grant the full equality dreamt of in the *Rights of Man.*[*] Thus even in 1789 those who possessed nothing acquired power and the resolve to employ it against property. Owing to the sudden and unrestricted freedom of the Press, and the equally unconditional right to hold meetings, the clubs and journals now became the real leaders of public affairs. The Breton club, still led by the triumvirate formed by Duport, Lameth and Barnave, had assembled since October in the Jacobin monastery in Paris, and the same Duport who had armed Paris, again gave proof of his talent for organising disorder by providing himself with agents and combinations in the departments, which, under the name of patriotic associations, operated in conjunction with his club in Paris, kept up the ferment and stirred up passion ; organising a system, both of *espionage* and of *propaganda,* which made it so impossible for quiet and circumspect citizens to exist, that the members and adherents of the club in the capital soon became the real masters of the situation, until they eventually fell into the hands of their successors and deadly enemies, the Jacobins. Madame de Staël compares this club to a mine which might cause an explosion at any moment.[†]

In April, 1790, an attempt was indeed made to counteract it by another; by the club founded by La Fayette, Bailly, La Rochefoucauld, Talleyrand, Cha-

[*] Jules Simon, *Une Académie sous le Directoire,* 289.

[†] Droz, *Histoire de Louis XVI.* iii. 102, 103. Sybel, *Geschichte der Revolutionszeit,* i. 121. Madame de Staël, *Considérations,* xii. 400.

pelier, and Roederer in 1789, supported by Mirabeau, and presided over by Sièyes, but like every future attempt it failed to check the torrent let loose. " The task of maintaining, limiting, forbidding, belongs to the Government, and not to a club," Madame de Staël rightly remarks. It was still less likely to succeed in this instance, as the difference between Duport and La Fayette or between Barnave and Talleyrand lay much more in the struggle for power than in the cause of principle. Both parties wished for the Revolution, and both wished to control it. An understanding with the conservative forces was not to be thought of. How could men of the strict uprightness of Clermont-Tonnerre or Malouet work together with A. de Lameth or Duport? The one was held by them to be as little to be relied upon as he was dangerous, and the other to be a fanatic who in order to reach his object would even stoop to a lie.*

Whilst the country was being turned upside down in feverish haste, the minister who was still nominally at the head of affairs had to meet the daily increasing expenses of the Revolution ; and it is reckoned that it cost several millions monthly to support the Parisian populace alone.† On the 6th of March, Necker was obliged to announce to the deputies that the deficit for

---

* Malouet, *Mémoires*, i. 281. Léouzon Le Duc, *Correspondance Diplomatique du Baron de Staël-Holstein*, 144. Dépêche No. 136. *Galerie Historique des Contemporains*, iv. 281 : A. Duport.

† A. Sorel, *L'Europe et la Révolution Française*, i. 206. Sybel *Geschichte der Revolutionszeit*, i. 130.

the next six months amounted to two hundred and ninety-four millions. The proposals he suggested on making this announcement were no longer pervaded by the former confidence. He now spoke of his failing health, caused by so many anxieties—of the necessity of a rest, if not of retirement. He begged the Assembly, who refused his request, to give him a finance commission chosen out of their midst, so that the responsibility might not rest entirely upon him. Instead of founding a national bank, guaranteed by the State as Necker intended, his demands for money had been met since November with a project for securing new loans, and, above all, for the issue of a paper currency by selling the Church property, beginning with that of the monasteries. It is to Necker's credit that he stood out this time; he gave himself up to no delusions regarding the financial point of view, and knew that without preliminary arrangements on the part of the Government as to the employment of the ecclesiastical funds which Mirabeau had also vainly demanded, such proposals would only lead to greater ruin, to farming the *assignats,* and to final bankruptcy. For while people undervalued the difficulty of alienating the Church property, they deceived themselves no less as to the extent of the riches of the Church. It was moreover expected that a portion of the hoped-for gain would be derived from a diminution of the cost of supporting the Church services, which was already determined by the transformation of the internal circumstances of the

Church. For the Left cherished the idea of dealing
a fatal blow to the Church by means of the confisca-
tion of its property.

Necker had unfortunately mere palliatives to offer
in order to avert this fresh danger. The *banque
d'escompte*, with the help of which he had hitherto
worked advantageously, was itself in debt, and the
fact that the State could no longer obtain credit
operated against the proposal to found a national
bank, which it was to have guaranteed.*

Although it was impossible to avert the decree of
the 19th December, which began by arranging for an
issue of *assignats* to the extent of four hundred
millions, its operation was hindered by the difficulty
of finding buyers at such an unfavourable moment for
goods so suddenly thrown into the market.

The Right built their hopes on this circumstance,
and Necker himself counted on carrying through his
proposal, when the Paris Commune suddenly interfered, and gave a different turn to the affair. The
dread of losing such an inimitable opportunity in
favour of a disturbance led it to offer to take over
monastic property to the amount of two hundred
millions under certain favourable conditions. Other
municipalities announced that they were ready to do
the same, and thus the sale of Church property was
secured to the extent of four hundred millions. No
one could any longer doubt that this was the first
step towards entire appropriation. In vain did the

* Jared Sparks, *Gouverneur Morris*, ii. 94.

clergy now offer an equal sum as hypothec upon their property. They were told that since the decision of the 2nd of November they had lost all right upon the Church property, which was now at the disposal of the nation, as there had been no authorised clerical order in France since the 27th of June. The most resolute defenders of the Church felt that the stormy disputes which now arose in the Assembly would be useless. It was all over; on the 14th and 17th April the *constituante* decided to give the clergy a salary, and to allow the State to bear the expense of the services ; to confiscate the whole of the Church property, and to issue *assignats* to the extent of four hundred millions.

Madame de Staël had hoped that with the introduction of parliamentary government in France, her father might succeed as Speaker in the Assembly, not only in forming a party around himself but also in dominating the man in whom she rightly felt was concentrated the whole strength and vitality of the Revolution,—namely, Mirabeau.* The disappointment was all the greater as Madame de Staël recognized that Mirabeau's talent combined wonderful "strength and originality, bitterness and irony," that his inimitable power over his hearers depended in no small degree on his capacity for self-restraint, and that "his presence in the tribune impressed every one."† Extraordinary conditions alone drew

* Madame de Staël, *Considérations*, xi. 264.

† Droz, *Histoire de Louis XVI.* iii. 288, note after contemporaneous evidence. Duc de Lévis, *Souvenirs et Portraits*, 217.

forth a challenging exclamation or fired the incomparable and instantaneous inspiration, hardly ever resisted by the *constituante*. Against such eloquence Necker's words were totally inadequate. Both verbally and in writing they were given out between long pauses, and hardly knew how to rise to the impassioned style of speech, at that time so much in vogue. " They are tired of always hearing M. Necker talk of his integrity," wrote the celebrated jurist Romilly, who spent 1789 in Paris, to his friend Dumont, after one of Necker's speeches.* Besides this, the minister's own conviction that since the October days the preservation of the king from personal danger had been offered on condition of his complete submission to the Assembly, was scarcely calculated to inspire eloquence.†

The eventful spring of 1790 had now been reached; foreign complications were added to internal difficulties. Worn out and disappointed, the Emperor Joseph II., the friend of man and chosen defender of philosophy, had closed his weary eyes.

In Belgium, on the borders of his empire, raged a revolution in favour of retaining and re-acquiring old established rights, which had little in common with the Revolution in France, but equally set the nation in uproar. This last was quite sufficient to ensure the sympathies of La Fayette and his friends although

* *Memoirs of the Life of Sir Samuel Romilly*, i. 378. Letter to Dumont, December, 1789.

† *De l'Administration de M. Necker, par lui-même*, vi. 167.

it was led by priests, noblemen, and peace-loving citizens. Against all evidence La Fayette and his adherents gave themselves up to the belief that this Revolution, undertaken in favour of historically established rights, might come to an understanding with their own Revolution.

Even the French ministry had begun to look upon war as the only prospect of release from the unbearable situation of internal affairs.

Montmorin, the Minister for Foreign Affairs, was no less inclined to intervene in a quarrel in favour of Spain against England, then was La Fayette to unsheath his sword, not merely in Brussels for his ideal of liberty, but in Amsterdam against the Prince of Orange, who was in league with England.*

Whilst war held out a prospect to the ministry of again controlling an armed force, it likewise gave General La Fayette a chance of personal success and of renewed popularity. The same reasons led the Jacobins and their numerous following in the assembly, in the tribunes, in the streets, and in Marat's "*L'ami du peuple*," to throw their whole influence into the opposite scale. Robespierre, who was afterwards to obtain the mastery by means of the war, meanwhile denounced it as treachery on the part of the king against the people, and the great question arose in the Assembly as to the right to decide on war and peace.

Another treaty of peace had previously been con-

* A. Sorel, *L'Europe et la Révolution Française*, ii. 54, 61, 93, 95.

cluded, in appearence at least, between the monarchy and Mirabeau.

Unknown to Necker and aided by Count de la Marck a reconciliation had been effected in April between him and the court, by the king's especial wish through Count Mercy, now ambassador from the Emperor Leopold to his sister's court. He had succeeded in convincing the queen that Mirabeau had no share in the offence of the 6th of October, and, once satisfied on this point, her personal aversion to La Fayette led to the idea of a reconciliation with Mirabeau. The old marquis, his father—" *l'ami des hommes* "— had died at the end of 1789 ; but this did not for the present improve the financial situation of his son. He therefore allowed the king to pay his debts, amounting to 208,000 livres, and, moreover, agreed that the king should place a monthly sum of 6,000 livres at his disposal. It might have appeared unbearable to the pride of an independent man to receive such a sum. Mirabeau got over it on the plea that his political attitude would not be altered thereby. As far as he could without endangering his popularity, he had long been an advocate of the royal prerogatives. De la Marck says of his friend that he felt the king's situation more deeply than the king did himself.[*]

Louis XVI., a monarch born, regarded the diminu-

---

[*] *Correspondance entre Mirabeau et de la Marck*, i. 150. A. Sorel, *L'Europe et de la Révolution Française*, ii. 39, 46. *Les plans de Mirabeau.*

tion of his responsibility as a personal gain. When
Madame de Staël lays down that it is not possible
for a king to resign himself to a loss of power, she
judges from her personal feeling.* The grandson of
Louis XVI. would have consented to any endurable
position. Mirabeau, on the contrary, desired a strong
monarchy quite as much at a time when, repudiated
by royalty, his popularity was due to the opposition
he offered to it, as now, when he accepted its pay in
order to save the throne if it still were possible. He,
who risked his head, was, strangely enough, the candid
party in this too tardy alliance; the indecisions, the
lack of confidence, the provoking restrictions, the
perpetual irresolution, came from those who were to
be saved. It is well known how Mirabeau returned
with an enthusiastic respect for the queen from the
interview granted to him by Marie Antoinette on the
3rd of July, 1790; how at St. Cloud he called her
"the only man the king had on his side," and how
he repeatedly asserted that to save her life the throne
must also be saved. With the one the other would be lost
as well. But the queen, ever incautious in her choice,
and therefore frequently deceived, showed herself incapable of any lasting confidence. The Duchess of
Polignac was an example of this when she no longer
enjoyed her favour, and the hatred of the populace forced
her to take refuge in a foreign land.† It might have
been thought that at least Count Mercy, her mother's

* Madame de Staël, *Considérations*, xi. 336.
† Duc de Lévis, *Souvenirs et Portraits*, 184.

faithful servant, and her own friend and counsellor from early youth, would not have suffered from any change in the queen's feelings. But we know from her own statement in 1792 to the Duchesse de Tourzel, that she accused Mercy of having no pity for their situation, and that she was assured that both he and her particular confidant, the Baron de Bréteuil, deceived her. "Bréteuil," she says, "has never allowed anything to influence him but self-advancement."* Although the severity of such a judgment may be put down chiefly to her misfortunes, Necker, and even La Fayette, to whom the queen was inclined in happier days, experienced the same alteration of sentiment. Necker had gone through every stage of favour and disfavour.† The insurmountable dislike, the instinctive aversion, Marie Antoinette had felt for La Fayette played no small part in the Revolution ever since its commencement. On this point she and Mirabeau appeared at any rate to be of one mind. This dislike did not prevent the king giving his solemn promise to have full confidence in La Fayette‡ concerning all constitutional questions, although the negociations with Mirabeau were already set on foot. Mirabeau was left in ignorance of the extent of the existing relations between the king and La Fayette,

* Duchesse de Tourzel, *Mémoires*, ii. 106.

† Léouzon Le Duc, *Correspondance Diplomatique du Baron de Staël-Holstein*, 116, 117, 125.

‡ Droz, *Histoire de Louis XVI.* iii. 194, 195. La Fayette, *Mémoires*, ii. 449, etc.

in the same way as the ministers were unaware of the transactions between him and the throne. On his own initiative, and well knowing that even opponents must be taken into account, Mirabeau endeavoured nevertheless to secure La Fayette's adhesion to his policy and to unite their efforts to save the State.[*]

In this he succeeded as little as in securing the full and lasting confidence of the queen and of Louis XVI.

There remained nothing therefore but the prodigious attempt to save the Revolution from itself; the monarchy in spite of the court; liberty in spite of the Jacobins; the social hierarchy in spite of the nobility—and this at a moment when Edmund Burke described France as politically expunged from the European system, and when he had his manifesto in preparation.[†] This gigantic struggle began with the transactions concerning the right of decision in peace and war, to which the rumours of war had given rise. Mirabeau desired peace; he had long recognised that war must give the mastery to these very Jacobins who opposed him; but he required means of defence to enable the Government to maintain a strong defensive, and that the "people's right to decide for war or peace" should be transferred to the king by the Assembly on condition that the National Assembly

[*] *Correspondance entre Mirabeau et de la Marck*, ii. 1-7, 15, 19-22. La Fayette, *Mémoires*, ii. 367.

[†] Burke's speech containing the sentence here referred to is dated Feb. 9, 1790. His remarks on the French Revolution followed in November.

should vote supplies, and that the ministers should be held responsible. Next day Paris was flooded with pamphlets and newspapers announcing "the great treachery of the Comte Mirabeau." The Left entrusted the matter to Barnave. The Right found an exponent in Maury who excelled himself on this occasion. But Mirabeau conquered, in so far at least that for the future the National Assembly could not decide on war or peace, unless suggested and sanctioned by the king.

La Fayette stood by Mirabeau on this occasion; the latter never experienced a greater oratorical triumph than that of the 22nd May; but the political victory was incomplete and isolated. This was at once seen in the events of the following week: the debates on the civil constitution of the clergy, in which Mirabeau took no part; the abolition of nobility as a preparation for the great fraternal rejoicings of liberty and equality; the federation which was to be inaugurated on the anniversary of the 14th of July in Paris.

On the 19th July that party in the nobility which had begun the Revolution, and which had sacrificed its privileges on the night of the 4th of August, now unhesitatingly sacrificed all that remained to it of outward honours, titles, escutcheons, and distinctions. Even names which in some cases might be traced back many hundred years had to be abolished. The Montmorencies were to be called Bouchard in future; the Mirabeaus Riquetti. "*Vous avez désorienté l'Europe*

pendant quatre jours avec votre nom de Riquetti,"
said Mirabeau to the journalist who had called him
Riquetti *l'âiné;* and he chose that moment to put
his servants into livery.

Unlike A. de Lameth, Noailles, the young Mathieu
de Montmorency, or La Fayette, who had specially
counselled the king to abolish the nobility, he dwelt
upon the power of tradition, the impossibility of
disturbing the real conception of nobility in this
way.† Lawful equality must be preserved, but any
other was only misplaced vanity. Mirabeau rightly
saw, and even the next transactions proved, how pre-
posterous it was to fight against things established by
nature itself, and therefore certain to come up again
in one form or another. Instead of abolishing the
existing distinctions, the Marquis de Condorcet proposed that every one should be at liberty to take
whatever title he liked, and Napoleon afterwards
remedied the blunder made by the *constituante* by
creating a military nobility in his own interest.

The next decree, which concerned the constitution of
the Church, had far more serious results than the preceding, which Necker had endeavoured vainly to prevent.‡

The reasons which induced the clergy to join the
movement for summoning the States-General have
already been given. From the first they gave such

---

* Duc de Lévis, *Souvenirs et Portraits,* 209.

† *Lettres de Mirabeau à un de ses amis d'Allemagne,* 519. Mirabeau
to Mauvillon, August 4, 1790.

‡ Necker, *Mémoire au Roi,* Mai, 1790. *Œuvres complètes.*

unmistakeable and decisive proof of sympathy for the cause of the people that nothing would have been easier than to preserve this sympathy. The more difficult problem would undoubtedly have been to trifle with their alliance, and to turn the French clergy into opponents. The year 1789 had hardly come to an end before the National Assembly had solved the problem ; and this time the fault lay not so much in the shortsightedness of their theorizing philosophers as in the encounter of their doctrines with other influences and motives of action. The political tendencies of the day, their levelling ideal of equality, must come into opposition with an organization founded like the Catholic Church on authority, even without the aid of the "Conspiracy of Atheism."

The past of the Gallican Church alone explains the common ground on which the disturbing powers of revolution were in sympathy with the struggles of this Church for reformation. By the Concordat of 1516 the Pope Leo X. had, in consideration of great material profit for the Curia, ceded to the crown of France the right, hitherto held by the chapters, of nominating the bishops and high dignitaries of the Gallican Church. From that moment dates the alliance of the clergy and the crown, at first unwillingly imposed upon the former. The clergy supported the power of the crown, and assisted to consolidate the nation. The great teachers upheld the doctrine that princes were answerable to God alone, and not to any earthly authority. They developed this theory with such

success that it was sufficiently established to be
advanced in the time of Louis XIV. against Rome
itself.*

The crown on the other hand robbed the clergy by
degrees of all sovereign power and political independence, but bestowed splendour and riches upon
them, made good the loss of their former influence
by appointments to the most important offices of the
State, and rewarded their devotion to the political
unity of the nation by the preservation of unity
in religious belief.   The same monarch who besieged
Avignon, called together a common council against the
Pope, and allowed his nuncio to be taken prisoner,—
persecuted heresy and revoked the Edict of Nantes.
The climax of the alliance between Church and State
was reached when the reign of Louis XIV. was in its
prime.†   It is easy to understand that from that
time a retrograde movement was inevitable.   The
importance of the Gallican Church rested not only on
an outward position but much more on the fact that
as the teacher of Christianity she had created a great
doctrinal system, and the theological school to which
she gave her name, and which she had preserved
intact by the help of famous doctors and divines.
The old Gallican doctrines were found to be in sharp
opposition to the teaching afterwards represented
by the order of Jesus; and when the struggle
against external enemies such as the Protestants and

* Bossuet, *La Politique tirée de l'Écriture Sainte.*
† See Chapter IV.

Huguenots began to cease, differences arose in the bosom of the French Church itself, in which men of the most distinguished intellect,—not merely bishops and theologians like St. Cyran, the Arnauds, Bossuet and Fénélon, but laymen of the genius of Blaise Pascal and the poetic distinction of Racine, — took part. The battle was not confined to the theological sphere alone. Accustomed to interfere where it was a question of warding off external attack and controlling heresy, the temporal power now interposed and favoured the Jesuits, who had gained the king's ear by means of his confessors, causing the Gallicans and the Jansenists, as their opponents, to feel the whole weight of religious persecution. Louis XIV. died, but the persecution continued to exist and to smother all spiritual life in the Church.

Outwardly peace was certainly restored, but it was the peace of the graveyard. The distinguished and educated men among the clergy were given up to pleasure, political intrigue, and too often to the irregularities of an immoral life. The field of theology lay uncultured. The spirit of opposition still flourished in the parlements, and led the French magistracy to that resistance which unintentionally prepared the Revolution.

Retribution did not fail to come upon the authors of this situation. The suppression of the order of Jesus was chiefly the work of the parlements, an act of retaliation proceeding from that portion of the magistracy which was Jansenist in its sentiments.

But the wound dealt to the French conscience could not be healed. Forced orthodoxy became unbelieving indifference; the suppression of freedom bred hypocrisy.

Materialistic doctrine found its way through the open breach. But religious consciousness, although forced back and condemned to silence, was not dead. The destructive teaching by which the great majority of educated people were swayed was counterbalanced by the practice in the lower order of those modest virtues which nurture civilisation and support nations; whilst a few learned theologians and pious laymen cherished the old Gallican doctrine and the strict Janseuist observance with that tenacity peculiar to all persecuted convictions.

Now that both in public and private life all chains were loosed, and Liberty, if not the aim was at least the watchword, nothing seemed more natural than that the parties in the Church so long oppressed should imagine the moment to have arrived for claiming the right to freedom of action, and for establishing a condition of things that would preclude any return to tyrannical despotism or to the compulsion formerly endured. Thus sincerely religious men like Lanjuinais, the advocate Camus, an authority on the subject of ecclesiastical law among the clergy, his colleagues Treilhard, Freteau, Durand - Maillane, shared in the work of the committee on clerical affairs, which produced the civil constitution for the clergy. These men sincerely desired reform and a return to the purity of apostolic times. In the midst of a generation inimical to every tradition, intent upon renewing all things from the beginning, they alone clung to the earlier rights and advanced the ancient constitution of the Gallican Church. Meanwhile they overlooked the difficulties presented by the surrounding circumstances, in the midst of which they hoped to reach their object. An experienced politician, afterwards Madame de Staël's son-in-law, spoke warningly of battles in which all doubtful elements would be sure to join, whilst orderly, peaceable people would be frightened into taking the opposite side.* A struggle of this sort was begun by the Jansenists and Gallicans composing the *constituante*.

The Left was already prepared to help them; for the Jacobins, by virtue of the same motives whereby a Camus or a Gregoire hoped to re-establish the Christianity of the first centuries, upheld the principle of the sovereignty of the people and the omnipotence of the State even in the Church; and whilst they demanded the restoration of the ancient prerogatives of the Gallican Church at the hands of the Roman See they extensively interfered in the internal affairs of the Church itself.

Through the diminution of the dioceses, caused by the eighty-three new departments, fifty-three of the former one hundred and thirty-six bishoprics lapsed; and, moreover, the mode of election was considerably

---

* Duc de Broglie, *Notices Biographiques inédites*, quoted by Thureau. Dangin, *Histoire de la Monarchie de Juillet*, i. 213.

altered. The electors in each district were for the future to elect their priest, and the electors in the departments to choose their bishop. It was in no wise essential to be a Catholic in order to exercise this right. It was only necessary to attend one mass in order to be qualified. All chapters and ecclesiastical jurisdiction were abolished. The bishops were for the future to announce their nomination to the pope, but they were forbidden to seek canonical installation at his hands, and he lost the right of bestowing dispensations.

Each individual elected was required to take the oath of fidelity to the nation, the king, and the constitution. Robespierre further demanded the abolition of celibacy, and Barnave declared conventual vows to be a violation of the Rights of Man. Far from regretting it, the Jacobins were enchanted to think that the success of these designs might alienate the clergy from the cause of the Revolution, and that it might create special opposition on the part of those who had sacrificed most to its cause. The prospect of destroying the Church was incomparably more welcome to them than any union with it could be.

Not only the king but the bishops, and amongst them the noble Boisgelin, archbishop of Aix, Cicé, archbishop of Bordeaux and keeper of the seal, and priests of the conciliatory tone of the abbé de Montesquieu, endeavoured to bring about an understanding between Rome and the French episcopate, and this for the sake of individually wise and useful arrangements, although they could not approve of the whole tenour of the civil constitution.   They succeeded, at least for the space of seven months, until the 10th of March, 1791, in delaying the condemnation of it by the gentle Pius VI., after it had been sanctioned by the king, on the 24th of August. *

Fully ten months before, since May 1790, several French provinces had replied with civil war to the interference of the National Assembly in the inner organisation of the Church.   When the country-folk saw that the ecclesiastical property, hitherto well-managed or economically farmed, had fallen into the hands of speculators or was to be taken from them by new owners, they sent petitions to the National Assembly against the demolition of the Catholic religion, and as this had no result they next resorted to armed opposition.   In Alsace, in Brittany, but principally in the south, in Provence, Aix, Marseilles, Nimes and Montauban, bloodshed ensued, and murderous encounters between Catholics and Protestants, between the adherents of the Revolution and its opponents.†
The *constituante* which regarded the people as sovereign, only when it went with the Jacobin majority, answered this demonstration on its part by advertising, or more correctly, by swallowing up all Church property not yet sold, by officially setting to

* Chauvelot, *Lettres de Louis XVI.* Louis XVI. à Pie VI. July 2, 1790.

† Taine, *Origines*, etc. *La Révolution*, i. 322, etc. René Lavollée, *L'Église et la Constituante. Correspondant*, September, 1873.

work to plunder churches and sacristies, convents
and monasteries, and by completing the civil constitution.

The portion of the nation still faithful to the Church
was now overwhelmingly convinced that nothing less
than a conspiracy against all religion was the chief
object. It was no longer a question of fresh reforms
in the Church, but the ranks closed up all the more
firmly against the new danger.

A disturbance of religious belief had failed in many
cases to accomplish that which pride of order and
the desire to hold together now brought about. "We
behaved like true noblemen in 1791," said the archbishop of Narbonne, "for most of us cannot assert
that we did it for the sake of religion.*

Only five bishops were subsequently found willing
to accept the civil constitution for the Church; three
of those bore the worst reputation in the French epis-
pate,—namely, Talleyrand, Loménie de Brienne, and
Jarente.

By the invitation of the Left, in reply to Mirabeau's threats, the Gallican Montlosier uttered the
words which the debates of three revolutionary Assemblies could not obliterate: "You chase the bishops
from their palaces; they will seek refuge in the huts of
the poor they have nourished. You rob them of their
golden crosses; they will find crosses made of wood:

---

* La Fayette, *Mémoires*, iii. 56. A. Sorel, *L'Europe et la Révolution Française*, ii. 119.

a wooden cross redeemed the world." *   Contrary to its adverse assertion of entire liberty and toleration the Assembly assumed power over religious matters; and on the 27th November, 1790, it forced all priests to take the oath to the constitution, on pain of dismissal from their office and of prosecution as disturbers of the public peace if they continued to fulfill it.†

From this decision dates the schism in the French Church, not restricted merely to its own limits but spreading over the whole nation and hastening its ruin. Much against his will, under pressure of the Assembly, amidst threats from the tribunes and in fear of uproar, after in vain hoping for a decision from Rome—Louis XVI. at length yielded, on the 23rd December, and signed the decree of the 27th November. To this step, taken against his conviction, may be ascribed his thoughts of flight and his plans for once again obtaining the mastery in France with aid from abroad.‡   "Rather be king at Metz than ruler of France under such conditions," he said at that time to Count Fersen.

The overwhelming sentiment of the untenability of his position overcame him on that day in April 1791 when a ferocious multitude forced him to

* Bardoux, *Le Comte de Montlosier*, 37. The words are engraved on his tombstone.

† Sybel, *Geschichte der Revolutionszeit*, i. 230, note 1.

‡ The king to Fersen. Droz, *Histoire de Louis XVI.* iii. 299, 320, etc. *Mémoires de Bouillé*, ix. x. A. Sorel, *L'Europe et la Révolution Française*, ii. 128.

give up the expedition to St. Cloud, whither, after
the pope's condemnation of the civil constitution, he
had intended to resort in order to receive the Easter
sacraments from a priest who had not taken the oath.

He was lost from the moment when on the 29th
of November, 1791, he refused to veto the decree of
the legislative which led from silent toleration to open
persecution, and awarded deprivation of office and
banishment to every priest who refused to take the
oath. Two-thirds of the Catholic clergy were made
liable to the penal law; the prisons were filled
with priests; nearly twenty-eight thousand were
deported; * others went of their own accord into
exile. It is calculated that two thousand one hundred
and eighty-three persons—priests, monks, and nuns—
lost their lives during the Revolution for the sake of
their sacred calling.†

It is to the honour of the authoress of *Les Considérations* that she never on this occasion hesitated to take
the part of the victims. The sense of justice which
the question of property failed to evoke was re-
awakened when persecution arose. "It is a fatal
error," she writes, "to require an oath from priests
which their conscience cannot accept, and to punish

* De Pradt, *Les quatre Concordats*, ii. 34.

† *Martyrologe du Clergé Française pendant la Révolution.* Paris,
1840. Abbé Carron, *Les Confesseurs de la Foi dans l'Église Gallicane
à la fin du xviii siècle.* Details on the subject. Delbos, *L'Eglise de
France.* Guettée, *Histoire de l'Eglise de France.* Sciout, *Histoire de
la Constitution Civile du Clergé.*

them for refusing to take it. It is to put political in the place of religious intolerance, and to excite the opposition of all honour and conscience." *

But this sketch of the Church question has anticipated events, for there previously arose a question of organising a *fête*, the first during the Revolution. On the anniversary of the 14th of July the oath was taken to the still unfinished constitution at the altar of the nation in the presence of the royal family, the National Assembly, deputations of the National Guard from every province, and an enormous crowd of people. At the altar—towards the erection of which, upon a high mound, monks and distinguished ladies had wheeled barrows of earth—stood Talleyrand, bishop of Autun, in pontifical robes, to celebrate mass and to bless the flags of the Nation, assisted by the abbé Louis, afterwards known as Baron Louis, the famous finance minister during the Restoration. It is said that cynical words passed between the two at that time and in that place.†

On the anniversary of the Revolution, when the oath was taken to the constitution, which, in a series of twenty thousand paragraphs of laws and decrees, took the power out of his hands, the king was received with indescribable enthusiasm. The Duchesse de Tourzel calls this feast of the federation "the last bright day for the queen," and mentions that on the return from Varennes Barnave told Madame Elizabeth

* Madame de Staël, *Considérations*, xii. 363, 409.

† Sainte-Beuve, *Talleyrand. Nouveaux Lundis*, xii. 12.

that if the king had understood how to use the predominant feeling and had gone to the provinces the revolutionary party would have had no further chance.*

The Duchesse de Tourzel's observation is further and curiously confirmed in the contents of a letter from La Fayette to Washington in August 1796, in which it is said that "the people are beginning to weary both of the Revolution and of the National Assembly." †

Baron de Staël and his wife as eye-witnesses have both described this day, which Necker's daughter under the impression of the prevailing excitement would still have been inclined to celebrate as the first of the new order of things and of a moderate monarchy had not the intense anxiety depicted on her father's features been a warning against such premature hopes.‡ In point of fact this first anniversary of the taking of the Bastille was scarcely less important than the day upon which that event had actually occurred. When the Jacobins realised the unmistakable signs of disgust called forth by the Revolution they collected all their strength, and renewed their efforts. Camille Desmoulins preached insurrection; Marat's monomania for murder came to a head. The notorious phrase, "five or six hundred heads cut off would have secured quiet, liberty, and happiness for you—

* Duchesse de Tourzel, *Mémoires*, i. 150.

† La Fayette, *Mémoires*, iii. 138.

‡ Léouzon Le Duc, *Correspondance Diplomatique du Baron de Staël-Holstein*, 166. Madame de Staël, *Considérations*, 377, 381.

a false humanity has stayed your arm," originated in those days. Marat's organ, *L'Ami du Peuple*, demanded "stones for all who still dared to preach royalist doctrines; and the life, not only of the ministers, but that of their adherents, those helots and sybarites, the agents of the executive. A gigantic scaffold in the Tuileries gardens should be the answer to the disgraceful attempt, and the daring demand for the reconstruction of the army." *

It was therefore towards this subject that the unfailing instinct of revolution continued to be directed. The abolition of the nobility had introduced a new element of discord into the army, it had strengthened the soldiers in their notions of equality and their resistance to their superiors, and in the same way it had disposed the officers unfavourably towards the Revolution. The daily efforts of the democratic press to promote uproar and disorder, to encourage the murder of treacherous officers, and to carry out foolish designs, bore due fruit. In June, 1790, Mirabeau called the army a tool for any one who might wish to carry on the trade of plunder and crime on a large scale. Town and country trembled, he said, before the doings of uproarious soldiers. The Nancy regiments replied with an armed rising to the decree at last voted by the National Assembly for suppressing the military clubs, and were quelled by the energetic

* Marat, *L'Ami du Peuple*.   Droz, *Histoire de Louis XVI.* iii. 247. Taine, *Origines*, etc.   *La Révolution*, ii. *Psychologie du Jacobin*, 333, 334.

Bouillé, with the aid of his still loyal garrison of Metz. This victory of order was, however, an exception; and discipline continued to be set aside. After the 14th July, Rivarol had already jestingly remarked, that whereas desertion had hitherto been considered a disgrace to the army, it had now become a claim for military distinction.* A proposition made by Mirabeau to disband and reorganize the whole army was negatived; but it was entirely remodelled. The king now had a voice in the highest military appointments only, whilst in every other respect the army was withdrawn from his influence. On the one side, discipline was strengthened, and on the other the soldiers were allowed a vote; at least on some trifling promotion. The National Assembly desired yet more eagerly to get the mastery of the armed force out of the hands of the Executive than to reorganise the army. They had prepared the soil for it by an increase of pay and other concessions; it was now a mere question of procuring the financial means towards the fulfilment of their promises.

In April the *assignats* were issued, in August three hundred and thirty of the four hundred millions were already exhausted, and the monthly deficit now amounted to three millions, without any prospect of further means of help. On similar occasions Necker's existence was usually recollected; but this time the finance committee of the National Assembly drew up

---

* Rivarol, Preface to the *Petit Dictionnaire des grands Hommes de la Révolution.*

a new plan to cancel the floating debt, which was not even imparted to the minister. The younger financial authorities in the Assembly did not attempt to conceal that he wearied them, and that they considered him to be worn out and past work. It was now a choice between an issue of fresh *assignats*, and State bankruptcy. Mirabeau had spoken his opinion upon both eventualities; his powerful speech of November, upon the fearful consequences of either, was not forgotten. But he considered paper money to be such a dangerous expedient that he was wont to call it the circulating pest.* Nevertheless, just as formerly, he now encouraged the further issue of *assignats* to the amount of eight hundred millions, and this time on no other security than raising mortgages on the State domains. The political motives were much stronger than the economical in this affair. In financial as in other matters everything was entirely in the power of the proletariat, especially in that of the Parisian populace, who would only consent to taxes which they had not to pay, and therefore made all reasonable financial systems impossible. Other considerations were added to this. By the issue of the *assignats* the fortunes of the proprietary classes became more or less dependant on the value of the paper. The sale of the State domains became necessary, the interests of all new purchasers of them were identified with those of the Revolution

* Mirabeau, Lettre à Cerutti, Janvier, 1789.

and accelerated one of its aims—the division of the soil among as many individuals as possible. Mirabeau chose to accept the *assignats* as hypothec on the land rather than as paper money, and to believe that the increase of peasant proprietors would afford a strong protection against the efforts of anarchy. One of Mirabeau's numerous notes to the court, indicated his own adviser in financial matters, the Genevan, Clavières, as the successor of Necker, whose retirement he regarded as a foregone conclusion.* On this occasion Necker met him half-way. He tendered a special memorial to the National Assembly earnestly warning it against issuing fresh *assignats*, and prophesying, what really came to pass, that without previous reform of the economy of the State these fresh sums would disappear like the four hundred millions derived from the Church property. He took the opportunity of uttering words of political wisdom concerning the danger of allowing abstractions to enter into public affairs, and of putting systems in the place of experience.† "*Le gros bon sens*," he said pointedly; "every day I would bow before it with increasing respect."‡ This memorial, listened to with frosty indifference by the Assembly, was read on the 27th of August. On the 31st of August, Bouillé suppressed the mutinous regiments at Nancy.

* *Correspondance entre Mirabeau et de la Marck*, ii. 149-156.
† *De l'Administration de M. Necker, par lui-méme*, vii. 448.
‡ Necker, *Du pouvoir exécutif dans les grands Etats*, viii. 46.

In its fury over this, the demagogic party in Paris made Necker responsible for the triumph of order. As far back as July, Marat had insanely accused Necker, in one of his pamphlets against him, of having devoted the quarter of his income — that patriotic gift which never was repaid—to the purpose of raising and arming 500,000 men to enslave France.[*]

Even earlier, towards the end of 1789, Robespierre assured Garat, afterwards minister of justice, that Necker plundered the State treasure; pack-horses had been met on the road to Geneva laden with his gold![†]

The king's prime minister found himself constantly forced to justify himself in the most humiliating manner, and to make useless attempts to invoke the protection of the Assembly against base accusations.[‡] In the first days of September things reached such a point that La Fayette, whilst an uproarious crowd in the streets of Paris demanded vengeance for the slaughter at Nancy, sent an *aide-de-camp* to Necker and warned him to take measures for his safety. He went to St. Ouen, where his arrival caused such excitement that he found it unadvisable to go to his own house, and passed the night wandering about

---

[*] *Pamphlet de Marat contre Necker*, Juillet, 1790. In Taine, *Origines*, etc. *La Révolution*, ii. *Psychologie du Jacobin.*

[†] Garat, *Mémoires*, i. 97.

[‡] Necker, *Troisième Ministère*, vii. 402.

the neighbourhood. Only in the morning did he join his terrified wife.*

He now no longer hesitated but tendered his resignation to the king under pretext of failing strength and ruined health. This was expected, and accepted without demur. The court felt no gratitude towards Necker for having, quite recently, endeavoured to preserve for it the right of appointments in the civil and military list, as well as the continued payment of pensions from the royal treasury, and for resolutely refusing to allow the National Assembly to scrutinize the so-called red-book in which was entered the secret outlay.† Party hatred profited even by his retirement to brand him with cowardice for withdrawing at a moment when, as Cazalès remarked, all good citizens ought to sacrifice their lives to the defence of their country.‡

As guarantee for his administration the retiring minister left the sum of two millions in the treasury which had been made over the year before for the purpose of laying in provisions of corn. It seemed the bitterest irony that the man, whom the hatred of the Right and the passions of the populace alike held responsible for ruining the nation, could find nothing more serious of which to accuse his conscience than the fact that he, who had always served

---

* Droz, *Histoire de Louis XVI.* iii. 265, 266.

† Duchesse de Tourzel, *Mémoires*, i. 167. Madame de Staël, *Considérations*, xii. 387.

‡ Cazalès, Discours du 16 Oct. 1790.

the nation gratuitously, had once accepted a consignment of fruit and Arabian coffee from Provence.*

It was hardly noticed amidst the disturbances of 1790 that Necker closed this third and last ministry with the same episode as his first. For in the letter announcing his retirement to the National Assembly he mentions the anxiety and care endured by a wife equally beloved and valued as one of the reasons for this step; in his subsequent justification of his third administration he added that he feared not again to call forth the ridicule of indifference by acknowledging the merits of one whose unexampled benevolence deserved recognition.†

Necker left Paris on the 8th of September, 1790, and was accompanied by his wife to Coppet. This time Madame de Staël did not accompany her parents. Her eldest son, Auguste de Staël, was born on the 31st August, and on this account she was obliged to remain behind, full of well-founded fears and anxiety as to the fate of her parents.

Four days after Necker's departure he sent a courier to her with the news, that, although provided with two sets of passports by the king and the National Assembly, he had been detained at Arcis-sur-Aube by a furious mob and taken prisoner as a traitor to the national cause. A special order from the National Assembly was required before he was allowed to

---

* De l'Administration de M. Necker, par lui-même, vi. 333, note.
† Idem, vi. 322. Madame de Staël, Considérations, xii. 387, 396.

proceed on his way to Switzerland, insulted and threatened with stone-throwing by the same population that thirteen months before had worshipped him. At Vesoul his life was in danger.

His calmness of temperament did not desert him, and no complaint passed his lips; but the thought of King Lear came into his mind, and the creation of his imagination, the idol he had reverenced in former days, *l'opinion public,* fell back into the region of dreams. He, who is described by Barnave as the first man whose popularity was European, thus writes: "I know not why public opinion is no longer as much to me as it used to be. The respect I once cherished for it is shattered since I have seen it tremble before the same men which it had condemned and disgraced shortly before." *

The ministry at the head of which Necker had stood did not fall till November, and then in consequence of a note of want of confidence from Mirabeau. Montmorin alone remained in the newly-formed cabinet as a faithful but irresolute observer and councillor, and was not alienated by the situation. As a last resource, the chaotic state of matters might be unravelled by Mirabeau's plans of re-construction. From June to the 3rd of February, 1791, the latter drew up the leading features of a policy for the court in fifteen notes, and thereby endeavoured with astounding energy to set agoing the whole remaining strength of resistance against the anarchy that had

* *De l'Administration de M. Necker, par lui-même,* 1791, vi. preface.

been let loose.   No return to the old state of things,
but the establishment of order ; no abolition of the
constitution, but a counter-constitution to replace it.
No surrender of what was already gained, no return
to privileges, to the unequal division of taxation, to the
independence of the provinces, to the existence of the
parlements, of the nobility and clergy as superior
orders,—was incessantly repeated by Mirabeau to the
court, and almost in the same words as Morris in his
letters to Washington.*   He held that it was no less
advantageous for the king than for the people to establish a uniform system of taxation; liberty, although
not entirely unrestrained, for the press ; toleration in
religious matters ; responsibility in the servants of
the Executive ; equality of every one before the law;
control of the finances by the nation.   On the other
hand, says Mirabeau, the king's authority must be
duly restored, the predominance of a faction broken
up, and an end put to the tyranny of the capital over
the provinces.

It was impossible to govern with two million armed
men ; the army was disorganised, the National Guard
on the contrary was in the hands of the municipality;
promises had been made to the people which no one
could keep ; and prospects of compensation held out
to the injured which could never be realised.   The
laws were disregarded; the newly created authorities,
the municipalities, districts, departments, mutually
thwarted and checked each other.   The constitution

* Jared Sparks, *Gouverneur Morris*, ii. 118.

was the work of fear and hatred, an unheard-of concession to the people to win its favour, to tempt it, and to impose a tyrannical yoke upon it instead of liberty. Expecting to last for ever, it only provided for the present. It must be altered, and from its materials a moderate monarchy built up.* That was the aim. The means, still according to Mirabeau, were support and encouragement of royalist tendencies throughout the land, by the press, the clubs, agents, pamphlets, and by adoption of the tactics of the opposition; † and the king must be set free from the trammels of La Fayette and the Parisian democracy, openly and before the whole world, "as becomes a king who desires to remain a king."‡

Mirabeau considered civil war to be inevitable, probably necessary; men must however decide whether it were to be allowed to come to pass, or whether they would initiate it. La Fayette was powerless as soon as he tried to do without the will of the Parisian populace, but as he still outwardly represented its power, his influence must be destroyed; the general of the Parisian National Guard must be rendered harmless. This actually came to pass, owing to the fact that Mirabeau was able to deprive him, at the beginning of 1791, of the gratuities he reserved from the civil list § for his private police. The result of these

---

* *Correspondance entre Mirabeau et de la Marck,* ii. 209, etc. and 223.   Notes of the 6th and 13th of Oct. 1790.

† *Idem,* ii. 78-418.

‡ *Idem,* ii. 34.

§ Sybel, *Geschichte der Revolutionszeit,* i. 216.

measures was so soon felt that Mirabeau had even to advise a delay in La Fayette's overthrow rather than that it should be unduly precipitated.*

In October he boldly proposed that were the ministers to be chosen from amongst the deputies, they should be selected from the ranks of the Jacobins, for *" les Jacobins ministres ne sont pas des ministres Jacobins"* — once in power, even they would be forced to restore the king's authority. In January he dwelt upon the necessity of fortifying the National Assembly in all its errors, and by this means luring it to its own destruction. It must wear marvellous spectacles, he wrote to his friend de la Marck, if the dismissal of twenty thousand parish priests does not open its eyes ; † but at the same time he took steps, especially in the Church question, which terrified the king's conscience, and again roused all his prejudices against Mirabeau. He never possessed the king's full confidence. As before, he was obliged to use his popularity as a weapon against the reactionary plans of the Right, the distrust of the court, and the hatred of the Jacobins. His last great triumph consisted in frustrating the plans of his personal opponents, Lameth, Duport, Barnave, and their adherents, when, in the celebrated apostrophe on the occasion of a discussion upon the laws against emigrants, he commanded the

* *Correspondance entre Mirabeau et de la Marck*, iii, 9, and 27. Note of January 17, 1791, and letter from de la Marck to Mercy, Jan. 26, 1791.

† *Correspondance entre Mirabeau et de la Marck*, ii. 360, 365, 370.

"thirty voices" to be silent. He often repeated that the thought was unbearable to him that he should merely have assisted to bring about great destruction ; ordinary strength was sufficient for destruction, pigmies might be employed ; but to reconstruct, *men* were necessary and there were none to be had : "You will have massacres of the people and slaughter," he once said from the tribune, "but never the dreadful renown of a civil war."[*]

The weighty question whether Mirabeau was in a position to stop the stone which had begun to roll, to bring the Revolution to a standstill, the king to act, to make use of the passive elements of society as a defensive weapon, was answered in the negative by the friend and sincere admirer we have so often quoted, the Prince Augustus of Arenberg, Count de la Marck. Mirabeau himself went through every stage of discouragement or of confidence, according as he dwelt most upon the weakness and insufficiency of the means of assistance, or allowed himself to be dominated by the inexhaustible strength of his genius. Much, such as the transactions between the king, Bréteuil and Bouillé, during the autumn and winter of 1790, remained unknown to him.[†] Apparently he had never been more powerful than in March, 1791, during his first brilliant presidency over the National Assembly, and after the scene in the

[*] Madame de Staël, *Considérations,* xii. 413. Dumont, *Souvenirs sur Mirabeau,* 218, etc.

[†] Droz, *Histoire de Louis XVI.* iii. 327.

Jacobin club, as the exponent of liberal opinions and the opponent of anarchy.

Then came Death, and the problem as to whether monarchical France was to be saved, remained unsolved.

Mirabeau died on the 2nd of April, 1791. The strong impression he had made on Madame de Staël, the interest and sympathy which he had wrung from her, increased to patriotic sorrow now that the curtain had fallen on his life, "strangled by his passions as the Laocoon was strangled by the serpents." Whilst still under the immediate impression of his loss, she extolled the man "who was strong enough to speak of order without fearing despotism, of the general safety without incurring the suspicion that he would make exceptions in favour of individuals." " The great oak has fallen " are the last words of the first volume of *Les Considérations;* "we cannot discern what is to follow." *

At this date Grimm's *Correspondence* ceases. He might feel that the policy he rejected derived its existence from those very productions, which, through him and Diderot, had cultivated the mind and taste of the great world of Europe, and had educated it in its theories. The southern Marmontel had come to the same conclusion as the clever, discreet, and even pessimist German. The long-cherished delusion that " If every one was not great most people were good,"

---

* Madame de Staël, *Considérations,* xii. 407, and *A quel signes peut on connaître, quelle est l'opinion de la majorité de la Nation,* 1792, xvii. 325.

the *naïve* belief that the world might be improved by
moral stories like those of the Inkas and Belisarius,[*]
now aroused in him an honourable indignation. Governeur Morris relates that when the current discussions were lost in metaphysical common-places, Marmontel used to demand clear definitions; and that on
one occasion, after dinner at his house, he had dis-
armed his opponent by insisting on such with regard
to the Rights of Man.[†] And Morris? Amongst all
his contemporaries this man who had assisted to found
a Republic had never changed his opinions with regard
to France. Events had only strengthened them.
Mirabeau's death he hardly considered to be a loss.
The gift of genius without the security of upright
principles was weighed in the balance and found
wanting. But he again paid tribute to human falli-
bility when he imagined that Talleyrand could
replace Mirabeau. This made the situation all the
more clear in the letters written by Morris to Washington upon French affairs. They are to this day
historical, and appear all the more valuable when
compared with other letters of that time, such as the
insignificant despatches of Lord Gower, the English
ambassador, [‡] or the letters written by La Fayette
to Washington. "All that existed," La Fayette
writes in 1790 to his greatest friend, "we have
destroyed. Perhaps it was the only means of over-

* Sainte-Beuve. Marmontel, *Causeries de Lundi*, iv. 516.

† Jared Sparks, *Gouverneur Morris*, i. 353, and ii. 89.

‡ *The Despatches of Earl Gower.* Cambridge University Press,
185.

coming innumerable obstacles. We have thereupon established a whole quantity of constitutional, legislative, and administrative decrees; of the latter— only too many. Happily I have been able to persuade the Assembly of the necessity for previously issuing a Declaration of the Rights of Men. Most of our decrees are in harmony with this. Our mistakes are mostly of a popular and speculative kind. We must reckon that the influence of the monarchy will amend them in a few years by means of a second convention. If we had stopped half-way it would have been impossible to overcome difficulties and to root out prejudices. It was this that kept up my determination to abolish the last remnants of all aristocratic institutions in our country."* A few months later Governeur Morris wrote to this same Washington :†
"This unhappy country, bewildered in the pursuit of metaphysical whimsies, presents to our moral view a mighty ruin. The sovereign humbled to the level of a beggar's pity, without resources, without authority, without a friend. The Assembly at once a master and a slave, new in power, wild in theory, raw in practice. It engrosses all functions though incapable of exercising any, and has taken from this fierce ferocious people every restraint of religion and respect. One thing only seems to be tolerably

* La Fayette, *Mémoires*, iii. 138. La Fayette to Washington, August 23, 1790.

† Jared Sparks, *Gouverneur Morris*, ii. 117. Morris to Washington, Paris, 22nd November, 1790.

ascertained, that the opportunity is lost, and (for the time at least) the Revolution has failed."*

The recipient of this letter left no doubt as to which of his correspondents he agreed with. "All that we hear from France," he wrote to La Fayette, "inspires us with more fear than hope."† Amongst all the powers of liberty, George Washington was one of the sincerest and greatest, and with the sure political instinct of his race he held to Edmund Burke.

Necker's book upon the Executive, which appeared in 1792, a year after his retirement, and almost simultaneously with the history of his third administration, was the most important of his political writings. In it he describes and criticizes the work done by the *constituante*.

He follows the building up of the constitution, which, proceeding from the monarchy and proclaiming it as the established form, surrounded the throne with republican institutions and by a single all-powerful chamber subject to no control and possessing complete power over the Government, until at last its seven hundred and forty-five deputies, with a salary of eighteen francs a day, made known their commands to the king of France as to their "head clerk," and he saw himself obliged, if he expected to retain so much as a gratuity of a hundred francs, to obtain their approval.

* Jared Sparks, *Gouverneur Morris*, ii. 117. Morris to Washington, Paris, 22nd November, 1790.

† La Fayette, *Mémoires*, ii. 118.

This powerless monarchy—"which now has become a mere name and will soon be too costly an article for the nation"—is compared by Necker with the position held by the President of the United States, with the authority possessed by the heads of European Republics; and he comes to the conclusion that the meaning of the Executive had simply been forgotten by the French law-givers. Undermined by the wave of equality, robbed of the protection afforded by reverence, the throne could not endure without the social hierarchy. It had been replaced by the sovereignty of the people resting on pure abstractions. Every one had asked himself in the presence of this new ruler which was the surest way of winning its favour.

In accordance with the French national character it was accomplished by above all flattering its vanity, by the decree passed on the 19th June, 1790, for the abolition of the nobility; and, starting from totally false premises, by making liberty conditional on equality, whereas all real liberty was negatived by the unlimited power of the National Assembly, which in its turn obeyed the popular current in the clubs and other political associations.*

The description agrees with that of Burke, but Necker's way out of the labyrinth is not that of Burke. The latter leaves on one side the much

---

* Necker, *Du pouvoir éxécutif dans les grands Etats*, viii. 23, 29, 33, 106, 108, 111, 279, 306, and ix. 290, 294, 379, 578, 582. Compare with Burke's *Reflections on the French Revolution*, Nov. 1790. Lecky, *History of England in the Eighteenth Century*, v. 469–473.

discussed question whether France possessed a constitution, and rather asserts that it had possessed all the elements of one—nobility, clergy, notables and orders, corporations and citizens, magistrates and soldiers—but that it had demolished them all. Necker agrees with him that confusion alone had ensued and that reform had been wrecked; but instead of seeking the remedy in the circumstances to hand he refers to the far distant British constitution. Contrary to Necker's views and those of his friends, Madame de Staël's ideas were strongly inclined towards the Left. She did not shrink from the depth of the abyss like Mirabeau; she did not express a sad renunciation of liberty like Burke and Gouverneur Morris. She knew nothing of the admission of Mounier and of Malouet, that a great experiment had failed, and that the class hatred of the *ancien régime* had increased into the manifold hydra of party hatred. Full of that hope peculiar to youth, and confident in the present, she delighted in the struggle and trusted to the future. She did indeed deprecate faction, but she held it to be natural that a generation emerging from servitude—to freedom—should dread nothing so much as a return to slavery, and should desire beyond all things to be protected from tyranny.

This tendency to advance showed itself all the more distinctly in an article written by Madame de Staël, although unsigned by her, in the paper styled *Les Indépendants*, and published by Suard and Lacretelle.

It busied itself with investigating the direction to-

wards which the majority of the nation really inclined,
and decided the question in favour of a middle party
retaining the monarchy as really necessary, although
any return to the ancient usages would be as blamable
as it would be impossible.   It considered that the
remedy might be found in the maintenance of a strong
legislative organization, such as Mirabeau desired
when on his death-bed, " to save liberty and equality."
She argued that " there were only two parties in
France, royalists and republicans ; why should the
one be condemned to silence and the other to hypocrisy, as if it were a question of servitude or sacri-
lege ? " The time when monarchical sympathies were
a sort of religion had passed for ever.   Royalty now
remained a matter of opinion, and its advantages and
disadvantages must be balanced against each other
like those of any other political institution.   Why
should one party attack it and the other defend it ?
People treated it like a prejudice instead of analysing
it as a principle.*   Her detailed statement leaves no
doubt that the authoress was not far from deciding in
favour of a republic if it came to be preferred to a
monarchy.   It sketched the path she was to tread
during the new phase of the Revolution, which began
in the spring of 1791, shortly before the flight to
Varennes, and closed with the first Girondin ministry.
Both the chances of politics, and those of her fate as
a woman, pointed to this path. She was now separated

* Madame de Staël, *A quels signes peut on connaître quelle est
l'opinion de la majorité de la Nation?* xvii. 318.

from her father's moderating influence and was under that of another. Necker must have been thinking to a certain extent of his daughter, when, in speaking of what had occurred in France, he says that not only the State but individual characters were revolutionized.*

* Necker, *Du pouvoir éxécutif, dans les grands Etats*, viii. 486.

· *11, Henrietta Street, Covent Garden, W.C.*

November, 1891.

A

Catalogue of Books

PUBLISHED BY

CHAPMAN & HALL,

LIMITED.

———————

A separate Illustrated Catalogue is issued, containing

Drawing Examples, Diagrams, Models, Instruments, etc.,

ISSUED UNDER THE AUTHORITY OF

THE SCIENCE AND ART DEPARTMENT,

SOUTH KENSINGTON,

FOR THE USE OF SCHOOLS AND ART AND SCIENCE CLASSES.

NEW AND FORTHCOMING BOOKS.

THE NATURALIST IN LA PLATA. By W. H. HUDSON, C.M.Z., Joint Author of "Argentine Ornithology." With numerous Illustrations. Demy 8vo.

A WEEK'S TRAMP IN DICKENS-LAND. Together with Personal Reminiscences of the "Inimitable Boz" therein collected. By W. R. HUGHES, F.L.S. With upwards of 100 Illustrations by F. G. KITTON, HERBERT RAILTON, and others. Demy 8vo, 16s.

THE TAROT OF THE BOHEMIANS. The most ancient book in the world. For the exclusive use of the Initiates. An Absolute Key to Occult Science. By PAPUS. Crown 8vo.

SIBERIA AS IT IS. By H. DE WINDT, Author of "From Pekin to Calais," "A Ride to India," &c. With numerous Illustrations. Demy 8vo.

A HISTORY OF ANCIENT ART IN PERSIA. By GEORGES PERROT and CHARLES CHIPIEZ. With numerous Illustrations. Royal 8vo.

A HISTORY OF ANCIENT ART IN PHRYGIA—Lydia and Caria—Lycia. By GEORGES PERROT and CHARLES CHIPIEZ. With numerous Illustrations. Royal 8vo.

AMONG TYPHOONS AND PIRATE CRAFT. By CAPTAIN LINDSAY ANDERSON, Author of "A Cruise in an Opium Clipper." With Illustrations. Crown 8vo.

RUSSIAN CHARACTERISTICS. By E. B. LANIN. Reprinted, with revisions, from *The Fortnightly Review.* Demy 8vo.

MY THOUGHTS ON MUSIC AND MUSICIANS. By H. H. STATHAM. Demy 8vo.

THE BIRDS OF OUR RAMBLES: a Companion for the Country. By CHARLES DIXON, Author of "Annals of Bird Life," "Idle Hours with Nature," &c. With Illustrations by A. T. ELWES. Crown 8vo, 7s. 6d.

TRAVELS IN AFRICA DURING THE YEARS 1879 to 1883. By DR. WILLIAM JUNKER. Second Volume. With numerous Full-page Plates and Illustrations in the Text. Translated from the German by PROFESSOR KEANE. Demy 8vo.

CHAPTERS ON SHIBBOLETHS. By W. S. LILLY. Demy 8vo.

LIFE IN ANCIENT EGYPT AND ASSYRIA. By G. MASPERO. With 188 Illustrations. Crown 8vo.

PARERGA; STRAY STUDIES IN LITERATURE. By W. L. COURTNEY, Author of "Studies Old and New," &c. Crown 8vo.

EVOLUTION AND ITS RELATION TO RELIGIOUS THOUGHT. By PROFESSOR JOSEPH LE CONTE. A new and revised Edition. Crown 8vo, 6s.

BOOKS

PUBLISHED BY

CHAPMAN & HALL, LIMITED.

ABOUT (EDMOND)—
HANDBOOK OF SOCIAL ECONOMY; OR, THE
WORKER'S A B C. From the French. With a Biographical and Critical
Introduction by W. Fraser Rae. Second Edition, revised. Crown 8vo, 4s.

ADAMS (FRANCIS)—
ALONG THE COAST: Australian Stories.

AFRICAN FARM, STORY OF AN. By Olive Schreiner
(Ralph Iron). New Edition. Crown 8vo, 1s. ; in cloth, 1s. 6d.
A New Edition, on Superior Paper, and Strongly Bound in Cloth, 3s. 6d.

AGRICULTURAL SCIENCE (LECTURES ON), and
OTHER PROCEEDINGS OF THE INSTITUTE OF AGRICULTURE,
SOUTH KENSINGTON, 1883-4. Crown 8vo, sewed, 2s.

ANDERSON (ANDREW A.)—
A ROMANCE OF N'SHABÉ: Being a Record of Startling
Adventures in South Central Africa. With Illustrations. Crown 8vo, 5s.

TWENTY-FIVE YEARS IN A WAGGON IN THE
GOLD REGIONS OF AFRICA. With Illustrations and Map. Second Edition.
Demy 8vo, 1 1s.

ANDERSON (CAPTAIN LINDSAY)—
AMONG TYPHOONS AND PIRATE CRAFT.
With Illustrations.

A CRUISE IN AN OPIUM CLIPPER. With Illustrations. Crown 8vo, 6s.

AVELING (EDWARD), D.Sc., Fellow of University College, London—
MECHANICS AND EXPERIMENTAL SCIENCE.
As required for the Matriculation Examination of the University of London.
    MECHANICS. With numerous Woodcuts. Crown 8vo, 6s.
        Key to Problems in ditto, crown 8vo, 3s. 6d.
    CHEMISTRY. With numerous Woodcuts. Crown 8vo, 6s.
        Key to Problems in ditto, crown 8vo. 2s. 6d.
    MAGNETISM AND ELECTRICITY. With Numerous Woodcuts.
    Crown 8vo. 6s.
    LIGHT AND HEAT. With Numerous Woodcuts. Crown 8vo, 6s.
    Keys to the last two volumes in one vol. Crown 8vo, 5s.

BAILEY (JOHN BURN)—
MODERN METHUSELAHS; or, Short Biographical
Sketches of a few advanced Nonagenarians or actual Centenarians. Demy 8vo,
10s. 6d.

BEATTY-KINGSTON (W.)—
A JOURNALIST'S JOTTINGS. 2 vols. Demy 8vo, 24s.

MY "HANSOM" LAYS: Original Verses, Imitations, and
Paraphrases. Crown 8vo, 3s. 6d.

THE CHUMPLEBUNNYS AND SOME OTHER
ODDITIES. Sketched from the Life. Illustrated by Karl Klietsch. Crown
8vo, 2s. ; paper, 1s.

A WANDERER'S NOTES. 2 vols. Demy 8vo, 24s.

MONARCHS I HAVE MET. 2 vols. Demy 8vo, 24s.

MUSIC AND MANNERS: Personal Reminiscences and
Sketches of Character. 2 vols. Demy 8vo, 30s.

A 2

BELL (JAMES, Ph.D., &c.), Principal of the Somerset House Laboratory—
THE CHEMISTRY OF FOODS.   With Microscopic
Illustrations.
PART I.   TEA, COFFEE, COCOA, SUGAR, ETC.   Large crown 8vo, 2s. 6d.
PART II.   MILK, BUTTER, CHEESE, CEREALS, PREPARED
STARCHES, ETC.   Large crown 8vo, 3s.

BENSON (W.)—
UNIVERSAL PHONOGRAPHY.   To classify sounds of
Human Speech, and to denote them by one set of Symbols for easy Writing and
Printing.   8vo, sewed, 1s.
MANUAL OF THE SCIENCE OF COLOUR.   Coloured
Frontispiece and Illustrations.   12mo, cloth, 2s. 6d.
PRINCIPLES OF THE SCIENCE OF COLOUR.   Small
4to, cloth, 15s.

BIRDWOOD (SIR GEORGE C. M.), C.S.I.—
THE INDUSTRIAL ARTS OF INDIA.   With Map and
174 Illustrations.   New Edition.   Demy 8vo, 14s.

BLACKIE (JOHN STUART), F.R.S.E.—
THE SCOTTISH HIGHLANDERS AND THE LAND
LAWS.   Demy 8vo, 9s.
ALTAVONA: FACT AND FICTION FROM MY LIFE
IN THE HIGHLANDS.   Third Edition.   Crown 8vo, 6s.

BLEUNARD (A.)—
BABYLON ELECTRIFIED: The History of an Expe-
dition undertaken to restore Ancient Babylon by the Power of Electricity, and how
it Resulted.   Translated from the French by F. L. WHITE, and Illustrated by
MONTADER.   Royal 8vo, 12s.

BLOOMFIELD'S (BENJAMIN LORD), MEMOIR OF—
MISSION TO THE COURT OF BERNADOTTE.   With Portraits.   2 vols.
Demy 8vo, 28s.

BONVALOT (GABRIEL)—
THROUGH THE HEART OF ASIA OVER THE
PAMIR TO INDIA.   Translated from the French by C. B. PITMAN.   With
250 Illustrations by ALBERT PÉPIN.   Royal 8vo, 32s.

BOWERS (G.)—
HUNTING IN HARD TIMES.   With 61 coloured
Illustrations.   Oblong 4to, 11s.

BRACKENBURY (COL. C. B.)—
FREDERICK THE GREAT.   With Maps and Portrait.
Large crown 8vo, 4s.

BRADLEY (THOMAS), of the Royal Military Academy, Woolwich—
ELEMENTS OF GEOMETRICAL DRAWING.   In Two
Parts, with Sixty Plates.   Oblong folio, half bound, each Part 16s.

BRIDGMAN (F. A.)—
WINTERS IN ALGERIA.   With 62 Illustrations.   Royal
8vo, 10s. 6d.

BRITISH ARMY, THE. By the Author of "Greater Britain,"
"The Present Position of European Politics," etc. Demy 8vo, 12s.

BROCK (DR. J. H. E.), Assistant Examiner in Hygiene, Science and Art
Department—
ELEMENTS OF HUMAN PHYSIOLOGY FOR THE
HYGIENE EXAMINATIONS OF THE SCIENCE AND ART
DEPARTMENT. Crown 8vo, 1s. 6d.

BROMLEY-DAVENPORT (the late W.), M.P.—
SPORT: Fox Hunting, Salmon Fishing, Covert Shooting,
Deer Stalking. With numerous Illustrations by General CREALOCK, C.B.
New Cheap Edition. Post 8vo, 3s. 6d.

BROWN (J. MORAY)—
POWDER, SPEAR, AND SPUR: A Sporting Medley.
With Illustrations. Crown 8vo, 10s. 6d.

BUCKLAND (FRANK)—
LOG-BOOK OF A FISHERMAN AND ZOOLOGIST.
With numerous Illustrations. Sixth Thousand. Crown 8vo, 3s. 6d.

BUCKMAN (S. S.), F.G.S.—
ARCADIAN LIFE. With Illustrations by P. BUCKMAN.
Crown 8vo., 1s.

JOHN DARKE'S SOJOURN IN THE COTTESWOLDS
AND ELSEWHERE: A Series of Sketches. Crown 8vo, 1s.

BURCHETT (R.)—
DEFINITIONS OF GEOMETRY. New Edition. 24mo,
cloth, 5d.

LINEAR PERSPECTIVE, for the Use of Schools of Art.
New Edition. With Illustrations. Post 8vo, cloth, 7s.

PRACTICAL GEOMETRY: The Course of Construction
of Plane Geometrical Figures. With 137 Diagrams. Eighteenth Edition. Post
8vo, cloth, 5s.

BURGESS (EDWARD)—
ENGLISH AND AMERICAN YACHTS. Illustrated
with 50 Beautiful Photogravure Engravings. Oblong folio, 42s.

BUTLER (A. J.)—
COURT LIFE IN EGYPT. Second Edition. Illustrated.
Large crown 8vo, 12s.

CAFFYN (MANNINGTON)—
A POPPY'S TEARS. Crown 8vo, 1s.; in cloth, 1s. 6d.

CARLYLE (THOMAS), WORKS BY.—See pages 29 and 30.
THE CARLYLE BIRTHDAY BOOK. Compiled, with
the permission of Mr. Thomas Carlyle, by C. N. WILLIAMSON. Second Edition.
Small fcap. 8vo, 3s.

CARSTENSEN (A. RIIS)—
TWO SUMMERS IN GREENLAND: An Artist's
Adventures among Ice and Islands in Fjords and Mountains. With numerous
Illustrations by the Author. Demy 8vo, 14s.

CHAPMAN & HALL'S SHILLING SERIES.

Bound in Cloth, 1s. 6d.

THE CHUMPLEBUNNYS AND SOME OTHER ODDITIES. Sketch-d from Life. By W. BEATTY-KINGSTON. Illustrated by KARL KLIETSCH. Crown 8vo.

A SUBURB OF YEIO. By the late THEOBALD A. PURCELL. With Numerous Illustrations.

ARCADIAN LIFE. By S. S. BUCKMAN, F.G.S. With Illustrations. Crown 8vo.

JOHN DARKE'S SOJOURN IN THE COTTESWOLDS AND ELSEWHERE. By S. S. BUCKMAN. With Illustrations.

SINGER'S STORY, A. Related by the Author of "Flitters, Tatters, and the Counsellor."

A POPPY'S TEARS. By MANNINGTON CAFFYN.

NOTCHES ON THE ROUGH EDGE OF LIFE. By LYNN CYRIL D'OYLE.

WE TWO AT MONTE CARLO. By ALBERT D. VANDAM.

WHO IS THE MAN? A Tale of the Scottish Border. By J. S. TAIT.

THE CHILD OF STAFFERTON. By CANON KNOX LITTLE.

THE BROKEN VOW: A Story of Here and Hereafter. By CANON KNOX LITTLE.

THE STORY OF AN AFRICAN FARM. By CLIVE SCHREINER.

PADDY AT HOME. By BARON F. DE MANDAT-GRANCEY.

CHARLOTTE ELIZABETH, LIFE AND LETTERS OF, Princess Palatine and Mother of Philippe d Orléans, Regent of France, 1652–1722. With Portraits. Demy 8vo, 10s. 6d.

CHARNAY (DÉSIRÉ)—

THE ANCIENT CITIES OF THE NEW WORLD. Being Travels and Explorations in Mexico and Central America, 1857—1882. With upwards of 200 Illustrations. Super Royal 8vo, 31s. 6d.

CHRIST THAT IS TO BE, THE: A Latter-day Romance. Third Edition. Demy 8vo, 3s. 6d.

CHURCH (PROFESSOR A. H.), M.A. Oxon.—Continued—

FOOD GRAINS OF INDIA. With numerous Woodcuts. Small 4to, 6s.

ENGLISH PORCELAIN. A Handbook to the China made in England during the Eighteenth Century, as illustrated by Specimens chiefly in the National Collection. With numerous Woodcuts. Large crown 8vo, 3s.

ENGLISH EARTHENWARE. A Handbook to the Wares made in England during the 17th and 18th Centuries, as illustrated by Specimens in the National Collections. With numerous Woodcuts. Large crown 8vo, 3s.

PLAIN WORDS ABOUT WATER. Illustrated. Crown 8vo, sewed, 6d.

FOOD: Some Account of its Sources, Constituents, and Uses. A New and Revised Edition. Large crown 8vo, cloth, 3s.

PRECIOUS STONES: considered in their Scientific and Artistic Relations. With a Coloured Plate and Woodcuts. Second Edition. Large crown 8vo, 2s. 6d.

COBDEN, RICHARD, LIFE OF. By the RIGHT HON. JOHN
MORLEY, M.P. With Portrait. New Edition. Crown 8vo, 7s. 6d.
Popular Edition, with Portrait, 4to, sewed, 1s.; cloth, 2s.

COLLINS (WILKIE) and DICKENS (CHARLES)—

THE LAZY TOUR OF TWO IDLE APPRENTICES;
NO THOROUGHFARE; THE PERILS OF CERTAIN ENGLISH
PRISONERS. With 8 Illustrations. Crown 8vo, 5s.

** These Stories are now reprinted for the first time complete.

COOKERY—

HILDA'S "WHERE IS IT?" OF RECIPES. Contain-
ing many old CAPE, INDIAN, and MALAY DISHES and PRESERVES;
also Directions for Polishing Furniture, Cleaning Silk, etc.; and a Collection of
Home Remedies in Case of Sickness. By HILDAGONDA J. DUCKITT. Inter-
leaved with White Paper for adding Recipes. Third Edition. Crown 8vo, 4s. 6d.

THE PYTCHLEY BOOK OF REFINED COOKERY
AND BILLS OF FARE. By MAJOR L——. Fourth Edition. Large crown 8vo,
8s.

BREAKFASTS, LUNCHEONS, AND BALL SUPPERS.
By MAJOR L——. Crown 8vo. 4s.

OFFICIAL HANDBOOK OF THE NATIONAL
TRAINING SCHOOL FOR COOKERY. Containing Lessons on Cookery;
forming the Course of Instruction in the School. Compiled by "R. O. C."
Twenty-first Thousand. Large crown 8vo, 6s.

BREAKFAST AND SAVOURY DISHES. By "R. O. C."
Ninth Thousand. Crown 8vo, 1s.

HOW TO COOK FISH. Compiled by "R. O. C."
Crown 8vo, sewed, 3d.

SICK-ROOM COOKERY. Compiled by "R. O. C."
Crown 8vo, sewed, 6d.

THE ROYAL CONFECTIONER : English and Foreign.
A Practical Treatise. By C. E. FRANCATELLI. With numerous Illustrations.
Sixth Thousand. Crown 8vo, 5s.

THE KINGSWOOD COOKERY BOOK. By H. F.
WICKEN. Crown 8vo, 2s.

COOPER-KING (LT.-COL.)—

GEORGE WASHINGTON. Large crown 8vo. With
Portrait and Maps. [*In the Press.*

COUPERUS (LOUIS)—

ELINE VERE. Translated from the Dutch by J. T.
GREIN. [*In the Press.*

COURTNEY (W. L.), M.A., LL.D., of New College, Oxford—

PARERGA; STRAY STUDIES IN LITERATURE.
Crown 8vo. [*In the Press.*

STUDIES NEW AND OLD. Crown 8vo, 6s.

CONSTRUCTIVE ETHICS: A Review of Modern Philo-
sophy and its Three Stages of Interpretation, Criticism, and Reconstruction.
Demy 8vo, 12s.

CRAIK (GEORGE LILLIE)—

ENGLISH OF SHAKESPEARE. Illustrated in a Philological Commentary on "Julius Cæsar." Eighth Edition. Post 8vo, cloth, 5s.

OUTLINES OF THE HISTORY OF THE ENGLISH LANGUAGE. Eleventh Edition. Post 8vo, cloth, 2s. 6d.

CRAWFURD (OSWALD)—

ROUND THE CALENDAR IN PORTUGAL. With numerous Illustrations. Royal 8vo, 18s.

BEYOND THE SEAS; being the surprising Adventures and ingenious Opinions of Ralph, Lord St. Keyne, told by his kinsman, Humphrey St. Keyne. Second Edition. Crown 8vo, 3s. 6d.

CRIPPS (WILFRED JOSEPH), M.A., F.S.A.—

COLLEGE AND CORPORATION PLATE. A Handbook for the Reproduction of Silver Plate. With numerous Illustrations. Large crown 8vo, cloth, 2s. 6d.

DAIRY FARMING—

DAIRY FARMING. To which is added a Description of the Chief Continental Systems. With numerous Illustrations. By JAMES LONG. Crown 8vo, 9s.

DAIRY FARMING, MANAGEMENT OF COWS, etc. By ARTHUR ROLAND. Edited by WILLIAM ABLETT. Crown 8vo, 5s.

DALY (J. B.), LL.D.—

IRELAND IN THE DAYS OF DEAN SWIFT. Crown 8vo, 5s.

DAS (DEVENDRA N.)—

SKETCHES OF HINDOO LIFE. Crown 8vo, 5s.

DAUBOURG (E.)—

INTERIOR ARCHITECTURE. Doors, Vestibules, Staircases, Anterooms, Drawing, Dining, and Bed Rooms, Libraries, Bank and Newspaper Offices, Shop Fronts and Interiors. Half-imperial, cloth, £2 12s. 6d.

DAVIDSON (ELLIS A.)—

PRETTY ARTS FOR THE EMPLOYMENT OF LEISURE HOURS. A Book for Ladies. With Illustrations. Demy 8vo, 6s.

DAY (WILLIAM)—

THE RACEHORSE IN TRAINING, with Hints on Racing and Racing Reform, to which is added a Chapter on Shoeing. Sixth Edition. Demy 8vo, 9s.

DE BOVET (MADAME)—

THREE MONTHS' TOUR IN IRELAND. Translated and Condensed by MRS. ARTHUR WALTER. With Illustrations. Crown 8vo., 6s.

DE CHAMPEAUX (ALFRED)—

TAPESTRY. With numerous Woodcuts. Cloth, 2s. 6d.

DE FALLOUX (THE COUNT)—

MEMOIRS OF A ROYALIST. Edited by C. B. PITMAN. 2 vols. With Portraits. Demy 8vo, 32s.

DE KONINCK (L. L.) and DIETZ (E.)—

PRACTICAL MANUAL OF CHEMICAL ASSAYING, as applied to the Manufacture of Iron. Edited, with notes, by ROBERT MALLET. Post 8vo, cloth, 6s.

DE LESSEPS (FERDINAND)—
  RECOLLECTIONS OF FORTY YEARS. Translated
  from the French by C. B. PITMAN. 2 vols. Demy 8vo, 24s.

DE LISLE (MEMOIR OF LIEUTENANT RUDOLPH),
  R.N., of the Naval Brigade. By the Rev. H. N. OXENHAM, M.A. Third
  Edition. Crown 8vo, 7s. 6d.

DE MANDAT-GRANCEY (BARON E.)—
  PADDY AT HOME; OR, IRELAND AND THE IRISH AT
  THE PRESENT TIME, AS SEEN BY A FRENCHMAN. Fifth Edition. Crown 8vo, 1s. ;
  in cloth, 1s. 6d.

D'OYLE (LYNN CYRIL)—
  NOTCHES ON THE ROUGH EDGE OF LIFE.
  Crown 8vo, 1s. ; in cloth, 1s. 6d.

DE STAËL (MADAME)—
  MADAME DE STAËL: Her Friends, and Her Influence
  in Politics and Literature. By LADY BLENNERHASSETT. Translated from the
  German by J. E. GORDON CUMMING. With a Portrait. 3 vols. Demy 8vo, 36s.

DE WINDT (H.)—
  SIBERIA AS IT IS. With Numerous Illustrations.
  [In the Press.
  FROM PEKIN TO CALAIS BY LAND. With nume-
  rous Illustrations by C. E. FRIPP from Sketches by the Author. Demy 8vo, 20s.
  A RIDE TO INDIA ACROSS PERSIA AND BELU-
  CHISTAN. With numerous Illustrations and Map. Demy 8vo, 16s.

DICKENS (CHARLES), WORKS BY—See pages 31—37.
  THE LETTERS OF CHARLES DICKENS. Two
  vols, uniform with "The Charles Dickens Edition" of his Works. Crown 8vo, 7s.
  THE LIFE OF CHARLES DICKENS—*See "Forster "*
  THE CHARLES DICKENS BIRTHDAY BOOK.
  With Five Illustrations. In a handsome fcap. 4to volume. 12s.
  THE HUMOUR AND PATHOS OF CHARLES
  DICKENS. By CHARLES KENT. With Portrait. Crown 8vo, 6s.

DICKENS (CHARLES) and COLLINS (WILKIE)—
  THE LAZY TOUR OF TWO IDLE APPRENTICES ;
  NO THOROUGHFARE; THE PERILS OF CERTAIN ENGLISH
  PRISONERS. With Illustrations. Crown 8vo, 5s.
  ** These Stories are now reprinted in complete form for the first time.

DILKE (LADY)—
  ART IN THE MODERN STATE. With Facsimile.
  Demy 8vo, 9s.

DINARTE (SYLVIO)—
  INNOCENCIA : A Story of the Prairie Regions of Brazil.
  Translated from the Portuguese and Illustrated by JAMES W. WELLS, F.R.G.S.
  Crown 8vo, 6s.

DIXON (CHARLES)—
  THE BIRDS OF OUR RAMBLES : A Companion
  for the Country. With Illustrations by A. T. ELWES. Large Crown 8vo, 7s. 6d.

  IDLE HOURS WITH NATURE. With Frontispiece.
  Crown 8vo, 6s.

  ANNALS OF BIRD LIFE : A Year-Book of British
  Ornithology. With Illustrations. Crown 8vo, 7s. 6d.

DOUGLAS (JOHN)—
SKETCH OF THE FIRST PRINCIPLES OF PHYSIO-
GRAPHY. With Maps and numerous Illustrations. Crown 8vo, 6s.

DRAYSON (MAJOR-GENERAL A. W.)—
THIRTY THOUSAND YEARS OF THE EARTH'S
PAST HISTORY. Large Crown 8vo, 5s

EXPERIENCES OF A WOOLWICH PROFESSOR
during Fifteen Years at the Royal Military Academy. Demy 8vo, 8s.

PRACTICAL MILITARY SURVEYING AND
SKETCHING. Fifth Edition. Post 8vo, cloth, 4s. 6d.

DUCKITT (HILDAGONDA J.)—
HILDA'S "WHERE IS IT?" OF RECIPES. Contain-
ing many old CAPE, INDIAN, and MALAY DISHES and PRESERVES;
also Directions for Polishing Furniture, Cleaning Silk, etc. Third Edition.
Crown 8vo, 4s. 6d.

DUCOUDRAY (GUSTAVE)—
THE HISTORY OF ANCIENT CIVILISATION. A
Handbook based upon M. Gustave Ducoudray's "Histoire Sommaire de la
Civilisation." Edited by Rev. J. VERSCHOYLE, M.A. With Illustrations. Large
crown 8vo, 6s.

THE HISTORY OF MODERN CIVILISATION. With
Illustrations. Large crown 8vo, 9s.

DUFFY (SIR CHARLES GAVAN), K.C.M.G.—
THE LEAGUE OF NORTH AND SOUTH. An Episode
in Irish History, 1850-1854. Crown 8vo, 8s.

DYCE (WILLIAM), R.A.—
DRAWING-BOOK OF THE GOVERNMENT SCHOOL
OF DESIGN. Fifty selected Plates. Folio, sewed, 5s.; mounted, 18s.

ELEMENTARY OUTLINES OF ORNAMENT. Plates I.
to XXII., containing 97 Examples, adapted for Practice of Standards I. to IV.
Small folio, sewed, 2s 6d.

SELECTION FROM DYCE'S DRAWING BOOK.
15 Plates, sewed, 1s. 6d.; mounted on cardboard, 6s. 6d.

TEXT TO ABOVE. Crown 8vo, sewed, 6d.

DYNAMIC ACTION AND PONDEROSITY OF MATTER
(FRESH LIGHT ON THE). By WATERDALE. Crown 8vo, 2s. 6d.

EARL (MRS.)—
DINNERS IN MINIATURE. Crown 8vo. [*In the Press.*

EDWARDS (MRS. SUTHERLAND)—
THE SECRET OF THE PRINCESS. A Tale of
Country, Camp, Court, Convict, and Cloister Life in Russia. Crown 8vo, 3s. 6d.

ELLIS (A. B., Major 1st West India Regiment)—
THE EWE-SPEAKING PEOPLE OF THE SLAVE
COAST OF WEST AFRICA. With Map. Demy 8vo, 1cs. 6d.

THE TSHI-SPEAKING PEOPLES OF THE GOLD
COAST OF WEST AFRICA: their Religion, Manners, Customs, Laws,
Language, &c. With Map. Demy 8vo, 10s. 6d.

SOUTH AFRICAN SKETCHES. Crown 8vo, 6s.

THE HISTORY OF THE WEST INDIA REGI-
MENT. With Maps and Coloured Frontispiece and Title-page. Demy 8vo, 18s.

THE LAND OF FETISH. Demy 8vo, 12s.

ENGEL (CARL)—
MUSICAL INSTRUMENTS. With numerous Woodcuts.
Large crown 8vo, cloth, 2s. 6d.

ESCOTT (T. H. S.)—
POLITICS AND LETTERS. Demy 8vo, 9s.

ENGLAND: ITS PEOPLE, POLITY, AND PURSUITS.
New and Revised Edition. Demy 8vo, 3s. 6d.

EUROPEAN POLITICS, THE PRESENT POSITION OF.
By the Author of "Greater Britain." Demy 8vo, 12s.

FANE (VIOLET)—
AUTUMN SONGS. Crown 8vo, 6s.

THE STORY OF HELEN DAVENANT. Crown 8vo,
3s. 6d.

QUEEN OF THE FAIRIES (A Village Story), and other
Poems. Crown 8vo, 6s.

ANTHONY BABINGTON: a Drama. Crown 8vo, 6s.

FARR (WILLIAM) and THRUPP (GEORGE A.)—
COACH TRIMMING. With 60 Illustrations. Crown 8vo,
2s. 6d.

FIELD (HENRY M.)—
GIBRALTAR. With numerous Illustrations. Demy 8vo,
7s. 6d.

FITZGERALD (PERCY), F.S.A.—
THE HISTORY OF PICKWICK. An Account of its
Characters, Localities, Allusions, and Illustrations. With a Bibliography. Demy
8vo, 8s.
A few copies are issued with impressions from the First Set of Steel Plates, 14s.

FLEMING (GEORGE), F.R.C.S.—
ANIMAL PLAGUES: THEIR HISTORY, NATURE,
AND PREVENTION. 8vo, cloth, 15s.

PRACTICAL HORSE-SHOEING. With 37 Illustrations.
Fifth Edition, enlarged. 8vo, sewed, 2s.

RABIES AND HYDROPHOBIA: THEIR HISTORY,
NATURE, CAUSES, SYMPTOMS, AND PREVENTION. With 8 Illustrations. 8vo, cloth, 15s.

FORSTER (JOHN)—
THE LIFE OF CHARLES DICKENS. Original
Edition. Vol. I., 8vo, cloth, 12s. Vol. II., 8vo, cloth, 14s. Vol. III., 8vo, cloth,
16s.

Uniform with the Illustrated Library Edition of Dickens's
Works. 2 vols. Demy 8vo, 20s.

Uniform with the Library and Popular Library Editions.
Post 8vo, 10s. 6d. each.

Uniform with the "C. D." Edition. With Numerous
Illustrations. 2 vols. 7s.

Uniform with the Crown Edition. Crown 8vo. [In the Pre s.

Uniform with the Household Edition. With Illustrations
by F. BARNARD. Crown 4to, cloth, 5s.

FORSTER, THE LIFE OF THE RIGHT HON. W. E.
By T. WEMYSS REID. With Portraits. Fourth Edition. 2 vols. Demy 8vo, 32s.
FIFTH EDITION in one volume with new Portrait. Demy 8vo, 10s. 6d.

FORSYTH (CAPTAIN)—
THE HIGHLANDS OF CENTRAL INDIA: Notes on
their Forests and Wild Tribes, Natural History and Sports. With Map and
Coloured Illustrations. A New Edition. Demy 8vo, 12s.

FORTESCUE (THE HON. JOHN)—
RECORDS OF STAG-HUNTING ON EXMOOR. With
14 full page Illustrations by EDGAR GIBERNE. Large crown 8vo, 16s.

FORTNIGHTLY REVIEW (see page 40)—
FORTNIGHTLY REVIEW.—First Series, May, 1865, to
Dec. 1866. 6 vols. Cloth, 13s. each.

New Series, 1867 to 1872. In Half-yearly Volumes. Cloth,
13s. each.

From January, 1873, to the present time, in Half-yearly
Volumes. Cloth, 16s. each.

CONTENTS OF FORTNIGHTLY REVIEW. From
the commencement to end of 1878. Sewed, 2s.

FORTNUM (C. D. E.), F.S.A.—
MAIOLICA. With numerous Woodcuts. Large crown
8vo, cloth, 2s. 6d.

BRONZES. With numerous Woodcuts. Large crown
8vo, cloth, 2s. 6d.

FOUQUÉ (DE LA MOTTE)—
UNDINE : a Romance translated from the German. With
an Introduction by JULIA CARTWRIGHT. Illustrated by HEYWOOD SUMNER.
Crown 4to, 5s.

FRANCATELLI (C. E.)—
THE ROYAL CONFECTIONER: English and Foreign.
A Practical Treatise. With Illustrations. Sixth Thousand. Crown 8vo, 5s.

FRANKS (A. W.)—
JAPANESE POTTERY. Being a Native Report, with an
Introduction and Catalogue. With numerous Illustrations and Marks. Large
crown 8vo, cloth, 2s. 6d.

FROBEL, FRIEDRICH ; a Short Sketch of his Life, including
Fröbel's Letters from Dresden and Leipzig to his Wife, now first Translated into
English. By EMILY SHIRREFF. Crown 8vo, 2s.

GALLENGA (ANTONIO)—
ITALY: PRESENT AND FUTURE. 2 vols. Dmy. 8vo, 21s.
EPISODES OF MY SECOND LIFE. 2 vols. Dmy. 8vo, 28s.
IBERIAN REMINISCENCES. Fifteen Years' Travelling
Impressions of Spain and Portugal. With a Map. 2 vols. Demy 8vo, 32s.

GASNAULT (PAUL) and GARNIER (ED.)—
FRENCH POTTERY. With Illustrations and Marks.
Large crown 8vo, 3s.

GILLMORE (PARKER)—
THE HUNTER'S ARCADIA. With numerous Illustrations. Demy 8vo, 10s. 6d.

GIRL'S LIFE EIGHTY YEARS AGO (A). Selections from
the Letters of Eliza Southgate Bowne, with an Introduction by Clarence Cook.
Illustrated with Portraits and Views. Crown 4to. 12s.

GLEICHEN (COUNT), Grenadier Guards—
WITH THE CAMEL CORPS UP THE NILE. With
numerous Sketches by the Author. Third Edition. Large crown 8vo, 9s.

GORDON (GENERAL)—
LETTERS FROM THE CRIMEA, THE DANUBE,
AND ARMENIA. Edited by DEMETRIUS C. BOULGER. Second Edition.
Crown 8vo, 5s.

GORST (SIR J. E.), Q.C., M.P.—
An ELECTION MANUAL. Containing the Parliamentary
Elections (Corrupt and Illegal Practices) Act, 1883, with Notes. Third Edition.
Crown 8vo, 1s. 6d.

GOWER (A. R.), Royal School of Mines—
PRACTICAL METALLURGY. With Illustrations. Crown
8vo, 3s.

GRESWELL (WILLIAM), M.A., F.R.C.I.—
OUR SOUTH AFRICAN EMPIRE. With Map. 2 vols.
Crown 8vo, 21s.

GRIFFIN (SIR LEPEL HENRY), K.C.S.I.—
THE GREAT REPUBLIC. Second Edition. Crown 8vo,
4s. 6d.

GRIFFITHS (MAJOR ARTHUR), H.M. Inspector of Prisons—
FRENCH REVOLUTIONARY GENERALS. Large
crown 8vo, 6s.
CHRONICLES OF NEWGATE. Illustrated. New
Edition. Demy 8vo, 16s.
MEMORIALS OF MILLBANK: or, Chapters in Prison
History. With Illustrations. New Edition. Demy 8vo, 12s.

HALL (SIDNEY)—
A TRAVELLING ATLAS OF THE ENGLISH COUN-
TIES. Fifty Maps, coloured. New Edition, including the Railways, corrected
up to the present date. Demy 8vo, in roan tuck, 10s. 6d.

HAWKINS (FREDERICK)—
THE FRENCH STAGE IN THE EIGHTEENTH
CENTURY. With Portraits. 2 vols. Demy 8vo, 30s.
ANNALS OF THE FRENCH STAGE: FROM ITS
ORIGIN TO THE DEATH OF RACINE. 4 Portraits. 2 vols. Demy 8vo, 28s.

HILDEBRAND (HANS), Royal Antiquary of Sweden—
INDUSTRIAL ARTS OF SCANDINAVIA IN THE
PAGAN TIME. With numerous Woodcuts. Large crown 8vo, 2s. 6d.

HILL (MISS G.)—
THE PLEASURES AND PROFITS OF OUR LITTLE
POULTRY FARM. Small 8vo, 3s.

HOLBEIN—
TWELVE HEADS AFTER HOLBEIN. Selected from
Drawings in Her Majesty's Collection at Windsor. Reproduced in Autotype, in
portfolio. £1 16s.

HOLMES (GEORGE C. V.), Secretary of the Institution of Naval Architects—
MARINE ENGINES AND BOILERS. With Sixty-nine
Woodcuts. Large crown 8vo, 3s.

HOPE (ANDRÉE)—
CHRONICLES OF AN OLD INN; or, a Few Words
about Gray's Inn. Crown 8vo, 5s.

HOUSSAYE (ARSENE)—
BEHIND THE SCENES OF THE COMÉDIE FRAN-
CAISE, AND OTHER RECOLLECTIONS. Translated from the French.
Demy 8vo, 14s.

HOVELACQUE (ABEL)—
THE SCIENCE OF LANGUAGE: LINGUISTICS,
PHILOLOGY, AND ETYMOLOGY. With Maps. Large crown 8vo, cloth, 5s.

HOZIER (H. M.)—
TURENNE. With Portrait and Two Maps. Large crown
8vo, 4s.

HUDSON (W. H.), C.M.Z. Joint Author of " Argentine Ornithology"—
THE NATURALIST IN LA PLATA. With numerous
Illustrations.   [*In the Press.*

HUEFFER (F.)—
HALF A CENTURY OF MUSIC IN ENGLAND.
1837—1887. Demy 8vo, 8s.

HUGHES (W. R.), F.L.S.—
A WEEK'S TRAMP IN DICKENS-LAND. With
upwards of 100 Illustrations by F. G. KITTON, HERBERT RAILTON, and others
Demy 8vo, 16s.

HUNTLY (MARQUIS OF)—
TRAVELS, SPORTS, AND POLITICS IN THE EAST
OF EUROPE. With Illustrations by the Marchioness of Huntly. Large
Crown 8vo, 12s.

INDUSTRIAL ARTS: Historical Sketches. With numerous
Illustrations. Large crown 8vo, 3s.

JACKSON (FRANK G.), Master in the Birmingham Municipal School of Art—
DECORATIVE DESIGN. An Elementary Text Book of
Principles and Practice. With numerous Illustrations. Second Edition. Crown
8vo, 7s. 6d.

JAMES (HENRY A.), M.A.—
HANDBOOK TO PERSPECTIVE. Crown 8vo, 2s. 6d.
PERSPECTIVE CHARTS, for use in Class Teaching. 2s.

JARRY (GENERAL)—
OUTPOST DUTY. With TREATISES ON MILITARY
RECONNAISSANCE AND ON ROAD-MAKING. By Major-Gen. W. C. E.
Napier. Third Edition. Crown 8vo, 5s.

JEANS (W. T.)—
CREATORS OF THE AGE OF STEEL. Memoirs of
Sir W. Siemens, Sir H. Bessemer, Sir J. Whitworth, Sir J. Brown, and other
Inventors. Second Edition. Crown 8vo, 7s. 6d.

JOKAI (MAURUS)—
PRETTY MICHAL. Translated by R. NISBET BAIN.
[*In the Press.*

JONES (CAPTAIN DOUGLAS), R.A.—
NOTES ON MILITARY LAW. Crown 8vo, 4s.

JONES. HANDBOOK OF THE JONES COLLECTION
IN THE SOUTH KENSINGTON MUSEUM. With Portrait and Wood-cuts. Large crown 8vo, 2s. 6d.

JOPLING (LOUISE)—
HINTS TO AMATEURS. A Handbook on Art. With
Diagrams. Crown 8vo, 1s. 6d.

JUNKER (DR. WM.) –
TRAVELS IN AFRICA DURING THE YEARS 1875
TO 1878. With 38 Full page Plates and 125 Illustrations in the Text and Map.
Translated from the German by Professor KEANE. Demy 8vo, 21s.

TRAVELS IN AFRICA DURING THE YEARS 1879
TO 1883. With numerous Full-page Plates, and Illustrations in the Text.
Translated from the German by Professor KEANE. Demy 8vo, 21s.

KENNARD (EDWARD)—
NORWEGIAN SKETCHES: FISHING IN STRANGE
WATERS. Illustrated with 30 beautiful Sketches. Second Edition. Oblong
folio, 21s.
Smaller Edition. 14s.

KING (LIEUT.-COL. COOPER)—
GEORGE WASHINGTON. Large crown 8vo. [*In the Press.*

KLACZKO (M. JULIAN)—
TWO CHANCELLORS: PRINCE GORTCHAKOF AND
PRINCE BISMARCK. Translated by Mrs. TAIT. New and cheaper Edition, 6s.

LACORDAIRE'S JESUS CHRIST; GOD; AND GOD AND
MAN. Conferences delivered at Notre Dame in Paris. New Edition.
Crown 8vo, 6s.

LAINÉ (J. M.), R.A.—
ENGLISH COMPOSITION EXERCISES. Crown 8vo,
2s. 6d.

LAING (S.)—
PROBLEMS OF THE FUTURE AND ESSAYS.
Eighth Thousand. Demy 8vo, 3s. 6d.

MODERN SCIENCE AND MODERN THOUGHT.
Twelfth Thousand. Demy 8vo, 3s. 6d.

A MODERN ZOROASTRIAN. Fifth Thousand. Demy
8vo, 3s. 6d.

LAMENNAIS (F.)—
WORDS OF A BELIEVER, and THE PAST AND
FUTURE OF THE PEOPLE Translated from the French by L. E.
MARTINEAU. With a Memoir of Lamennais. Crown 8vo, 4s.

LANDOR (W. S.)—
LIFE AND WORKS. 8 vols.
VOL. 1. Out of print.
VOL. 2. Out of print.
VOL. 3. CONVERSATIONS OF SOVEREIGNS AND STATESMEN, AND
FIVE DIALOGUES OF BOCCACCIO AND PETRARCA.
Demy 8vo, 14s.
VOL. 4. DIALOGUES OF LITERARY MEN. Demy 8vo, 14s.
VOL. 5. DIALOGUES OF LITERARY MEN (*continued*). FAMOUS
WOMEN. LETTERS OF PERICLES AND ASPASIA. And
Minor Prose Pieces. Demy 8vo, 14s.
VOL. 6. MISCELLANEOUS CONVERSATIONS. Demy 8vo, 14s.
VOL. 7. GEBIR, ACTS AND SCENES AND HELLENICS. Poems.
Demy 8vo, 14s.
VOL. 8. MISCELLANEOUS POEMS AND CRITICISMS ON THEO-
CRITUS, CATULLUS, AND PETRARCH. Demy 8vo, 14s.

LANIN (E. B.)—
> RUSSIAN CHARACTERISTICS. Reprinted, with Re-
> visions, from *The Fortnightly Review.*   *[In the Press.*

LAVELEYE (ÉMILE DE)—
> THE ELEMENTS OF POLITICAL ECONOMY.
> Translated by W. POLLARD, B.A., St. John's College, Oxford. Crown 8vo, 6s.

LE CONTE (JOSEPH), Professor of Geology and Natural History in the University of California—
> EVOLUTION: ITS NATURE, ITS EVIDENCES,
> AND ITS RELATIONS TO RELIGIOUS THOUGHT. A New and
> Revised Edition. Crown 8vo, 6s.

LEFÈVRE (ANDRÉ)—
> PHILOSOPHY, Historical and Critical. Translated, with
> an Introduction, by A. W. KEANE, B.A. Large crown 8vo, 3s. 6d.

LE ROUX (H.)—
> ACROBATS AND MOUNTEBANKS. With over 200
> Illustrations by J. GARNIER. Royal 8vo, 16s.

LESLIE (R. C.)—
> OLD SEA WINGS, WAYS, AND WORDS, IN THE
> DAYS OF OAK AND HEMP. With 135 Illustrations by the Author. Demy
> 8vo, 14s.
>
> LIFE ABOARD A BRITISH PRIVATEER IN THE
> TIME OF QUEEN ANNE. Being the Journals of Captain Woodes Rogers,
> Master Mariner. With Notes and Illustrations by ROBERT C. LESLIE. Large
> crown 8vo, 9s.
>
> A SEA PAINTER'S LOG. With 12 Full-page Illustrations
> by the Author. Large crown 8vo, 12s.

LETOURNEAU (DR. CHARLES)—
> SOCIOLOGY. Based upon Ethnology. Large crown
> 8vo, 3s. 6d.
>
> BIOLOGY. With 83 Illustrations. A New Edition.
> Demy 8vo, 3s. 6d.

LILLY (W. S.)—
> CHAPTERS ON SHIBBOLETHS.   *[In the Press.*
>
> ON RIGHT AND WRONG. Second Edition. Demy
> 8vo, 12s.
>
> A CENTURY OF REVOLUTION. Second Edition.
> Demy 8vo, 12s.
>
> CHAPTERS ON EUROPEAN HISTORY. With an
> Introductory Dialogue on the Philosophy of History. 2 vols. Demy 8vo, 21s.
>
> ANCIENT RELIGION AND MODERN THOUGHT.
> Second Edition. Demy 8vo, 12s.

LITTLE (THE REV. CANON KNOX)—
> THE CHILD OF STAFFERTON: A Chapter from a
> Family Chronicle. New Edition. Crown 8vo, boards, 1s.; cloth, 1s. 6d.
>
> THE BROKEN VOW. A Story of Here and Hereafter.
> New Edition. Crown 8vo, boards, 1s.; cloth, 1s. 6d.

LITTLE (THE REV. H. W.)—
> H. M. STANLEY: HIS LIFE, WORKS, AND
> EXPLORATIONS. Demy 8vo, 10s. 6d.

LLOYD (COLONEL E.M.), R.E.—
VAUBAN, MONTALEMBERT, CARNOT : ENGINEER
STUDIES. With Portraits. Crown 8vo, 5s

LLOYD (W. W.), late 24th Regiment—
ON ACTIVE SERVICE. Printed in Colours. Oblong
4to, 5s.

SKETCHES OF INDIAN LIFE. Printed in Colours.
4to, 6s.

LONG (JAMES)—
DAIRY FARMING. To which is added a Description of
the Chief Continental Systems. With numerous Illustrations. Crown 8vo, 9s.

LOVELL (ARTHUR)—
THE IDEAL OF MAN. Crown 8vo, 3s. 6d.

LOW (WILLIAM)—
TABLE DECORATION. With 19 Full Illustrations.
Demy 8vo, 6s.

McCOAN (J. C.)—
EGYPT UNDER ISMAIL: a Romance of History.
With Portrait and Appendix of Official Documents. Crown 8vo, 7s. 6d.

MALLESON (COL. G. B.), C.S.I.—
PRINCE EUGENE OF SAVOY. With Portrait and
Maps. Large crown 8vo, 6s.

LOUDON. A Sketch of the Military Life of Gideon
Ernest, Freicherr von Loudon. With Portrait and Maps. Large crown 8vo, 4s.

MALLET (ROBERT)—
PRACTICAL MANUAL OF CHEMICAL ASSAYING,
as applied to the Manufacture of Iron. By L. L. DE KONINCK and E. DIETZ.
Edited, with notes, by ROBERT MALLET. Post 8vo, cloth, 6s.

MARCEAU (SERGENT)—
REMINISCENCES OF A REGICIDE. Edited from
the Original MSS. of SERGENT MARCEAU, Member of the Convention, and
Administrator of Police in the French Revolution of 1789. By M. C. M. SIMPSON.
Demy 8vo, with Illustrations and Portraits, 14s.

MASKELL (ALFRED)—
RUSSIAN ART AND ART OBJECTS IN RUSSIA.
A Handbook to the Reproduction of Goldsmiths' Work and other Art Treasures.
With Illustrations. Large crown 8vo, 4s. 6d.

MASKELL (WILLIAM)—
IVORIES : ANCIENT AND MEDIÆVAL. With nume-
rous Woodcuts. Large crown 8vo, cloth, 2s. 6d.
HANDBOOK TO THE DYCE AND FORSTER COL-
LECTIONS. With Illustrations. Large crown 8vo, cloth, 2s. 6d.

MASPÉRO (G.)—
LIFE IN ANCIENT EGYPT AND ASSYRIA.
With 188 Illustrations. Crown 8vo, 5s.

MAUDSLAY (ATHOL)—
HIGHWAYS AND HORSES. With numerous Illustrations. Demy 8vo, 21s.

C

GEORGE MEREDITH'S WORKS.

A New and Uniform Edition.   Crown 8vo, 3s. 6d. each.

Copies of the Six-Shilling Edition are still to be had.

ONE OF OUR CONQUERORS.   [*In the Press.*

DIANA OF THE CROSSWAYS.

EVAN HARRINGTON.

THE ORDEAL OF RICHARD FEVEREL.

THE ADVENTURES OF HARRY RICHMOND.

SANDRA BELLONI.

VITTORIA.

RHODA FLEMING.

BEAUCHAMP'S CAREER.

THE EGOIST.

THE SHAVING OF SHAGPAT; AND FARINA.

MERIVALE (HERMAN CHARLES)—

BINKO'S BLUES. A Tale for Children of all Growths.
Illustrated by EDGAR GIBERNE. Small crown 8vo, 5s.

THE WHITE PILGRIM, and other Poems. Crown 8vo, 9s.

MILLS (JOHN), formerly Assistant to the Solar Physics Committee—

ADVANCED PHYSIOGRAPHY (PHYSIOGRAPHIC
ASTRONOMY). Designed to meet the Requirements of Students preparing for
the Elementary and Advanced Stages of Physiography in the Science and Art
Department Examinations, and as an Introduction to Physical Astronomy.
Crown 8vo, 4s. 6d.

ELEMENTARY PHYSIOGRAPHIC ASTRONOMY.
Crown 8vo. 1s. 6d.

ALTERNATIVE ELEMENTARY PHYSICS. Crown
8vo, 2s. 6d.

MILLS (JOHN) and NORTH (BARKER)—

QUANTITATIVE ANALYSIS (INTRODUCTORY
LESSONS ON). With numerous Woodcuts. Crown 8vo, 1s. 6d.

HANDBOOK OF QUANTITATIVE ANALYSIS. Crown
8vo, 3s. 6d.

MILNERS, THE; OR, THE RIVER DIGGINGS. A Story of
South African Life. Crown 8vo, 6s.

MOLESWORTH (W. NASSAU)—

HISTORY OF ENGLAND FROM THE YEAR 1830
TO THE RESIGNATION OF THE GLADSTONE MINISTRY, 1874.
Twelfth Thousand. 3 vols. Crown 8vo, 18s.

ABRIDGED EDITION. Large crown, 7s. 6d.

MOLTKE (FIELD-MARSHAL COUNT VON)—

POLAND: AN HISTORICAL SKETCH. With Biographical Notice by E. S. BUCHHEIM. Crown 8vo, 1s.

MOOREHEAD (WARREN K.)—

WANNETA, THE SIOUX. With Illustrations from Life.
Large crown 8vo, 6s.

MORLEY (THE RIGHT HON. JOHN), M.P.—
RICHARD COBDEN'S LIFE AND CORRESPON-
DENCE. Crown 8vo, with Portrait, 7s. 6d.
Popular Edition. With Portrait. 4to, sewed, 1s. Cloth, 2s.

MURRAY (ANDREW), F.L.S.—
ECONOMIC ENTOMOLOGY. APTERA. With numerous Illustrations. Large crown 8vo, 3s. 6d.

MURRAY (HENRY)—
A DEPUTY PROVIDENCE. Crown 8vo, 3s. 6d.

NECKER (MADAME)—
THE SALON OF MADAME NECKER. By VICOMTE
D'HAUSSONVILLE. 2 vols. Crown 8vo 18s

NESBITT (ALEXANDER)—
GLASS. With numerous Woodcuts. Large crown 8vo,
cloth, 2s. 6d.

NICOL (DAVID)—
THE POLITICAL LIFE OF OUR TIME. Two vols.
Demy 8vo, 24s.

NORMAN (C. B.)—
TONKIN; OR, FRANCE IN THE FAR EAST. With
Maps. Demy 8vo, 14s.

O'BYRNE (ROBERT), F.R.G.S.—
THE VICTORIES OF THE BRITISH ARMY IN
THE PENINSULA AND THE SOUTH OF FRANCE from 1808 to 1814.
An Epitome of Napier's History of the Peninsular War, and Gurwood's Collection
of the Duke of Wellington's Despatches. Crown 8vo, 5s.

O'GRADY (STANDISH)—
TORYISM AND THE TORY DEMOCRACY. Crown
8vo, 5s.

OLIVER (PROFESSOR D.), F.R.S., &c.—
ILLUSTRATIONS OF THE PRINCIPAL NATURAL
ORDERS OF THE VEGETABLE KINGDOM, PREPARED FOR THE
SCIENCE AND ART DEPARTMENT, SOUTH KENSINGTON. With
109 Plates. Oblong 8vo, plain, 16s.; coloured, £1 6s.

OLIVER (E. E.), Under-Secretary to the Public Works Department, Punjaub—
ACROSS THE BORDER; or, PATHAN AND BILOCH.
With numerous Illustrations by J. L. KIPLING, C.I.E. Demy 8vo, 14s.

PAPUS—
THE TAROT OF THE BOHEMIANS. The most
ancient book in the world. For the exclusive use of the Initiates. An Absolute
Key to Occult Science. [In the Press.

PATERSON (ARTHUR)—
A WESTERN PARTNER. [In the Press.

PAYTON (E. W.)—
ROUND ABOUT NEW ZEALAND. Being Notes from
a Journal of Three Years' Wandering in the Antipodes. With Twenty Original
Illustrations by the Author. Large crown 8vo, 12s.

PERROT (GEORGES) and CHIPIEZ (CHARLES)—

A HISTORY OF ANCIENT ART IN PERSIA.
With Numerous Illustrations. *[In the Press.*

A HISTORY OF ANCIENT ART IN PHRYGIA—
LYDIA, AND CARIA—LYCIA. With numerous Illustrations. *[In the Press.*

A HISTORY OF ANCIENT ART IN SARDINIA,
JUDÆA. SYRIA, AND ASIA MINOR. With 395 Illustrations. 2 vols.
Imperial 8vo, 36s.

A HISTORY OF ANCIENT ART IN PHŒNICIA
AND ITS DEPENDENCIES. With 654 Illustrations. 2 vols. Imperial
8vo, 42s.

A HISTORY OF ART IN CHALDÆA AND ASSYRIA.
With 452 Illustrations. 2 vols. Imperial 8vo, 42s.

A HISTORY OF ART IN ANCIENT EGYPT. With
600 Illustrations. 2 vols. Imperial 8vo, 42s.

PETERBOROUGH (THE EARL OF)—

THE EARL OF PETERBOROUGH AND MON-
MOUTH (Charles Mordaunt): A Memoir. By Colonel FRANK RUSSELL, Royal
Dragoons. With Illustrations. 2 vols. demy 8vo. 32s.

PIERCE (GILBERT)—

THE DICKENS DICTIONARY. A Key to the Charac-
ters and Principal Incidents in the Tales of Charles Dickens, with Additions by
WILLIAM A. WHEELER. New Edition. Demy 8vo, 10s. 6d.

PILLING (WILLIAM)—

LAND TENURE BY REGISTRATION. Second Edition
of "Order from Chaos," Revised and Enlarged. Crown 8vo, 5s.

PITT TAYLOR (FRANK)—

THE CANTERBURY TALES. Selections from the Tales
of GEOFFREY CHAUCER rendered into Modern English. Crown 8vo, 6s.

POLLEN (J. H.)—

GOLD AND SILVER SMITH'S WORK. With numerous Woodcuts. Large crown 8vo, cloth, 2s. 6d.

ANCIENT AND MODERN FURNITURE AND
WOODWORK. With numerous Woodcuts. Large crown 8vo, cloth, 2s. 6d.

POOLE (STANLEY LANE), B.A., M.R.A.S.—

THE ART OF THE SARACENS IN EGYPT. Pub-
lished for the Committee of Council on Education. With 108 Woodcuts. Large
crown 8vo, 4s.

POYNTER (E. J.), R.A.—

TEN LECTURES ON ART. Third Edition. Large
crown 8vo, 9s.

PRATT (ROBERT), Headmaster School of Science and Art, Barrow-in-Furness—

SCIOGRAPHY, OR PARALLEL AND RADIAL
PROJECTION OF SHADOWS. Being a Course of Exercises for the use of
Students in Architectural and Engineering Drawing, and for Candidates preparing
for the Examinations in this subject and in Third Grade Perspective conducted by
the Science and Art Department. Oblong quarto, 7s. 6d.

PURCELL (the late THEOBALD A.), Surgeon-Major, A.M.D., and Principal Medical Officer to the Japanese Government)—

A SUBURB OF YEDO. With numerous Illustrations. Crown 8vo, 2s. 6d.

RADICAL PROGRAMME, THE. From the *Fortnightly Review,* with additions. With a Preface by the RIGHT HON. J. CHAMBERLAIN, M.P. Thirteenth Thousand. Crown 8vo, 2s. 6d.

RAB (W. FRASER)—

AUSTRIAN HEALTH RESORTS THROUGHOUT THE YEAR. A New and Enlarged Edition. Crown 8vo, 5s.

RAMSDEN (LADY GWENDOLEN)—

A BIRTHDAY BOOK. Containing 46 Illustrations from Original Drawings, and numerous other Illustrations. Royal 8vo, 21s.

RANKIN (THOMAS T.), C.E.—

SOLUTIONS TO THE QUESTIONS IN PURE MATHEMATICS (STAGES 1 AND 2) SET AT THE SCIENCE AND ART EXAMINATIONS FROM 1881 TO 1886. Crown 8vo, 2s.

RAPHAEL: his Life, Works, and Times. By EUGENE MUNTZ. Illustrated with about 200 Engravings. A New Edition, revised from the Second French Edition. By W. ARMSTRONG, B.A. Imperial 8vo, 25s.

READE (MRS. R. H.)—

THE GOLDSMITH'S WARD; A Tale of London City in the Fifteenth Century. With 27 Illustrations by W. BOWCHER. Crown 8vo, 6s.

REDGRAVE (GILBERT)—

OUTLINES OF HISTORIC ORNAMENT. Translated from the German. Edited by GILBERT REDGRAVE. With numerous Illustrations. Crown 8vo, 4s.

REDGRAVE (RICHARD), R.A.—

MANUAL OF DESIGN. With Woodcuts. Large crown 8vo, cloth, 2s. 6d.

ELEMENTARY MANUAL OF COLOUR, with a Catechism on Colour. 24mo, cloth, 9d.

REDGRAVE (SAMUEL)—

A DESCRIPTIVE CATALOGUE OF THE HIS-TORICAL COLLECTION OF WATER-COLOUR PAINTINGS IN THE SOUTH KENSINGTON MUSEUM. With numerous Chromo-lithographs and other Illustrations. Royal 8vo, £1 1s.

REID (T. WEMYSS)—

THE LIFE OF THE RIGHT HON. W. E. FORSTER. With Portraits. Fourth Edition. 2 vols. Demy 8vo, 32s.
FIFTH EDITION, in one volume, with new Portrait. Demy 8vo, 10s. 6d.

RENAN (ERNEST)—

THE FUTURE OF SCIENCE: Ideas of 1848. Demy 8vo, 18s.

HISTORY OF THE PEOPLE OF ISRAEL.
FIRST DIVISION. Till the time of King David. Demy 8vo, 14s.
SECOND DIVISION. From the Reign of David up to the Capture of Samaria. Demy 8vo, 14s.
THIRD DIVISION. From the time of Hezekiah till the Return from Babylon. Demy 8vo, 14s.

RECOLLECTIONS OF MY YOUTH. Translated from the French, and revised by MADAME RENAN. Crown 8vo, 8s.

RIANO (JUAN F.)—
THE INDUSTRIAL ARTS IN SPAIN. With numerous
Woodcuts. Large crown 8vo, cloth, 4s.

RIBTON-TURNER (C. J.)—
A HISTORY OF VAGRANTS AND VAGRANCY AND
BEGGARS AND BEGGING. With Illustrations. Demy 8vo, 21s.

ROBINSON (JAMES F.)—
BRITISH BEE FARMING. Its Profits and Pleasures.
Large crown 8vo, 5s.

ROBINSON (J. C.)—
ITALIAN SCULPTURE OF THE MIDDLE AGES
AND PERIOD OF THE REVIVAL OF ART. With 20 Engravings. Royal
8vo, cloth, 7s. 6d.

ROBSON (GEORGE)—
ELEMENTARY BUILDING CONSTRUCTION. Illus-
trated by a Design for an Entrance Lodge and Gate. 15 Plates. Oblong folio,
sewed, 8s.

ROCK (THE VERY REV. CANON), D.D.—
TEXTILE FABRICS. With numerous Woodcuts. Large
crown 8vo, cloth, 2s. 6d.

ROGERS (CAPTAIN WOODES), Master Mariner—
LIFE ABOARD A BRITISH PRIVATEER IN THE
TIME OF QUEEN ANNE. With Notes and Illustrations by ROBERT C.
LESLIE. Large crown 8vo, 9s.

ROOSE (ROBSON), M.D., F.C.S.—
THE WEAR AND TEAR OF LONDON LIFE.
Second Edition. Crown 8vo, sewed, 1s.
INFECTION AND DISINFECTION. Crown 8vo, sewed, 6d.

ROOSEVELT (BLANCHE)—
ELISABETH OF ROUMANIA: A Study. With Two
Tales from the German of Carmen Sylva, Her Majesty Queen of Roumania.
With Two Portraits and Illustration. Demy 8vo, 12s.

ROLAND (ARTHUR)—
FARMING FOR PLEASURE AND PROFIT. Edited
by WILLIAM ABLETT. 8 vols. Crown 8vo, 5s. each.

DAIRY-FARMING, MANAGEMENT OF COWS, etc.
POULTRY-KEEPING.
TREE-PLANTING, FOR ORNAMENTATION OR PROFIT.
STOCK-KEEPING AND CATTLE-REARING.
DRAINAGE OF LAND, IRRIGATION, MANURES, etc.
ROOT-GROWING, HOPS, etc.
MANAGEMENT OF GRASS LANDS, LAYING DOWN GRASS,
ARTIFICIAL GRASSES, etc.
MARKET GARDENING, HUSBANDRY FOR FARMERS AND
GENERAL CULTIVATORS.

ROSS (MRS. JANET)—
EARLY DAYS RECALLED. With Illustrations and
Portrait. Crown 8vo, 5s.

SCHREINER (OLIVE), (RALPH IRON)—

THE STORY OF AN AFRICAN FARM. Crown 8vo,
1s.; in cloth, 1s. 6d.
A New Edition, on Superior Paper, and Strongly Bound in Cloth. Crown 8vo, 3s. 6d.

SCHAUERMANN (F. L.)—

WOOD-CARVING IN PRACTICE AND THEORY,
AS APPLIED TO HOME ARTS. With Notes on Designs having special
application to Carved Wood in different styles. Containing 124 Illustrations.
Large crown 8vo, 7s. 6d.

SCIENCE AND ART: a Journal for Teachers and Scholars.
Issued monthly. 3d. See page 38.

SCOTT (JOHN)—

THE REPUBLIC AS A FORM OF GOVERNMENT;
or, The Evolution of Democracy in America. Crown 8vo, 7s. 6d.

SCOTT (LEADER)—

THE RENAISSANCE OF ART IN ITALY: an Illus-
trated Sketch. With upwards of 200 Illustrations. Medium quarto, 18s.

SCOTT-STEVENSON (MRS.)—

ON SUMMER SEAS. Including the Mediterranean, the
Ægean, the Ionian, and the Euxine, and a voyage down the Danube. With a
Map. Demy 8vo, 16s.

OUR HOME IN CYPRUS. With a Map and Illustrations. Third Edition. Demy 8vo, 14s.

OUR RIDE THROUGH ASIA MINOR. With Map.
Demy 8vo, 18s.

SEEMAN (O.)—

THE MYTHOLOGY OF GREECE AND ROME, with
Special Reference to its Use in Art. From the German. Edited by G. H.
Bianchi. 64 Illustrations. New Edition. Crown 8vo, 5s.

SETON-KARR (H. W.), F.R.G.S., etc.—

BEAR HUNTING IN THE WHITE MOUNTAINS;
or, Alaska and British Columbia Revisited. Illustrated. Large Crown, 4s. 6d.

TEN YEARS' TRAVEL AND SPORT IN FOREIGN
Lands; or, Travels in the Eighties. Second Edition, with additions and Portrait
of Author. Large crown 8vo, 5s.

SHEPHERD (MAJOR), R.E.—

PRAIRIE EXPERIENCES IN HANDLING CATTLE
AND SHEEP. With Illustrations and Map. Demy 8vo, 10s. 6d.

SHIRREFF (EMILY)—

A SHORT SKETCH OF THE LIFE OF FRIEDRICH
FRÖBEL; a New Edition, including Fröbel's Letters from Dresden and Leipzig
to his Wife, now first Translated into English. Crown 8vo, 2s.

HOME EDUCATION IN RELATION TO THE
KINDERGARTEN. Two Lectures. Crown 8vo, 1s. 6d.

SHORE (ARABELLA)—

DANTE FOR BEGINNERS: a Sketch of the "Divina
Commedia." With Translations, Biographical and Critical Notices, and Illustrations. With Portrait. Crown 8vo, 6s.

SIMKIN (R.)—
  LIFE IN THE ARMY: Every-day Incidents in Camp,
  Field, and Quarters. Printed in Colours. Oblong 4to, 5s.

SIMMONDS (T. L.)—
  ANIMAL PRODUCTS: their Preparation, Commercial
  Uses and Value. With numerous Illustrations. Large crown 8vo, 3s. 6d.

SIMPSON (M. C. M.)—
  REMINISCENCES OF A REGICIDE. Edited from
  the Original MSS. of Sergent Marceau, Member of the Convention, and
  Administrator of Police in the French Revolution of 1789. Demy 8vo, with
  Illustrations and Portraits, 14s.

SINNETT (A. P.)—
  ESOTERIC BUDDHISM. Annotated and enlarged by
  the Author. Sixth and cheaper Edition. Crown 8vo, 4s.

  KARMA. A Novel. New Edition. Crown 8vo, 3s.

SMITH (MAJOR R. MURDOCK), R.E.—
  PERSIAN ART. With Map and Woodcuts. Second Edition.
  Large crown 8vo, 2s.

STANLEY (H. M.): HIS LIFE, WORKS, AND EXPLORA-
  TIONS. By the Rev. H. W. LITTLE. Demy 8vo, 10s. 6d.

STATHAM (H. H.—)
  MY THOUGHTS ON MUSIC AND MUSICIANS.
  Demy 8vo.   [*In the Press.*

STOKES (MARGARET)—
  EARLY CHRISTIAN ART IN IRELAND. With 106
  Woodcuts. Demy 8vo, 7s. 6d.
  Cheaper Edition, Crown 8vo, 4s.

STORY, (W. W.)—
  CASTLE ST. ANGELO. With Illustrations. Crown
  8vo, 10s. 6d.

SUTCLIFFE (JOHN)—
  THE SCULPTOR AND ART STUDENT'S GUIDE
  to the Proportions of the Human Form, with Measurements in feet and inches of
  Full-Grown Figures of Both Sexes and of Various Ages. By Dr. G. SCHADOW.
  Plates reproduced by J. SUTCLIFFE. Oblong folio, 31s. 6d.

SUVÓROFF, LIFE OF. By LIEUT.-COL. SPALDING. Crown
  8vo, 6s.

SWIFT: THE MYSTERY OF HIS LIFE AND LOVE.
  By the Rev. JAMES HAY. Crown 8vo, 6s.

SYMONDS (JOHN ADDINGTON)—
  ESSAYS, SPECULATIVE AND SUGGESTIVE. 2 vols.
  Crown 8vo, 18s.

TAINE (H. A.)—
  NOTES ON ENGLAND. With Introduction by W.
  FRASER RAE. Eighth Edition. With Portrait. Crown 8vo, 5s.

TAIT (J. S.)—
  WHO IS THE MAN? A Tale of the Scottish Border.
  Crown 8vo, 1s. ; in cloth, 1s. 6d.

TANNER (PROFESSOR), F.C.S.—

HOLT CASTLE; or, Threefold Interest in Land. Crown 8vo, 2s.

JACK'S EDUCATION; OR, HOW HE LEARNT FARMING. Second Edition. Crown 8vo, 2s.

TAYLOR (EDWARD R.), Head Master of the Birmingham Municipal School of Art—

ELEMENTARY ART TEACHING: An Educational and Technical Guide for Teachers and Learners, including Infant School-work; The Work of the Standards; Freehand; Geometry; Model Drawing; Nature Drawing; Colours; Light and Shade; Modelling and Design. With over 600 Diagrams and Illustrations. Imperial 8vo, 10s. 6d.

TEMPLE (SIR RICHARD), BART., M.P., G.C.S.I.—

COSMOPOLITAN ESSAYS. With Maps. Demy 8vo, 16s.

THOMSON (D. C.)—

THE BARBIZON SCHOOL OF PAINTERS: Corot, Rousseau, Diaz, Millet, and Daubigny. With 130 Illustrations, including 36 Full-Page Plates, of which 18 are Etchings. 4to, cloth, 42s.

THRUPP (GEORGE A.) and FARR (WILLIAM)—

COACH TRIMMING. With 60 Illustrations. Crown 8vo, 2s. 6d.

THRUPP (THE REV. H. W.), M.A.—

AN AID TO THE VISITATION OF THOSE DISTRESSED IN MIND, BODY, OR ESTATE. Crown 8vo, 3s. 6d.

TOPINARD (DR. PAUL)—

ANTHROPOLOGY. With a Preface by Professor PAUL BROCA. With 49 Illustrations. Demy 8vo, 3s. 6d.

TOVEY (LIEUT.-COL., R.E.)—

MARTIAL LAW AND CUSTOM OF WAR; or, Military Law and Jurisdiction in Troublous Times. Crown 8vo, 6s.

TRAHERNE (MAJOR)—

THE HABITS OF THE SALMON. Crown 8vo, 3s. 6d.

TRAILL (H. D.)—

THE NEW LUCIAN. Being a Series of Dialogues of the Dead. Demy 8vo, 12s.

TROLLOPE (ANTHONY)—

THE CHRONICLES OF BARSETSHIRE. A Uniform Edition, in 8 vols., large crown 8vo, handsomely printed, each vol. containing Frontispiece. 6s. each.

THE WARDEN and BAR-CHESTER TOWERS. 2 vols. DR. THORNE. FRAMLEY PARSONAGE.	THE SMALL HOUSE AT ALLINGTON. 2 vols. LAST CHRONICLE OF BARSET. 2 vols.

LIFE OF CICERO. 2 vols. 8vo. £1 4s.

TROUP (J. ROSE)—

WITH STANLEY'S REAR COLUMN. With Portraits and Illustrations. Second Edition. Demy 8vo, 16s.

VANDAM (ALBERT D.)—

WE TWO AT MONTE CARLO. Second Edition. Crown 8vo, 1s.; in cloth, 1s. 6d.

VERON (EUGENE)—

ÆSTHETICS. Translated by W. H. ARMSTRONG. Large crown 8vo, 3s. 6d.

WALFORD (MAJOR), R.A.—
PARLIAMENTARY GENERALS OF THE GREAT
CIVIL WAR. With Maps. Large crown 8vo, 4s.

WALKER (MRS.)—
UNTRODDEN PATHS IN ROUMANIA. With 77
Illustrations. Demy 8vo, 10s. 6d.

EASTERN LIFE AND SCENERY, with Excursions to
Asia Minor, Mitylene, Crete, and Roumania. 2 vols., with Frontispiece to each
vol. Crown 8vo, 21s.

WALL (A.)—
A PRINCESS OF CHALCO. With Illustrations.
[In the Press.

WARD (JAMES)—
ELEMENTARY PRINCIPLES OF ORNAMENT.
With 122 Illustrations in the text. 8vo, 5s.

WATSON (JOHN)—
POACHERS AND POACHING. With Frontispiece.
Crown 8vo, 7s. 6d.

SKETCHES OF BRITISH SPORTING FISHES. With
Frontispiece. Crown 8vo, 3s. 6d.

WEGG-PROSSER (F. R.)—
GALILEO AND HIS JUDGES. Demy 8vo, 5s.

WELLS (HENRY P.)—
CITY BOYS IN THE WOODS ; or, A Trapping Venture
in Maine. With upwards of 100 Illustrations. Royal 8vo, 9s.

WHITE (WALTER)—
A MONTH IN YORKSHIRE. With a Map. Fifth
Edition. Post 8vo, 4s.

A LONDONER'S WALK TO THE LAND'S END, AND
A TRIP TO THE SCILLY ISLES. With 4 Maps. Third Edition. Post
8vo, 4s.

WORNUM (R. N.)—
ANALYSIS OF ORNAMENT: THE CHARACTER-
ISTICS OF STYLES. An Introduction to the History of Ornamental Art.
With many Illustrations. Ninth Edition. Royal 8vo, cloth, 8s.

*WRIGHTSON (PROF. JOHN), M.R.A.C., F.C.S., &c.; President of the
College of Agriculture, Downton.*
PRINCIPLES OF AGRICULTURAL PRACTICE AS
AN INSTRUCTIONAL SUBJECT. With Geological Map. Second Edition.
Crown 8vo, 5s.

FALLOW AND FODDER CROPS. Crown 8vo, 5s.

WORSAAE (J. J. A.)—
INDUSTRIAL ARTS OF DENMARK, FROM THE
EARLIEST TIMES TO THE DANISH CONQUEST OF ENGLAND.
With Maps and Woodcuts. Large crown 8vo, 3s 6d.

YOUNG OFFICER'S "DON'T"; or, Hints to Youngsters
on Joining. 32mo, 1s.

YOUNGE (C. D.)—
PARALLEL LIVES OF ANCIENT AND MODERN
HEROES. New Edition. 12mo, cloth, 4s. 6d.

SOUTH KENSINGTON MUSEUM SCIENCE AND ART HANDBOOKS.

Handsomely printed in large crown 8vo.

Published for the Committee of the Council on Education.

MARINE ENGINES AND BOILERS. By GEORGE C. V.
HOLMES, Secretary of the Institution of Naval Architects, Whitworth Scholar.
With Sixty-nine Woodcuts. Large crown 8vo, 3s.

EARLY CHRISTIAN ART IN IRELAND. By MARGARET
STOKES. With 106 Woodcuts. Crown 8vo, 4s.
A Library Edition, demy 8vo, 7s. 6d.

FOOD GRAINS OF INDIA. By PROF. A. H. CHURCH, M.A.,
F.C.S., F.I.C. With Numerous Woodcuts. Small 4to, 6s.

THE ART OF THE SARACENS IN EGYPT. By STANLEY
LANE POOLE, B.A., M.A.R.S. With 108 Woodcuts. Crown 8vo, 4s.

ENGLISH PORCELAIN: A Handbook to the China made in
England during the 18th Century. By PROF. A. H. CHURCH, M.A. With
numerous Woodcuts. 3s.

RUSSIAN ART AND ART OBJECTS IN RUSSIA: A
Handbook to the reproduction of Goldsmiths' work and other Art Treasures from
that country in the South Kensington Museum. By ALFRED MASKELL. With
Illustrations. 4s. 6d.

FRENCH POTTERY. By PAUL GASNAULT and EDOUARD
GARNIER. With Illustrations and Marks. 3s.

ENGLISH EARTHENWARE: A Handbook to the Wares
made in England during the 17th and 18th Centuries. By PROF. A. H. CHURCH,
M.A. With numerous Woodcuts. 3s.

INDUSTRIAL ARTS OF DENMARK. From the Earliest
Times to the Danish Conquest of England. By J. J. A. WORSAAE, Hon. F.S.A.,
&c. &c. With Map and Woodcuts. 3s. 6d.

INDUSTRIAL ARTS OF SCANDINAVIA IN THE PAGAN
TIME. By HANS HILDEBRAND, Royal Antiquary of Sweden. With numerous
Woodcuts. 2s. 6d.

PRECIOUS STONES: Considered in their Scientific and
Artistic relations By PROF. A. H. CHURCH, M.A. With a Coloured Plate and
Woodcuts. 2s. 6d.

INDUSTRIAL ARTS OF INDIA. By Sir GEORGE C. M.
BIRDWOOD, C.S.I., &c. With Map and Woodcuts. Demy 8vo, 14s.

HANDBOOK TO THE DYCE AND FORSTER COLLEC-
TIONS in the South Kensington Museum. With Portraits and Facsimiles. 2s. 6d.

INDUSTRIAL ARTS IN SPAIN. By JUAN F. RIAÑO.
With numerous Woodcuts. 4s.

GLASS. By ALEXANDER NESBITT. With numerous Woodcuts.
2s. 6d.

GOLD AND SILVER SMITHS' WORK. By JOHN HUNGER-
FORD POLLEN, M.A. With numerous Woodcuts. 2s. 6d.

TAPESTRY. By ALFRED DE CHAMPEAUX. With Woodcuts. 2s. 6d.

BRONZES. By C. DRURY E. FORTNUM, F.S.A. With numerous
Woodcuts. 2s. 6d.

SOUTH KENSINGTON MUSEUM SCIENCE & ART HANDBOOKS—*Continued.*

PLAIN WORDS ABOUT WATER. By A. H. CHURCH, M.A.
Oxon. With Illustrations. Sewed, 6d.

ANIMAL PRODUCTS: their Preparation, Commercial Uses,
and Value. By T. L. SIMMONDS. With Illustrations. 3s. 6d.

FOOD: Some Account of its Sources, Constituents, and Uses.
By PROFESSOR A. H. CHURCH, M.A. Oxon. New Edition, enlarged. 3s.

ECONOMIC ENTOMOLOGY. By ANDREW MURRAY, F.L.S.
APTERA. With Illustrations. 7s. 6d.

JAPANESE POTTERY. Being a Native Report. With an
Introduction and Catalogue by A. W. FRANKS, M.A., F.R.S., F.S.A. With
Illustrations and Marks. 2s. 6d.

HANDBOOK TO THE SPECIAL LOAN COLLECTION
of Scientific Apparatus. 3s.

INDUSTRIAL ARTS: Historical Sketches. With Numerous
Illustrations. 3s.

TEXTILE FABRICS. By the Very Rev. DANIEL ROCK, D.D.
With numerous Woodcuts. 2s. 6d.

JONES COLLECTION IN THE SOUTH KENSINGTON ·
MUSEUM. With Portrait and Woodcuts. 2s. 6d.

COLLEGE AND CORPORATION PLATE. A Handbook
to the Reproductions of Silver Plate in the South Kensington Museum from
Celebrated English Collections. By WILFRED JOSEPH CRIPPS, M.A., F.S.A.
With Illustrations. 2s. 6d.

IVORIES: ANCIENT AND MEDIÆVAL. By WILLIAM
MASKELL. With numerous Woodcuts. 2s. 6d.

ANCIENT AND MODERN FURNITURE AND WOOD-
WORK. By JOHN HUNGERFORD POLLEN, M.A. With numerous Woodcuts.
2s. 6d.

MAIOLICA. By C. DRURY E. FORTNUM, F.S.A. With
numerous Woodcuts. 2s. 6d.

THE CHEMISTRY OF FOODS. With Microscopic Illus-
trations. By JAMES BELL, Ph.D., &c., Principal of the Somerset House Laboratory.
· Part I.—Tea, Coffee, Cocoa, Sugar, &c. 2s. 6d.
Part II.—Milk, Butter, Cheese, Cereals, Prepared Starches, &c. 3s.

MUSICAL INSTRUMENTS. By CARL ENGEL. With numerous Woodcuts. 2s. 6d.

MANUAL OF DESIGN. By RICHARD REDGRAVE, R.A. By
GILBERT R. REDGRAVE. With Woodcuts. 2s. 6d.

PERSIAN ART. By MAJOR R. MURDOCK SMITH, R.E. With
Map and Woodcuts. Second Edition, enlarged. 2s.

CARLYLE'S (THOMAS) WORKS.

THE ASHBURTON EDITION.

New Edition, handsomely printed, containing all the Portraits and Illustrations, in Seventeen Volumes, demy 8vo, 8s. each.

THE FRENCH REVOLUTION AND PAST AND PRESENT. 2 vols.
SARTOR RESARTUS; HEROES AND HERO WORSHIP. 1 vol.
LIFE OF JOHN STERLING—LIFE OF SCHILLER. 1 vol.
LATTER-DAY PAMPHLETS—EARLY KINGS OF NORWAY—
ESSAY ON THE PORTRAIT OF JOHN KNOX. 1 vol.
LETTERS AND SPEECHES OF OLIVER CROMWELL. 3 vols.
HISTORY OF FREDERICK THE GREAT. 6 vols.
CRITICAL AND MISCELLANEOUS ESSAYS. 3 vols.

LIBRARY EDITION COMPLETE.

Handsomely printed in 34 vols., demy 8vo, cloth, £15 8s.

SARTOR RESARTUS. With a Portrait, 7s. 6d.

THE FRENCH REVOLUTION. A History. 3 vols., each 9s.

LIFE OF FREDERICK SCHILLER AND EXAMINATION
OF HIS WORKS. With Supplement of 1872. Portrait and Plates, 9s.

CRITICAL AND MISCELLANEOUS ESSAYS. With Portrait.
6 vols., each 9s.

ON HEROES, HERO WORSHIP, AND THE HEROIC
IN HISTORY. 7s. 6d.

PAST AND PRESENT. 9s.

OLIVER CROMWELL'S LETTERS AND SPEECHES. With
Portraits. 5 vols., each 9s.

LATTER-DAY PAMPHLETS. 9s.

LIFE OF JOHN STERLING. With Portrait, 9s.

HISTORY OF FREDERICK THE SECOND. 10 vols.,
each 9s.

TRANSLATIONS FROM THE GERMAN. 3 vols., each 9s.

EARLY KINGS OF NORWAY; ESSAY ON THE POR-
TRAITS OF JOHN KNOX; AND GENERAL INDEX. With Portrait
Illustrations. 8vo, cloth, 9s.

CHEAP AND UNIFORM EDITION.
23 vols., Crown 8vo, cloth, £7 5s.

THE FRENCH REVOLUTION:
A History. 2 vols., 12s.

OLIVER CROMWELL'S LET-
TERS AND SPEECHES, with Eluci-
dations, &c. 3 vols., 18s.

LIVES OF SCHILLER AND
JOHN STERLING. 1 vol., 6s.

CRITICAL AND MISCELLA-
NEOUS ESSAYS. 4 vols., £1 4s.

SARTOR RESARTUS AND
LECTURES ON HEROES. 1 vol., 6s.

LATTER-DAY PAMPHLETS.
1 vol., 6s.

CHARTISM AND PAST AND
PRESENT. 1 vol., 6s.

TRANSLATIONS FROM THE
GERMAN OF MUSÆUS, TIECK,
AND RICHTER. 1 vol., 6s.

WILHELM MEISTER, by Göethe.
A Translation. 2 vols., 12s.

HISTORY OF FRIEDRICH THE
SECOND, called Frederick the Great.
7 vols., £2 9s.

PEOPLE'S EDITION.
37 vols., small crown 8vo, 37s.; separate vols., 1s. each.

SARTOR RESARTUS. With Portrait of Thomas Carlyle.

FRENCH REVOLUTION. A
History. 3 vols.

OLIVER CROMWELL'S LET-
TERS AND SPEECHES. 5 vols.
With Portrait of Oliver Cromwell.

ON HEROES AND HERO
WORSHIP AND THE HEROIC
IN HISTORY.

PAST AND PRESENT.

CRITICAL AND MISCELLA-
NEOUS ESSAYS. 7 vols.

THE LIFE OF SCHILLER,
AND EXAMINATION OF HIS
WORKS. With Portrait.

LATTER-DAY PAMPHLETS.

WILHELM MEISTER. 3 vols.

LIFE OF JOHN STERLING.
With Portrait.

HISTORY OF FREDERICK
THE GREAT. 10 vols.

TRANSLATIONS FROM
MUSÆUS, TIECK, AND RICHTER.
2 vols.

THE EARLY KINGS OF NOR-
WAY; Essay on the Portraits of Knox.

Or in sets, 37 vols. in 18, 37s.

CHEAP ISSUE.

THE FRENCH REVOLUTION. Complete in 1 vol. With Portrait.
Crown 8vo, 2s.

SARTOR RESARTUS, HEROES AND HERO WORSHIP, PAST
AND PRESENT, AND CHARTISM. Complete in 1 vol. Crown 8vo, 2s.

OLIVER CROMWELL'S LETTERS AND SPEECHES. Crown 8vo,
2s. 6d.

CRITICAL AND MISCELLANEOUS ESSAYS. 2 vols. 4s.

WILHELM MEISTER. 1 vol. 2s.

SIXPENNY EDITION.
4to, sewed.

SARTOR RESARTUS. Eightieth Thousand.

HEROES AND HERO WORSHIP.

ESSAYS: BURNS, JOHNSON, SCOTT, THE DIAMOND NECKLACE.
The above in 1 vol., cloth, 2s. 6d.

DICKENS'S (CHARLES) WORKS.

ORIGINAL EDITIONS.

In demy 8vo.

THE MYSTERY OF EDWIN DROOD. With Illustrations
by S. L. Fildes, and a Portrait engraved by Baker. Cloth, 7s. 6d.

OUR MUTUAL FRIEND. With Forty Illustrations by Marcus
Stone. Cloth, £1 1s.

THE PICKWICK PAPERS. With Forty-three Illustrations
by Seymour and Phiz. Cloth, £1 1s.

NICHOLAS NICKLEBY. With Forty Illustrations by Phiz.
Cloth, £1 1s.

SKETCHES BY "BOZ." With Forty Illustrations by George
Cruikshank. Cloth, £1 1s.

MARTIN CHUZZLEWIT. With Forty Illustrations by Phiz.
Cloth, £1 1s.

DOMBEY AND SON. With Forty Illustrations by Phiz.
Cloth, £1 1s.

DAVID COPPERFIELD. With Forty Illustrations by Phiz.
Cloth, £1 1s.

BLEAK HOUSE. With Forty Illustrations by Phiz. Cloth,
£1 1s.

LITTLE DORRIT. With Forty Illustrations by Phiz. Cloth,
£1 1s.

THE OLD CURIOSITY SHOP. With Seventy-five Illus-
trations by George Cattermole and H. K. Browne. A New Edition. Uniform with
the other volumes, £1 1s.

BARNABY RUDGE: a Tale of the Riots of 'Eighty. With
Seventy-eight Illustrations by George Cattermole and H. K. Browne. Uniform with
the other volumes, £1 1s.

CHRISTMAS BOOKS: Containing—The Christmas Carol;
The Cricket on the Hearth; The Chimes; The Battle of Life; The Haunted House.
With all the original Illustrations. Cloth, 12s.

OLIVER TWIST and TALE OF TWO CITIES. In one
volume. Cloth, £1 1s.

OLIVER TWIST. Separately. With Twenty-four Illustrations
by George Cruikshank. Cloth, 11s.

A TALE OF TWO CITIES. Separately. With Sixteen Illustrations by Phiz. Cloth, 9s.

✱ *The remainder of Dickens's Works were not originally printed in demy 8vo.*

DICKENS'S (CHARLES) WORKS.—*Continued.*

LIBRARY EDITION.

In post 8vo. With the Original Illustrations, 30 vols., cloth, £12.

		s.	*d.*
PICKWICK PAPERS ... ... 43 Illustrns., 2 vols.	16	o
NICHOLAS NICKLEBY ... ... 39 ,, 2 vols.	16	o
MARTIN CHUZZLEWIT ... ... 40 ,, 2 vols.	16	o
OLD CURIOSITY SHOP & REPRINTED PIECES 36 ,, 2 vols.	16	o
BARNABY RUDGE and HARD TIMES ... ... 36 ,, 2 vols.	16	o
BLEAK HOUSE ... ... 40 ,, 2 vols.	16	o
LITTLE DORRIT ... ... 40 ,, 2 vols.	16	o
DOMBEY AND SON ... ... 38 ,, 2 vols.	16	o
DAVID COPPERFIELD ... ... 38 ,, 2 vols.	16	o
OUR MUTUAL FRIEND ... ... 40 ,, 2 vols.	16	o
SKETCHES BY "BOZ" ... ... 39 ,, 1 vol.	8	o
OLIVER TWIST ... ... 24 ,, 1 vol.	8	o
CHRISTMAS BOOKS ... ... 17 ,, 1 vol.	8	o
A TALE OF TWO CITIES ... ... 16 ,, 1 vol.	8	o
GREAT EXPECTATIONS ... ... 8 ,, 1 vol.	8	o
PICTURES FROM ITALY & AMERICAN NOTES 8 ,, 1 vol.	8	o
UNCOMMERCIAL TRAVELLER ... . 8 ,, 1 vol.	8	o
CHILD'S HISTORY OF ENGLAND ... ... 8 ,, 1 vol.	8	o
EDWIN DROOD and MISCELLANIES ... ... 12 ,, 1 vol.	8	o
CHRISTMAS STORIES from "Household Words," &c. 14 ,, 1 vol.	8	o

Uniform with the above, 10s. 6d.

THE LIFE OF CHARLES DICKENS. By JOHN FORSTER. With Illustrations.

A NEW EDITION OF ABOVE, WITH THE ORIGINAL ILLUSTRATIONS, IN LARGE CROWN 8vo, 30 VOLS. IN SETS ONLY.

THE "CHARLES DICKENS" EDITION.

In Crown 8vo. In 21 vols., cloth, with Illustrations, £3 16s.

	s.	*d.*
PICKWICK PAPERS ... ... 8 Illustrations ...	4	o
MARTIN CHUZZLEWIT ... ... 8 ,, ...	4	o
DOMBEY AND SON ... ... 8 ,, ...	4	o
NICHOLAS NICKLEBY ... ... 8 ,, ...	4	o
DAVID COPPERFIELD ... ... 8 ,, ...	4	o
BLEAK HOUSE ... ... 8 ,, ...	4	o
LITTLE DORRIT ... ... 8 ,, ...	4	o
OUR MUTUAL FRIEND ... ... 8 ,, ...	4	o
BARNABY RUDGE ... ... 8 ,, ...	3	6
OLD CURIOSITY SHOP ... ... 8 ,, ...	3	6
A CHILD'S HISTORY OF ENGLAND ... ... 4 ,, ...	3	6
EDWIN DROOD and OTHER STORIES ... ... 8 ,, ...	3	6
CHRISTMAS STORIES, from "Household Words" ... 8 ,, ...	3	6
SKETCHES BY "BOZ" ... ... 8 ,, ...	3	6
AMERICAN NOTES and REPRINTED PIECES ... 8 ,, ...	3	6
CHRISTMAS BOOKS ... ... 8 ,, ...	3	6
OLIVER TWIST ... ... 8 ,, ...	3	6
GREAT EXPECTATIONS ... ... 8 ,, ...	3	6
TALE OF TWO CITIES ... ... 8 ,, ...	3	o
HARD TIMES and PICTURES FROM ITALY ... 8 ,, ...	3	o
UNCOMMERCIAL TRAVELLER 4	3	o

Uniform with the above.

THE LIFE OF CHARLES DICKENS. Numerous Illustrations. 2 vols. 7 o
THE LETTERS OF CHARLES DICKENS ... ...2 vols. 7 o

DICKENS'S (CHARLES) WORKS.—*Continued.*

THE ILLUSTRATED LIBRARY EDITION.

(WITH LIFE.)

Complete in 32 Volumes. Demy 8vo, 10s. each; or set, £16.

This Edition is printed on a finer paper and in a larger type than has been employed in any previous edition. The type has been cast especially for it, and the page is of a size to admit of the introduction of all the original illustrations.

No such attractive issue has been made of the writings of Mr. Dickens, which, various as have been the forms of publication adapted to the demands of an ever widely-increasing popularity, have never yet been worthily presented in a really handsome library form.

The collection comprises all the minor writings it was Mr. Dickens's wish to preserve.

SKETCHES BY "BOZ." With 40 Illustrations by George Cruikshank.

PICKWICK PAPERS. 2 vols. With 42 Illustrations by Phiz.

OLIVER TWIST. With 24 Illustrations by Cruikshank.

NICHOLAS NICKLEBY. 2 vols. With 40 Illustrations by Phiz.

OLD CURIOSITY SHOP and REPRINTED PIECES. 2 vols. With Illustrations by Cattermole, &c.

BARNABY RUDGE and HARD TIMES. 2 vols. With Illustrations by Cattermole, &c.

MARTIN CHUZZLEWIT. 2 vols. With 40 Illustrations by Phiz.

AMERICAN NOTES and PICTURES FROM ITALY. 1 vol. With 8 Illustrations.

DOMBEY AND SON. 2 vols. With 40 Illustrations by Phiz.

DAVID COPPERFIELD. 2 vols. With 40 Illustrations by Phiz.

BLEAK HOUSE. 2 vols. With 40 Illustrations by Phiz.

LITTLE DORRIT. 2 vols. With 40 Illustrations by Phiz.

A TALE OF TWO CITIES. With 16 Illustrations by Phiz.

THE UNCOMMERCIAL TRAVELLER. With 8 Illustrations by Marcus Stone.

GREAT EXPECTATIONS. With 8 Illustrations by Marcus Stone.

OUR MUTUAL FRIEND. 2 vols. With 40 Illustrations by Marcus Stone.

CHRISTMAS BOOKS. With 17 Illustrations by Sir Edwin Landseer, R.A., Maclise, R.A., &c. &c.

HISTORY OF ENGLAND. With 8 Illustrations by Marcus Stone.

CHRISTMAS STORIES. (From "Household Words" and "All the Year Round.") With 14 Illustrations.

EDWIN DROOD AND OTHER STORIES. With 12 Illustrations by S. L. Fildes.

LIFE OF CHARLES DICKENS. By John Forster. With Portraits. 2 vols. (Not separate.)

DICKENS'S (CHARLES) WORKS.—*Continued.*

THE POPULAR LIBRARY EDITION

In 30 *Vols., large crown* 8vo*, price* £6 ; *separate Vols.* 4s. *each.*

An Edition printed on good paper, each volume containing 16 full-page Illustrations, selected from the Household Edition, on Plate Paper.

SKETCHES BY "BOZ."
PICKWICK. 2 vols.
OLIVER TWIST.
NICHOLAS NICKLEBY. 2 vols.
MARTIN CHUZZLEWIT. 2 vols.
DOMBEY AND SON. 2 vols.
DAVID COPPERFIELD. 2 vols.
CHRISTMAS BOOKS.
OUR MUTUAL FRIEND. 2 vols.
CHRISTMAS STORIES.
BLEAK HOUSE. 2 vols.
LITTLE DORRIT. 2 vols.

OLD CURIOSITY SHOP AND REPRINTED PIECES. 2 vols.
BARNABY RUDGE. 2 vols.
UNCOMMERCIAL TRAVELLER.
GREAT EXPECTATIONS.
TALE OF TWO CITIES.
CHILD'S HISTORY OF ENGLAND.
EDWIN DROOD AND MISCELLANIES.
PICTURES FROM ITALY AND AMERICAN NOTES.

HOUSEHOLD EDITION.
(WITH LIFE.)

In 22 *Volumes. Crown* 4to*, cloth,* £4 8s. 6d.

MARTIN CHUZZLEWIT, with 59 Illustrations, 5s.
DAVID COPPERFIELD, with 60 Illustrations and a Portrait, 5s.
BLEAK HOUSE, with 61 Illustrations, 5s.
LITTLE DORRIT, with 58 Illustrations, 5s.
PICKWICK PAPERS, with 56 Illustrations, 5s.
OUR MUTUAL FRIEND, with 58 Illustrations, 5s.
NICHOLAS NICKLEBY, with 59 Illustrations, 5s.
DOMBEY AND SON, with 61 Illustrations, 5s.
EDWIN DROOD ; REPRINTED PIECES ; and other Stories, with 30 Illustrations, 5s.
THE LIFE OF DICKENS. By JOHN FORSTER. With 40 Illustrations, 5s.
BARNABY RUDGE, with 46 Illustrations, 4s.
OLD CURIOSITY SHOP, with 32 Illustrations, 4s.
CHRISTMAS STORIES, with 23 Illustrations, 4s.
OLIVER TWIST, with 28 Illustrations, 3s.
GREAT EXPECTATIONS, with 26 Illustrations, 3s.
SKETCHES BY "BOZ," with 36 Illustrations, 3s.
UNCOMMERCIAL TRAVELLER, with 26 Illustrations, 3s.
CHRISTMAS BOOKS, with 28 Illustrations, 3s.
THE HISTORY OF ENGLAND, with 15 Illustrations, 3s.
AMERICAN NOTES and PICTURES FROM ITALY, with 18 Illustrations, 3s.
A TALE OF TWO CITIES, with 25 Illustrations, 3s.
HARD TIMES, with 20 Illustrations, 2s. 6d.

DICKENS'S (CHARLES) WORKS.—*Continued.*

THE CROWN EDITION,
(WITH LIFE.)

The Volumes contain ALL THE ORIGINAL ILLUSTRATIONS,

And the Letterpress is printed from Type expressly cast for this Edition.
In 18 Vols.

LARGE CROWN OCTAVO.
PRICE FIVE SHILLINGS EACH.

The Volumes Now Ready are:

1.—**THE PICKWICK PAPERS.** With Forty-three Illustrations by SEYMOUR and PHIZ.

2.—**NICHOLAS NICKLEBY.** With Forty Illustrations by PHIZ.

3.—**DOMBEY AND SON.** With Forty Illustrations by PHIZ.

4.—**DAVID COPPERFIELD.** With Forty Illustrations by PHIZ.

5.—**SKETCHES BY "BOZ."** With Forty Illustrations by GEO. CRUIKSHANK.

6.—**MARTIN CHUZZLEWIT.** With Forty Illustrations by PHIZ.

7.—**THE OLD CURIOSITY SHOP.** With Seventy-five Illustrations by GEORGE CATTERMOLE and H. K. BROWNE.

8.—**BARNABY RUDGE :** a Tale of the Riots of 'Eighty. With Seventy-eight Illustrations by GEORGE CATTERMOLE and H. K. BROWNE.

9.—**OLIVER TWIST** and **TALE OF TWO CITIES.** With Twenty-four Illustrations by CRUIKSHANK and Sixteen by PHIZ.

10.—**BLEAK HOUSE.** With Forty Illustrations by PHIZ.

11.—**LITTLE DORRIT.** With Forty Illustrations by PHIZ.

12.—**OUR MUTUAL FRIEND.** With Forty Illustrations by MARCUS STONE.

13.—**AMERICAN NOTES ; PICTURES FROM ITALY ; and A CHILD'S HISTORY OF ENGLAND.** With Sixteen Illustrations by MARCUS STONE.

14.—**CHRISTMAS BOOKS and HARD TIMES.** With Illustrations by LANDSEER, MACLISE, STANFIELD, LEECH, DOYLE, F. WALKER, etc.

15.—**CHRISTMAS STORIES AND OTHER STORIES,** including **HUMPHREY'S CLOCK.** With Illustrations by DALZIEL, CHARLES GREEN, MAHONEY, PHIZ, CATTERMOLE, etc.

16.—**GREAT EXPECTATIONS. UNCOMMERCIAL TRAVELLER.** With Sixteen Illustrations by MARCUS STONE.

17.—**EDWIN DROOD** and **REPRINTED PIECES.** With Sixteen Illustrations by LUKE FILDES and F. WALKER.

18.—**THE LIFE OF CHARLES DICKENS.** By JOHN FORSTER. With Portraits and Illustrations. Will be added at the request of numerous Subscribers.

DICKENS'S (CHARLES) WORKS.—*Continued.*

THE CABINET EDITION.

In 32 vols. small fcap. 8vo, Marble Paper Sides, Cloth Backs, with uncut edges, price Eighteenpence each.

Each Volume contains Eight Illustrations reproduced from the Originals.

In Sets only, bound in blue cloth, with cut edges, £2 8s.

CHRISTMAS BOOKS.
MARTIN CHUZZLEWIT, 2 vols.
DAVID COPPERFIELD, 2 vols.
OLIVER TWIST.
GREAT EXPECTATIONS.
NICHOLAS NICKLEBY, 2 vols.
SKETCHES BY "BOZ."
CHRISTMAS STORIES.
THE PICKWICK PAPERS, 2 vols.
BARNABY RUDGE, 2 vols.
BLEAK HOUSE, 2 vols.
AMERICAN NOTES AND PICTURES FROM ITALY.

EDWIN DROOD; AND OTHER STORIES.
THE OLD CURIOSITY SHOP, 2 vols.
A CHILD'S HISTORY OF ENGLAND.
DOMBEY AND SON, 2 vols.
A TALE OF TWO CITIES.
LITTLE DORRIT, 2 vols.
MUTUAL FRIEND, 2 vols.
HARD TIMES.
UNCOMMERCIAL TRAVELLER
REPRINTED PIECES.

CHARLES DICKENS'S CHRISTMAS BOOKS.

REPRINTED FROM THE ORIGINAL PLATES.

Illustrated by JOHN LEECH, D. MACLISE, R.A., R. DOYLE, C. STANFIELD, R.A., etc.

Fcap. cloth, 1s. each. Complete in a case, 5s.

A CHRISTMAS CAROL IN PROSE.

THE CHIMES: A Goblin Story.

THE CRICKET ON THE HEARTH: A Fairy Tale of Home.

THE BATTLE OF LIFE. A Love Story.

THE HAUNTED MAN AND THE GHOST'S STORY.

SIXPENNY REPRINTS.

COPYRIGHT EDITION OF DAVID COPPERFIELD.
By CHARLES DICKENS. Clearly printed on good paper. from new type. With numerous Illustrations by FRED BARNARD. Medium 8vo.

READINGS FROM THE WORKS OF CHARLES DICKENS.
As selected and read by himself and now published for the first time. Illustrated.

A CHRISTMAS CAROL, AND THE HAUNTED MAN.
By CHARLES DICKENS. Illustrated.

THE CHIMES: A GOBLIN STORY, AND THE CRICKET ON THE HEARTH. Illustrated.

THE BATTLE OF LIFE: A LOVE STORY, HUNTED DOWN, AND A HOLIDAY ROMANCE. Illustrated

DICKENS'S (CHARLES) WORKS.—*Continued.*
A NEW EDITION, ENTITLED

THE PICTORIAL EDITION,

Now being issued in MONTHLY PARTS, royal 8vo, at

ONE SHILLING EACH.

Each Part containing 192 pages of Letterpress, handsomely printed, and, besides full-page Plates on plate paper, about 24 Illustrations inserted in the Text.

The Edition will be completed in about THIRTY-SEVEN PARTS, of which Twenty-five are now ready, and will contain in all—

UPWARDS OF NINE HUNDRED ENGRAVINGS.

The Volumes now ready are:

DOMBEY AND SON. With 62 Illustrations by F. BARNARD. 3s. 6d.

DAVID COPPERFIELD. With 61 Illustrations by F. BARNARD. 3s. 6d.

NICHOLAS NICKLEBY. With 59 Illustrations by F. BARNARD. 3s. 6d.

BARNABY RUDGE. With 46 Illustrations by F. BARNARD. 3s. 6d.

OLD CURIOSITY SHOP. With 39 Illustrations by CHARLES GREEN. 3s. 6d.

MARTIN CHUZZLEWIT. With 59 Illustrations by F. BARNARD. 3s. 6d.

OLIVER TWIST and A TALE OF TWO CITIES. With 28 Illustrations by J. MAHONEY, and 25 Illustrations by F. BARNARD. 3s. 6d.

OUR MUTUAL FRIEND. With 58 Illustrations by J. MAHONEY. 3s. 6d.

BLEAK HOUSE. With 61 Illustrations by F. BARNARD. 3s. 6d.

PICKWICK PAPERS. With 57 Illustrations by PHIZ. 3s. 6d.
[Now being issued in Parts.

LITTLE DORRIT. With 58 Illustrations by J. MAHONEY. 3s. 6d.

GREAT EXPECTATIONS & HARD TIMES. With 30 Illustrations by J. A. FRASER and 20 by H. FRENCH.

THE TWO SHILLING EDITION.

Each Volume contains a Frontispiece.   Crown 8vo, 2s.

The Volumes now ready are—

DOMBEY AND SON.
MARTIN CHUZZLEWIT.
THE PICKWICK PAPERS.
BLEAK HOUSE.

OLD CURIOSITY SHOP.
BARNABY RUDGE.
DAVID COPPERFIELD
NICHOLAS NICKLEBY *(In Press.*

OUR MUTUAL FRIEND. *(In the Press.)*

MR. DICKENS'S READINGS.

Fcap. 8vo, sewed.

CHRISTMAS CAROL IN PROSE. 1s.

CRICKET ON THE HEARTH. 1s.

CHIMES: A GOBLIN STORY. 1s.

STORY OF LITTLE DOMBEY. 1s.

POOR TRAVELLER, BOOTS AT THE HOLLY-TREE INN, and MRS. GAMP. 1s.

SCIENCE AND ART,
AND TECHNICAL EDUCATION.
A Journal for Teachers and Students.

The Official Organ of the Science and Art Teachers' Association.

Edited by JOHN MILLS.

MONTHLY, THREEPENCE; POST FREE, FOURPENCE.

The Journal contains contributions by distinguished men; short papers by prominent teachers; leading articles; correspondence; answers to questions set at the May Examinations of the Science and Art Department; and interesting news in connection with the scientific and artistic world.

PRIZE COMPETITION.

With each issue of the Journal, papers or drawings are offered for Prize Competition, extending over the range of subjects of the Science and Art Department and City and Guilds of London Institute.

There are thousands of Science and Art Schools and Classes in the United Kingdom, but the teachers connected with these institutions, although engaged in the advancement of identical objects, are seldom known to each other except through personal friendship. One object of the Journal is to enable those engaged in this common work to communicate upon subjects of importance, with a view to an interchange of ideas, and the establishment of unity of action in the various centres.

TERMS OF SUBSCRIPTION.

ONE YEAR'S SUBSCRIPTION (including postage)	..	..	.. **4s. 0d.**
HALF ,, ,,	..	..	.. **2s. 0d.**
SINGLE COPY ,, ,,	..	..	.. **4d.**

Cheques and Post Office Orders to be made payable to
Messrs. **CHAPMAN & HALL, Limited,**
Agents for the Science and Art Department of the Committee of Council on Education.

SOLUTIONS TO THE QUESTIONS IN PURE MATHE-
MATICS—Stages 1 and 2—SET AT THE SCIENCE AND ART
EXAMINATIONS from 1881 to 1886. By THOMAS T. RANKIN, C.E.,
Rector of the Gartsherrie Science School, and West of Scotland Mining
College. Crown 8vo, 2s.

SOLUTIONS TO THE QUESTIONS SET IN THE
FOLLOWING SUBJECTS AT THE MAY EXAMINATIONS
OF THE SCIENCE AND ART DEPARTMENT ANTERIOR
TO 1887.

1. Animal Physiology ...	From 1881 to 1886.	
2. Hygiene	,, 1884 to 1886	{ with Notes and Index.
3. Building Construction ...	,, 1881 to 1886.	
4. Machine Construction ...	,, 1881 to 1886.	
5. Agriculture	,, 1881 to 1886.	
6. Magnetism and Electricity	,, 1881 to 188 .	
7. Physiography	,, 1881 to 1886.	
8. Sound, Light, and Heat	,, 1881 to 1886.	

Each Subject dealt with in a Separate Volume, containing Complete Answers to the Elementary and Advanced Papers for the Years noted.

Price 1s. 6d. each.

Works Published at Three Shillings and Sixpence each.

THE SECRET OF THE PRINCESS: a Tale of Country, Camp, Court, Convict, and Cloister Life in Russia. By Mrs. SUTHERLAND EDWARDS.

STORY OF AN AFRICAN FARM. By OLIVE SCHREINER.

CHRIST THAT IS TO BE, THE: A Latter-day Romance. Third Edition.

BEYOND THE SEAS; being the surprising Adventures and ingenious Opinions of Ralph, Lord St. Keyne, told by his kinsman, Humphrey St. Keyne. By OSWALD CRAWFURD. Second Edition.

THE STORY OF HELEN DAVENANT. By VIOLET FANE.

A DEPUTY PROVIDENCE. By HENRY MURRAY.

MY "HANSOM" LAYS: Original Verses, Imitations, and Paraphrases. By W. BEATTY-KINGSTON.

SPORT: Fox Hunting, Salmon Fishing, Covert Shooting, Deer Stalking. By the late W. BROMLEY DAVENPORT, M.P. With Illustrations by GENERAL CREALOCK, C.B.

LOG-BOOK OF A FISHERMAN AND ZOOLOGIST. By FRANK BUCKLAND. With Illustrations. Fifth Thousand.

THE HABITS OF THE SALMON. By MAJOR TRAHERNE.

BRITISH SPORTING FISHES. By JOHN WATSON.

ENGLAND: ITS PEOPLE, POLITY, AND PURSUITS. By T. H. S. ESCOTT. New and Revised Edition.

PROBLEMS OF THE FUTURE AND ESSAYS. By SAMUEL LAING. Eighth Thousand.

MODERN SCIENCE AND MODERN THOUGHT. By SAMUEL LAING. Twelfth Thousand.

A MODERN ZOROASTRIAN. By SAMUEL LAING. Fifth Thousand.

THE SCIENCE OF LANGUAGE: LINGUISTICS, PHILO-LOGY, AND ETYMOLOGY. By ABEL HOVELACQUE. With Maps.

SOCIOLOGY. Based upon Ethnology. By DR. CHARLES LETOURNEAU.

BIOLOGY. By DR. CHARLES LETOURNEAU. With 83 Illustrations.

PHILOSOPHY, Historical and Critical. By ANDRÉ LEFÈVRE.

ANTHROPOLOGY. By DR. PAUL TOPINARD. With a Preface by PROFESSOR PAUL BROCA. With 49 Illustrations.

ÆSTHETICS. By EUGENE VERON.

THE IDEAL OF MAN. By ARTHUR LOVELL.

AN AID TO THE VISITATION OF THOSE DIS-TRESSED IN MIND, BODY, OR ESTATE. By the REV. H. W. THRUPP.

ANIMAL PRODUCTS: their Preparation, Commercial Uses, and Value. By T. L. SIMMONDS. With Illustrations.

ECONOMIC ENTOMOLOGY. By ANDREW MURRAY, F.L.S. APTERA. With Illustrations.

THE FORTNIGHTLY REVIEW.

THE FORTNIGHTLY REVIEW is published on the 1st of every month, and a Volume is completed every Six Months.

The following are among the Contributors:—

ADMIRAL LORD ALCESTER.
GRANT ALLEN.
SIR RUTHERFORD ALCOCK.
AUTHOR OF "GREATER BRITAIN."
PROFESSOR BAIN.
SIR SAMUEL BAKER.
PROFESSOR BEESLY.
PAUL BOURGET.
BARON GEORGE VON BUNSEN.
DR. BRIDGES.
HON. GEORGE C. BRODRICK.
JAMES BRYCE, M.P.
THOMAS BURT, M.P.
SIR GEORGE CAMPBELL, M.P.
THE EARL OF CARNARVON.
EMILIO CASTELAR.
RT. HON. J. CHAMBERLAIN, M.P.
PROFESSOR SIDNEY COLVIN.
THE EARL COMPTON.
MONTAGUE COOKSON, Q.C.
L. H. COURTNEY, M.P.
G. H. DARWIN.
SIR GEORGE W. DASENT.
PROFESSOR A. V. DICEY.
PROFESSOR DOWDEN.
RT. HON. M. E. GRANT DUFF.
RIGHT HON. H. FAWCETT, M.P.
ARCHDEACON FARRAR.
EDWARD A. FREEMAN.
J. A. FROUDE.
MRS. GARRET-ANDERSON.
J. W. L. GLAISHER, F.R.S.
SIR J. E. GORST, Q.C., M.P.
EDMUND GOSSE.
THOMAS HARE.
FREDERIC HARRISON.
ADMIRAL SIR G. P. HORNBY.
LORD HOUGHTON.
PROFESSOR HUXLEY.
PROFESSOR R. C. JEBB.
ANDREW LANG.
E. B. LANIN.
EMILE DE LAVELEYE.
T. E. CLIFFE LESLIE.
W. S. LILLY.
MARQUIS OF LORNE.
PIERRE LOTI.

SIR JOHN LUBBOCK, BART., M.P.
THE EARL OF LYTTON.
SIR H. S. MAINE.
W. H. MALLOCK.
CARDINAL MANNING.
DR. MAUDSLEY.
PROFESSOR MAX MÜLLER.
GEORGE MEREDITH.
RT. HON. G. OSBORNE MORGAN,
    Q.C., M.P.
PROFESSOR HENRY MORLEY.
RT. HON. JOHN MORLEY, M.P.
WILLIAM MORRIS.
PROFESSOR H. N. MOSELEY.
F. W. H. MYERS.
F. W. NEWMAN.
PROFESSOR JOHN NICHOL.
W. G. PALGRAVE.
WALTER H. PATER.
RT. HON. LYON PLAYFAIR, M.P.
SIR HENRY POTTINGER, BART.
PROFESSOR J. R. SEELEY.
LORD SHERBROOKE.
PROFESSOR SIDGWICK.
HERBERT SPENCER.
M. JULES SIMON.
    (DOCTOR L'ACADEMIE FRANCAISE).
HON. E. L. STANLEY.
SIR J. FITZJAMES STEPHEN, Q.C
LESLIE STEPHEN.
J. HUTCHISON STIRLING.
A. C. SWINBURNE.
DR. VON SYBEL.
J. A. SYMONDS.
SIR THOMAS SYMONDS,
    (ADMIRAL OF THE FLEET).
THE REV. EDWARD F. TALBOT
    (WARDEN OF KEBLE COLLEGE).
SIR RICHARD TEMPLE, BART.
HON. LIONEL A. TOLLEMACHE.
COUNT LEO TOLSTOI.
H. D. TRAILL.
PROFESSOR TYNDALL.
ALFRED RUSSELL WALLACE
A. J. WILSON.
GEN. VISCOUNT WOLSELEY.
THE EDITOR.

ETC. ETC. ETC.

THE FORTNIGHTLY REVIEW *is published at 2s. 6d.*

CHAPMAN & HALL. LIMITED, 11, HENRIETTA STREET,
COVENT GARDEN, W.C.

CHARLES DICKENS AND EVANS, PRINTERS, CRYSTAL PALACE PRESS.

1

Lightning Source UK Ltd.
Milton Keynes UK
UKOW06n1830060116

265944UK00009B/83/P